Private Practice, Public Payment:
Canadian Medicine and the Politics of
Health Insurance, 1911–1966

Private Practice, Public Payment is the first detailed overview of
medical interest-group activity during the formative period of the
Canadian health insurance system. David Naylor follows the evolution
of Canadian health insurance from 1911, when attention was focused
on the issue by British developments, to the enactment of the Medical
Care Act by Parliament in 1966.

Naylor's particular concern is with the nature and extent of
opposition by the medical profession to government-administered
systems of health insurance at both the provincial and the federal
levels. He details various developments in medical politics and
policies, including the dispute over a state health insurance plan
in British Columbia during the Depression, the national health
insurance program drafted by the King government, the doctors' strike
in Saskatchewan in 1962, and the development and eventual governmental rejection of prepayment plans sponsored by organized medicine.

The author concludes that physicians regarded medical insurance
schemes over which they had little administrative control, or where
coverage was not limited to the indigent or to those earning below
a modest wage, as threats to professional incomes and autonomy.
His analysis of the evolution of the professional perspectives, policies,
and pressure-group activities suggests that in dealing with regulatory
legislation, organized medicine is as likely to act in defence of its
members' economic and social interests as any other occupational
collection. The final chapter touches on the role of professional
ideology in legitimizing this interest-group activity, and also briefly
links current conflicts to policial precedents described in the book.

David Naylor is a medical historian and physician currently spe-
cializing in internal medicine. He lives in Ontario.

Private Practice, Public Payment

Canadian Medicine and the Politics of Health Insurance 1911–1966

C. DAVID NAYLOR

McGill-Queen's University Press
Kingston and Montreal

© McGill-Queen's University Press 1986
ISBN 0-7735-0557-1 (cloth)
ISBN 0-7735-0568-7 (paper)

Legal deposit third quarter 1986
Bibliothèque nationale du Québec

Printed in Canada

This book has been published with the help of a grant
from the Social Science Federation of Canada, using
funds provided by the Social Sciences and Humanities
Research Council of Canada. Publication has also been
assisted by the Canada Council under its block grant
program.

Canadian Cataloguing in Publication Data

Naylor, C. David (Christopher David), 1954-
    Private practice, public payment
    Includes bibliographical references and index.
    ISBN 0-7735-0557-1 (bound) ISBN 0-7735-0568-7 (pbk.)
    1. Insurance, Health – Canada – History.
    2. Medicine – Canada – History – 20th century.
    3. Medical policy – Canada – History – 20th century.
    I. Title.
    HD7102.C3N39 1986   368.4'2'00971   c86-093893-X

For Thomas and Edna Naylor

Contents

Tables

Acknowledgments

Many individuals and institutions have contributed in diverse ways to making this study possible. I cannot list all of them and send apologies and thanks to any who should be mentioned but are not. However, I must acknowledge several special debts.

This project evolved out of an Oxford University doctoral dissertation, and my stay in England was made possible by the Rhodes Scholarship Trust. The Ontario Arts Council provided some much-needed financial assistance while I was doing research in Canada during 1980-1. More recently, the Social Sciences and Humanities Research Council has helped fund some work of mine that proved relevant to this book.

A special nod of gratitude must go to Dr D.W. Millard of Oxford's department of social and administrative studies, who supervised my academic sojourn in England. Although he was not directly involved in this work, Professor Malcolm G. Taylor deserves mention as a Canadian pioneer in the field of health insurance studies. His seminal analyses of the role and viewpoints of organized medicine kindled my interest in the area, and my debt to Professor Taylor's scholarship is obvious from the chapter notes. It is also a pleasure to acknowledge the constructive criticism provided by Professors Samuel E.D. Shortt and Ronald Hamowy in their capacity as expert reviewers. Editorial commentary on matters of form and substance was given in detail by Professor William G. Watson for McGill-Queen's University Press. Of course, it should not be assumed that any of these scholars agrees with the interpretations presented here.

Mrs Joan McGilvray of McGill-Queen's University Press efficiently managed the logistics of publication. Ms Catherine Frost did the copy-editing in a rigorous fashion that considerably improved the style and flow of the text. For secretarial assistance I am greatly indebted to Ms Anne Donovan and Mrs Paula Hugin.

Like many other authors, I have come to see librarians and archivists as a remarkable subspecies possessed of superhuman patience and courtesy. The locations where members of this *genus* were encountered include a variety of library facilities at Oxford University, the University of Toronto, and the University of Western Ontario, as well as the Public Archives of Canada.

It is more difficult to thank the many friends from Oxford days who tolerated my preoccupation with medical history and health care politics and who served as sounding boards during the gestation of certain chapters. When I suffered through a bout or two of what Will Durant once called "intellectual measles," these intrepid spirits gave injections of antibodies against extremism to hasten the healing process. Latterly, I have had the good fortune to do post-graduate work in the department of medicine at the University of Western Ontario, and again have learned much from informal discussions with mentors and peers. It is impossible to compile a reasonable list of names, and I can only hope that these friends and colleagues will know who they are and how much I owe them.

Finally, my family, as always, was a fount of assistance of every possible description. Dr Ilse Treurnicht must be singled out for the unofficial dedication, however, on the grounds that she had the misfortune to be at close quarters with me during the production of both a thesis and a book: *baie dankie en baie liefde*.

Responsibility for any errors and shortcomings in this monograph is mine alone.

CDN
London, Ontario
March 1986

Abbreviations

AALL	American Association for Labor Legislation
AMA	American Medical Association
AMS	Associated Medical Services, Incorporated
BCHA	British Columbia Hospital Association
BCMA	British Columbia Medical Association
BMA	British Medical Association
CAMSI	Canadian Association of Medical Students and Interns
CCF	Co-operative Commonwealth Federation
CCL	Canadian Congress of Labour
CFA	Canadian Federation of Agriculture
CHA	Canadian Hospital Association
CHIA	Canadian Health Insurance Association
CHSA	Community Health Services Association
CLIOA	Canadian Life Insurance Officers Association
CMA	Canadian Medical Association
CMAJ	Canadian Medical Association Journal
COA	Canadian Osteopathic Association
CPSO	College of Physicians and Surgeons of Ontario
FMOQ	La Féderation des Médecins omnipracticiens du Québec
GMS	Group Medical Services, Incorporated (Regina)
GP	general practitioner
HIDS	Hospital Insurance and Diagnostic Services Act
HSPC	Health Services Planning Commission
KODC	"Keep Our Doctors" Committees
MCIC	Medical Care Insurance Commission
MD	medical doctor
MLA	member of the legislative assembly

MMA	Manitoba Medical Association
MMC	Maritime Medical Care
MMS	Manitoba Medical Services
MP	member of parliament
MPP	member of provincial parliament
MSA-BC	Medical Services Associated, British Columbia
MSI (Alberta)	Medical Services (Alberta), Incorporated
MSI-BC	Medical Services Incorporated, British Columbia
MS(S)I	Medical Services (Saskatoon), Incorporated
NDP	New Democratic Party
NHI	national health insurance
NHS	National Health Service (United Kingdom)
OMA	Ontario Medical Association
OMSIP	Ontario Medical Services Insurance Plan
PSI	Physicians' Services Incorporated
QHSA	Quebec Hospital Services Association
RCAMC	Royal Canadian Army Medical Corps
SCPS	Saskatchewan College of Physicians and Surgeons
SMA	Saskatchewan Medical Association
TCMP	Trans-Canada Medical Plans, Incorporated
TCMS	Trans-Canada Medical Services
TLCC	Trades and Labour Council of Canada
UFA	United Farmers of Alberta
VMA	Vancouver Medical Association
VON	Victorian Order of Nurses
WMA	World Medical Association

Private Practice, Public Payment

CHAPTER ONE

Introduction

One hundred years have elapsed since Chancellor Otto von Bismarck began organizing a state-sponsored sickness insurance program for German wage-earners. Over the past century, universal health care systems have been implemented with varying degrees of state involvement in the vast majority of industrialized nations. Canada has followed suit. As of April 1972, when the Yukon Territory inaugurated its medical services insurance plan, Canadians in all ten provinces and both northern territories were insured against basic medical and hospital expenses through a set of publicly administered programs generally referred to as medicare.[1]

The evolution of Canada's health insurance system has occurred piecemeal over several decades, and almost every step towards universal and comprehensive coverage has been dogged by controversy. In consequence, to study the evolution of health insurance is also to affirm one's faith in the democratic process, if only because so many segments of Canadian society have been vigorously represented in the debate. Big business, organized labour, agriculture, the churches, ethnic and consumer groups, the insurance industry, hospital administrators, and the health professions – these are just some of the voices through the years that have spoken to the issue of state-sponsored medical and hospital services prepayment in Canada.

For obvious reasons, the medical profession has played a particularly important role in the political evolution of health care insurance. The actual reactions of Canadian doctors and organized medicine to government initiatives in the financing of health services have varied considerably across provinces and decades. While generally suspicious of politicians' motives and bureaucratic blueprints, organized medicine at times took a very positive view of state-administered health insurance. More recently, of course, it has become clear that there is considerable professional dissatisfaction with government's role in the health services marketplace. In 1982 the National Council of Welfare went so far as to describe the Canadian Medical Association (CMA) as the "harshest critic" of current health insurance arrangements.[2] Although that assessment is debatable, since 1979 spokesmen for organized medicine have made a variety of privatization proposals aimed at eliminating the first-dollar coverage provisions of medicare. User-fees, deductibles, and supplemental private insurance all have been endorsed as policy options by medical associations or their leaders.

Controversy has also arisen in the last six years about the billing practices of doctors in some provinces who make additional charges above the fee schedule negotiated between provincial medical associations and their respective health ministries.[3] Initially, most provincial divisions of the CMA defended the right of practitioners to extra-bill as they saw fit and pointed out that only a small percentage of the total number of physician services was affected at any time. However, the federal government viewed these practices as a potential threat to the egalitarian principles of the medicare program. In April 1984, with the unanimous passage of the Canada Health Act by parliament, provinces that did not eliminate physician extra-billing were subjected to financial penalties under federal-provincial cost-sharing arrangements. (The penalties also applied against provinces levying hospital user-fees.) The last eighteen months have therefore seen relatively amicable negotiations to bring about the elimination of extra-billing in Manitoba, Nova Scotia, and Saskatchewan. As of March 1986 additional charges by physicians are a rarity in all provinces except Alberta, Ontario, and, to a lesser extent, New Brunswick, either because of legislative curbs or because practitioners have simply agreed to accept payments at the standard rates without extra-billing.[4]

Concerned by the compliance of several provinces with the intent of the Canada Health Act and encouraged by favourable legal opinions, the CMA has filed a claim with the Ontario Supreme Court in support of a challenge to the legislation. However, it is possible that this legal challenge will have to wend its way through the Supreme Court of Ontario, the Ontario Court of Appeal, and ultimately the Supreme Court of Canada – a process that could easily take two or three years.[5] In the interim, although Alberta's Conservative government seems temporarily prepared to tolerate extra-billing by physicians, a Liberal minority government in Ontario has encountered strong resistance from the Ontario Medical Association (OMA) as it endeavours to end extra-billing.[6] (The latter dispute is still unfolding as this book goes to press.)

Regardless of the outcome of the controversy over physician billing practices, further conflicts seem likely to arise between organized medicine and the state as technological progress and demographic change strain the organizational and fiscal fabric of medicare. In such a situation the historian's role is marginal. He can merely look backwards, hoping, if nothing else, to bring to light a record of the problems of the past; hoping, too, that analysis of that record will be helpful in understanding the problems of the present and those that could develop.

This particular historical study centres on doctors and health insurance. It was undertaken in part out of curiosity about the roots of current disputes between governments and organized medicine, and in part as an academic response to a gap in the literature on Canadian medicine and health insurance. From a historiographic viewpoint, the pivotal public policy decisions that shaped the Canadian health insurance system since the 1940s have already been superbly documented and analysed by Professor Malcolm G. Taylor.[7] Saskatchewan, too, has received considerable attention. Not only was that province the pioneer in public hospitalization and medical care insurance, but also the introduction of medicare precipitated a tremendous controversy and doctors' strike in 1962. Several books bearing on Saskatchewan medical politics have accordingly been published by individuals with first-hand knowledge of events in that province.[8]

In this study, however, the focus is neither on one province nor on public policy per se, but rather on the Canadian medical profession as an interest group concerned with developments in the field of state health insurance. While even brief sketches of policy development give some sense of the profession's role and its pressure-group strategies,[9] only one monograph has been published that takes a general view of the Canadian medical profession's reactions to state mediation in the health services marketplace. That volume, Professor Bernard Blishen's *Doctors and Doctrines*, emphasizes the origins, content, and function of professional ideology, using a sociological rather than historical framework.[10] Although sociological theory helps form the analytic backbone of the study at hand, it nonetheless is best approached as social historiography.

A historical orientation naturally implies that the author sets temporal boundaries on his or her work. In this case the narrative spans the fifty-five formative years from 1911, when leaders of Canadian

medicine took notice of Britain's national sickness insurance legislation, to 1966, when the Canadian federal government passed legislation guaranteeing financial assistance for any province implementing universal and comprehensive medical services insurance. The
concluding chapter does cursorily review some of the links between
these pre-medicare years and more current controversies. However,
a detailed discussion of the profession's policies and perspectives in
the years after 1966 has been deferred until the ramifications of the
1984 Canada Health Act become clearer.

A few caveats are in order at the outset. First, this book deals with
the political issue that has arguably been of greatest concern to
Canadian organized medicine in this century. Some medical readers
may be disappointed that the focus on health insurance precludes
consideration of the large amount of public service performed through
the years by various committees of the CMA and its provincial divisions.
The fact that these services are not better known is arguably a matter
for the public relations committees of organized medicine to address;
they are not directly relevant to the analysis here.

Second, because it is concerned with doctors and their organizations,
this volume necessarily understates the role of other individuals and
interest groups and also may at times appear to over-emphasize the
attention that governments gave to the viewpoints of organized
medicine. Political scientists long ago abandoned the notion that
governments serve simply to referee and respond to a continuing
contest between interest groups. Indeed, the records of the Department
of National Health and Welfare in the Public Archives of Canada
bear reviewing by anyone who believes that senior civil servants sit
passively waiting for policy ideas and analyses to be generated in
academe or the private sector. However, the activism of politicians
and civil servants is naturally seen most clearly in a study of public
policy such as Professor Taylor's, rather than in this work with its
emphasis on the policy preferences and strategies of a single private-
interest group.

Third, as with any historiographic portrait of a social group,
methodological problems arise; for every group is composed of
individuals who may or may not share the characteristics and
viewpoints imputed to a mythical average member. This is obviously
a concern when one describes the policies and perspectives of the
medical profession, since its members are well educated and accustomed to exercising their independent judgment on a daily basis in
clinical practice. On the other hand, the exigencies of a busy practice
may simply serve to limit the political involvement of the rank and
file, with the result that Michel's law of organizational oligarchy holds

sway, and a leadership corps self-selected by virtue of its political concern and commitment is better able to influence group opinions and actions.[11]

More specifically, it should be noted that speeches and articles by leaders of organized medicine, formal policy statements from medical associations, and reports of medical association committees form a substantial part of the documentation in this book. All these sources have limitations. As already mentioned, the view of political activists and leaders in the profession might not reflect rank-and-file opinion. Formal policy statements adopted at major medical conventions are more reliable, but here, too, there are difficulties: a clique may have swayed the delegates, or the delegates themselves may not be representative of the profession at large. Even committee reports have their drawbacks; for the final consensus is all that emerges, and the antecedent disagreements are buried. Unfortunately, only a limited amount of formal survey data concerning doctors' attitudes and policy preferences is available for the years 1911 to 1966, although it will be cited where appropriate. The result is a group portrait that inevitably blurs some of the differences within the medical profession during the period under discussion. It is to be hoped that other historians may be able to flesh out these details using this work as a preliminary sketch.

CHAPTER TWO

The Canadian Medical Profession: Theoretical and Historical Background

Among the professions, medicine is both the paradigmatic and the exceptional case: paradigmatic in the sense that other professions emulate its example; exceptional in that none have been able to achieve its singular degree of economic power and cultural authority.

Paul Starr, *The Social Transformation of American Medicine*, 1982

In 1960 Professor Malcolm Taylor aptly summed up organized medicine's reactions to government intervention in the health services market as typical of any group in society responding to a "presumed threat to its control over its physical and social environment."[1] Yet the medical profession is, in certain respects, far from a typical social group. A minimum of seven or eight years post-secondary training is required before one can apply for a general licence to practise medicine in Canada today; specialization can add three to six years to the training period. Medical incomes are reported by Statistics Canada to be the highest of any major occupational group. And, while Canadian doctors in every decade of the twentieth century have lamented the decline in status of their profession, physicians and surgeons continue to enjoy considerable public esteem and confidence.

The very fact that one refers to medicine as a profession means that a series of assumptions is being made. Many occupational groups aspire to professional status, but none in the twentieth century has been as successful as medicine – a truism that becomes more interesting in the light of the uncertain standing of doctors in Canadian society as recently as 150 years ago. In this chapter, then, certain aspects of professionalism as an occupational form will be examined with special reference to medicine. A background sketch of the profession's pre-1911 development will also be presented to provide historical context.

MEDICINE AS A PROFESSION

The special position of medicine in society is due in no small measure to the fact that doctors are linked with two powerful and paired sources of cultural authority: science and technology on the one hand, and health and illness and its treatment on the other.[2] But although medicine is therefore perceived and portrayed as the paradigmatic profession, sociologists have not always agreed on what actually demarcates a profession from other occupational groups.[3] Unique sets of traits said to be characteristic of professions turn out to be applicable to many other occupations. Take, for example, higher education by members of the skill-group, practice based on a standardized and explicit body of theory, barriers to entry based on competence assessments, and mechanisms of occupational self-discipline. These criteria, singly and in various combinations, could be applied not only to most occupations commonly thought of as professions, but also to a variety of skilled trades whose practitioners lay no claims to professional status.

Similar problems arise with features such as codes of ethics. These documents, which amount to public promises of performance, help foster an image of innate occupational altruism. Sociologists have sometimes taken ethical codes at face value and argued that professions are distinguished from more ordinary occupational groups by their commitment to public service. One might, as did Plato, claim that since medicine was invented for the noble aim of healing the sick, the doctor's aims are always similarly altruistic.[4] But this argument confuses the purpose of a task with the moral character of those who do it and throws into question the status of professions other than medicine. For example, the daily work of many accountants and lawyers cannot really be said to embody the same humanitarian goals as are inherent in the work of, say, an employee of a charitable organization. Moreover, adoption of an ethical code may be a strategic manoeuvre whereby a skill-group formulates its own rules and indicates a willingness to enforce them in hopes of avoiding external regulation.[5] How, then, does one determine whether an occupation is genuinely professionalized or merely engaged in self-serving mimicry? Certainly there is no validated scale of service-orientation and occupational altruism to permit such determinations.[6]

This is not to deny that codes of behaviour are useful. In the particular case of medicine many ethical tenets obviously help reduce the psychological tensions inherent in a situation where the doctor, as a stranger or near-stranger, takes an intimate medical history or performs a physical examination. Certain aspects of medical ethics – including promises that the physician will put the patient's interests first, proscriptions against sexual relations with patients, and assurances of confidentiality – have been important in defusing anxieties and building a legacy of trustworthiness that gives doctors extraordinary access both to their patients' bodies and to the details of patients' personal lives. Taboos concerning emotional involvement also enhance medical objectivity, which in turn is necessary given the emotional stress of illness for the patient and his or her friends and family.[7]

In a classic essay on medicine published in 1951 the American sociologist Talcott Parsons suggested that the anti-competitive and anti-commercial features of medical ethics should also be seen in a positive light. Overt commercialization of medicine might produce the image of the doctor as huckster or predator; patients would become more suspicious and less co-operative. On the one hand, the doctor's job of helping the sick would be made difficult. On the other, patients would be forced to cope with even more anxiety and the beneficial psychosomatic spin-offs of trust in the doctor would be reduced. Prohibitions against advertising, agreement on fee schedules, and the use of a sliding scale of charges, all demarcated the profession from the business world. And according to Parsons, all these practices supposedly served to "cut off the physician from many immediate opportunities for financial gain which are treated as legitimately open to businessmen."[8]

Despite the cogency of Parsons' reasoning, some questions arise at this point. Does the prohibition against advertising only safeguard the patient, or does it widen existing gaps in public information and reduce the accountability of the professional? Do fee schedules simply ensure that individual doctors do not exploit individual patients? Or do they also prevent price competition of potential benefit to the consumer and abet the economic advancement of doctors as monopoly sellers of an essential service?

The sliding scale of fees is equally problematic. Long held out as evidence of medical altruism, the sliding scale was given a more practical meaning by Dr D.W. Cathell in a book of business advice popular with American and Canadian practitioners of the 1890s. Doctors, Cathell wrote, should display a sign in a "semi-prominent place" stating that fees are from "$1–$10 CASH": "Having your charge from $1–$10 will enable you to get an extra fee from cases of an extraordinary character, and still allow you to charge minimum fees for ordinary cases. Such a schedule will also make those who get off by paying the lowest fee feel gratified, and will show everybody that you assume to be skillful enough to attend $10 cases."[9] More importantly, economist Reuben Kessel's oft-cited 1958 paper demonstrated that the profession's "Robin Hood" function in settings where a sliding scale was used might in fact be seen as profitable price discrimination.[10] (Price discrimination is the practice of varying the charges for identical goods and services depending on the perceived ability or willingness of the purchaser to pay.)

Thus it is plain that most aspects of medical ethics can be viewed as promoting or protecting the interests of both patients *and* doctors. That they do so does not mean that they should be condemned or abandoned but rather emphasizes our earlier reservations about the automatic attribution of a distinctive professional service orientation to occupations that uphold an ethical code.

The sociological debate about what makes professions unique is ongoing; analysts such as Eliot Freidson and Terence Johnson, however, have persuasively argued that occupational autonomy is the most important cornerstone of professionalism. In general terms, *professionalism as a form of occupational institutionalization is unique in the extent to which the members of the occupation themselves control their daily work, along with the social institutions and subordinate occupations associated with professional practice.* Given this privileged position in the working world and an understandable pride in both the collective achievements of the profession and their own clinical attainments, it is to be expected that doctors should strongly resist any encroachment on their autonomy. State intervention in the medical services marketplace has been particularly threatening, because any government has, in theory, legal and fiscal power to produce sweeping changes in the technical and socioeconomic terms of practice. Thus, to modify Professor Taylor's observation, the medical profession's response to a presumed or actual threat to "its control over its physical and social environment" will be atypically vigorous precisely because that control is so marked.

PROFESSIONAL AUTONOMY: FURTHER CONSIDERATIONS

Professional autonomy has both technical and socio-economic aspects. The medical profession's collective technical autonomy consists in its freedom, as an international community of scholarly and consulting experts, to arrive at definitions of disease and formulate continually updated principles for the prevention, palliation, and cure of illness.

State agencies, together with the research divisions of drug companies and medical equipment manufacturers, have taken a larger role in the production and control of innovations over the years. But medical academicians nonetheless remain the key formulators and disseminators of information on the evolving theory and practice of medicine.

An important feature of professionalism is the extent to which the technical autonomy accorded the occupation extends to its individual members.[11] In medicine the importance of applying general principles with reference to the particular needs of individual patients underpins the practitioner's freedom to diagnose and treat as he sees fit.

This freedom is apparent in diverse settings, because third parties are usually in no position to evaluate the fiduciary and clinical interactions between individual doctors and individual patients. Even in bureaucratic settings, such as hospitals or large clinics, lay administrators can be expected to tread carefully when their decisions impinge on technical aspects of medical practice. The profession's monopoly of diagnostic expertise also limits the extent to which other health care workers can interfere in the daily clinical work of doctors.[12] Indeed, the most reliable source of direct checks and balances is interaction with – and evaluation by – professional peers and mentors.

Where the doctor is self-employed and working either solo or as part of a small group, opportunities for colleague control are few. Bureaucratic settings do open up more possibilities for peer evaluation. However, except as part of formal professional training programs, doctors seem generally reluctant to criticize their fellow practitioners, let alone invoke disciplinary proceedings upon them.[13] The clear lines of authority associated with bureaucracies are therefore supplanted by a loose collegial network that leaves the individual practitioner's clinical freedom more or less unchecked. This independence stands in definite contrast to the situation of "semi-professions," such as social work and nursing, where formal supervision and discipline are built into the institutional setting of work.[14]

Freidson has been so impressed with the durability of technical autonomy in widely disparate practice situations[15] that he views it as the single most important feature of medical professionalism: "So long as a profession is free of the technical evaluation and control of other occupations in the division of labor, its lack of ultimate freedom from the State, and even its lack of control over the socioeconomic terms of work do not significantly change its essential character as a profession."[16] As we shall see in the chapters that follow, long before medical sociologists made this distinction, advocates of state-administered health care services used the same point in attempting to reassure both doctors and the general public that the clinical freedom of medicine would not be undermined by prepayment mechanisms.

But while the distinction between socio-economic and technical autonomy can be drawn in theory, the process by which abstract concepts of client needs are translated into professional practices is inevitably affected by social and material factors. For example, it has been noted that practitioners struggling to build a clientele in a private-fee setting can, through fear of professional and financial failure, become "particularly responsive to their patients' demands for hospitalization and for acceptable diagnoses and types of treatment."[17] Surgery rates are higher when doctors are paid on a fee-for-service basis rather than by salary.[18] Conversely, it has been suggested that doctors on salary have less incentive to serve their patients well.[19] Rates of hospital bed utilization also appear to vary depending on how a medical practice is organized and financed.[20] In short, since social and economic factors do have some influence on clinical practice, technical autonomy is at least subject to indirect constraints.

Also vital in terms of practice patterns is the availability of resources. It has become well recognized that Say's Law finds application in health economics: supply seldom outstrips demand when insurance creates a zero price market. Instead, hospital beds and doctors' offices are overloaded in response to consumer-initiated and supplier-induced demand,[21] and rationing by price has sometimes given way to rationing by queue when prepayment mechanisms are introduced. The availability of resources has accordingly been a frequent source of conflict between doctors and third parties intervening to organize consumer prepayment of health care costs. Specialists practising on a fee basis may be disturbed when shifts in resource allocation curb the availability of hospital beds necessary to their livelihood. In salaried situations, too, although the financial sting is drawn, clinicians may face discomfiting professional and ethical dilemmas when hospital beds or vital medical technologies are in short supply.

These links between technical and socio-economic matters not only heighten professional concern over third party mediation in the medical services marketplace; they also provide organized medicine with an important weapon in political battles to ensure that intervention by the state or other agencies occurs in patterns salutary to professional status, incomes, and working conditions. Disputes over remuneration can, for instance, be turned into crusades for better-quality care, as organized medicine's spokesmen argue that lower fees force doctors to see too many patients for a livelihood. And although any profession will "lay great stress on the need for occupational and individual independence as a precondition of fulfilling obligations to consumers,"[22] no other occupational group is able to muster these arguments with such emotive life-and-death connotations.

The actual socio-economic form of practice that has traditionally been associated with professionalism finds the majority of practitioners self-employed, working solo or in small groups, and providing their services to individual consumers on a fee basis. This pattern is still commonplace in medical practice in many parts of the world and appears to be preferred by large numbers of doctors. Reasons for the appeal of private-fee practice are varied. It definitely provides a practitioner with a sense of being his or her "own boss" and also allows considerable latitude for the doctor to choose place of work, colleagues, office arrangements, and – depending on facilities and referral networks – areas of special technical interest. Where services are sold direct to individuals without mediation by a third party, the practitioner retains the prerogative of setting his or her fees with reference to guidelines adopted by medical organizations. This gives the practitioner some of the economic benefits of what may be termed "cartelization,"[23] and additional market strength is provided through price discrimination.

When organizations rather than individuals become the predominant purchasers of professional services, however, the individual professional may be hired directly on a salaried basis. This trend accounts for the contrast in the organization of accountancy practice between the nineteenth and twentieth centuries.[24] The medical profession has been better able to maintain its socio-economic autonomy for the obvious reason that its members' services are generally provided to consumers on a one-to-one basis. Consumers themselves have occasionally organized to strengthen their position in dealing with providers of medical services. Historically, the best-known example is the development of contract practice under the auspices of fraternal organizations in the United Kingdom and North America between 1880 and 1910.

Rather than paying doctors on an individual fee-per-item-of-service basis, members of a fraternal organization would hire general practitioners either on an annual retainer, or on a capitation basis where the practitioner would receive a set amount per patient regardless of the volume of services given. Hence the economic leverage of the doctor was curtailed, because he was forced to haggle over his retainer with an organization instead of adjusting his fees to individual consumers on a per service basis that permitted price discrimination.

In another respect, too, the balance of power was altered. The doctor in private-fee practice with a clientele of individuals would, of course, have a financial interest in maintaining and building his practice, but he could afford to lose the occasional client who was excessively demanding or unpleasant. In "lodge" or "club" practice, one disagreeable patient could agitate against renewal of the doctor's contract with the entire fraternal organization. (General practitioners in Canada referred to these patients as "kickers" – a sobriquet borrowed from the farmers' term for domestic cattle and horses that kicked without warning.) As we shall see in chapter 3, the influence of the fraternal organizations was much weaker in Canada than in Britain, and private fee-for-service practice remained prevalent in Canadian medicine during the period under discussion in this study. Hence, in the absence of major intervention in the medical services market by consumer-sponsored organizations, a challenge to the profession's position could come only from the state.

Interestingly, the profession's early perception of government intervention tended to be positive, particularly in the period from 1870 to 1910.[25] State support was recognized as an important adjunct in the development of medical education, hospitals, and public health regulations and facilities. Moreover, doctors were also well aware that government regulation played a central role in the organization and maintenance of an autonomous medical profession. Any occupation whose members control specialized services will enjoy some degree of occupational autonomy, simply because of its information advantage over consumers. However, a key aspect of professionalism is the extent to which the state has intervened to support the self-regulatory claims of a given occupation and to confer a legalized monopoly of expertise on its members. In this respect there is an obvious contrast in legal status between doctors or other professionals and providers of technical services such as auto mechanics or television repairmen. The propensity of nation-states to regulate private markets has varied considerably in Europe and North America over the past two centuries, so that the success of occupational groups in marshalling support for their claims to statutory self-regulation has sometimes been a function of when those claims were made and the strength of the occupational lobby rather than a reflection of the public interest to be served by thwarting the free play of market forces. Nonetheless, medicine was able to make a particularly strong case for occupational monopoly and professional autonomy because of public health considerations and the ability of doctors to embrace and abet the rise of biomedical science and technology in the nineteenth and twentieth centuries. With these concepts in mind, let us turn now to an examination of the pre-1911 backdrop of the Canadian medical profession.

CANADIAN MEDICINE: THE INSTITUTIONALIZATION OF A PROFESSION

When sociologists speak of a profession of medicine, they are referring to a particular occupational form that evolved in Europe and first became clearly identifiable in the nineteenth century. Indeed, if the nation-state was the midwife of the industrial revolution, it was also *accoucheur* to medicine and other professions in the nineteenth century. A deregulatory impulse cleared away guild and mercantilist statutes to make way for industrial capitalism;[26] a regulatory impulse abetted the professions as they organized and controlled specialized service markets.[27] Certainly if one looks back merely as far as eighteenth-century Europe, one sees not the medical profession but rather an array of squabbling practitioners of diverse stripes. Medical education was provided in guild academies, apprenticeship situations, and proprietary schools, in addition to universities. Barber-surgeons, apothecaries, and surgeon-apothecaries lingered on as urban guild atavisms; while even within the universities surgery and medicine had yet to be fully reconciled. Independent fee practice was common, although formal fee schedules were seldom used and large numbers of high-status physicians worked on direct retainer for the houses of European nobles. Partly as a result of the continuation of medieval guild statutes, licensing mechanisms were in existence in many jurisdictions. However, these regulations were inconsistently applied and often flouted by leading practitioners. The lower classes of society had little contact with "official medicine," and there is in any case no evidence that the legally recognized factions had much advantage over the many self-taught healers and charlatans who still did a brisk trade. Clinical attainments and the judgment of one's peers were less important for advancement than the ability to curry favour either with aristocratic patrons or with a wealthy clientele culled from the expanding merchant class.[28]

The situation in Canada naturally reflected the influence of institutions and trends in Britain and Europe. As is usually the case with professions, state regulation of the Canadian medical services market came at the behest not of consumers but of practitioners. The first initiative was in 1710, when indigenous barber-sugeons and surgeon-apothecaries persuaded the colonial governor to issue an edict forbidding practice by any other than those already established in practice in New France (later Quebec). This edict was never enforced. A more effective enactment followed in 1750, warning of "the evil" done by "strangers whose ability is unknown" and entrenching formal mechanisms for the evaluation of credentials and expertise.[29]

Licensing legislation in Quebec fell into disuse after the English invasion of 1759. A new act was therefore promulgated in 1788 that relegated the dwindling numbers of barber-surgeons and surgeon-apothecaries to secondary status and elevated an elite group of British-trained practitioners to positions on a licensing board. This act was part of a broader movement that saw government authority marshalled to create a more homogeneous and better-qualified occupational group. In Prussia, for example, an 1825 edict restricted barber-surgeons and surgeon-apothecaries to practising under the surveillance of a higher-grade doctor. First-class surgeons were to have three years' theoretical and practical studies in a university-affiliated institute; but, while given full practice rights in surgery, they could practise *medicine* only in areas where no holder of a university-conferred medical doctorate (MD) was available. Those holding MD degrees, still at the top of the ladder, were now pushed to study surgery and know its applications. The impetus clearly was towards single-category licensure, with uniportal entry to practice for doctors trained in basic medicine and surgery in Prussian universities. Albeit with many variations, this same trend was evident elsewhere in Europe.[30] It is likely that the coalescence and upgrading of the profession occurred more rapidly in Canada simply because guild academies and statutes did not exist to perpetuate European and British divisions in the skill-group.

On the other hand, the weakness of colonial authority and lack of trained personnel meant that medical licensing legislation was not well enforced. New Brunswick and Nova Scotia passed their first licensing acts in 1816 and 1828, respectively, but as historian Ronald Hamowy has noted, "the only penalty associated with practising in violation of these statutes was that the practitioner was prohibited from suing for the recovery of fees." Even the practitioners who were appointed to sit on the licensing board in New Brunswick did not bother to take out licences.[31] Feeble attempts to enforce medical licensure were also made in Upper Canada (eventually Ontario) starting in 1795, although the first licensing board was not appointed until 1818.[32]

Difficulties with enforcement notwithstanding, Canadian provincial governments hereafter continuously maintained some mechanism for regulating the medical services marketplace. This was in contrast to the situation in the United States, where a deregulatory impulse contributed to the repeal of medical licensing laws in most jurisdictions during the 1830s and 1840s.[33] In fact, the Canadian medical community at this juncture began pressing for the establishment of formal professional *self-government* to supplant licensing boards appointed by colonial administrators. In Ontario conflict between English and Scottish trainees led rival factions to seek control of licensing procedures. A provincial College of Physicians and Surgeons was incorporated in 1839, but its charter was disallowed in 1840 because the powerful London (England) licensing corporations claimed infringement on their fiat to regulate medicine and surgery throughout the Empire. In Quebec there were also intraprofessional rivalries, as a rising group of indigenous practitioners, predominantly but not exclusively francophone, sought to undercut the British elite who controlled the licensing board and the McGill University medical faculty. From 1831 to 1837 licensing boards were elected by the practitioners themselves, but thereafter the boards were again appointed by the governor.[34] In 1846 the Quebec doctors made another bid for professional self-government, a movement prompted in part by the proliferation of unlicensed practitioners and the petitions for formal licensure by Thomsonian (botanic) healers. A College of Physicians and Surgeons was incorporated the following year and assisted in heading off not only the self-taught Thomsonian herbalists, but later the homeopaths and eclectics – two splinter groups that rejected certain of the theories and practices of the mainstream profession.[35]

The Quebec case illustrates some important points about the form of occupational authority that has been described by social theorist Max Weber as "collegial." In Quebec the profession's political lobbying was clearly the result of an impulse – first, to level out differences within the group, and second, to generate autonomy and protect the exclusive status of all the group's members. Weber has therefore contended that the creation of such private governments "is in no sense specifically 'democratic.'" Diverse social groups in different societies "have tended to set up and maintain collegial bodies to supervise or even take over powers," and these bodies are then used to guard their members' privileges "against those who were excluded from them."[36]

The emergence of rival schools such as homeopathy and eclecticism can be taken as evidence that there was no firm scientific consensus concerning most aspects of practice. Until the latter third of the nineteenth century the substantive bodies of theory and practice developed by practitioners of the healing arts were usually fanciful or downright dangerous.[37] Hence in the general case, the existence of such systems need not be seen as a criterion of professionalism per se, but rather as an adjunct in bolstering "the claim that there is such an unusual degree of skill and knowledge involved in professional work that non-professionals are not equipped to evaluate or regulate it."[38]

In Ontario the regular profession was less successful in pressing this claim on legislators than was its counterpart in Quebec. Petitions for reinstatement of professional self-government were showered upon the legislators, and actual bills to this effect were introduced in 1845, 1846, 1849, 1859, and 1860. None passed. There was widespread scepticism about the effectiveness of mainstream medicine. Moreover, the political atmosphere in the anglophone province was influenced both by the American trend to deregulation and by the laissez-faire aspects of the 1858 British Imperial Medical Act which eliminated earlier penalties for unlicensed practice.[39] Pursuing a liberal rather than libertarian course,[40] the Ontario assemblymen licensed both the homeopaths (1859) and the eclectics (1861). Indeed, these "irregulars" were given the right to elect their own licensing boards, a step towards self-government the regulars had yet to win. By 1865 the main body of the profession in Ontario had also moved towards self-government through an act creating an administrative council on which elected territorial representatives sat with medical school delegates. And in 1869 an Ontario College of Physicians and Surgeons was incorporated, albeit with the homeopaths and eclectics included as a concession to win political support.[41]

In Ontario and Quebec, where professional self-government was attained prior to the formation of province-wide *voluntary associations*, local medical societies abounded. The Quebec City Medical Society, founded in 1826, was the first such association, and others followed rapidly. Local medical societies proclaimed various goals, including promotion of science and professional fellowship, suppression of practice by irregulars, and, almost invariably, creation of a fee schedule to be used by all local practitioners.[42] Coalescence of local medical societies into province-wide associations permitted stronger legislative lobbying and in the western and maritime provinces was soon followed by conferral of self-regulatory privileges. In the Maritimes, the provincial medical societies themselves were given self-government privileges, and this legislative approach accordingly produced a single body charged with both promoting professional interests and protecting the public interest. In the other provinces the voluntary association and College of Physicians and Surgeons were legally separate entities. Table 1 shows the year

TABLE 1
Professional Self-Government in Canadian
Medicine

Province or Territory	Date Inaugurated
Quebec	1847
Ontario	1869
Nova Scotia	1872
Manitoba	1877*
New Brunswick	1881
British Columbia	1886
Prince Edward Island	1890
Northwest Territories	1888–1905†
Alberta	1906
Saskatchewan	1906

* The Manitoba profession, although incorporated in 1871, does
  not seem to have had significant self-government privileges
  until 1877.
† The Northwest Territories' professional corporation was dissolved into the Alberta and Saskatchewan colleges.

professional self-government was attained in each province.

Among voluntary associations the most important group was eventually to be the Canadian Medical Association (CMA). It was born in 1867, the year that Ontario, Quebec, Nova Scotia, and New Brunswick federated into the Dominion of Canada; but it had little influence for more than twenty-five years. In the 1890s thought was given to abandoning annual meetings of the CMA or to disbanding the association altogether. Although the national organization's profile was enhanced when the *Canadian Medical Association Journal* (*CMAJ*) began publication in 1911, it was not until the 1920s that the CMA gained a large membership, secure funding, and considerable political influence.[43]

One of the important early contributions of the CMA, however, was its code of ethics, adopted at an 1868 meeting and styled almost identically after the code devised by the American Medical Association in 1847.[44] A variety of paternalistic instructions to patients appeared. For example, a patient's "first duty" was to consult only "regular" practitioners. Patients should see the doctor even for "trivial cases," lest "fatal results" supervene. And a patient should "never permit his crude opinion as to their fitness" to undercut his obedience to doctors' orders and prescriptions.

For CMA members themselves the code sternly forbade consultations with irregular practitioners, while it encouraged shared patient care by regular doctors. An elaborate etiquette of consultation was provided which was designed to promote solidarity and reduce disagreements in the presence of laymen. Other anti-competitive measures were also given prominence. For instance, while "individuals in indigent circumstances" should be "cheerfully and freely accorded" professional services, a rich practitioner should never give free service to the well-to-do lest others come to demand discounts from his poorer brethren in practice. So far as possible, doctors "in every town and district" should adhere to a single fee schedule as "a point of honour." Advertising, medical reports to lay journals, use of secret remedies, and practitioner patents on medicines or surgical instruments were all implicitly or explicitly discouraged as well.[45]

Some sections of the code can be seen as promoting – or advertising – an altruistic service-ideal; and, consonant with our earlier discussion of Parsons's view of medical ethics, many can be interpreted as benefiting the profession and public simultaneously. At the same time, the overall effect of the document would be to encourage professional behaviour and public perceptions that might foster an image of the doctor as part of a community of ethical gentlemen for whom the crass practices of the commercial realm had no appeal.[46] This image in turn could assist "in generating public trust in a system in which members of the community judged the competence of one another."[47]

Rules from the CMA code were applied during the 1880s and 1890s, when the self-governing colleges won the right to discipline their members for "infamous or disgraceful conduct in a professional respect." Such practices as guaranteeing cures, advertising successful cases in a newspaper, or distributing handbills that claimed superior ability were curtailed.[48] Thus, while the CMA's code of ethics embodied voluntary measures oriented to the creation of a professional collective whose members would appear to be equally superior practitioners of the healing arts, the self-governing colleges formally institutionalized this movement. By co-opting a variety of disciplinary privileges from their respective governments, the colleges helped transform the profession from a community within a community to a state within a state. And by policing themselves, albeit loosely, the doctors minimized the likelihood of some external regulatory agency having a significant say in how the profession conducted its affairs.

Only in Ontario did a political group contest these legal privileges. The Patrons of Industry, a rural populist party, gained legislative representation in 1894,[49] and as an Ontario Medical Association (OMA) president later complained, a "prominent feature" of their policy "was obnoxious opposition to all kinds of class legislation."[50] The Patrons introduced a bill in 1895 to license midwives; add government appointees to the College of Physicians and Surgeons' board of examiners; reduce medical school and college examination fees to open the profession to poorer students; remove disciplinary proceedings from college auspices to magistrates' courts; and give the legislature, rather than the college, the legal right to approve the fee schedules set by local medical societies. Only the last point was accepted by the Liberals and Conservatives. However, the provincial legislature never did roll back a fee increase, and the only consequence was that in cases where a doctor sued for his fee, the courts were no longer bound to use his medical society schedule as a guideline for settlement. After 1896, with the Patrons gone from the political scene, the Ontario Medical Association pressed successfully for restoration of the college's power to approve fee schedules.[51] Thus, in the early part of the twentieth century the profession's self-government privileges were firmly established in all provinces.

In the early post-Confederation period, the CMA had led the way in the battle against irregular practitioners, and the Association's "ethical" injunction against consulting with them was strictly enforced.[52] At that time, however, the number of irregulars outside Ontario was not very large. Only one homeopath was registered among forty-nine practitioners on Manitoba's provincial roster between 1873 and 1883,[53] for example, and the Northwest Territories College of Physicians and Surgeons made arrangements to test homeopaths only twice in its eleven years of formal examination proceedings.[54] In Ontario, although the eclectics died out rapidly, fierce infighting between the homeopaths and their mainstream rivals persisted for some years within the College of Physicians and Surgeons.[55] The revolution in biomedical science during the latter part of the nineteenth century undercut both the allopathic dogma of the mainstream and the homeopathic paradigm.[56] By the 1890s there were almost certainly less than 100 homeopaths practising across Canada; by 1925 there were only forty in the entire nation, thirty-two of whom practised in Ontario.[57]

Although the profession's authority and status were greatly increased by the discoveries and applications of biomedical science, other groups at the turn of the century were perceived as potential threats to medicine's newly consolidated position. Because nurses, like doctors, were given increasingly rigorous training, medical spokesmen protested vigorously against nurses who dared make "ill-directed excursions beyond their proper latitude."[58] The OMA criticized both the Victorian Order of Nurses (VON) and British-trained midwives, and the Winnipeg Medical Society soon added a western voice to the anti-VON campaign.[59] Midwives were officially barred from practice in Ontario as early as 1865, although many remained active in rural areas. In Quebec they were subject to strict control by the College of Physicians and Surgeons. Throughout the Maritimes and the western provinces they were regulated more loosely and continued to be an important source of obstetrical care for decades. However, by the Second World War traditional midwifery was almost entirely absent from the Canadian medical scene.[60]

Organized medicine's strongest reactions were reserved for osteopaths and chiropractors, who began to immigrate from the United States in the late 1890s. No osteopathic training institute was ever opened in Canada, and the number of osteopaths north of the forty-ninth parallel was small. Moreover, the osteopaths split into two warring camps early in the twentieth century. An older faction of "ten-fingered osteopaths" relied on spinal manipulation alone, whereas more progressive osteopaths effected a gradual rapprochement with the medical mainstream.[61] Despite opposition from organized medicine, between 1906 and 1918 osteopaths won full practice rights (except for major surgery) in the west and the Maritimes, although only a handful of osteopaths practised in those provinces.[62] In Quebec a very limited number of osteopaths moved into the province before the College of Physicians and Surgeons acted to curb osteopathic immigrant practitioners. However, in Ontario, where well over 100 osteopaths eventually settled, there was especially heavy infighting between the osteopaths and the regular profession. In 1925 the osteopaths were finally relegated to subordinate status by the Drugless Practitioners' Act, which confined their practice to spinal manipulation alone.[63]

Unlike the osteopaths the chiropractors had little credibility with the legislators. They put blind faith in spinal manipulation as a panacea, and completely rejected the scientific paradigm of the then rapidly advancing medical sciences.[64] Some 200 to 300 practitioners were estimated to be working in Canada by 1914, about two-thirds of them in Ontario. At that time the only Canadian training institute for chiropractors was in Hamilton, Ontario and the facilities and instructor alike were judged wholly inadequate by a royal commission in 1917.[65] The first chiropractic act was passed by Alberta in 1923, and Ontario's 1925 Drugless Practitioners' Act also offered legal recognition to chiropractors. Further recognition came slowly, however, and chiropractors in diverse provinces practised outside the law on into the 1940s and 1950s, by which time more judicious claims were being made for chiropractic therapy.

Last among potential rivals to the regular profession, we must consider the opticians. At the turn of the century, a split was developing between those opticians who simply sold pre-ground spectacles or ground lenses to a doctor's specifications, and those who took greater pains in diagnostic refractions. The former were eventually classified as opticians and the latter evolved into modern optometrists. Attempts by reform-minded opticians to upgrade their skill-group were derided by regular doctors,[66] but because of the limited scope of optometric practice, competition was never as intense as it was with other groups. By the First World War clearer and higher standards for optometry began to emerge, and optometrists were legally recognized in ensuing years.[67] (Infighting between optometrists and regular doctors did not again pose a problem until the 1960s, when the number of ophthalmologists increased. Ophthalmologists were ethically barred from teaching optometrists; they also campaigned against independent practice by optometrists and in favour of their subordination to a paramedical role as ophthalmological assistants. This conflict died out once ophthalmology was securely established as a surgical specialty.)

No background sketch of professional institutions would be adequate without data on medical education. Formal medical education began in Canada in the 1820s with the creation of the Montreal Medical Institute, later the medical faculty of McGill University. Various proprietary schools sprang up and flourished from the 1850s to the 1870s. However, in contrast to the United States, the proprietary schools were not in themselves degree-granting institutions. Hence the number of proprietary schools in Canada tended to be limited by the number of universities with which they could affiliate for bestowal of degrees, and competition for students never attained the cutthroat level of America's "diploma mills."

McGill first and later Laval (Quebec City) had been the only universities to maintain very close ties with their medical faculties, but starting in the 1880s and 1890s the proprietary schools began to be reabsorbed into the universities. New scientific subjects were added to the curriculum, and both matriculation requirements and the length of the medical course were increased. There were at times mixed motives for raising standards. For example, in Ontario, where the profession was believed to be overcrowded, councillors of the College of Physicians and Surgeons argued in 1891, 1895, and 1898 for higher matriculation requirements and a lengthening of the medical curriculum on the grounds that this would limit enrolments and ultimately reduce the competition that was driving incomes down.[68] Together with a desire to improve practice standards, similar concern about overcrowding led Maritimes medical reformers to seek lengthened courses and tougher admission requirements.[69]

By 1910, when Abraham Flexner toured Canadian medical schools to prepare his famous Carnegie Foundation report, many reforms had already taken place. Medical faculties at McGill, Toronto, and Laval (Quebec City) universities merited high praise for their standards of admission, curricula, and facilities. The Manitoba Medical College also was judged a good teaching institute, and the connection between the University of Manitoba and the medical school was, as Flexner saw it, "in process of becoming organic."[70] However, Flexner's criticisms of Queen's, Laval (Montreal), Western Ontario, and Dalhousie universities struck home. Protests were raised against his assessments,[71] but changes were initiated almost overnight. In particular, both Western and Dalhousie, which Flexner castigated mercilessly for lending their prestige and degrees "to proprietary medical schools for which they can hope to do nothing and which they cannot possibly control,"[72] entirely reorganized their medical training to create a proper medical faculty with professorial chairs and good facilities.[73]

Thus, by 1911, when state health insurance first warranted official reaction from Canadian organized medicine, the proprietary school was a thing of the past.[74] Medical education was in the hands of the universities, and both curricula and admission requirements were well on their way to being standardized. Although irregular practitioners remained in evidence, they were clearly in a subordinate position. Professional self-government bodies were firmly established in every province, and despite low enrolment in the CMA, local and provincial medical associations were flourishing. Unlike manual workers of the period, who sold their labour to capitalist intermediaries, doctors sold their services directly to consumers. Unlike various other experts, who sold their knowledge and skills to organizations and businesses and might be taken into actual employment, most doctors were self-employed and sold their expertise to a large and heterogeneous clientele of individuals. And finally, unlike self-employed artisans, who controlled their own craft processes but otherwise worked "to order," the doctors' therapeutic authority put them in a position to give "orders" to clients. Professionalization, seen as a state-aided process by which doctors gradually established a high degree of socio-economic and technical control of their own occupation, was now complete. And from here on, consumers, governments, and other third parties would face considerable resistance whenever they attempted to reverse the trend and curtail professional power.

CHAPTER THREE

Canadian Medicine and Health Insurance: Pre-Depression Ambivalence

We are living in a commercial age and, I believe, the solution to this problem will be arrived at by studying commercial methods.

A.R. Munroe, "Health Insurance and the Medical Profession," *CMAJ*, 1914

The medical man is willing to be exploited and to do any amount of work for nothing; but when it comes to making an arrangement whereby he can be sure of being paid, he wants the earth; at least, some of them do.

J.H. MacDermot, "Health Insurance," *CMAJ*, 1925

In state health insurance Canada and its medical profession were subject to strong international influences from the outset. The first European health insurance law was passed in the German Empire in 1883 and was the brainchild of that master of *Realpolitik*, Chancellor Otto von Bismarck. Bismarck did not dissemble about his motivation: increasing support for the German socialist movement led the chancellor to implement sickness insurance that would "bribe the working classes" and help undermine political opposition.[1] The 1883 Sickness Assurance Act legislated compulsory contributions to an insurance fund by workers in industry and their employers but did not affect the higher-income groups.

Political unrest helped spur the spread of sickness insurance to other European nations, as did concern about the links between health and industrial productivity and the need for a fit working class to supply vigorous soldiers in a world of competing imperial powers. For whatever reasons, state-sponsored schemes for the provision of medical and wage benefits to manual workers and employees below a certain income level were initiated by Austria in 1883, by Hungary in 1891, Luxembourg in 1901, Norway in 1909, and Serbia in 1910. Despite this steady growth, prior to 1911, the Canadian medical profession registered little or no reaction to the idea of state health insurance. Not until the innovation crossed the English Channel did it seem close enough to excite commentary from Canadian practitioners.

HEALTH INSURANCE IN
"THE OLD COUNTRY"

As already noted, the latter half of the nineteenth century saw the Canadian medical profession following a developmental course different from that of either the United Kingdom or the United States. Complaints about the proliferation of specialties were voiced in Canadian medical circles during the 1880s and 1890s, but no serious friction existed between general practitioners (GPs) and specialists.

In Britain, however, a class barrier of sorts separated the medical and surgical consultants from general practitioners, the former being descended, as it were, from Royal College stock, while the latter found their ancestry among the apothecaries and, before that, the trade-tainted grocers' and spicers' guild.[2] This division became of increasing importance as both consumer organizations and the state intervened in the medical services marketplace. From the 1880s on, an increasing number of Friendly Societies, lodges, and other fraternal organizations hired GPs on contract. The "club doctors," as they were called, found conditions of work for the consumer collectives to be less than satisfactory. Capitation fees were generally low and the volume of work high. So long as GPs underbid one another in an effort to win the yearly contract to attend a given consumer organization, there was little chance of pushing the capitation fees up. Moreover the complaint was made that some patients tended to call the doctor in for no good reason, and the doctor in turn was unable to refuse a call for fear that a disgruntled patient would then agitate against renewal of his contract with the organization at the year's end. Conflicts between doctors and the various fraternal organizations came to a head in the 1890s. Local medical societies were formed and boycotted some of the clubs, seeking higher capitation fees and other improvements in the GPs' lot.[3] However, the consultants, who regarded GP activism as a threat to their own status, were not always supportive of the medical societies' attempts to drive a better bargain with the lodges and clubs.[4]

Despite their drawbacks, club work and contract practice were vital to the livelihood of many general practitioners. They could not really compete with the elite of physicians and surgeons, who acted both as consultants and as providers of primary care to the upper and middle classes of British society on a predominantly fee-for-service basis. Thus, by 1911, when the Liberal government first proposed a national sickness insurance plan, about 10,000 of Britain's 20,000 GPS were believed to be involved in some form of contract practice. Of these, historian Frank Honigsbaum has estimated that 5,000 were dependent for their very subsistence on the capitation rates offered by the consumer organizations.[5] Club doctors were accordingly interested in state health insurance as a means of escaping the economic pressures of contract practice.

Not surprisingly, the British Medical Association (BMA) was split on the issue. The BMA, formed in 1856, was actually the outgrowth of the Provincial Medical and Surgical Association, which had been organized in 1832 to protect the interests of the apothecary-GPS. Consultants later joined the body, but they saw themselves as "scientists" in a learned professional association; the "unionist" outlook of the club doctors was a source of internal squabbles. Initial acceptance of national health insurance by the BMA thus reflected an apparent victory for the general practitioners. Freed of contract practice, they might improve their status within the profession and society at large.

The actual national insurance bill, however, was drawn up with only minimal consultation between the governing Liberals and the medical profession. Protests poured in on all sides, and David Lloyd George, then chancellor of the exchequer, courted the BMA unsuccessfully through lengthy negotiations. While the doctors had misgivings on several scores as their marriage to the state loomed ever closer, the size of the dowry appears to have been a major consideration. The government offered six shillings per head per year. This offer was 50 percent more than what a BMA survey showed the average rate to be in lodge or contract practice, but the doctors remained opposed.[6]

Although Canadian medical journals of the late nineteenth and early twentieth centuries devoted considerable space to political and economic matters, they mirrored their American counterparts by taking virtually no notice of state health insurance until the controversy began in Britain.[7] The oldest Canadian medical periodical at this time was the *Canada Lancet*, a Toronto-based monthly published regularly since 1870; in September 1911 its editors, Drs John and Ewart Ferguson, offered a brief and accurate synopsis of the conflict over the British insurance bill. No obvious editorial judgments were rendered, but the Fergusons did note that the government plan had a "decided advantage" from the profession's standpoint, because control of the insurance funds was to be taken away from the consumer organizations that had "made the club or contract form of practice very onerous" for doctors.[8]

That same month, a more opinionated view of British developments was given in a new medical periodical, the *Canadian Medical Association Journal (CMAJ)*. The founding editor of the *CMAJ*, Dr Andrew Macphail, was a prominent literary figure of the period who had a considerable interest in politics and philosophy. Macphail was a throughgoing conservative with a strong suspicion of social progress and a disdain for measures that sought to move people from their appointed place in nature's hierarchy.[9] He accordingly took a dim view of the national insurance bill: "We have heard much of the doctor's dilemma. We are likely to hear more of the patient's dilemma, as the free play of the profession is impeded by unconsidered legislation." The English profession, claimed Macphail, had nothing to fear. Doctors were, to some extent, now to be paid "for doing what they have hitherto done for nothing." But the public would suffer, for philanthropically endowed hospitals would eventually become state-funded institutions, "and the spirit of charity will be replaced by a cold, official atmosphere which is not congenial to a member of a free profession." The best doctors would leave the hospitals; "the rich will be gainers and the last state of the poor will be worse than the first."[10]

Macphail returned to the topic early in 1912, sounding the same warning. The "socialist doctors were also taking a hand," and among these radicals, voices were already being raised in favour of a full-blown salaried medical service and "public management and control of the voluntary hospitals."[11]

By this time the *Canada Lancet* was expressing greater mistrust of the insurance bill as well. An editorial comment over the signature of Dr G.A. Sterling Ryerson, a prominent Toronto ear, nose, and throat specialist and sometime MLA, contended that "the average medical man will be nothing but a contract doctor at poor remuneration." However, in the absence of any formal policy statement by organized medical groups, it is impossible to know how representative such sentiments were. (For that matter, organized medicine itself may not have been altogether representative – the CMA had a membership of only about 1,400 in a total medical population of over 7,000.) Certainly those affiliated with the public health movement took a different view from either Macphail or Ryerson. In February 1912, for example, an unsigned editorial in the Toronto-based *Public*

Health Journal welcomed the British legislation on the grounds that it provided for compulsory notification of tuberculosis and would therefore assist in the battle against this urban scourge. Even the British profession's division over health insurance was seen as beneficial, since it would "do much to clear the atmosphere of professional mists which exclude for many medical men a proper prospective of the future." The editorial continued: "Thoughtful physicians now recognize the ultimate meaning of the growth of public health sentiment and understand that certain of their number must inevitably suffer in the natural evolution of medicine from the research-quelling commercialism of modern practice to a more dignified place in state ministry."[12]

Despite BMA opposition, the National Insurance Act came into force on 15 July 1912. Although dependants were not covered, some 15 million wage-earners in the lower-income brackets were insured for GP services and against wages lost due to illness. On 24 July, meeting at Liverpool, the BMA threw down a challenge to Lloyd George. Its members would not serve under the act unless the capitation rate were increased from six shillings to eight shillings/six pence. Public criticism of the profession's demands and tactics mounted steadily.

In the autumn of 1912 Macphail altered his editorial emphasis. Acknowledging the rapid growth in preventive medicine, the *CMAJ* editor suggested that doctors might soon have to be paid for keeping people well: "We can, indeed, go further and lay down that just as preventive medicine, as public medicine, is calculated not for the benefit of any particular individual, but for the well-being of the community at large, so, not the individual but the community must recompense the doctor, and the general practice of medicine must become a national service, endowed by the State." The British GPs, noted Macphail accurately, "would rejoice to be delivered from the thraldom of the Friendly Societies, and from the miserable rates which the struggle for existence makes it necessary to accept from those organizations." Money really was not the issue, he claimed. Rather, Lloyd George – like another Welshman, "Fluellen" of Shakespeare's *King Henry the Fifth* – had been high-handed and had not consulted the doctors before telling them "to eat his uncooked leek."[13]

Money, however, turned out to be the overriding issue. Although 26,000 members of the BMA were supposedly bound by a pledge not to work under the NHI scheme, the government's final offer was sufficiently above prevailing lodge rates to tempt many practitioners. By early 1913, faced with evidence that more than half the association's general practitioners had ignored their pledge and begun taking on insurance patients, the BMA was forced to abandon all resistance. The wisdom of those who broke ranks was quickly demonstrated; for as the London correspondent for the *Journal of the American Medical Association* remarked in 1914, GPs' incomes were doubled in some poor industrial areas, while those practising in more affluent regions still were able to augment their incomes by 20 to 50 percent.[14]

THE CANADIAN CONTEXT

The political evolution of the Canadian medical services marketplace in this period had followed a course that differed from that in Britain and the United States. As noted above, divisions in the profession were much less pronounced than in the United Kingdom, where guild affiliations with their roots in the sixteenth century had a lingering effect. Canadian doctors also enjoyed greater legislative protection through licensing mechanisms and professional self-government in the nineteenth century than doctors in either the United States or Britain. In consequence, the population per physician remained comparatively high: the United States, for example, stood at 637 in 1900, while Canada registered 987 in 1901; by 1921 the population per physician in Canada had climbed to 1,008, with that of America standing at 746.[15]

As early as 1883 employers in the Glace Bay colliery district of Nova Scotia were making approved deductions from the wages of miners to underwrite doctors' charges and hospitalization costs. A certain number of mining and lumbering centres across the nation developed similar arrangements, and doctors seeking economic security would enter into contracts with unions and companies to provide medical services on a salaried or capitation basis.[16] Presumably, such arrangements were relatively rare; for they do not seem to have evoked any commentary from leaders of organized medicine prior to the First World War.

City lodge or club practice was a source of some concern, however, especially in turn-of-the-century Ontario, where the growth of working-class culture was associated with the creation of many fraternal orders and benevolent societies. By the 1890s editorial attacks on lodge practice had become fairly commonplace in Canadian medical journals. The Ontario Medical Association adopted a resolution condemning lodge practice at its 1894 annual meeting and unsuccessfully pressed the College of Physicians and Surgeons for disciplinary action against doctors taking club contracts.[17] In 1898 the president of the OMA, Dr William Britton, decried the ongoing spread of lodge practice, claiming in his valedictory address that the practice was "everywhere." Although it was "contrary to his nature," the doctor was "forced into this objectionable line of work" for "self-protection." Bemoaning the willingness of medical men "to acept the beggarly pittance of one hundred and fifty dollars a year or less for looking after the health of a hundred members of some lodge or other," the OMA president went on to assert: "With all my heart and soul I stigmatize the system as a rotten plank in the platform of gentlemanly dignity and independence."[18]

Editorialists at the *Canadian Medical Review* were equally forthright in assailing the lodge-contract system and quoted an illuminating American critique: "The working classes are organized to secure the highest wage going for their own. In the case of the doctor, however, they are combined to secure the doctor on the cheapest terms." Doctors were actually bidding against one another for the security of the lodge contract and the possibility of extra fees from work done for the family members of the lodgers. In consequence, "The lodge system completely destroys the possibility of maintaining a proper fee system. When a man finds that for one dollar a year he can be attended through such diseases as typhoid fever, it is difficult to collect a bill of $50.00 for attending a case of typhoid in his family." All in all, "The lodge system degrades the dignity of the profession. The doctor becomes the hired man. He gives away his independence; and has to hob-nob with those who are his inferiors in every way in order to retain his hold on the lodge."[19]

The actual extent of lodge practice in Ontario and across the nation in this period remains uncertain.[20] However, the peak years of concern were the late 1890s; thereafter the lodge system provoked an ever-diminishing number of criticisms, in part because local medical societies actively discouraged tenders by their members. Indeed, letters appear in Ontario medical journals of this period publicizing mutual undertakings by doctors in smaller centres to refuse all club work in their city or town.[21]

Another potential source of economic conflict was municipal contract practice. Such local government mediation first took place in 1914, when the Saskatchewan rural municipality of Sarnia – about to lose its only doctor – paid him a $1,500 retainer to stay on. But although the Rural Municipalities Act was amended in 1916 to allow tax levies for such contracts, Saskatchewan's famous Municipal Doctor program was still in its infancy, and no other province had a similar scheme.

Thus, in the first two decades of the twentieth century, the situation in the Canadian medical services marketplace contrasted markedly with that in the United Kingdom. Whether through lodges, the workplace, or local government, consumer collectivism in Canada had much less impact on the medical profession's market strength. Fee-for-service practice with independent price discrimination according to the patient's income was seldom displaced by bargaining over capitation fees or salaries. In consequence, there was neither reason for the doctors to view state health insurance as the lesser of two evils, nor was there an existing framework for insurance practice upon which governments could build.

Through 1913 and 1914, as the British experiment got under way, leaders of Canadian organized medicine began to offer their reactions to the innovation. Dr H.A. McCallum, the 1913 CMA president, warned that Canadian government action in the health insurance sphere might come "in the very near future" and called for a membership drive to head it off:

The splendid service of the British Medical Association to the profession of the British Isles, in dealing with the terms of Lloyd George's Insurance Bill, points out what an association can do for each individual member of the profession. The future outlook of Canadian medicine demands a strong association to confront legislation that would make us a despised arm of the Civil Service . . . If four-fifths of the profession belonged to the Association, instead of one-fifth, as at present, no attempt could get under way to bring us into the Service without our consent.[22]

Later that year Dr Herbert Hamilton touched on British developments in an address to the Toronto Academy of Medicine. Government support for diagnostic laboratories and medical research was deemed acceptable; state health insurance was beyond the pale. However, a form of "National Medical Service" seemed to be inevitable.[23]

Some of these themes were taken up at the 1914 CMA annual meeting, where two committees had turned their attention to health insurance. The CMA Committee on Applied Sociology was apparently imbued with the reform spirit of a decade during which social welfare measures were steadily gaining popularity. Its members advised that the old principles of political economy, with their emphasis on "individualistic competition," should give way to "a higher ideal, and that is that members of society should exist for the good of one another." Since preventive medicine was very much under the wing of government, curative medicine should surely follow. The Committee on Public Health Legislation echoed the latter notion, but with much less optimism: "If we do not take our full part in shaping aright the coming changes, it will fare ill with our profession at some later date."[24] However, the 1914 CMA president, Dr Murray MacLaren, made no mention of health insurance in his valedictory address to the doctors assembled at Saint John, New Brunswick.

Not until late 1914 did an analysis appear that weighed the potential benefits of health insurance for medical incomes. Dr A.R. Munroe of Edmonton contended that the medical profession was already being exploited "in the name of charity or religion," an obvious allusion to unpaid office fees and free services supplied to public hospitals. Lloyd George was now exploiting doctors "in the name of politics," proof positive that recent scientific progress in medicine had not been matched by progress on "the business side." Like Andrew Macphail, Munroe recognized that Lloyd George's insurance program gave doctors better payment from the poorer segment of society, and he succinctly summed up the situation:

A fair percentage of patients pay us a full fee, a few pay us a partial fee, and more than a few pay us nothing at all ... We are living in an age when the "gold standard" determines one's station in society – the day is past when the doctor is respected because of his profession alone, and most of us are guilty of evaluating our practices by our cash receipts for the year ... we would welcome a method of converting this loss to gain ... By accepting the good points of present insurance methods and supplying what is lacking to make it acceptable to the medical profession, we can arrive at a scheme that would guarantee the insured public medical, surgical, and hospital attendance, and guarantee the medical profession their fees.

Munroe rejected both a British-style insurance plan and a salaried medical service. Instead, "commercial methods" should be applied to a four-point plan:

1. The services of the whole of the medical profession should be at the disposal of the whole public.
2. No one should be made the object of charity.
3. The average medical income should be increased.
4. The basis of reckoning from which the actuary obtains his rate of insurance to the public should be the medical schedule of fees.

Understandably, then, Munroe insisted health insurance was "worth every man's while studying."[25]

WARFARE AND WELFARE: A PASSING FANCY

Although leaders of organized medicine apparently viewed health insurance as an imminent development, this concern became secondary during the early years of the First World War. A great many doctors abandoned private practice to serve in the Royal Canadian Army Medical Corps (RCAMC). Further attention was focused on the RCAMC because of both a continuing need for medical recruits and a bitter controversy over its administration. Professional life was sufficiently disrupted in this period that the CMA cancelled its annual meetings for 1915 and 1916.

The war effort, however, prepared the ground for a more widespread interest in health insurance to take root in Canada during the final years of conflict. The population inevitably came to be seen as a biological resource without which the war effort could not function. When a substantial number of Canadian recruits were rejected as unfit for active service, the importance of health care and social welfare was underscored. The war also brought acceptance of a new and expanded role for government,[26] so that intervention by the state – be it with health insurance or other legislation – was no longer viewed as untenable. At the same time, evidence of wartime profiteering by certain domestic businesses[27] led to a public backlash against private enterprise, accompanied by a greater sensitivity to the plight of the poor and the labouring classes. It was, after all, these groups that supplied the bulk of Canada's armed forces. And when Johnny Canuck came marching home, he might well expect – even demand – some measure of social reform as a reward for his patriotic efforts.

In a reversal of the pattern that would prevail in later decades, some of the impetus for state health insurance in Canada came from the United States. The American Association for Labor Legislation (AALL), founded in 1906, had about 3,000 members by 1913, including a large number of prominent academics in the social sciences. The AALL had been instrumental in convincing many states to adopt workmen's compensation acts, and in 1912 it formed a committee to investigate health insurance and similar measures. That same year Theodore Roosevelt's Progressive party expressed support for old age pensions, unemployment insurance, and health insurance in its electoral platform; and by late 1915, armed with research data and their own draft health insurance bill, the Social Insurance Committee of the AALL embarked on a national campaign. Private insurance companies lobbied furiously against public insurance, but many industrialists were supportive. And although Samuel F. Gompers, the conservative president of the American Federation of Labor, was opposed to health insurance, most labour leaders endorsed the concept.[28]

In 1916 two state commissions reported favourably on health insurance; another six state commissions were evaluating the AALL

proposals by the following year. Health insurance committees were
set up by influential bodies such as the American Public Health
Association, the American Academy of Medicine, the National Conference of Charities and Corrections, and the New York Chamber
of Commerce. The American Medical Association also had a committee working on this subject, with none other than Dr I.M. Rubinow,
a committed socialist and the leading AALL campaigner, as its
secretary.[29] Indeed, the editor of the *Journal of the American Medical
Association* was known to support national health insurance, and
both the New York and the Wisconsin State Medical Societies formally
endorsed legislative plans for such policies in 1916. Medical opinion,
however, was far from formed: only twenty-three of thirty-two state
medical societies polled in late 1916 had specifically considered the
question, and of the six states where health insurance was still under
review by doctors' committees, four were felt to be against the measure
and one was doubtful.[30]

As in the United States, physicians with a special interest in public
health matters tended to spearhead the Canadian debate. Dr J.D.
Fitzgerald, one of the founders of Toronto's School of Hygiene, helped
organize a group of practitioners from Toronto, London, Niagara
Falls, and Hamilton, who began meeting in 1916 to discuss state
medicine and health insurance.[31]

Sparked, perhaps, by wartime idealism and an awareness of the
campaign underway in the United States, some Canadian doctors
openly endorsed health insurance. Among them was Major J.W.
McIntosh, a member of the British Columbia legislative assembly.
An internist, former president of the Vancouver Medical Association,
and a dissident Liberal who sometimes talked of forming a Returned
Soldiers' Party, McIntosh later played an active role in pushing the
BC government to appoint the nation's first social insurance commission. In the spring of 1917 McIntosh had already informed the
legislature that it was "only a question of time before the workmen's
compensation act would be extended to include sickness as well as
accident."[32]

On 27 June 1917 the Edmonton Medical Academy and Dental
Association held a joint meeting at which it was decided that an
education committee should be established "to organize a campaign
of social reform." Creation of a federal Department of Public Health
was one priority. Health insurance was another: "The committee is
of the opinion that a good workable social or public insurance scheme
would prove of invaluable assistance in reducing the number of cases
requiring provincial or charitable assistance, and recommends that
the same be put into operation at the earliest possible moment."[33]

In the same month, Dr A.D. Blackader reviewed the burgeoning American literature on health insurance in his presidential address to the CMA annual meeting and urged the formation of "a strong committee" to study health insurance lest events in England repeat themselves. Blackader's outlook was nevertheless positive: "I feel assured that with broad and friendly consideration from the profession, the details of an insurance scheme can be arranged so as to secure entirely dignified terms for our members, and to accomplish mutual benefit for all parties."[34] Blackader noted accurately that "thus far, very little attention has been given to a measure of this character" in Canada. But at that same CMA meeting, the Canadian health insurance campaign was given impetus by Dr Charles J. Hastings, Toronto's medical officer of health. Hastings was in close touch with the AALL and served on the executive of the American Public Health Association. In a wide-ranging address he summarized developments in the United States and Europe and offered a strong endorsement of health insurance. Even Lloyd George drew praise as "the most outstanding character in Great Britain today" – a rather striking contrast with Andrew Macphail's 1912 allusion to "that strange, uncomfortable demagogue enthusiast."[35]

The movement gathered force in the fall of 1917. A special symposium on health insurance – the first such event in Canada – was held at Ottawa during the annual meeting of the Canadian Public Health Association. Charles Hastings discussed "the National Importance of Health Insurance," and two spokesmen for the Social Insurance Committee of the AALL came north to share the rostrum with him. A month later economist Irving Fisher of Yale, another American apostle, extolled the virtues of state health insurance to a large medical audience at Toronto General Hospital. The Toronto-based *Public Health Journal* published several papers on the topic, and offered editorial support in November 1917. Indeed, the *Journal* gently reproached the British profession for its earlier intransigence and fully approved the "underlying principles" of health insurance.[36]

The public health doctors, of course, had a different vantage point from their colleagues in private practice. Already in receipt of government salaries, they saw little to fear from further state intervention in the medical services marketplace. Moreover their overview of community health logically moved them towards social engineering and collectivist measures of medical care delivery. But a reform spirit also animated other professional factions in this period. Dr J. Gibb Wishart, 1917 president of the Toronto Academy of Medicine, took aim against creeping commercialism in private practice in his valedictory address. The war, said Wishart, had brought "a fresh outlook, an upsetting of accepted aspects of truth," and an appreciation of "the unimportance of individuality." The prevention and treatment of various diseases had been placed successfully under state aegis:

May these not be signs of the times that the day of the competitive physician and surgeon is over and that presently he must become a member of a panel and have removed from him the opportunity to exploit his experience for mere gain – that as his training is even now largely paid for by the state, so his employer hereafter may be that same body ... I am not a prophet, but let us not mistake, there are great changes coming.[37]

During 1918 the *Public Health Journal* continued its campaign for socialist reforms. The editors assailed big business and the "selfish luxury-seeking class"; they heaped praise on the policies of the British Labour party.[38] A clarion call was sounded for the creation of a federal Department of Public Health, "one which would make certain that every Canadian present and future, enjoyed a maximum of good health, reasonable hours of labour, health insurance and other benefits which as citizens of a country of great natural wealth, we are entitled to."[39]

In May 1918 at the Canadian Medical Week in Hamilton the OMA president, Dr John Morton, painted a rosy picture of health insurance:

The cost of this so-called health insurance system would be divided between the patient, the firm, and the government. Hospitals and other properly equipped diagnostic centres would be established, where all necessary examinations for arriving at correct diagnosis would be carried out. The greatest gain of this plan would be the abolition of charity work, the very name of which has a stigma attached to it.[40]

Dissatisfaction with the status quo was also evident at a round-table session convened as part of the Hamilton conference. Seventy-five practitioners from across Canada, discussing "The Ethics of Commerce," criticized the traditional Robin Hood billing method of private medicine and expressed concern about the overworked doctors who, because they served poor patients, lacked the wherewithal to take a holiday, let alone refresher courses. To this lament the editors of the *Public Health Journal* offered a ready response:

National Health Insurance in England, at first bitterly opposed by the physicians, now meets with almost universal approval. It has meant in large measure state control of the medical profession in England. It has also meant that a more rational point of view has been adopted towards matters of health. It has in some degree divorced the medical profession from the 'Ethics of Commerce.' All of which is better for everyone concerned.[41]

But there were already signs that the health insurance bandwagon was losing momentum. The president of the CMA did not so much as mention health insurance or state medicine in his keynote address to the Hamilton conference. Only one paper was read on the topic during the week-long proceedings: Charles Hastings again took up the torch at a session sponsored by the Canadian Public Health Association and the Ontario Health Officers Association.[42]

In fact, a few weeks after the Hamilton conference, Dr J. Heurner Mullin, the first vice-president of the OMA, openly dissented from the positive verdict on health insurance that had been handed down by the association's chief. Mullin warned a gathering of St Thomas and Elgin County medical men that they must gird themselves for "the struggle which is sure to come between the medical profession on the one hand and the legislators and their more or less expert advisers." Mullin acknowledged the benefits of health insurance and outlined the provisions of the AALL draft bill which he deemed more reasonable than "anything presented in other countries." Yet the OMA's second-in-command rejected the concept, harkening back instead to the principles of political economy that the CMA Committee on Applied Sociology had declared obsolete four years before:

Sickness in this country is still looked on as a personal misfortune and *not* as an economic calamity for which all members of the community are more or less responsible ... The central principle of our system in the government under democracy lies in the proposition that every man has a right to a full and complete individual liberty limited only by the liberty of every other man ... Why not give everyone a decent living and the money wherewith to pay for the needed attention supplemented if necessary by some insurance scheme?

Mullin believed that this approach, bolstered by programs of continuing medical education and perhaps a certain number of multi-specialty diagnostic clinics, could obviate any need for state health insurance.[43]

Mullin's viewpoint was a harbinger of things to come. South of the border the health insurance movement had aroused ever-greater professional opposition, and Canadian doctors were influenced by the attitudes of their American confreres. In New York, for example, county medical groups pressed the state medical society to rescind its endorsement of health insurance. America's declaration of war on Germany in April 1917 gave those opposed to sickness insurance a new propaganda tool: doctors fighting against the innovation in California denounced the very idea as a "mess of German pottage," a theme also used by the insurance industry and the federal government's wartime information committee. Although the opponents of sickness insurance were increasingly numerous and vocal, several state commissions reported favourably on the question during 1917 and 1918.[44] Canada's first commission on health insurance was appointed the following year.

BRITISH COLUMBIA:
THE FIRST INITIATIVE

November 1918 brought an armistice in Europe, but conflict continued on the home front. Labour unrest in Quebec was limited by the balance-wheel of Catholic conservatism, while in Ontario craft unionism and ties to American labour organizations steered wage-workers away from a militant course. But in the west the influence of the Industrial Workers of the World and other radical labour groups had grown considerably during the war years.

In the final weeks of 1918 Conservative Prime Minister Robert Borden authorized a crackdown on the militant socialists. Fourteen left-wing organizations, including the Industrial Workers of the World and several socialist parties, were declared illegal by the federal government. Scores of radicals were arrested, labour meetings throughout the west were monitored by federal agents, and socialist newspapers were shut down. These measures were ineffective. Western unrest swept along on the crest of a wave of strikes through early 1919, culminating in a General Strike in Winnipeg during May-June of that year.[45]

By this juncture opponents of health insurance in the United States were steadily winning the upper hand, not least because the entire issue of state intervention in health care was tainted by anxiety about both the new communist regime in Russia and the potential for like-minded domestic radicals to disrupt the social fabric of America. The 1919–20 president of the American Medical Association was, in fact, an ardent supporter of health insurance: Dr Alex Lambert, professor of medicine at Cornell University and a member of the AALL campaign committee from its inception. Although Lambert personally avoided raising the issue, the 1919 AMA annual meeting brought considerable grassroots agitation for passage of a resolution condemning health insurance.[46]

In contrast, during the CMA's 1919 annual meeting there was little controversy about health insurance. The sole address that touched on the topic in any detail was given by Dr P.H. Bryce, the chief medical officer for the federal department of immigration. Bryce outlined the possible activities of a federal department of health and, in arguing for state health insurance, underscored the fact that consumer-sponsored insurance had only limited scope. For example, in Ontario there were 172,000 members of Friendly Societies in 1917, but less than 13 percent of the financial benefits paid out was for medical services, even though 33,468 members reported sick for a total of 166,782 weeks. Bryce accordingly contended that the "socializing of medicine," as had been effected in England, would do much to improve public health.[47]

Later that summer, Dr G.D. Shortreed of Grandview, Manitoba offered a similar endorsement in a remarkably Fabian presidential address to the Manitoba Medical Association (MMA). It is likely that many Manitoba practitioners were disturbed by events in Winnipeg during the General Strike, but one must suspect that few would have endorsed the solutions suggested by Shortreed. The MMA president denounced "the old order" as "military, individualistic in the extreme, and exploitative." "The new order will be humanitarian, altruistic, co-operative." In this new society, "free hospital, nursing and medical service" would be available to all. And in a flight of dialectical rhetoric Shortreed called for the medical profession – despite its "middle class position" – to use its understanding of all classes for the reconciliation of "apparently irreconcilable opposites," thereby aiding "in this great task of ushering in, as painlessly as possible, a new and better day."[48]

But British Columbia rather than Manitoba provided the locale for the most concrete action in the health and welfare field. The province had long suffered the stormiest industrial relations in the country. In the company towns of the interior strikebreakers and their police allies were not infrequently joined in bloody battles with striking miners or loggers. And in the election of 1916 an assortment of social democrats, socialists, and labourites contested seats. The Liberals were installed to govern for the first time in the province's history, but the prompt establishment of a Department of Labour and enactment of minimum wage laws did little to quell working-class unrest.

A complex concatenation of factors therefore combined to make health insurance seem an attractive proposition. Such a social reform measure might, of course, help ease the problems in British Columbia's industrial relations. With 6,225 native sons dead in the war and more than 13,000 wounded returning to the province, some improvement in domestic conditions seemed called for as a gesture of gratitude for sacrifices made in Europe. In addition, public health considerations were imperative: more than 8,500 of the province's "able-bodied men" had been found unfit for active service, and the worldwide Spanish influenza epidemic swept British Columbia in 1918–19, killing almost 3,000 persons and inflicting serious illness on thousands more.[49] Medical aid for rural British Columbia was brought in from neighbouring Alberta and the north-west United States. Certainly on a national scale the influenza epidemic sparked considerable reorganization of health services and served as a catalyst for the long-delayed creation of a federal Department of Health.

A more immediate reason for action on health insurance was a legislative motion from Major J.W. McIntosh, the internist and maverick Liberal mentioned above. On 24 February 1919 McIntosh called for a debate on "the question of 'State Health Insurance' with a view to discussing the advisability of appointing a Committee to bring in a Bill before the close of this session of the House." Liberal front-benchers hastened to recast the motion in weaker form,[50] but the cabinet faced mounting public pressure in ensuing days. Deputations from various church, labour, and veterans' groups urged action on health insurance and other reforms; encouraging resolutions were passed by post-war reconstruction committees and the Trades and Labour Council of Victoria. Finally, in mid-March 1919 a cabinet spokesman announced that "before committing the province to so radical a change in her social fabric," a commission of inquiry into public insurance schemes should be appointed.[51]

No commission was set up during the spring session, but inter-sessional prompting came from two sources. The Winnipeg General Strike sparked off sympathy strikes in Vancouver, Victoria, and Prince Rupert during the summer of 1919. And in August the federal Liberal party took an apparent leftward turn at its national convention, choosing W.L. Mackenzie King – an industrial relations specialist – as its leader. The social policy planks of the platform adopted at the August convention were reputed to be very much the work of the new leader; among them was the cautious promise that, "so far as may be practicable, having regard for Canada's financial position," an "adequate" sickness insurance system should be instituted by the federal government in co-operation with the provinces.

On 19 November 1919 a BC Social Welfare Commission was appointed. Its chairman, E.S.H. Winn, also headed the provincial Workmen's Compensation Board. The other three members were D. McCallum, a former president of the BC Federation of Labour; Cecilia Spofford, a welfare worker and leader of the Women's Christian Temperance Union; and Dr T.B. Green, a New Westminster physician representing the medical profession, employers, and returned soldiers. In a press release Winn indicated that the commission was to investigate mothers' pensions, maternity benefits, state health insurance, and public health nursing arrangements. Its goal was to submit actual legislative proposals to the government as soon as possible.[52]

Evidence at the hearings conducted by the commission ran strongly in favour of legislation on all fronts. Health insurance in particular was seen by women's, labour, veterans', and fraternal organizations as a valuable means of decreasing tension between the classes in British Columbia society.[53] J.W. McIntosh later noted that although "the general public" was "more or less disinterested and uninformed," "employers of labour were found, unexpectedly, to be more or less favourable."[54] However, the opinion expressed by the Victoria Medical Society at the hearing in the provincial capital was clearly unfavourable. Speaking on behalf of the Society, Dr George A. Hall stated that the profession could support health insurance "academically" but would "not accept such an act as at present in force in Great Britain." The province should wait and observe state health insurance in other jurisdictions before enacting this legislation; for there was "no immediate need for it in British Columbia." The society's final riposte was carefully aimed: "We as taxpayers are considering the financial aspect. Where are we to get the money to establish such a scheme? We do not want any ill-advised legislation on this matter."[55] Three years later, the Victoria doctors' statement on the need for health insurance was disproved when their confreres in the Vancouver Medical Association arranged a survey of the working population and found less than 5 percent had insurance of any kind, let alone against the costs of illness per se.[56]

During 1920 the Social Welfare Commission submitted unanimous endorsements of mothers' pensions, maternity insurance, and public health nursing programs. But the report on health insurance, last to be written, was not submitted until 19 March 1921, more than a year behind schedule. Dr T.B. Green, dissenting from the other three commissioners, who strongly supported health insurance, did not contribute to the report. Indeed, by 1929, the last boom year for the Canadian economy and Canadian doctors' incomes, Dr Green would be informing a CMA committee that he had "never heard, with one exception, any voice favouring health insurance" in British Columbia medical circles.[57]

The report on health insurance itself reflected an odd blend of compassion and calculation. It envisioned employers taking a renewed interest in occupational safety and working conditions to reduce their share of the insurance premiums. And through preventive action, a sickness insurance scheme would allow more employees to hang on to their jobs in later life. "Fewer workmen will be thrown on the scrap heap in their early forties with all the tragic consequences involved to their families as well as to themselves." But there were considerations other than public health per se:

Old world radicalism with its propaganda is sinuously forcing its way into every community ... The bolsheviks of today are mainly the neglected children of yesterday ... It is not enough that your own child is healthy, well-nurtured and trained; the other fellow's child must have his chance, must be healthy, properly developed and trained, or your boy when he reaches maturity and seeks to take his father's place in the world's work will find that the other fellow's boy has also reached the state of manhood a radical, who refuses to allow your son to work.[58]

The Liberals introduced mothers' pensions in 1921 but were hardly in a position to consider a volatile and expensive project such as health insurance. Medical opposition seemed certain; the party was in power by only a slim margin; the province was over $50 million in debt and the post-war slump still prevailed.[59] Perhaps it is understandable that the health insurance report, with its siren song of social serenity, was never officially acknowledged, never published, and in fact remained a rather shadowy document for some years. In November 1922, when two Labour members in the legislature called for a health insurance bill to be drafted, Premier John Oliver amended their motion into a rather long apology for lack of government action. The premier took note of a recent dominion-provincial conference where health and unemployment insurance had been adjudged a federal concern, quoted the federal Liberal convention's resolution on health insurance from August 1919, bemoaned the $500,000 per annum already consigned to mothers' pensions, and called on the federal government to shoulder its responsibility by enacting a variety of social insurance schemes.[60] The buck thus passed adroitly, nothing more was heard of health insurance in the BC legislature for five years.

THE LATENCY PERIOD

In 1919, when the flush of war-induced collectivism had yet to pass, Professor D. Fraser Harris had gone far beyond an endorsement of health insurance in a speech to the Nova Scotia health officers. Harris, a distinguished physiologist at Dalhousie, outlined a detailed plan for state medicine with doctors on salary. If all went well, medical men could "give up the worrisome, unorganized competition of private practice and become the valued (and pensioned) officers of the noblest state service than can be conceived of." Provided appointments were made on the basis of merit rather than through political patronage, this would be "true socialism" but might best be called "co-operationism" to avoid the bolshevik taint. Andrew Macphail had left his post as *CMAJ* editor; and some months after Harris spoke, the new editorial staff at the *CMAJ* recapitulated his arguments in a lengthy leader and offered a surprisingly positive assessment: "The present may not be just the right time to create the State Medical Service, but with the Public Health Department already created, there occurs no valid reason why the scheme advocated in this interesting address should not be attempted in the near future."[61]

By late 1920, however, the *CMAJ* editors were taking sober note of the British profession's negative reactions to proposals for a salaried medical service in the United Kingdom.[62] Thereafter, the national association suffered organizational difficulties and little attention was paid to health insurance or state medicine for several years.[63] At the end of the First World War, for example, the CMA enjoyed inconsistent support from less than a quarter of Canadian practitioners. It carried a debt of $14,000, and consideration was given to dissolving the association in 1921. Instead, a plan of revitalization was adopted, with Dr T. Clarence Routley, the energetic young secretary of the OMA, henceforth devoting time to recruitment at the national level as well as in Ontario.

The CMA's travails aside, enthusiasm for state intervention was decidedly absent in most medical circles in the early 1920s. The end of wartime collectivism was undoubtedly one factor influencing medical attitudes, and it seems probable that the strength of anti-insurance sentiment in United States medical circles also had an effect. Indeed, in 1920 health insurance had been unequivocally rejected by the American Medical Association, when more than 90 percent of delegates to the annual meeting voted in favour of a blanket motion opposing any such federal or state policies.[64]

In British Columbia, as noted above, representatives of the profession warned against health insurance in 1920. Ontario was an interesting case, in that one of the governing parties made health insurance a part of its platform. The Independent Labour party, founded in 1917, had managed to win twelve seats in the provincial election of October 1919 and subsequently formed a coalition government with the United Farmers of Ontario. The Labour party had been on record since the war years as supporting social insurance of all kinds, and while the United Farmers had yet to set out a platform on social security measures, there remained the possibility that action might be taken. A 1920 OMA membership recruitment pamphlet accordingly stressed that not only did "Medical fees require revision and Province-wide collaboration," but also "Various aspects of State Medicine now in vogue or being inaugurated demand the urgent attention of a united medical profession." Dr Frank Billings of Chicago, one of the leaders of the AMA, was invited to address the Ontario Medical Association meeting in June 1921 and left little doubt about his own antipathy to health insurance:

A majority of the medical profession of the United States is opposed to it on the rational ground that it is class legislation which benefits the insured alone, tends to the moral and financial degradation of the medical profession, interferes with the patient in the selection of the individual physician, encourages inefficient medical practice and other evils not necessary to mention.[65]

By this time Heurner Mullin had advanced to become president of the OMA, and in a valedictory address to the same meeting spoke of his efforts to steer the association "between the extremes of reactionary and radical opinions." Mullin stressed the benefits of a strong organization and warned that "State Medicine" should be "considered as a threat, not a solution." As in 1918 he claimed that professional initiative in fostering more efficient forms of practice was the best response to health care delivery problems. Mullin also suggested that OMA members should visit the headquarters of the AMA in Chicago to see "what it has been possible to accomplish with perfection of organization and plenty of money."[66]

Elsewhere, studied indifference to the issue was in evidence. In 1923, when T.C. Routley visited points west on behalf of the CMA, he was unable to convince Saskatchewan doctors that health insurance was a serious proposition and deserving of study. The secretary of the Saskatchewan Medical Association contended that "this is just a flight of imagination in Dr Routley's mind, and if he keeps quiet about it the country will never hear of it again."[67]

The tenor of the times had clearly changed. Trade union influence and industrial unrest fell off sharply during the 1920s. The Independent Labour Party gradually lost ground, and while the United Farmers/Progressives enjoyed continuing electoral success in the west, their eastern membership dwindled and they were defeated in the 1923 Ontario election. Although several provincial economies slumped immediately following the First World War, from 1922 to 1928 the Canadian economy boomed; and from all appearances social security measures had lost much of their public appeal.

Doctors, like Canadians in all sectors of the economy, did well during the 1920s. Whereas gross medical incomes were reputed to have climbed above an average of $2,000 per year for the first time in Ontario during the early 1900s,[68] a survey of 500 Ontario physicians' gross receipts for the last five years of the 1920s revealed an average annual inflow of $6,262. Manitoba rural practitioners were reported as grossing an average of $5,010; while in Winnipeg generalists averaged $6,523 and specialists earned $11,368. British Columbia data from a 1923 survey of sixty-six doctors in Vancouver and suburbs reveal a similar picture. Average gross income was $6,575, with about one-fifth of the doctors taking in over $8,000 per year. Although practice overheads might be expected to consume around 30 percent of gross incomes, these figures nonetheless compare quite favourably with the average for Canadian industrial wage-earners in the boom year of 1928: $1,024.[69] The change in status for doctors in Quebec by the mid-1920s was happily acknowledged by one francophone GP who recalled that at the turn of the century, medical prices in rural Quebec were very low. A home visit had been $1; an office visit was $.50; and attendance at childbirth cost from $5 to $10: "Everything has changed happily, on account of the cost of living and social exigencies; at the current fee schedule, the young doctor can aspire to ease and comfort if not to a fortune."[70] Not until the Depression ended this period of unprecedented medical affluence would the profession as a whole look favourably on state payment for doctors' services.

Only in British Columbia, it seems, did a sizeable segment of the profession take concrete action in the matter of health insurance. Because injured workmen often had trouble paying their doctors' bills, the Vancouver Medical Association (VMA) had joined forces with organized labour during the war to press for inclusion of medical aid in the workmen's compensation benefits. Medical bills were eventually underwritten at two-thirds of the British Columbia Medical Association (BCMA) fee schedule, an arrangement that pleased all parties. Spurred both by this success, and by an awareness that the BC Social Welfare Commission had considered health insurance in 1920-1, the VMA, in co-operation with its parent provincial organization, hired a statistician to review the matter in 1923. The need for health insurance was felt to be evident from the fact that less than 5 percent of industrial employees had "any insurance of any kind against illness, accident, or death."[71]

Dr J.H. MacDermot, who spearheaded the VMA initiative, also interviewed E.S.H. Winn concerning the still-unpublished health insurance report of the Social Welfare Commission. Early in 1925

MacDermot presented the VMA's findings on health insurance to a special Conference on Medical Services at Ottawa, reminding his audience several times that Canadian doctors must be prepared lest events similar to those in pre-war Britain overtake them. MacDermot pointed out that the "average working man's family in British Columbia has about one week's supply of money in case of illness attacking the wage earner: when this is spent they must run into debt." He contended that organized medicine should work with the labour movement and recognize its concerns: "It is Labour that is hardest hit. They have adopted health insurance as a plank in their platform. The demand is there, and the facts I have cited seem to show that the need exists."

MacDermot went on to outline the Vancouver profession's health insurance plan. The VMA proposed an extension of the workmen's compensation arrangement, so that doctors could offer better quality service to wage-earners in the lower income brackets. A voluntary scheme was rejected on the grounds that insurance company overheads were too high and only those already insured would be likely to enrol. Coverage should therefore be compulsory for those "of the class affected" and the plan publicly administered by an "extra-political board." Both these tenets would later become part of organized medicine's national policy. MacDermot left open the question of income limits on participation but noted that E.S.H. Winn had suggested a ceiling of $3,000 a year. This figure was higher than the VMA had envisioned; for at least 85 percent of Vancouver households would have fallen under the insurance program, leaving the medical profession with a very small private sector of self-pay patients.[72] (Much lower ceilings were advocated by British Columbia doctors when they revised their health insurance blueprint during the Depression.) The VMA members had come to "a unanimous conclusion" that they would "utterly reject the panel system or any system involving salaried medical men except in cases such as x-ray or other laboratory workers." These innovations would destroy the "valuable and salutory" competitive element in prevailing private fee-for-service practice.[73]

The VMA saw many benefits from such a scheme. First, the scope of practice would be broadened through removal of financial impediments to full diagnosis and treatment for lower-income groups, which would bring an end to "the really enormous amount of work done for nothing or for trifling fees." Second, the "prevalence of quackery" would be curtailed; for "nobody can suppose that any intelligent commission administering an act would allow patients to go to practitioners of cult medicine; this would not be from any love of us, but from simple economic reasons." Third, the doctor "who lets himself slump, who gets rustier and rustier," would be checked, because health insurance would require more careful record-keeping and open up the possibility of practice cross-comparisons. And lastly, "over-specialization, and specialization by men who are not fit to be specialists, would be checked, because results are tabulated, and results count."[74] Discussants of MacDermot's paper agreed that they must be better prepared than were their British counterparts. They arranged for the VMA data to be distributed to other provinces and referred the question of health insurance to the CMA executive committee.[75]

The VMA plan, while forward-looking in some respects, would have served above all to buttress the economic position of private-fee practitioners. As will be shown below, this protective impulse was becoming widespread.

PROTECTING PRIVATE PRACTICE

Traditional forms of private fee-for-service practice maximized professional control over conditions of medical work and remuneration. The Vancouver doctors' plan for health insurance obviously sought to minimize the impact of state intervention on these advantageous arrangements. At this time, however, there were other worrisome encroachments on private practice. In the absence of state health insurance, a growing number of benevolent schemes were set up to provide selected medical services to those in the lower socio-economic strata. A doubled-edged threat was contained in many lay-sponsored charitable endeavours. The services offered were frequently used by those who could, in fact, pay some portion of their medical bills, with the result that private practitioners lost business. This abuse had been a source of annoyance to the profession since the 1890s.[76] At the same time, because these public service organizations tended to hire doctors on salary, they provoked fears of lay control and employee status for increasing numbers of MDs.

In 1914, for example, the City School Board in Calgary started a free clinic for school children with eye, ear, nose and throat problems. Medical inspectors would examine children and refer them to the clinic for treatment if necessary, without regard for whether their parents could pay a private specialist's fee. The clinic was staffed by a salaried specialist in the employ of the school board. Pressure from local MDs brought an end to the system in 1924. Henceforth, school medical inspectors referred children to private practitioners who would then charge at reduced rates if necessary. A Calgary surgeon nevertheless warned: "Of late years other organizations have stepped in keen and expectant and eager to develop new fields of free health work. Through all this the legitimate field of the practising physician has been greatly encroached upon and toiling hard for a meagre reward he has found it difficult to eke out an existence. Some solution should be found to ease up existing conditions."[77]

Similar problems had developed in Winnipeg, where hospital governors were designating wards as public, that is, for non-paying patients, without consulting the medical staff. Since doctors gave a considerable amount of free service to public-ward patients, they expected in return that private wards would remain available for them to do more remunerative work among the upper-income groups. In the ensuing controversy, a committee of the Manitoba Medical Association was formed and investigated seventy-three different charities in Winnipeg. Abuse of free out-patient clinics by those who could afford to pay for private care was found to be commonplace, while on the other hand, free service was being given by private practitioners for work in "the Indian Department" that should have been underwritten by tax dollars. The MMA concluded that "the chief difficulty arose out of the fact that an attempt was being made to take the matter of free medical services out of the hands of the medical profession and to dispose of and direct it without consultation with the profession ... We must, as far as possible, regain control of our free work."[78]

This alarm was not confined to the western section of the profession. Writing in 1926, Dr L.A. Gagnier warned Quebec's francophone practitioners of the coming deluge. Anti-venereal disease dispensaries set up during the war to treat soldiers were still functioning but with a broader clientele. A public tuberculosis clinic staffed by salaried doctors had recently been founded in Montreal, and it was giving free service to patients hitherto attended by competent private practitioners. Moreover medical charity at hospital in-patient and out-patient facilities was being exploited everywhere, and an official means test should be developed to check this phenomenon: "If the public powers continue to cut into every medical domain, if philanthropic organizations pursue medical services left and right, the practitioner will have only one thing to do; close his office and look for a place among the unemployed."[79]

A related area of concern was the employment of doctors under salaried contracts by municipalities in remote rural areas. Starting with the rural municipality of Sarnia in 1914, many outlying Saskatchewan townships retained GPs on salary. By 1930 there were thirty-two "municipal doctors" working in the province and a small number in neighbouring Manitoba and Alberta as well. Organized medicine seems to have viewed the municipal doctor concept as a necessary evil whose proliferation should not be encouraged. Some city practitioners resented the fact that farmers and their families no longer travelled to them with medical problems;[80] and municipal doctors themselves did not paint glowing portraits of the system for their colleagues. Seven Saskatchewan GPs, replying to a query from the CMA Committee on Municipal Physicians in 1928, expressed general satisfaction but complained of mediocre salaries, too many unnecessary calls, and a perception that they were tied into being available to the public at all times. When a private practitioner turned down a suggestion that an out-of-hours call be made, both doctor and patient knew that the practitioner was forgoing fee income. The municipal doctor, in contrast, would simply seem to be shirking duties that had already been paid for by local taxpayers. The CMA committee noted "Most of them would rather practise as before, could they finance as easily."[81]

The underlying issue for all parties was one of market power. Not unlike his city lodge practice counterpart at the turn of the century, the salaried rural doctor had ceased to be an independent, fee-earning service-seller dealing with an individualized clientele. A rural practitioner operating successfully on a fee-for-service basis was accountable only to individual patients who, if dissatisfied, had little recourse save finding another doctor locally – an improbable occurrence – or travelling to the nearest urban centre for care. The municipal doctor scheme undercut the doctor's position as a self-employed monopoly seller of an essential service, substituting a local near-monopsony situation wherein the doctor was subject to dismissal by municipal councillors.

Not just the municipal doctor schemes but contract practice of any kind obviously threatened the profession's position. In Alberta, for example, the College of Physicians and Surgeons was vexed by the fact that both municipalities and industries were hiring doctors on salary. After the war mining centres and lumber camps in remote parts of the province increasingly made contract arrangements for medical services, sometimes driving hard bargains in the process. In 1922 the Alberta College of Physicians and Surgeons took aim at contract practice when it added a new clause to its code of ethics: "It is unprofessional for a physician to dispose of his services under conditions that make it impossible to render adequate service to his patient or which interfere with reasonable competition among the physicians of a community. To do this is detrimental to the public and to the individual physician, and lowers the dignity of the profession."[82]

Despite this dictate, contract practice persisted, and the college council continued receiving complaints, presumably both from those who had been tied into difficult contracts and from others who found segments of their local markets closed off by prearrangement. In 1924 the college council resolved that "Contract Practice, as it exists today, is not satisfactory to the profession." A circular letter was sent to all college members, and warned:

The time may come and may be nearer at hand than many think, when all men holding contracts may be asked to consider seriously whether in the interest of the patient and the profession they should not be cancelled ... the Council views with apprehension and disfavour any development in the matter of contract practice, and especially as the question of contracts already in existence has been the cause of considerable difficulties.[83]

In 1929 the college was cool in its response to proposals by the province for expansion of the municipal doctor program, and over the next several years medical spokesmen frequently criticized both municipal and industrial contract practice. The college again threatened to institute centralized auditing of all contracts so that they would be "fair to both the public and the profession."[84] But consumers, in fact, had reason to be pleased with the decentralized bargaining; for as one Alberta practitioner complained, the system allowed purchase of medical services at "wholesale rates" and reflected "a desire to get more for the patients and give less to the physician."[85]

It may seem paradoxical that the college ethics called for maintenance of competition at a time when the CMA code still made it "a point of honour" for doctors to collude in fee-setting and contained an assortment of anti-competitive clauses. Indeed, the problem was not too little but too much competition, as Alberta doctors bid against one another to win contracts with municipalities and industries. The college, charged with protecting the public interest but already actively safeguarding the profession's socio-economic position, subsequently merged with the provincial voluntary association to strengthen the profession's hand in dealing with consumerist or state mediation in the marketplace.[86]

AGITATION ON THE
WESTERN FRONT

Leaders of organized medicine in Alberta were disturbed not only by contract practice, but also by conflicts with the ruling United Farmers Association of Alberta. As noted above, the United Farmers held office in Ontario from 1919 to 1923. They also won their first electoral contests in Alberta (1921) and Manitoba (1922). In Alberta, the UFA – or Progressives – totally dominated the legislature and were ostensibly committed to implementing a state medical service. But as the wheat boom continued, these plans were abandoned. Radicals who had envisaged greater social reform split off in 1924, leaving the leadership largely in the hands of those who saw the movement primarily as a way for farmers and other small producers to win a fairer share in the private enterprise system.[87] Finally in 1927, as a concession to earlier campaign promises, a "travelling clinic" was organized to bring cheap medical services to those in the outlying areas of the province. George Hoadley, the Farmers' health minister, proudly claimed that the cost of minor surgery performed by salaried doctors in the "travelling clinic" was almost one-third less than the going rates in private practice. More than 2,300 tonsillectomies were carried out by the clinic in its first year of operation, much to the displeasure of private practitioners across the province. Despite Hoadley's assurances that the government did not wish to interfere with any local doctor's business, the Alberta correspondent of the *CMAJ* complained that the clinic frequently operated in more populated areas where there were "competent physicians well able to take care of all such cases." He added, 'This is a form of state-medicine for which there is no possible excuse. To say that physicians are not in any way 'interfered with' is begging the question."[88]

On 22 November 1927 the Provincial Constituency Association of the UFA passed a resolution endorsing state medical services. The resolution noted that "the cost of medical services under the present system is extremely prohibitive for the great majority of people." As in Great Britain and some European countries, there should be "government control" of hospitals, not least because "a medical system operated and controlled by the State tends to eliminate unnecessary treatment in the form of too frequent surgical operations, etc. as well as any element of profit or advantage to practitioners who may be inclined to place such consideration before the welfare of the patient or the health of the community." The convention therefore pronounced itself "in favour of the Provincial Legislative Assembly adopting an act which is, as far as possible, a duplication of the Medical Act of Great Britain," and that "such a law be enacted and put into force at the earliest possible date."[89]

Word of events in Alberta moved east, and early in 1928 the editor of the *Nova Scotia Medical Bulletin* wrote on the shortcomings of "the panel system in the Old Country" and called for good attendance at the CMA annual meeting in Charlottetown: "Do we want this law in Canada? Do we want state medicine here? Prophecy need not be invoked to convince us that these problems are not far ahead. Will our profession meet them, speaking as a unit through a national organization?''[90]

In February 1928 the motion for a formal inquiry into state medical services came in the Alberta legislature, not from the United Farmers, but from Fred White, leader of the small Labour faction in the House. The motion carried unanimously. The CMA executive was clearly displeased, for an editorial in the *CMAJ* curtly noted: "It will be interesting to learn Mr White's views and aims in desiring an investigation of the practice of a profession demanding from its members a high standard of education, whose aims are so altruistic, and upon whose services the health of a community is so dependent." There followed sundry acerbic comments on the British insurance system, the "travelling clinic," and the wisdom of putting farmers in the health ministry.[91]

When its report was tabled in February 1929, the Alberta committee did not, in fact, endorse either a state medical service with physicians on salary or a British-style panel program. Nor were hospitals to be transferred to government control. Instead, a fee-for-service insurance system was deemed "feasible," with "municipalized" hospitals and municipal doctors on salary in rural districts where normal insurance practice could not be expected to support a practitioner. Moreover the report cautioned that "while these proposals are feasible, their cost to the province would be considerable." It would therefore be "prudent to weigh carefully the probable value of such a program in the improvement of public health as against the result of a similar expenditure along preventive lines."[92]

Given the report's doubting tone, one can hardly be surprised to find little ardour for systems of state medicine in the United Farmers' caucus, which from all appearances was more conservative than the party rank and file. Shortly after the report was tabled a Labour member called for concrete government action in response to its recommendations but was rebuffed by George Hoadley. The health minister argued that the financial position of the province did not really warrant anything more than continued efforts to augment public health services; meanwhile Alberta, "in cooperation with other provinces," should continue its studies of health insurance.[93] There the issue lay fallow in Alberta for three years.

Hoadley's reference to studies "in cooperation with other provinces" was obviously directed at British Columbia; for the health insurance cauldron had again started to bubble on the west coast. As early as 1926 the British Columbia Hospital Association (BCHA) had endorsed health insurance, seeing in a state-run hospitalization scheme the best way to place its member institutions on a firmer financial footing. A past-president of the bcha, Dr Horace Wrinch (Liberal – Skeena), spoke in favour of state health insurance during the 1927 spring session of the legislature, but he made little impact on his fellow politicians.[94]

Public pressure, however, was building. The Farmers' Institute of British Columbia called for a province-wide health insurance scheme. E.S.H. Winn, a key contributor to the 1921 report on state health insurance, spoke out as compensation board chairman in favour of extending medical benefits to cover sickness as well as workplace accidents. The city of Kamloops sent a memorandum in support of health insurance to the provincial government, even as it contacted other municipalities, asking for their support. Trades unions also petitioned for action.[95]

Although Liberal front-benchers tried to downplay the extent of the groundswell, in March 1928 Horace Wrinch joined with another back-bencher to sponsor a private bill on health insurance. They reviewed the history of the previous commission of inquiry and pronounced that "there is now a much more general demand for such a provision to be made to conserve the health of the people of this Province, as is shown by the numerous appeals from widely differentiated sources of origin that are being made to the Government for such legislation." Their resolution calling for appointment of an investigative committee of five mlas was carried unanimously.[96]

All these developments were conveyed to the cma annual meeting at Charlottetown in June 1928 through the Committee on Municipal Physicians (there being, as yet, no committee on economics). One bc correspondent felt sure the average family could pay its medical bills and suggested that notions to the contrary were being put about by chiropractors and other irregular practitioners. The real problem, he wrote, lay in the costs of hospital care, X-rays, and laboratory tests; a "health tax" might be imposed to cover these necessities, but medical fees should be left totally aside. Other bc doctors writing to the committee were equally convinced of the need – and inevitability – of some kind of change but deferred to the expertise of Dr J.H. MacDermot. MacDermot had headed the Vancouver Medical Association's health insurance study group earlier in the 1920s and was now chairman of similar groups in both the bcma and the national association. Not surprisingly, then, the official bcma plan bore a definite resemblance to the proposals originally put forward by the Vancouver doctors: an extension of the workmen's compensation benefits to cover sickness in lower-income groups, salaried doctors only in mining areas and small towns, and traditional fee-for-service practice maintained in all other respects.[97]

Reports from other jurisdictions were generally less comprehensive but included several endorsements of the principle of state health insurance for wage-earners on the grounds that the bulk of consumers and providers of medical services would be better off. A lengthy analysis of professional "disintegration and degeneration" under the British panel system was also mailed to the CMA's Committee on Municipal Physicians. Most alarming, perhaps, was a bulletin from Saskatchewan, where a Liberal government was being pressured by the provincial United Farmers' group for introduction of free consultative clinics: "The Government got by this session without directing that an inquiry be made into health insurance as was done in British Columbia and Alberta, but we are satisfied that it will not be long before the continual pressure from all sides will force the government to take action."[98]

Not only did fears of a Saskatchewan inquiry prove groundless, but the machinery in British Columbia was stalled while the voters rendered judgment on J.D. MacLean's Liberal regime. A negative verdict was delivered on 18 July 1928, shortly after the CMA met in Charlottetown; the Conservatives, under former veterinarian Dr S.F. Tolmie, took power. And the inquiry into health insurance was laid aside until January 1929, when Dr Wrinch, now on the opposition benches, once more attempted to prod the government into action.[99]

Wrinch was successful, and on 1 February 1929, even as the Alberta Commission of Inquiry into Systems of State Medicine was preparing to table its cautionary report, the BC legislative assembly set out the terms of reference for a Royal Commission on State Health Insurance and Maternity Benefits. The commission was to examine national and international experience in these areas, "inquire as to whether and to what extent the public interest requires the introduction of similar laws into the Province of British Columbia," and provide information on costs and distribution of the financial burden of any new scheme.[100] On 16 April 1929 the members were selected and the inquiry began its deliberations.[101]

At about the same time, Dr J.H. MacDermot took to the pages of the *CMAJ* to present the BC profession's perspective on these developments:

What should be the attitude of the medical profession towards health insurance? At present, I take it, mainly expectant. We are not supporting, even less initiating, any scheme; nor are we opposed to health insurance. We should be willing, and, I am sure, we are willing, to support and help to implement any wisely designed measure calculated to improve social conditions, to lessen sickness, and to prevent disease. We should be ready and equipped to advise the Legislature as to what is sane and wise, and what would be short-sighted and dangerous legislation.[102]

This attitude of cautious expectancy towards state intervention was soon to be transformed. In October 1929 came the crash on Wall Street; the boom years were over. Unemployment mounted steadily, reaching its peak late in 1932 when a quarter of Canada's workforce was without a job. Doctors meanwhile faced a growing number of bad debts and falling incomes. If properly arranged, state health insurance could provide the practitioner with guaranteed payment from his augmented proportion of non-paying patients; badly handled, it could leave the doctor enmeshed in the state regulatory apparatus and no further ahead. And so, as the Depression wore on, Canada's medical profession turned to government with hope and trepidation, seeking economic salvation on the best possible terms.

CHAPTER FOUR

Depression Developments: The British Columbia Health Insurance Feud

The chief fear of the medical men seems to be that their earnings will be threatened.

> George Pearson, BC Minister of Labour, *Victoria Times*, 24 September 1935

Above everything else, the profession protests – and will continue to protest – against the lack, either inside or outside the scheme, of any provision for the indigent, the low wage earner and widow pensioner.

> Dr Wallace Wilson, *Vancouver Daily Province*, 5 February 1937

As already suggested, the economic collapse of 1929 sharply lowered the ability of a large fraction of the Canadian population to pay for life's necessities – including medical care. Every Canadian province was hit hard. Because of drought conditions and a deflated world price for wheat, Saskatchewan and Alberta suffered the largest declines in per capita income during the Depression. But national data indicate that the industrial provinces shared fully in the disaster: average per capita money income across the nation fell by 48 percent between 1928 and 1933, with small businessmen and professionals of all stripes registering a 36 percent average decline.[1] Although the cost-of-living index declined by 25 percent in the same period,[2] many physicians found themselves in unprecedentedly difficult financial straits.

In rural Ontario, for example, practitioners who had hitherto prospered now found their farmer clients paying in kind, if at all.[3] In rural Saskatchewan conditions were so bad that some doctors themselves were forced into relief queues. One general practitioner would later recall the humbling experience of lining up with his patients to receive rations of dried fish sent out from Ottawa.[4] As for urban doctors, the toll of the Depression was clearly indicated by a survey of practitioners in Hamilton, Ontario. Between 1929 and 1932 the total volume of services delivered fell an average of 36.5 percent. In 1929, 77.5 percent of work done was remunerative; but in 1932 half of the patients were non-paying. Almost one-half of the doctors in the Hamilton survey sample claimed to be unable to provide the necessities of life for their households. There was also a definite awareness that many patients, whether paying or non-paying, were putting off visits to the doctor, even though their illnesses were serious.[5]

With unemployment running as high as 20 to 30 percent across the nation, the federal and provincial governments were forced to provide assorted relief measures. Medical care of the "indigent," however, had traditionally been the responsibility of the municipalities. Those unable to pay their medical or hospital bills received free in-patient services. For ambulatory care they were expected variously to attend hospital out-patient clinics, to be seen by municipal health officers, or to rely on the charity of private practitioners. Debt-ridden municipalities could seldom afford to provide full medical services for the unemployed and their families. In any case, many of these individuals were long-standing patients of private practitioners, and they continued to consult their doctors in the hope that an economic recovery would soon restore their ability to pay. If other levels of government could be persuaded to step in and pay doctors for their non-remunerative work – work, after all, that now accounted for half their practices – then the profession could expect a dramatic improvement in its fortunes. This, in large measure, was the issue at stake during the British Columbia health insurance dispute.

BRITISH COLUMBIA:
THE HONEYMOON PHASE

On 11 February 1930 the British Columbia Royal Commission on State Health Insurance and Maternity Benefits submitted an interim report. This document summarized the international experience with health insurance, surveyed the constitutional aspects of the question in Canada, and offered a preliminary assessment of employers' reactions to participating in a plan to cover employees. The commissioners' interim commentary was positive: "Our investigations thus far convince us that there is justification and a general demand for the introduction in British Columbia of an economically sound and equitable public health insurance plan in the interests of the majority of provincial wage-earners, of provincial industries and of the State."[6] The commissioners then requested and received additional time to complete their report.

Meanwhile, the Depression steadily undermined the BC economy. With its resource-based industries, the province had always been sensitive to the slump-and-boom cycles of the market mechanism. More than a quarter of the work force was unemployed by mid-1931, and many municipalities were deeply in debt. Hospitals, in particular, faced substantial deficits, both because the number of paying patients was reduced and because the municipalities could no longer afford generous operating grants.[7]

Like their colleagues in all parts of Canada, doctors in British Columbia lost ground rapidly during this period. The average medical income in the province fell by 40 percent between 1929 and 1933, with more than half the doctors earning less than $3,000 per year (gross), and some taking in under $500 per year. Whereas 29 percent of all patients had been non-paying in 1929, four years later more than half were either unable or unwilling to pay anything for medical attention.[8]

Thus, in its recommendations to the royal commission, the BCMA understandably viewed a provincial health insurance plan as providing some measure of economic redress. The extension of the workmen's compensation plan that had won the support of the Vancouver Medical Association in the 1920s continued to be the framework of organized medicine's proposals.[9] Payments should be on a fee-for-service basis at two-thirds of the BCMA tariffs. All those below a certain income level should participate, and dependants must be covered. Those unable to contribute were to be subsidized by government funds, so that ultimately no charity care by doctors would be required. In short, any state plan should insure all those who were currently unable to pay the doctor or unlikely to call him in because of expected financial hardship.

Two other points in the BCMA submission bear notice. First, the BCMA was willing to give a health insurance administrative board the "power to discipline or suspend any practitioner for just cause." In later years there would be greater preoccupation with keeping such disciplinary measures under the umbrella of the College of Physicians and Surgeons. Second, "insurance companies and benevolent societies" were to be barred as carriers.[10] This mistrust of intermediary agencies may have been related, as one analyst claimed in 1932, to a dislike of the idea that a third party would profit from doctor-patient transactions.[11] Or, since Canadian doctors kept close watch on events in Great Britain, it may have reflected a reaction to the BMA's funding squabbles with "approved societies" during the 1920s.[12]

The commissioners submitted their final report in February 1932. This document included an international survey of health insurance and a detailed plan for the implemention of health insurance in British Columbia. One of its most striking sections was several pages of statements from doctors, nurses, and a variety of prominent citizens of the province, offering strong endorsements of the insurance concept. The commissioners recommended the establishment of a compulsory health insurance scheme "at an early date" with enrolment of all wage-earners between the ages of sixteen and seventy who had incomes of less than $2,400 per year. Those with higher incomes could enrol on a voluntary basis. Financing was to be primarily by contributions from employees and other insured persons, but employers and the state would also be required to support the health insurance fund. Coverage should extend to all medical services, hospitalization costs, drugs, and appliances, with a dental benefit included as soon as financially possible. The insured were to have "reasonable freedom of choice" in selecting a doctor. Ideally, the plan would be administered by a permanent central commission, supported by regional advisory committees on which would sit representatives of the insured, contributing employers, the medical profession, and the municipalities.[13]

Apart from the *Vancouver Sun*, which opposed health insurance on principle as "unsound morally and socially,"[14] the newspapers generally praised the proposals. The profession also responded favourably, since many of the commission's recommendations were compatible with the BCMA's stated policy. Dr C.H. Bastin, BC correspondent for the *CMAJ*, later enthused that "Even the most jealous critic will fail to find any suggestion of an attempt to exploit the medical profession."[15]

But for Premier Simon Fraser Tolmie and the ruling Conservatives, state health insurance was simply another measure that would have to wait until the Depression eased. Increasingly shaken by the attacks of Liberal opposition members and the appearance of divisions within his cabinet, Tolmie turned for economic advice to a special ad hoc advisory body – the so-called Kidd Committee. Composed entirely of prosperous businessmen, the Kidd Committee rejected all suggestions of experimentation with deficit financing and social reforms, recommending instead a series of belt-tightening measures to balance the budget. Predictably, public support for the Conservatives plummetted, and the government caucus collapsed into bickering factions.[16]

Meanwhile, the medical profession in urban areas of the province had become increasingly disgruntled about the burden of charity work doctors were forced to carry. The situation was particularly difficult in Victoria and Vancouver; each city had only two municipal doctors on salary to deal with the unemployed, and they were unable to handle even the day-time emergencies.[17] An editorial in the *Bulletin of the Vancouver Medical Association* for February 1933 acknowledged that the profession traditionally had provided free care to the poor, but it complained that "this tradition does not apply in the present situation and our generosity and idealism are being exploited and abused."[18] Under pressure from organized medicine, Victoria agreed to pay some fraction of the doctors' bills for relief work; however, a ceiling of only $10 per practitioner per month was set on payments. In Vancouver no progress was made in negotiations with the city during the spring of 1933. Since the out-patient department of the Vancouver General Hospital was the largest source of demand for unpaid services, every doctor in the city signed an undertaking on 1 August 1933 refusing further work in the hospital clinic except in emergency or on referral from another practitioner. The city responded in the autumn by offering to pay partial fees for medical attendance at childbirth.[19] This concession was welcomed by doctors but deemed inadequate to warrant an end to the restrictions on out-patient services at the hospital.

By this time the editor of the *Bulletin of the Vancouver Medical Association* was openly calling for a system of state health insurance as "the only answer" to the profession's difficulties.[20] An editorial published in October 1933 was especially noteworthy; it warned against the British insurance plan as being too limited and hobbled by vested interests. Indeed, the question arose as to whether any plan of health insurance "would go far enough" and be "sufficiently generous" to the public: "For good or evil, the feet of our civilization are set on the path that leads to socialization of every department of life. For ourselves, we are frank to say that we think it is for good ... [C]andor and generosity on our part will do more than anything else to restore the medical profession to the pinnacle on which it once stood, and from which to a great extent, as a profession, it has slipped."[21]

In the election of November 1933 British Columbians faced a choice between the Liberals and the newly organized Co-operative Commonwealth Federation (CCF) – a choice, in essence, between what Liberal leader T.D. Patullo called "socialized capitalism" and the eclectic socialism of a farm-labour coalition spawned by the Depression.[22] When the ballots were tallied, the Liberals had taken thirty-four seats, the CCF held seven, and an assortment of independents and fringe party candidates filled the other six seats in the legislature.[23] The new government intervened with a subsidy to assist in resolving the dispute over medical relief payments in Vancouver, and concrete action on provincial health insurance seemed sure to follow.

In Patullo's cabinet the provincial secretary and minister responsible for health, welfare, and education was George Moir Weir, PH D, a highly respected professor of education at the University of British Columbia who was noted for his progressive views on educational opportunity and equality. Hired to assist Weir as director of social welfare was Harry M. Cassidy, PH D, a former lecturer in social science at the University of Toronto and a member of the left-leaning League for Social Reconstruction.[24] The Liberal government's first session, that of spring 1934, brought, in historian Martin Robin's words, "a flurry of social and labour legislation." An investigating committee was set up for the summer recess to look into practical aspects of implementing a health insurance scheme.[25] Before this committee could begin probing professional attitudes and formulating concrete policy, a key document became available that provided much useful information about organized medicine's standpoints.

NATIONAL DEVELOPMENTS

In June 1934 the CMA Committee on Economics produced a landmark report that summarized the financial plight of doctors in the Depression and outlined a national health insurance plan as one possible solution. The genesis of that report is best understood by reviewing the developments in medical economics on a national scale.

British Columbia doctors were not alone in their enthusiasm for state intervention. In New Brunswick, for example, doctors claimed that 50 percent of their work was non-remunerative and demanded medical relief payments.[26] In every other province of the Dominion, the same cry went up, as organized medicine pressed for municipal or provincial assistance. During the early 1930s, however, debt-ridden municipalities were frequently unable or unwilling to help. Small centres across the Prairies and the Maritimes were especially reluctant to underwrite the medical bills of the unemployed and their families. Large cities generally hired physicians on salary to help lighten the burden of unpaid work on private practitioners, but as already noted for Victoria and Vancouver, the magnitude of the problem was such that two or three salaried doctors made little difference.[27]

The actual amount of unpaid work done by Canadian doctors on an annual basis during the Depression is difficult to estimate.

However, the data available suggest that prior to the Depression the average urban general practitioner grossing between $5,000 and $6,000 did at least $2,000 worth of unpaid work – of which about 40 percent was purely charitable and another 60 percent represented bad debts. The economic downturn probably doubled the latter amount, except in the case of those practitioners who catered to what was known as "the carriage trade."[28] Doctors were accordingly faced with an unprecedented decline in their incomes and were further vexed by the fact that they continued to work without pay, even though relief funds were used for groceries, rent, and other necessities of life.

Drawn together by their shared grievances, doctors mobilized politically and mounted strong campaigns for medical relief payments. But each level of government – be it the municipality, the relevant provincial ministry, or the federal Conservatives under Prime Minister R.B. Bennett – either disclaimed responsibility or pleaded financial embarassment. Small cities occasionally offered doctors a tax rebate as a gesture of gratitude. However, in Moose Jaw, Saskatchewan, the city council refused to accept a request by the medical society for credits on property or business taxes in lieu of other payments. The doctors retaliated by forcing paperwork on the city officials: relief recipients were to produce a letter from the relief commission requesting medical care every time they saw a private practitioner.[29]

Other work-actions were more serious. The reduction in services at the out-patient department of the Vancouver General Hospital has already been described. By far the most remarkable events were in Winnipeg, where the dispute over medical relief culminated in a doctors' strike that denied all except emergency services to over 50,000 relief recipients in Winnipeg and adjoining suburbs. Frustrated by the refusal of either the provincial or the municipal government to offer a payment plan, the Winnipeg Medical Society implemented this work-action on 1 July 1933 and sustained it for seven months. The Victoria Hospital, alone among the city's hospitals, rejected the concept of providing only emergency care for relief recipients and instead maintained full out-patient services. After warning the hospital's trustees in the autumn of 1933, the Winnipeg Medical Society requested a mass resignation of the medical staff, and eleven of fourteen specialists complied. The organizers of the strike had assumed that the increased amount of illness in winter would force the issue, but perhaps because a low-profile minority was the sole group denied services, the city officials seemed prepared to tolerate the situation indefinitely. Since a liberal definition of emergency care was being applied, the profession voted in January 1934 to refuse treatment of any kind except where life was in imminent danger. Faced with this threatened escalation in the work-action, the city council capitulated and implemented a full-scale medical relief plan. It is a measure of public sympathy for the profession's plight that both the *Winnipeg Free Press* and the *Winnipeg Tribune* offered editorial support for the doctors' cause during the entire course of the dispute.[30]

This plan cost the city and suburbs about $10,500 a month in its first year and a half of operations; however, requests for financial assistance from the provincial government were repeatedly turned down.[31] Indeed, the only provincial government to take the initiative in medical relief was Ontario. Rather than intrude directly on municipal autonomy, the government issued an order-in-council on 19 September 1932 offering a subsidy to any municipality that set up a medical relief plan on the following lines: doctors were to be paid 50 percent of the OMA minimum tariffs, in-hospital work was not included, and no doctor could collect more than $100 per month from the plan.[32] By the spring of 1933 only a few municipalities were participating, and the OMA board of directors resolved that medical relief should be removed from municipal jurisdiction and administered on a province-wide scale by an independent commission.[33] More municipalities enrolled, and between January and November 1933, 1,269 practitioners, about 35 percent of the province's doctors, received payments totalling $306,693.52.[34] However, many cities and towns still did not participate; the payments were still subject to a monthly ceiling. Scarborough experimented by removing the $100 ceiling on a six-month trial basis and found that hospitalization costs dropped enough to more than cover the additional payments to physicians. To Dr W.S. Caldwell, head of the OMA's newly appointed Committee on the Care of the Near-Indigent, this was an important signpost: "It is now the considered opinion of many, including probably the majority of York County physicians, that some form of Province-wide or Dominion-wide state-aided health insurance is as inevitable as the daylight after dark."[35]

Provincial health insurance also found favour with doctors in Alberta and Saskatchewan, where drought conditions and economic hardship were widespread. Alberta's United Farmers' government was again prompted by the Labour opposition to inquire into public health care systems, and in late 1932 a commission chaired by George Hoadley convened hearings on the matter. The council of the Alberta College of Physicians and Surgeons, now entrenched in its double role as public protector and professional advocate, advised the commission that

There has always been a large number of people whose illnesses have been looked after adequately, although they have been unable to pay for these services. The ethical wisdom, or the economic soundness of continuing this state of affairs may be seriously doubted ... In our opinion, a considerable majority of the profession of this province would welcome a scheme of State Health Insurance which would include certain important provisions.

Among those provisions was coverage of all with an income under $1,800 per year, including indigents, in a fee-for-service plan. Salary was explicitly rejected as a payment mode.[36] This representation of medical opinion was later proved valid by a formal college survey (see table 2). Although the Hoadley commission reported favourably in 1933, no attempt was made to implement a province-wide plan.

Saskatchewan's doctors, too, showed marked interest in state health insurance. Like British Columbia, Saskatchewan was giving strong support to the new Co-operative Commonwealth Federation party.[37] Saskatchewan doctors therefore not only lived and worked in a province with the highest decrease in per capita income of any during the Depression – a 72 percent fall-off in four years[38] – but also were troubled by the ccf's apparent commitment to abolition of private-fee practice. Their endorsement of state health insurance was strategic on two counts: first, to alleviate the profession's financial plight; and second, to entrench existing practice patterns instead of "state medicine." A special medical committee on a "System of Health Insurance" for Saskatchewan was appointed in 1932, and its report outlining a fee-for-service health insurance program to cover low-income groups was adopted at the sma annual meeting in February 1933. It was also agreed that a committee of the sma should be struck to make overtures concerning health insurance to "the various social organizations who are, or may become, interested in the provision of adequate medical care to the people of the Province, at as reasonable a cost as possible, for the purpose of discussing with them, and, if possible, obtaining their approval."[39]

The cma was naturally very much alive to these various provincial developments. And in 1933, while the provincial associations lobbied for medical relief payments or health insurance schemes in their jurisdiction, the cma took action as well. If the provinces and municipalities would not help the profession, the federal government might nonetheless be persuaded to do so. A cma delegation accordingly met with Prime Minister R.B. Bennett for an hour on 6 October 1933, making the case for a national program of medical relief. The cma brief noted that the profession, "adhering to its ideals and

TABLE 2

Medical Viewpoints on Health Insurance, Ontario and Alberta, 1933–4

Alberta 1933

Respondents: 227 of 550 practitioners. Results expressed as numerical ratio of positive to negative responses to given statement.

Financial conditions in medical practice are unsatisfactory: 9:1

Physicians could give better service if patients were not afraid of the expense: 10:1

Would favour state health insurance if a satisfactory program were devised: 20:1

An insurance plan should be compulsory for low-income groups, but not universal: 3:2

Fee-for-service is preferred payment mode: 26:1

State medicine with payment on salary is not acceptable: 7:1

Ontario 1934

Respondents: approx. 1,000 out of 4,088. Replies as yes (Y), no (N), or undecided (U) in response to statement.

Approve health insurance to apply for persons below a given income level: 887 Y, 30 N, 17 U.

Would be willing to work as an insurance practitioner if a satisfactory scheme were arranged: 853 Y, 35 N, 31 U.

Ontario Medical Association should take initiative in promoting health insurance: 818 Y, 62 N, 39 U.

Favour professional initiative in consultation with government: 783 Y, 51 N, 26 U.

Favour negotiating with interested organizations other than government: 465 Y, 146 N, 55 U.

Sources: For the Alberta data, see G.E. Learmonth, "Medical Services in Alberta," *CMAJ* 30 (Feb. 1934): 202–3. The actual wording of the questions can be found in idem, "Health Insurance," *Manitoba Medical Association Review* 14 (Jan. 1934): 11–12. The Ontario survey was organized by the OMA; see *OMA Bulletin* 2, no. 1 (Feb. 1935): 20–2.

traditions and having in mind that its first duty is the protection of the public health," was willing to accept payment at half the usual provincial tariff, and "would respectfully suggest that the other half of the cost of their professional services be assumed by the State." Bennett expressed sympathy for the doctors, but was immovable on the question of responsibility, stating that "the matters you have presented are strictly the business of the provinces."[40] Shortly there-

after, the CMA Committee on Economics arrived at the same conclusion.

THE 1934 CMA POLICY STATEMENT

A standing Committee on Economics had been formed by the CMA
in 1930 in response to BC developments and depressed economic
conditions across the country. Drawing on surveys and policy statements by provincial medical bodies, this committee produced a major
report on state-supported medical services for the CMA annual meeting
at Calgary in June 1934. The document was reputed to be mainly
the work of Dr A. Grant Fleming, a professor of public health and
epidemiology at McGill. It summarized international experience with
health insurance, examined the federal-provincial division of powers
in Canada, and highlighted the inadequate assistance offered to the
nation's beleaguered medical practitioners during the Depression. By
refusing to deal with the medical relief problem governments had
put the financial burden of caring for the indigent and unemployed
onto the profession. As in the past, the well-to-do ended up underwriting the costs of care for the needy, but on an inadequate and
ad hoc basis through the sliding scale of fees: "This is not a sound
economic system. There is no reason why anyone should be over-
charged simply because he can afford to pay such overcharge." The
use of the sliding scale was particularly imprecise among lower-
income groups, because it presumed the physician was able to judge
ability to pay. Indeed, the "thrifty" would be penalized, because they
would help subsidize the bills of those who were financially solvent
yet refused to pay the doctor some portion of his fee.[41] To remedy
this situation the CMA committee presented a detailed plan for state
health insurance, together with seventeen principles to guide legislators. Certain of these principles bear review.

The CMA committee favoured administration by provincial departments of public health, a definite contrast with later years, when
organized medicine's policy placed special emphasis upon administration by independent, non-political commissions in each province.
This early preference for administration by the health department
is best understood in relation to the profession's general unease about
third-party mediation between doctor and patient. As already suggested, the record of insurance companies and mutual societies as
state-approved carriers in Britain made doctors wary; these intermediaries were hard bargainers and were also under total lay control.
The department of health, on the other hand, was perceived as an
ally in the war against disease. Indeed, the senior staff of the provincial

health departments were invariably medical doctors, and qualified physicians held the deputy minister's post in every province at this time.

The CMA plan recommended the creation of two central advisory committees: one "representative of all interested" to consider broad questions of administration; and a central medical services committee, its appointees selected by organized medicine, "to consider and advise on all questions affecting the administration of the medical benefit." A parallel pair of committees would operate at regional and local levels.

On the issue of financing, the CMA planners supported a contributory scheme, with employers, government, and employees all paying into a health insurance fund. The state was to pay premiums on behalf of the indigent, "who then receive medical care under exactly the same conditions as the insured person." The plan would be compulsory for those with dependants and incomes under $2,500 a year and for single persons with incomes under $1,200 a year. Above those levels, however, only hospital insurance should be available on a voluntary basis.

In the light of the report's criticism of the sliding fee scale, the inclusion of an income ceiling on compulsory participation seems inconsistent, as does the statement that those above the income ceiling could purchase state hospital insurance but not medical services coverage. However, there is no doubt that these provisions would have considerably strengthened the profession's economic position by guaranteeing payments from those who were non-paying or poor payment risks, while ensuring that upper-income groups could still be charged higher fees instead of the lower tariffs likely to prevail under any state scheme.

International experience with those plans where cash benefits and medical services benefits were intertwined had shown that friction between doctors and patients commonly resulted. Doctors resented the additional paperwork of certifying a patient's entitlement to cash benefits, and patients in turn were angered if a practitioner refused to certify that they were too sick to work. The CMA therefore specified that health care services alone should be covered.

In keeping with the profession's suspicion of salaried systems as tending to state medicine and lay control, any contract-salary arrangements were to be limited to those areas in which a GP could not make a livelihood through insurance-supported practice. Although each local group of practitioners would be free to choose its own preferred method of remuneration, the central medical services committee would be responsible for deciding "the relationship between specialist and general practitioner fees, and between medical and surgical fees." Presumably, the actual dollar value for service units would be negotiated and relative prices fixed from this negotiated baseline.

Finally, apart from the insured's paying part of the costs of prescribed medicines, "no economic barrier" should be imposed between doctor and patient.[42] This provision reflected not only the deterrent effects of direct payments, but also the practitioner's problems in collecting some portion of his fees directly from insured patients. Full coverage of low-income patients would improve both doctor-patient relationships and the average practitioner's financial situation.

BRITISH COLUMBIA:
MEDICAL OPPOSITION BEGINS

The CMA economics committee report, although not formally endorsed until the following annual meeting,[43] naturally proved a valuable aid to Weir, Cassidy, and others charged with implementing a health insurance scheme in British Columbia. As the summer of 1934 drew to a close, the provincial secretary began receiving replies to a questionnaire his department had sent out to the medical profession. Speaking to the BCMA annual meeting in September, George Weir claimed that only 10 percent of doctors replying to the survey were opposed to health insurance, and support among dentists and nurses ran even higher.[44] However, the BC correspondent of the *CMAJ* gently cautioned against accepting Weir's claims; for less than half of the province's doctors had responded, and there had been a similarly low response rate to a survey on health insurance mailed out by organized medicine.[45]

In July 1933, following the Alberta precedent, the BCMA had voted to transfer all but its scientific and education work to the College of Physicians and Surgeons.[46] This transference of negotiating and lobbying functions to the college improved the profession's financial and political position, since, unlike the BCMA, the college governed all licensed practitioners in the province and was empowered to draw annual fees from them. It was therefore to the health insurance committee of the college that Harry Cassidy wrote when he began drafting an insurance bill. Cassidy posed two fundamental questions. First, did the college accept the health insurance principles as laid down by the CMA Committee on Economics earlier in the year? Second, were there any amendments to that report that the profession in British Columbia would suggest? The college's health insurance committee replied in writing on 17 December 1934: "As regards your first question, our answer would be 'yes.' As regards any amendments, there might be some small items of local importance that might require modification, but on the whole this report is thoroughly in accord with our opinion."[47]

The social welfare director maintained his diplomatic approach by asking the college to appoint a representative who would assist in preparing the legislation. A logical choice seemed to be Dr Grant Fleming, and at the request of his BC colleagues Fleming made the long trip from Montreal to Victoria in January 1935. Fleming met with the health insurance committee of the College of Physicians and Surgeons on 16 January and found definite divisions of opinion within it – divisions apparently reflected in the profession at large. Although this was a dangerous omen, the committee had gone on record as supporting the CMA principles, and it further specified:

That, while as a profession, we believe that the principle of payment for services should be followed whenever possible, we would not oppose a system of payment by capitation fee, provided that the fee per person, for general practitioner services, be approximately three dollars and fifty cents, with extra payments on a proportional basis for specialist services. It being understood that a complete service be provided for, including hospitals and specialist services.

Fleming therefore concluded that his mandate was to incorporate as many of the CMA principles as possible into the draft legislation, and to ensure that GP services would be remunerated at the levels suggested by the college committee.[48] The resulting draft bill was presented to the legislature in March 1935. It was also bound together with a twenty-one-page explanatory preamble, and thousands of copies of the resulting pamphlet were distributed throughout the province. In his foreword to the pamphlet Weir made it plain that it was meant to serve as a basis for discussion by all interested parties.[49]

At first glance, there was little in the draft bill to displease the BC doctors. Points in the proposed legislation could be matched up with almost every one of the CMA principles. Indeed, when Dr Grant Fleming later performed this exercise, he claimed that the bill's only failing lay in its coverage of cash sickness benefits: "It seems to me to be fair to state that the 'Principles,' as accepted by the Canadian Medical Association, have been included, with one exception, i.e., the provision of Cash Benefits, but even here we are met halfway by having the responsibility for certification placed with the full-time medical staff of the Commission."

At this time the profession's perspective was still positive. Dr H.E. MacDermot, the *CMAJ* editor, praised the British Columbia government for its "courageous and sensible attempt" to implement health insurance. The *Bulletin of the Vancouver Medical Association* reserved judgment on the draft bill pending further study but stressed that the province's doctors must "recognize the need for radical change" and "welcome reform."[50]

In July 1935 a Hearings Committee on health insurance was appointed by the government to tour the province and sample public reactions to the draft bill and explanatory memorandum that had been circulated in the spring. The Hearings Committee was chaired by the government's newly appointed technical adviser on insurance, Dr Allon Peebles. Peebles held a PhD in economics from Columbia University and had served on the research staff of America's famous Committee on the Cost of Medical Care before returning to work as a life insurance executive in Canada.[51] Other members included representatives of the business community, organized labour, the BC Hospital Association, and the nursing profession. In an astute move, Dr A. Grant Fleming was also invited to sit on the Hearings Committee. Fleming returned from Montreal and met behind the scenes with doctors and the college health insurance committee to assist them in preparing their brief for the hearings. Teaching commitments at McGill University forced Fleming to leave British Columbia in early autumn, and the BC doctors did not consult him again. As quickly became clear, their view of the proposed legislation was totally at odds with Fleming's analysis.

Presented at Victoria on 24 September 1935, the doctors' brief was accompanied by a letter stating that the college committee was "unanimously and unalterably opposed to the present enactment" on the grounds that the draft bill did not "indicate a reasonable assurance or indeed any likelihood of a high standard of scientific medical practice."[52] When the brief was read, however, it was apparent that the issues were more economic than clinical.

The college wanted cash benefits eliminated; the "halfway" compromise of the draft bill was rejected. There should also be "a reserve fund to protect against cutting down on remuneration to medical men and benefits to the insured." The draft legislation had called for payments for indigent care to be made at one-half the rate for other insured parties. This the college rejected flatly, and indeed the provision did fly in the face of the CMA principle calling for indigents to be covered on the same terms and conditions as others who were insured. The college committee therefore demanded that "all references to payments for indigents at half rates be eliminated and one rate apply to all those insured."[53]

But rigorous adherence to CMA principles was not the sole issue; for the college committee departed sharply from CMA policy on a different count. The draft bill had called for compulsory coverage of those with dependants who earned less than $200 per month and those without dependants earning $100 per month. Voluntary coverage for hospitalization might be made available to higher-income groups. This was exactly in line with the CMA principles of health insurance; however, the college objected: "It seems perfectly clear that the person earning $200 per month, with or without dependants, needs no assistance."[54] The ceilings should therefore be lowered to $125 per month for medical services, although hospital insurance would continue to be compulsory for all those earning less than $200 per month. These ceilings would have reduced the proportion of the population covered by the plan from over 85 percent to around 70 percent. Analysing this complaint, the *Victoria Daily Times* observed that "the doctors would lose out" if medical insurance and the attendant uniform fee schedule applied to the higher income group who were already "the best paying patients they have."[55]

As to medical remuneration, the draft bill stated that an administrative commission, "after obtaining the advice of the Medical Committee," would "arrange for payment of medical practitioners, including specialists, by capitation fee, fee for services rendered, or otherwise." Harry Cassidy was aware of the profession's preference for fee-for-service, and in an article on the bill published earlier by the *CMAJ*, he emphasized that the final choice rested with the doctors.[56] However, the college health insurance committee was clearly uneasy about the wording of the legislation and now requested that the bill indicate fee-for-service as the only payment mode except in special cases such as rural salary-contract practice. (The profession's fears were well founded, since the government later proposed to pay GPs exclusively by capitation.) The actual payment levels provided by the bill were in line with those suggested by the college itself: the budget for GP services was "not less than three dollars nor more than four dollars per annum per insured person." Although no comment was made by the college on these figures, the doctors were clearly suspicious of the entire scheme. Indeed, their final comment was that the insurance program would be better set aside until the federal government had appointed a royal commission to investigate health conditions and health services coast to coast.

Dr George Weir was of course displeased by the medical criticisms.

Weir remarked that a federal royal commission would take three to five years to report, and in a thinly veiled threat as to the possibilities of a full-blown state medical service, he suggested that 60 to 75 percent of doctors might in fact prefer to have an assured salary, regular vacations, and retirement on good superannuation. An even stronger reaction came from George S. Pearson, the minister of labour in Patullo's cabinet and former member of the 1929 Royal Commission on Health Insurance. Pearson warned:

The chief fear of the medical men seems to be that their earnings will be threatened. This plan protects them to a certain extent as well as it protects a section of the people against the costs of sickness. Those who can afford to pay are left as fair game for the doctors. Some of my socialist ideas would give me the tendency to socialize the whole thing, but I really don't think we're ready for that yet and I'm sure the doctors don't want us to go that far.[57]

One of the most barbed responses to the college's criticisms came from none other than Dr Grant Fleming. Reporting to the CMA executive committee in Ottawa on 31 October 1935, Fleming scolded the BC college health insurance committee for its misuse of his services and its bargaining tactics. Fleming remarked that the BC government had consulted the profession in drafting their legislation; adopted the CMA principles, "practically *in toto*"; and "followed a most democratic procedure in putting up a Draft Bill for discussion. The response of the medical profession has, I fear, been such as to discharge any other government from following along these lines."[58]

Following Fleming's analysis of the BC situation, members of the CMA executive committee discussed strategy. Two major options were open. Hugh Wolfenden, an actuary and leading member of the Association of Canadian Life Insurance Officers, might be sent west to analyse the situation. This choice of consultants was significant. In 1932 Wolfenden had published a monograph attacking social insurance schemes generally and concluding that private insurance had important advantages over public insurance for health care or other purposes.[59] Dr T.C. Routley, the CMA general secretary, suggested that because the BC Royal Commission on Health Insurance had not included an actuary, the government might be persuaded to delay until Wolfenden had assessed the data base. Fleming and others replied that proper statistics to create actuarial tables for health insurance were unavailable in Canada and Wolfenden could do nothing constructive. Routley's suggestion was therefore rejected.

The executive committee turned next to the second delaying tactic

– a federal royal commission. Routley said, "What they really need is time. Could we not communicate with the Prime Minister of Canada and take this matter up again?" The general secretary was accordingly empowered to visit Parliament Hill and to press the federal government for a national survey of health services.[60]

THE REVISED BILL

Soon after the CMA executive had discussed the BC imbroglio, the Hearings Committee produced its recommendations for revisions to the draft bill. Reporting on the results of hearings at eighteen centres, the committee stressed that very few of the 139 submissions expressed opposition to the principle of health insurance. Indeed, by far the most frequent suggestion was elimination of all income ceilings and extension of the plan either to every employee or to every BC resident. However, in an apparent attempt to satisfy conflicting pressure groups, the Hearings Committee recommended a more limited plan.

Whereas the original bill had provided that employers would contribute an amount equal to 2 percent of their payrolls, the committee proposed a revision to 1 percent, primarily because of complaints from BC industrialists that a payroll tax would compromise their already weak position of competition for international markets with eastern manufacturers. Once the employers' contribution was reduced, fairness dictated that the employees receive a reduction as well. There had in any case been complaints from labour groups about the size of the proposed payroll deductions, and the CCF was known to favour complete elimination of premiums with financing of the insurance fund from general taxation revenue. Hence the committee suggested a revision from 3 percent to 2 percent for the maximum deduction from an employee's weekly pay cheque.

Three additional modifications were suggested that might have appeased the college health insurance committee. First, because of financial stringency payments of cash benefits to sick workers should be postponed. Second, full rates instead of half rates should apply for indigents. And finally, the Hearings Committee proposed that the ceiling on annual incomes of participants be reduced to $1,800. If not the $1,500 the doctors originally sought, this was nevertheless a substantial reduction from the original $2,400 ceiling for those with dependants. According to their private report to George Weir, "The major consideration of the Committee in suggesting that the limit of $2,400 be reduced to $1,800 is the desirability of obtaining the co-operation of the medical profession."[61] The new income limit was formally opposed by Percival Bengough, the labour representative on the committee, who claimed in a radio broadcast on 18 December 1935 that the new bill "would compel the poor to help the poor and carry what are now the 'bad debts' of the medical profession."[62]

An examination of the financial ramifications of the Hearings Committee's recommendations reveals the roots of later problems. Revenues from employers were halved. Revenues from employees were decreased by at least half, since the new lowered ceiling and 33 percent reduction in maximum pay-packet deduction would combine to reduce both the number of enrolled employees and the amount paid on average. While elimination of cash benefits and diminution of the insured population improved the balance sheet, a doubling of expenses for indigent services could be anticipated.

Accordingly the Hearings Committee proposals, if implemented, would impose an augmented burden on the BC government which it could not easily pass on to middle-class taxpayers. Federal assistance might help, but throughout 1934 and most of 1935, T.D. Patullo and his cabinet colleagues had little success in persuading Conservative Prime Minister R.B. Bennett to loosen the federal purse-strings. Without the backing to float a provincial bond issue and therefore the capital for social welfare measures and public works programs, the BC Liberals found their reformist initiative blunted and their popularity waning. In October 1935, when W.L. Mackenzie King and the Liberals returned to power, Patullo nursed hopes that his federal confreres would prove more willing to experiment with deficit financing. These hopes were dashed at a dominion-provincial conference in December 1935. The BC Liberals therefore faced the 1936 legislative session with a sizeable provincial debt, little room for financial manoeuvring, and an expensive health insurance program of uncertain popularity.[63]

Despite these fiscal and political constraints, in late November 1935 Dr George Weir delivered a half-hour radio broadcast that confirmed the government's commitment to an insurance program. Praising health insurance and rebutting criticisms of the BC scheme, the provincial secretary averred that the time was "over-ripe" for action. There was no point in waiting for a federal royal commission: this was merely "a red herring across the trail" and a "stalling device." Medical men, in particular, were reminded that the CMA Committee on Economics had acknowledged that health insurance was under provincial jurisdiction. But Weir's broadcast left one major question unanswered. The hearings had been held and changes in the draft bill recommended. Nobody, however, was entirely certain what revisions would actually be made. The BC correspondent for the *CMAJ* cautioned: "It was apparent throughout the address that the revised

Bill, and not the one placed before the public for consideration, was being referred to. Except that, as Dr Weir stated, in many respects this Bill did not go as far as he would wish there was no other indication as to the manner in which the Bill had been modified."[64] Nor in the early part of the new year was any description of the revisions forthcoming from the provincial government, perhaps because the possibility of a federal windfall had not been ruled out. In February 1936 there was a $4.3 million loan from Ottawa to British Columbia, but this sum was to cover a maturing bond issue. No other assistance was offered.

Rumours concerning the new form of the health insurance bill began to circulate in the BC press. Although firm data were still lacking, the British Columbia Loggers' Association, representing the businessmen who controlled the province's forestry concerns, submitted a brief to the government calling for postponement of health insurance until a national program was in effect, lest eastern competition be given further market advantages. Shortly before the assembly convened for the opening session of 1936, a delegation from the British Columbia Manufacturers' Association met with the cabinet to advance the same argument.[65]

When the throne speech was read on 25 February outlining the program for the third sitting of British Columbia's eighteenth legislature, health insurance was the only weighty measure scheduled for debate. It was immediately apparent, however, that the province's straitened finances had a major influence in the revisions to the draft bill.[66] The Hearings Committee recommendations were followed in only two respects. Contributions from employers and employees were bumped downwards by a percentage point, and the ceiling on participation was lowered to $1,800. The latter concession to organized medicine was sweetened by an increase in the per capita funding for physician payments. Previously the insurance fund was to contain not more than $4.60 per insured person for all GP and specialist services. The new maximum was $5.50. Of course, the doctors' raise and reduced revenues built into the bill sat badly together. In order to close the revenue gap the government first disclaimed any responsibility for administrative expenses and then, in a move totally contrary to the direction suggested by the Hearings Committee, eliminated any provision for indigent coverage.

The health insurance committee of the BC College of Physicians and Surgeons had attempted unsuccessfully to get advance information on the nature of the revisions. Once the committee learned of the proposed terms, a telegram was sent to every member of the profession in the province stating that the bill was "absolutely unsatisfactory." Doctors were urged to telegraph the premier and their local representatives at once, protesting passage of the bill. Dr A.T. Bazin, a veteran member of the CMA executive and professor of surgery at McGill University, was sent west with T.C. Routley to assist the British Columbia profession. On 28 February the CMA representatives met with the Liberal cabinet to warn that the proposed scheme was unsound from both an actuarial and a medical standpoint. Strong caucus discipline has traditionally limited the impact of pressure groups in Canadian party politics, but in this instance two doctors in the Liberal caucus – J.J. Gillis and W.H. Sutherland – had broken ranks and actually joined Routley and Bazin to present the profession's criticisms.[67] The participation of Gillis was especially damaging, since he had served on the 1929 Royal Commission on Health Insurance along with George Pearson, the minister of labour. George Weir had already asked two leading actuaries from eastern Canada to analyse the bill, and they independently confirmed its financial integrity. Weir released their report to the press the day after the medical delegation's visit.[68]

When the Act to Provide for the Establishment of a Provincial System of Health Insurance formally began its first reading on 3 March, the debate inside and outside the legislature split the province along ideological lines. On one side, supporting the legislation, were employees in the lower-income bracket and those who sympathized with their position: the unions, women's and church groups, left-wing Liberals, and CCF members. On the opposing side stood many businessmen and professionals. Boards of trade and chambers of commerce registered strong opposition; and property-owning rate-payers expressed concern that health insurance would lead to increased urban hospital utilization, the costs of which would be subsidized through municipal taxes rather than spread out on a province-wide basis. Eighteen Vancouver corporation heads who met with Premier Patullo to protest the measure advanced the now familiar argument about eastern competition, although in addition a financial lure was trolled. If action were postponed for a year, BC industries would supply funds for an actuarial survey. Alluding to actuarial opinions already tendered, George Weir rejected this offer.[69]

Opposition mounted on the medical front as well. It was widely rumoured that the CMA had endowed a $10,000 lobbying fund and was prepared to back the BCMA totally.[70] The provincial secretary therefore took to the offensive in dealing with medical opposition and publicly quoted Dr Grant Fleming's opinion, as presented to the CMA executive committee, that the bill embodied the CMA principles. Spokesmen for the BCMA replied cogently that Fleming's analysis had applied to the draft bill, not the revised version. Fleming, opined the BCMA, was in any case "an enthusiast for health insurance, who is anxious to see the experiment tried out immediately, and in that, he is in perfect accord with Dr Weir. Where it is tried out does not matter much to Dr Fleming."[71]

Additional pressure was applied by British Columbia's commercial interests on 9 March, when a mammoth delegation of industrialists and businessmen met with the majority of the Liberal caucus and called for postponement. The Victoria Trades and Labour Council responded with a telegram to the premier, urging the government not to waver. But by this time the Liberals were already wavering badly. A handful of caucus members had opposed the plan from the outset, and under the leadership of Mr Gordon Wismer (Liberal – Vancouver Centre) they began a plebiscite movement: no action should be taken until the voters were polled for their opinions on health insurance.[72] Wismer, in fact, was the legal counsel of the College of Physicians and Surgeons and had been paid a special retainer to prepare and present the doctors' brief to the Hearings Committee in 1935.[73]

The CCF caucus found the bill too limited and regressive, but most members were prepared to support it as a step in the right direction. Thus, although five Liberals voted against it, the bill passed its second reading on 26 March by twenty-eight to ten.

On 27 March the College of Physicians and Surgeons reiterated its criticisms in an open letter to Dr Weir. The bill, claimed the doctors, was actuarially unsound and should be delayed. The provincial secretary, who had acquired yet another favourable expert opinion on the bill's actuarial integrity,[74] was unimpressed and he steered the legislation forward, although two last-minute changes were made. First, the provincial treasurer's responsibility for underwriting the scheme had previously been limited to $50,000 per year, and this limit was removed altogether. Second, at the instigation of Dr W.H. Sutherland, who now also sat on the college health insurance committee, the budgetary ceiling of $5.50 per person per annum for medical services was lifted.[75] The final vote on 31 March saw a margin of twenty-five to fourteen, with seven Liberals voting against. Royal assent was granted through the lieutenant-governor on 1 April 1936.

THE FINAL DEADLOCK

The doctors had by no means given up their fight to have health insurance on better terms – or not at all. By eliminating provision for the unemployed and pensioners, the government not only had left the profession with an excessive burden of unpaid work but also had given medical spokesmen a powerful rhetorical weapon. Henceforth the BCMA and the College of Physicians and Surgeons were not simply battling for guaranteed fees from the expanded population of medical indigents; they were fighting on behalf of better medical services for low-income groups. While George Weir boasted that the legislation covered 275,000 British Columbians,[76] Dr William Ainley of the college health insurance committee lamented the fact that more than 100,000 of the truly needy were left without insurance by the new law.[77]

Shortly after the bill was read into law, the college arranged the release to the press of a letter sent to Weir by the Canadian Life Insurance Officers Association (CLIOA). Seven actuaries comprising the CLIOA Committee on Social Insurance indicated their support in principle for the aims of the BC legislation, but warned against proceeding without impartial review by a group of insurance experts. Their letter specifically condemned the lack of any mechanism to appeal decisions made by the administrative commission. The actuaries also stated that it "would seem to be necessary to prescribe equitable bases of remuneration for the medical profession ... rather than to place unlimited and punitive powers in the hands of the commission," since the doctors might simply refuse to work under the terms of the legislation.[78] Dr W.E. Ainley drove home these points by announcing that the profession's own estimates projected the cost of the health insurance plan to be 35 percent above the program's actual revenues.[79]

A tartly worded summary of the profession's grievances was printed in the *Bulletin of the Vancouver Medical Association* for May 1936. The *Bulletin*'s editors noted that the original draft bill of 1935, while "not in any way perfect," was definitely superior to the final legislation:

It *did* purport to look after all the members of the community whose yearly income, whether from indigence or low wages, fell below a certain level. It *did* acknowledge the fact that the Government should contribute to the Act, by at least half the cost of administration. It *did* acknowledge the medical profession. It seemed to recognize the fact that medical men will be necessary in the working of this Act, and it gave us a certain amount of say in the administration of the Act.

However, the insurance act failed on all these scores. The financial terms would mean "economic slavery for the majority of medical men," but the "main reason" for the *Bulletin*'s objection to the law was that its financing simply could not "give what was promised to those who came under it, namely, a complete and adequate medical service." The editors also acknowledged the business community's fears about the negative impact of payroll deductions to fund the plan and concluded with a tribute to Dr W.H. Sutherland for his assistance in the legislature.[80]

The same issue of the *Bulletin* carried an open letter to "All Members of the Medical Profession in British Columbia" from the chairman of the college health insurance committee, calling for total solidarity. Dr W.E. Ainley, the committee chairman, observed that the administrative commission of the government plan had wide latitude to negotiate on financial issues, especially since the last set of revisions to the legislation had removed the previous limit on payments for medical services: "We believe that there is still room for negotiation and that terms satisfactory to both parties can be arranged – but this can only be secured if we act as a unit. Independent action on the part of any medical man can only lead to disaster for himself as well as for all the members of the profession."[81]

Solidarity-building continued by other means. A luncheon meeting of the BCMA was held at the Hotel Georgia in Vancouver on 20 May, with health insurance the topic of addresses by Dr Wallace Wilson, standing in for the ailing Dr Ainley as college committee chairman, and by Dr M.W. Thomas, newly recruited as full-time executive secretary of the BCMA. Thomas departed shortly thereafter for a tour of the province to drum up support among practitioners in outlying areas.[82]

In June the CMA met at Victoria for its 1936 annual convention. The CMA Committee on Economics spent considerable time discussing health insurance and "socialized medicine" and was warned by a BC delegate that "the present situation in our province is the thin edge of the wedge, and that sooner or later, every province in Canada will be concerned."[83]

The British Columbia profession, which held its annual meeting in conjunction with the CMA convention, naturally focused on the health insurance dispute in depth. The guest speaker was Dr W.K. Colbeck, president-elect of the Ontario Medical Association, who outlined the new arrangements for medical relief in his province. As already mentioned, although the Ontario government had offered a conditional subsidy to all municipalities setting up medical relief schemes, many municipalities were unwilling or financially unable to participate. The OMA's requests for a uniform provincial plan were turned down. Worse yet, after a change of government in 1934, the health ministry indicated on 6 February 1935 that the existing program was an administrative nuisance and proposed to cancel it altogether unless the OMA would take over the administration of the plan. After two and a half weeks of negotiations the OMA council was convened and voted in favour of this new role for organized medicine. Under the agreement the government paid $3 per annum to the OMA for each person on relief, with a higher subsidy going to designated northern areas where more of the population was out of work. These funds were disbursed locally on a prorated, fee-for-service basis, and all auditing was done by local committees. This experiment proved successful, and the OMA found itself administering a medical relief plan with about 3,000 practitioners, 400,000 patients, and an annual budget of well over $1 million per year. Understandably then, Dr Colbeck urged the BC profession to "exhaust every avenue of conciliation and co-operation" before giving up "hope of obtaining satisfactory terms."[84] This detailed report on the OMA plan probably hardened the resolve of the BC profession to reject the proposed health insurance program unless some payment for indigent care were included.

Dr Wallace Wilson spoke next and emphasized that the profession should "play a waiting game ... One or two meetings have been held with the Health Insurance commission and they wish to co-operate. They realize that we hold the key. They do not know as yet the solution of the indigent problem, but the Premier has promised legislation, also Dr Weir."[85]

While the profession waited, there was steady activity in the government camp. Dr Allon Peebles, the health economics expert who had chaired the Hearings Committee, was appointed chairman of the Health Insurance Commission,[86] and representatives of employers and employees were also selected. However, the medical spokesman appointed to the commission had no special ties to the organized profession and was known to be a close personal friend of Premier Patullo.[87] Through the summer and autumn the commission and its administrative staff systematically registered all employers and employees who would be participating in the plan. There is no question that some in the provincial secretariat had reservations about the legislation they were charged with implementing. Writing to a federal colleague in November 1936, Dr Harry Cassidy remarked that the original health insurance proposals were "in the private opinion of those of us who have worked on the problem ... a good deal better than the act which was finally passed last March."[88] In any case, other events were already afoot which sharply altered the political backdrop against which the last scene in the BC health insurance drama unfolded.

Economic recovery was beginning, and British Columbia led the nation in rate of commercial resurgence. The CCF, which until mid-1936 had represented a growing electoral threat to the Liberals, was weakened by internal squabbles and gradually lost ground. With the Conservative party regaining momentum after its 1933 electoral disaster, the safe thing for the Liberals to do now was to steer from left to centre and take credit for having led the province through the slump. Although the Liberals' ideological commitment to health insurance was weakening,[89] the government could scarcely renege on its oft-repeated promise at this late date.

On 8 January 1937 Premier Patullo announced that the health insurance program would be operational by 1 March, with benefit eligibility commencing on 29 March. This assessment proved unduly optimistic; for negotiations between the medical profession and the Health Insurance Commission were proceeding badly. On 20 January a lengthy meeting of the college health insurance committee was held in Vancouver. The committee, expanded by additional delegates from all parts of the province, dissected the tentative operating plan clause by clause and pronounced it unsatisfactory. Discussions were held with the Health Insurance Commission that evening and the final verdict rendered: the committee must poll the profession formally, but it would definitely recommend that the plan be rejected.

The college's list of complaints was daunting: there were no mileage payments for house calls; the provisions for hospitalization were inadequate; deductibles and exemptions built into the plan would damage doctor-patient relations. But the major source of disgruntlement was remuneration per se. The total pool of funds for specialist and GP services rested still on the allowance of $5.50 per insured person. Despite the profession's earlier objections, the commissioners insisted on paying GPs by capitation fee, and the college again rejected this as an unsatisfactory alternative to fee-for-service. The actual GP capitation fee offered was about $4 per patient per year, obviously an improvement on the $3.50 the college had suggested eighteen months previously but now deemed inadequate. Specialists were to be paid on a prorated, fee-for-service basis, using the remaining pool of funds. This proposal, too, was rejected emphatically: "No man in any other line of life would undertake to do work without knowing how much he could be sure of receiving – no business man would sign any such contract as this."[90] The college committee therefore insisted that either the range of medical services be decreased or the overall assessments be increased from $5.50 by at least one dollar per person.

Finally they reiterated the complaint about failure to cover low-income groups – "the indigent, those on relief, domestic servants, old-age and mothers' pensioners, casual and part-time labourers, and those earning less than ten dollars a week." While this omission was presented as a signpost of the act's inadequacy from "the public standpoint," the committee added that "the medical profession must still continue to carry this whole load of unpaid work, both in and out of the hospital, without any compensation whatever ... After we had made many requests for action along this line – which in our belief, was promised again and again, with no result – we finally obtained a statement from Premier Patullo that the question of the indigent would be taken up and settled *after the Health Act was in force*. We frankly cannot accept this as of any value at all."[91]

Meetings of the profession were quickly convened at Victoria and Vancouver, and the college officials presented their case against the health insurance legislation. Doctors from the lower mainland voted 191 to four against participating in the plan; at Victoria, the negative vote was unanimous. A press release detailing the college's objections was published in extenso by the *Vancouver Daily Province*.[92] The college health insurance committee also published an account of their negotiations and their criticisms of the commission's plan in the February *Bulletin of the Vancouver Medical Association*. The *Bulletin*'s editor reinforced the college committee's position, encouraged general refusal of the terms that had been offered, and warned, "We are undoubtedly at a very vital crossroads in the history of medicine, not only in British Columbia but throughout Canada ... Not temporary expediency, and not apparent self-interest, must guide us, for what may seem of benefit at the moment may later turn out to be the first step to suicide."[93]

From here, as the newspapers became vehicles for acrimonious exchanges between the two sides, matters moved rapidly to an impasse. Dr Allon Peebles, the Health Insurance Commission chairman, defended the plan, insisting that remuneration was the major stumbling block to agreement with the profession and pointing out that all those earning above $1,800 per year could be billed by the doctors as they saw fit.[94] Dr Wallace Wilson, neatly side-stepping this thrust, responded that while the remuneration was inadequate, "Above everything else, the profession protests – and will continue to protest – against the lack, either inside or outside the scheme, of any provision for the indigent, the low wage earner and widow pensioner."[95] Dr Weir entered the debate at this stage, claiming that no plan of health insurance in the world covered indigents. The province and municipalities between them had in any case paid out some $350,000 for indigent medical services during the fiscal year 1935-6, and this sum did not include the costs of free hospitalization.

But, as the *Vancouver Daily Province* accurately remarked, the fate of health insurance had "ceased to be a fight between the Health Insurance Commission and medical men of British Columbia."[96] Provincial business interests were again making their voices heard in protest, and the college committee astutely saw the opportunity for a joint public protest. On 9 February a mammoth luncheon meeting of the Vancouver Board of Trade was arranged under BCMA auspices at the Hotel Georgia. Dr Wallace Wilson reiterated the profession's criticisms of the bill in a public address broadcast across the provincial radio network. Four hundred professional and business men attended, and an informal vote showed almost unanimous opposition to the legislation.[97]

This proved to be the last straw. Over the next week, it became apparent that the cabinet would back down, and on 19 February Dr Weir announced that the premier, away in Ottawa at a conference, had telegraphed instructions to postpone operation of the Health Insurance Commission *sine die*. The commission's headquarters were radically reduced over the next several days from sixty or seventy employees to a skeleton staff. Rumours meanwhile were circulating that the plan would be delayed until after the imminent provincial election during which a plebiscite might be held on the issue.

The BC college health insurance committee had already organized its own plebiscite. On 3 February ballots had been sent to each practitioner with a covering letter, signed on behalf of the committee by the registrar of the College of Physicians and Surgeons – that is, the doctor employed by the self-governing body to attend to licensing and discipline matters. The letter referred to the February *Bulletin of the Vancouver Medical Association* but noted that the committee "wishes to approach you more directly and personally than through the pages of a journal ... for our struggle is not yet over, and will only be settled satisfactorily by the absolute solidarity of the profession in a determination not to betray the trusts which are imposed upon us, namely, the protection of the science of medicine, and the protection of the public in health matters." The letter outlined once more all the previous criticisms of the bill and closed with a call for unity: "Do not delay! Never have we been faced with such a serious problem. Never has the profession been so united!"[98] Whether these voting instructions played a role must remain unknown; however, the BCMA vice-president later claimed the profession's solidarity, "revealed by the secret ballot on their stand has not only amazed the government and the public at large but has astonished the doctors themselves."[99] The final tally, accounting for more than 99 percent of registered practitioners, showed 622 against participation in the health insurance plan and only thirteen in favour.[100]

The legislature was dissolved on 15 April and an election called for 1 June 1937. At that time a referendum on health insurance would be presented. The wording, however, was more than a little vague. Voters would simply be asked: "Are you in favour of a comprehensive Health Insurance plan, progressively applied?" The *Victoria Daily Colonist*, which had joined Vancouver's *Province* and *Sun* in baiting the Liberals, pointed out trenchantly that the plebiscite would merely leave more questions unanswered. Who was to draft the new bill? What exactly did "comprehensive" and "progressive" mean? In short, the electorate was "asked to commit themselves one way or another on the subject of health insurance without the slightest inkling of what is projected, and having the experience that after a long period of intensive research work and more intensive propaganda the Government failed to devise a workable scheme."[101]

Liberal newspaper advertisements contended that a health insurance scheme would be implemented if the plebiscite were positive, but health insurance was a side issue in the election. Premier Patullo, on the campaign stump in May, waffled elegantly: "I am not going to tell you now what we are going to do about health insurance. I don't know. But we are not going to ram it down everyone's throat. We will iron out all difficulties." In fact, Patullo concentrated his campaign energies on portraying the Liberals as the only provincial party capable of slaying the federal dragon and winning a new division of powers - and finances - within Confederation. The CCF strongly supported a universal health insurance scheme; while the rejuvenated Conservatives warned that the province was visibly overgoverned and called for a return to free enterprise, but were willing to consider an "actuarially sound" health insurance scheme.[102]

In the event, the health insurance plebiscite was carried favourably by a majority of 35,000, winning support from 59 percent of the voters. However, the Liberals lost four seats, and Dr Weir, the health insurance exponent in the cabinet, only narrowly escaped defeat. With economic recovery under way and the electorate's temper demonstrably uncertain, Premier Patullo abandoned "socialized capitalism."[103] Despite advocacy from the Liberal back benches, prodding from the CCF and labour groups, and the occasional public plea by George Weir,[104] health insurance was temporarily removed from the British Columbia government agenda.

THE BC HEALTH INSURANCE
FEUD: A RETROSPECT

Glancing back over the tangled chain of events that led to indefinite postponement of the BC health insurance act of 1936, it is clear that while the opposition of business interests had some impact, the pivotal factor was organized medicine's rejection of the government plan. The conflicting actuarial assessments of the insurance act undermined the profession's confidence in the program, and the wide-ranging powers of the administrative commission were perceived as a threat to professional autonomy. However, the most important points of disagreement were about modes and amounts of remuneration.

In January 1935 the college had indicated a preference for fee-for-service payment of GPs yet was willing to accept an annual capitation fee. The government, too, suggested the mode of remuneration was negotiable. But in the ensuing months both sides took increasingly inflexible positions on this issue. The profession's stand against capitation fees was linked to what the *Bulletin of the Vancouver Medical Association* termed the "deplorably low" standard of "panel practice" under the British insurance system, and during the 1930s the quality of British general practice had indeed sagged.[105] However, economic self-interest was also involved. It was not that capitation fees meant loss of the doctors' ability to price-discriminate with higher-income patients, since they remained outside the plan, and all lower-income patients would be insured on a uniform basis regardless of whether fee-for-service or capitation payment was applied. Nevertheless the college was aware that the insurance program would lead to increased demands on doctors, and only under a fee-for-service system would incomes rise in lockstep with the greater volume of services delivered. This coupling of every item of service with a given payment sustained the doctors' self-image as a small businessman and also meant that the more enterprising practitioners could increase their incomes by altering the volume and mix of services provided. As for the prorated fee-for-service payment plan for specialists, here the doctors faced the straightforward prospect of diminishing marginal returns for increasing amounts of work.

Many of the college's other criticisms of proposed and actual legislation reflected its concern that the terms of health insurance should be favourable to income maximization through a combination of guaranteed fees and opportunities for price discrimination. With insured payments from all low-income groups and a free hand to charge higher fees for identical services rendered to patients who were better off, the average doctor's cash flow would be markedly improved. This point readily explains both the college committee's insistence on changing the income ceiling for participation in the plan and its repeated demands that indigents and pensioners be covered at the same rates as contributing employees.

The united front put up by specialists and GPs underscores an observation made in chapter 3 about the comparative lack of division in the Canadian profession. Specialists usually took appointments at major public hospitals, receiving in some cases a small honorarium; they were expected to tend the poor as "social rent" for use of the hospital's beds and operating theatres in their private practices. GPs attended patients in and out of hospital in smaller centres and, albeit less frequently as the years passed, could also obtain admitting privileges in large hospitals. Complaints about inappropriate specialization were in any case less common in the 1930s than in the 1920s, in part because the Royal College of Physicians and Surgeons was chartered in 1929 to standardize specialty requirements.[106]

The pressure-group strategies used by the BC profession were numerous and surprisingly successful, considering that organized medicine had relatively little experience with such high-profile and intense political activity. One might note, in passing, the transference of negotiating and lobbying power from the BCMA to the College of Physicians and Surgeons; the assistance from Drs Gillis and Sutherland in the legislature; the effective use of press releases throughout the campaign; and the mustering of support from the CMA and the BC business community. The college was also careful to keep its own ranks united with many meetings, articles and editorials in the *Bulletin of the Vancouver Medical Association*, and direct mailings to doctors across the province.

What gave the doctors' campaign additional momentum was the profession's ability to project its interests in an altruistic light. It is logical that pressure groups of any kind will tend to present their particular interests in a fashion that highlights the common good, but just as decades before, when the profession sought licensing and self-governance privileges, the doctors were in a position to legitimize their political actions convincingly. By stressing, for example, that inclusion of low-income groups in the plan was really a matter of justice for indigents and widow pensioners, spokesmen for the BCMA and the college health insurance committee doubtless sparked the profession's morale, hardened its resistance, and won considerable public support.

Indeed, when Professor H.F. Angus of the University of British Columbia had examined the developing stalemate in the April 1937

Canadian Forum, his assessment of the profession's role was uncertain. "To a neutral spectator," wrote Angus, "it was not apparent where the doctors' real interests lay." Left-wing commentators were further confused by the profession's apparent transformation from a loosely knit group of small businessmen into a hard-nosed labour union. Some, reported the professor, were sympathetic: the doctors deserved payment for their work with the unemployed; the plan was flawed and the income ceiling on coverage was so low that the measure could hardly be construed as progressive in any case.

Others, legalistically minded, pointed out that for a trade union to bargain for rates of pay and conditions of work was wholly reasonable, but that a syndicalistic dictation of policy, (analogous to a claim by typesetters to censor an editorial or to a refusal by railway men to move munitions of war), was a bad example for a learned bourgeois profession to set its less erudite proletarian brethren, who are confirmed by it in their suspicion that all human behaviour can be explained by economic interest.[107]

THE CHANGING NATIONAL CONTEXT

The British Columbia health insurance dispute was unquestionably the most important episode in medical politics during the Depression, but intense activity took place in other jurisdictions as well. The withdrawal of indigent services by doctors in Winnipeg from July 1933 to February 1934 has already been mentioned. Montreal, too, was a site of professional agitation in this period, with Dr Norman Bethune playing a key role. During 1935 Bethune had developed an increasing interest in preventive and social medicine and eventually helped to organize a weekly clinic for the unemployed and their families in the Montreal suburb of Verdun. His belief in the need for medical reforms led to a visit to the Soviet Union in August, and before the year was over Bethune had not only joined the Communist party but also founded the Montreal Group for the Security of the People's Health. Its membership included Communists, CCFers, and a certain number of those who were, as Bethune told J.S. Woodsworth, "humanitarians of no political hue, but of progressive views."[108] Doctors, nurses, dentists, social workers, and statisticians participated in the group's endeavours.[109]

As chief of the tuberculosis unit at Sacre Coeur Hospital, Bethune enjoyed a professional standing that allowed him to press his new-found enthusiasm for "socialized medicine" on the Montreal medical establishment.[110] His speeches were dramatic, if not always very diplomatic. For example, in an address to the Montreal Medico-Chirurgical Society on 17 April 1936, Bethune declared,

The people are ready for socialized medicine. The obstructionists to the people's health security lie within the profession itself. Recognize this fact. It is the all-important fact of the situation. These men with the mocking face of the reactionary ... proclaim their principles under the guise of 'maintenance of the sacred relationship between doctor and patient' ... These are the enemies of the people and make no mistake. They are the enemies of medicine too.[111]

The response from the profession at large was lukewarm at best, in part because by the summer of 1936 a civic Unemployment Medical Relief Commission was in operation to assist doctors with the problem of services for non-paying patients. Bethune's group nonetheless pressed for further relief measures and prior to the provincial election of 17 August 1936 sent all candidates in Montreal an open letter seeking support for an ambitious plan of reforms in health care delivery. Bethune and his colleagues proposed not one but several alternative modes of prepaid health care, including fee-for-service practice and salaried clinics; results would be tabulated and the best plan extended to as many citizens as possible.[112] Their proposals were also published by the *CMAJ*,[113] although after Bethune's departure for Spain later that year, the Montreal Group for the Security of the People's Health kept a lower profile.

By the late 1930s the political climate in any case was less and less conducive to professional interest in health insurance or state medicine. Signs of economic recovery could be seen in most parts of Canada, and with unemployment rates falling, the profession's burden of unpaid work fell off as well. Some urban relief plans, as in Montreal and Winnipeg, were comprehensive; other municipalities set up more limited programs. But all such programs further lightened the doctors' load. Ontario's unique province-wide relief plan, for example, distributed over $2 million to doctors in its first two years, and the OMA negotiated an increase in the government subsidy in March 1937. There was some professional dissatisfaction with the Ontario plan on two counts: only out-patient services were covered and the prorating of fees led to payments averaging 38.1 percent of the OMA official tariff. However, the new subsidy level brought 1938 payments up to 50 percent of the OMA tariff, and the plan remained popular with most doctors, not least because its administration was entirely in the hands of the OMA.[114]

Complaints concerning medical relief remained prevalent only in the drought-stricken provinces of Alberta and Saskatchewan. Although Calgary's city council finally started a monthly payment program in 1936, the sums available were small. One doctor calculated that his colleagues were paid an average of $.33 per call and revised this figure downwards four months later.[115] Alberta's outlying municipalities were inconsistent. While some offered reasonable compensation, those in the dust bowl offered nothing. The College of Physicians and Surgeons of Alberta had petitioned the new Social Credit government for implementation of a general policy to supplant these haphazard arrangements and eventually submitted a plan similar to that of the Ontario Medical Association. However, the Social Credit cabinet rejected this proposal.[116]

Saskatchewan's economy was even more devastated than Alberta's. There, provincial medical relief payments had become a matter of subsistence. Doctors in the 103 rural municipalities comprising Relief Area "B" received $50 per month, while those in fifty-six other municipalities – the harder hit Area "A" – received $75 per month.[117] Drought conditions contributed to the spread of salaried-contract practice in outlying areas. By 1938 there were seventy-five municipal doctors,[118] more than double the number in 1930. Bankrupt municipalities were occasionally forced to pay their salaried doctors less than the agreed-upon sum; indeed, some offered payment in kind from municipal stocks of hardware and cordwood. Such situations provided further evidence for organized medicine across Canada on the dangers of salaried systems.

In 1937 the CMA petitioned the federal government repeatedly for more assistance to doctors in the dust-bowl areas of Alberta and Saskatchewan. A revision of the association's code of ethics was also undertaken, acknowledging new socio-economic dilemmas. A warning about contract practice was added to the code, and hospital boards were directed to ensure that "the free services of physicians are not asked for, or given to, or exploited for those who can and should pay, or for whom payment should be made." Perhaps understandably there was an important deletion. The code in force since 1868 promised that medical services would "always be cheerfully and freely accorded" to indigents. But the revised code read: "While what have been called God's poor should always be cared for with charity, the growing numbers of what might be called the State's poor, or the State's wards, should be cared for on some basis that allows proper remuneration for services."[119]

Another set of revisions to CMA policy took place at this time. In 1936 the CMA Committee on Economics had been instructed to "clarify and amplify" the 1934 health insurance principles. This move had been prompted by the quarrel about interpretation of the principles that had arisen between the BC profession, Dr Grant Fleming, and the BC provincial secretariat. The new chairman of the CMA Committee on Economics was Dr Wallace Wilson, a major figure in the BC conflict. Moreover, Wilson and his co-workers prepared their revisions of the CMA principles in early 1937, when that conflict was at its most heated. Logically, the revisions reflected a heightened anxiety about the terms of state intervention.

Although several minor changes were made, four alterations are especially noteworthy. First, since the income ceilings set by the CMA had been rejected by the BCMA as unfavourable to optimum price discrimination, any plan was now to be compulsory for those with incomes "below a level which upon investigation by competent local authorities proves to be insufficient to meet the costs of adequate medical care." Second, the 1934 statement had suggested that "whether or not under a Commission," any health insurance plan should ultimately be administered through the provincial department of public health. The 1937 statement allowed that co-operation with the public health department would be crucial but called for top-level administration by "an independent Health Insurance Commission." Removing management from the political arena had become imperative. Third, both 1934 and 1937 statements indicated that the health insurance fund should receive payments from the insured, employers, and the state. The 1937 version, however, spelled out in greater detail the state's obligations to pay premiums on behalf of indigents and others. A fourth change reflected the profession's heightened desire to control both mode and level of remuneration. Each statement affirmed that practitioners should be paid according to the method they preferred. But the 1934 statement had suggested that the central medical services committee, an advisory body of professional representatives, should decide "the relationship between specialist and general practitioner fees, and between medical and surgical fees." This principle was replaced by two rather categorical statements asserting the profession's economic autonomy:

(a) That the Schedule of Fees in any Health Insurance Scheme shall be the Schedule of Fees accepted by the organized profession in the province concerned.
(b) That all Schedules of Fees be under complete control of the organized medical profession in each Province.[120]

Late in 1937 the federal government announced that a Royal Commission on Dominion-Provincial Relations would begin hearings in early 1938. Before being swept out of office by the Liberals, R.B. Bennett's Conservative government had passed the federal Employment and Insurance Act of 1935. This legislation was struck down by the British Privy Council as an encroachment on provincial jurisdictions set out in the British North America Act, and the royal commission, better known as the Rowell-Sirois Commission, was appointed to review the division of powers that should exist between Ottawa and the provinces. Since matters in British Columbia were still unresolved, the CMA executive committee promptly sent a resolution asking the commissioners to endorse a federal health insurance inquiry. Mention was also made of the need for greater federal involvement in medical relief to drought-stricken areas.[121]

Both these themes were taken up again in 1938 when the formal brief of the CMA was presented at the Rowell-Sirois hearings in Ottawa. In addition, the CMA brief went to some lengths in spelling out the need for federal support in paying the medical bills of a list of groups ranging from the indigents and unemployed to war veterans and old age pensioners. (Weighing this list in the light of the revised CMA code of ethics, one senses that "the State's poor" far outnumbered "God's poor.") On the health insurance front, however, a new strategic caution was evident. The CMA principles were presented, but the brief specified that the national association had "not authorized an expression of opinion either in favour of, or opposed to, the institution of health insurance in Canada."[123]

Through 1938, what with improvements in the economic outlook and the bitter after-taste left by events in British Columbia, strategic caution continued to be the corner-stone of the CMA's approach to state health insurance. Dr T.C. Routley returned from Europe carrying detailed analyses of government action on the other side of the Atlantic. Experiments in profession-sponsored medical services plans were set in motion. A watchful eye was kept on contract practice, private hospitalization programs, and industrial arrangements for employees' medical insurance. Whether in the private sector or in the public sector, the growth of prepayment schemes for medical services seemed certain to continue. But when the CMA Committee on Economics polled the provinces, no policy consensus emerged. The ground, it seems, was shifting too rapidly; the profession's footing was too uncertain for a firm stance to be taken.

Thus in 1939, as war in Europe became inevitable, the CMA's economics experts simply recommended further study of public and private health insurance. No plans should be drafted: "Government must be the lead horse ... the Canadian Medical Association should be an essential and recognized running mate."[123] Shortly after this pronouncement, a national health insurance derby got underway in Ottawa and continued throughout the Second World War. Government was indeed to be "the lead horse"; but although the CMA was second from the gate, the doctors' position was soon challenged by many other pressure groups with a stake in state-sponsored health services.

CHAPTER FIVE

War Years:
Pressure Group Politics
in Ottawa

The first and most important characteristic of Canadian government is that it is a democracy, a government which is controlled by the greater part of the people. It rests on the will of the people and is at all times responsive to their opinions. It exists to serve the citizen and provide him with a better life.

R. MacGregor Dawson, *Democractic Government in Canada*, 1949

The Depression was an important watershed in the political life of Canadian organized medicine. In the 1920s systematic state mediation in health care had been a matter for academic debate. But in the 1930s commissions of inquiry in some provinces and an acrimonious dispute over the BC health insurance plan forced organized medicine to formulate clearly defined policies designed to protect the profession's socio-economic position. An unprecedented variety of pressure group activities was also undertaken by organized medicine. The profession's policies, as we have seen, reflected two major concerns: to restore medical incomes by winning payments from the state on behalf of expanded numbers of non-paying patients and to preserve professional autonomy while buttressing the market position of the private practitioner against any inroads consequent upon state intervention.

A new corporatism became evident in the professional ranks. Structural changes were one sign of this development. As already noted, in Alberta, British Columbia, and Saskatchewan the College of Physicians and Surgeons amalgamated with the provincial medical association to create a combined lobbying and negotiating body. In each case the architects of amalgamation advertised the potential

TABLE 3
Practitioners Belonging to Provincial Medical
Association, 1932–3

Approximate Total Number of Practitioners		Percentage
Ontario	4000	35
Quebec	2650	23
British Columbia	650	100
Manitoba	600	50
Saskatchewan	575	100
Alberta	550	100
Nova Scotia	450	30
New Brunswick	285	100

Source: The data in this table are drawn from *OMA Bulletin*
1, no. 1 (March 1934): 16.

importance of "closed shop" conditions for dealing with public and
political agencies.[1] (Membership figures in table 3 confirm the effect
of amalgamation.) Although no other province followed suit, doctors
in both Manitoba and Ontario gave serious consideration to this
and similar measures designed to strengthen their hand in the arena
of medical politics and economics.[2]

As well, the CMA launched a campaign for national reorganization,
hoping to pull the provincial associations into closer orbit. Doctors
who belonged to their provincial medical body frequently did not
pay the separate dues required for CMA membership. The new CMA
plans called for a conjoint annual membership fee and also set out
a framework for better federal-provincial co-operation in organized
medicine. Dr T.C. Routley, secretary of both the OMA and the CMA
since 1921, spearheaded the campaign for reorganization and in 1938
took on full-time duties with the expanded national association.
Events in British Columbia and the national scope of the medical
relief dilemma ensured that CMA overtures were received warmly by
most provinces.[3] By the end of 1938 seven out of nine provincial
medical societies were full-fledged divisions of the CMA, and Manitoba
was soon to enter the federation. The other hold-out, the New
Brunswick Medical Society, was restrained more by legal impediments
than by lack of interest. The New Brunswick profession's nineteenth-
century charter of incorporation had given self-government powers
direct to the provincial medical association without creating a separate
College of Physicians and Surgeons, and the statutory implications
of federation with the CMA were uncertain.

Structural change aside, both recruiting appeals and addresses by medical spokesmen reflected a heightened politicization and new emphasis on shared medical interests in the face of possible state mediation.[4] For obvious reasons, these sentiments were most prominent in British Columbia, but they also surfaced to varying degrees in every other province. The 1936 OMA president's assessment of his association's medical relief plan speaks volumes about the changes wrought by the Depression: "What has been the result? A solidity and welding of the medical profession that has never before been attained, so that now the Ontario Medical Association has the backing of almost every man in the province. It has *won the confidence* of these men, and now no man can afford to stay out."[5] Indeed, the OMA membership rolls showed steady growth. The peak membership prior to the Depression had been 1,836, and by 1934 the number of OMA members had dropped to 1,729. After the OMA took over administration of the medical relief plan, membership climbed to 2,121 by the end of 1935 and 2,400 the following year.

Partly because of federation arrangements and partly as a result of active recruitment by T.C. Routley and other enthusiasts, the CMA's membership also rose. While just over 20 percent of Canadian doctors belonged to the CMA in the early 1920s, by the start of the Second World War more than 35 percent of the profession held CMA membership. The new strength was mirrored financially. In 1921 the association was $18,000 in debt. Seventeen years later, despite the intervening Depression, its assets were $85,000 and growing steadily.[6] As fate would have it, the national association's star was rising at a propitious time. For the federal government, once seen as a potential brake on unfavourable developments in British Columbia, launched its own attempt to implement health insurance during the Second World War.

THE POLITICAL INITIATIVE

From 1935 to 1939, the Liberal government of W.L. Mackenzie King had an uncertain legal position in the social policy field. As already noted, the Bennett "New Deal" reforms had been rejected by the British Privy Council, and the Rowell-Sirois Commission had yet to decide on the division of powers in Confederation. The outbreak of war in 1939 also turned government attention away from more mundane domestic issues. Nonetheless there was a prompt government response to the final report of the Rowell-Sirois Commission in 1940. The commissioners called for equalizing grants to poorer provinces and a federal unemployment insurance scheme; and before the end of 1940 an unemployment insurance act was in the national statute books. There remained the problem of other forms of social insurance, including coverage for hospitalization and medical services. Although the Rowell-Sirois report indicated that old age pensions should fall under the federal aegis, the commissioners felt that neither workmen's compensation nor health insurance was of an inherently national character. Provincial administration of health insurance was therefore favoured. But the commissioners opened the door for federal financial initiatives by suggesting that a given province might entrust the dominion with collection of premiums from employees. Particularly if Ottawa were already levying taxes for other social insurance schemes, this might prove a more efficient modus operandi.[7]

Ian A. Mackenzie, previously defence minister, had been transferred to the Department of Pensions and National Health in September 1939. Mackenzie had been a member of the BC legislature before shifting to federal politics and was naturally familiar with the health insurance story in his province. Even before the end of 1939 Mackenzie wrote to King urging legislation of a health insurance plan. Not only might this be an important part of eventual post-war reconstruction, but also the political climate – with eight of nine provinces then under Liberal rule – had seldom been better. When in 1940 the cabinet rejected this proposal, Mackenzie decided to act on his own.[8]

A logical route, and one that would stir public interest, was to bring the matter before the Dominion Council of Health. The council consisted of the deputy minister of pensions and national health as chairman; the chief medical officer of each province; representatives of labour, farm, and women's groups; and a scientific adviser. Mackenzie convened a meeting of the council in June 1941 with the express purpose of initiating a comprehensive study that would lead to the adoption of a health insurance plan for the Dominion.

Dr John J. Heagerty, the federal director of public health, opened the conference by reviewing some Canadian health statistics. The incidence of tuberculosis, for example, had declined, but the disease still killed about 6,000 Canadians per year. Venereal disease was another problem: Sweden had seven new cases of syphilis per 10,000 population per year; Canada had ten times that many. Maternal mortality was high, especially when compared with European countries where government medical care schemes were in effect. And between 1930 and 1940 an average of 15,000 children under one year of age died every year.[9] With this disturbing keynote the tone of the conference could scarcely help but be favourable to health insurance.

From here Mackenzie initiated action on two fronts. First, through Dr Heagerty, he asked that the health professions, agriculture, labour and women's groups all set up health insurance committees to communicate with his ministry. Second, Mackenzie pressured the cabinet for an official inquiry into health services. Somewhat reluctantly, his colleagues acquiesced, and an Advisory Committee on Health Insurance was appointed in February 1942. J.J. Heagerty took the chair, and the committee included a group of senior civil servants and government statisticians who would provide the data base for the report.

Although the first tentative steps towards national health insurance had been taken, the King government was understandably preoccupied with the war effort rather than with any plans for post-war reconstruction. Domestic discontent, however, was on the rise. Canada's military endeavours unquestionably had a broad base of popular support, but resentment of the high price paid to earn victories abroad led Canadians to look for a better deal on the home front. Membership in trades unions and the CCF grew apace. And the Liberals, pushed leftward by this political threat, eventually steered a health insurance program to the brink of implementation.

THE PROFESSION'S PERSPECTIVE

At the 1941 CMA annual meeting due notice was taken of events in Ottawa. The executive committee firmly rejected any possibility of a state medical service where practitioners might be "employed, directed and paid by the State on a salary basis or otherwise." But the CMA executive suggested that professional support should be forthcoming for any fair insurance plan that would make curative and preventive services available to all Canadians regardless of income.[10]

This positive perspective was not atypical. During the early 1940s renewed enthusiasm for state action became evident in Canadian medicine. Some of the interest was simply financial. Medical incomes across Canada had still not climbed to their pre-Depression levels, and in any event the 1930s had sensitized doctors to their loss of potential income through free or reduced-price care given to indigents and those in the lower-income brackets generally. No doubt wartime idealism also played a role. But an important consideration seems to have been the technological transformation that was taking place in medical practice. Laboratory tests and X-ray techniques proliferated; more surgical procedures became feasible, and hospital utilization rates began to climb. Moreover, the disease patterns of the population had clearly shifted; tuberculosis and pneumonia continued to claim a large toll, but the other leading causes of death were heart disease, stroke, cancer, and nephrological disorders. An era of chronic – and expensive – diseases had arrived, and the costs of health services bore heavily on a larger proportion of the population. Saskatchewan data provide evidence of this trend in the hospital sector: in 1934, 5.5 percent of the population was hospitalized with average provincial per capita costs of $1.93; while in 1944, 11.7 percent of the population spent time in hospital with an increase in per capita costs to $5.20.[11]

Doctors therefore found themselves in a disquieting position. Wealthy patients could, of course, pay their own way. Those below the poverty line were assured free hospitalization and diagnostic services, although their medical attendants would still go unpaid in many parts of the nation. Wage-workers and salaried employees with modest incomes were hardest hit; for they could not always afford hospital charges or specialist fees. Even out-patient laboratory tests might be vetoed on financial grounds. Dr Gordon S. Fahrni, a leading surgeon and 1942 CMA president, spoke for many conscientious practitioners when he said: "Only too often this has resulted in inadequate investigation and inadequate treatment, much to the disappointment of the medical attendant."[12]

Obviously, voluntary health insurance programs were one possible solution to this dilemma. Private investor-owned carriers had barely entered the field. But during the late 1930s a variety of prepayment plans for hospital, diagnostic, and medical services grew up in all parts of Canada. Provincial hospital associations sponsored Blue Cross schemes. In Saskatchewan two urban medical service co-operatives were organized; and the number of municipal doctors under contract in rural areas climbed above 100 by 1941. Employee group coverage became more popular, although the arrangements varied. For example, the International Nickel Company in Sudbury, Ontario, hired doctors on salary and underwrote hospitalization costs for its employees. Hollinger Mines in Timmins set up a plan that found greater favour with organized medicine, since the local doctors remained in ordinary, fee-for-service, private practice and were paid at 75 percent of the OMA fee schedule whenever they looked after any of the 9,300 Hollinger employees and dependants.

Organized medicine also experimented in the voluntary health insurance field. First off the mark were doctors in Essex County, Ontario. As early as 1933 the Essex County Medical Society had passed resolutions unanimously opposing both state medicine and private health insurance, and instead supported compulsory insurance for low- and middle-income groups. Since government had done nothing about these groups, the Windsor-area doctors asked that the OMA take

the lead.[13] These resolutions did not lead to concrete action until
1936. By this time, the OMA had already undertaken the administration
of the provincial medical relief scheme, and the Essex County doctors
used their local experience with medical relief to devise a contributory
plan for employees with modest incomes and their dependants. In
1936 the incoming OMA president, Dr W.K. Colbeck, strongly endorsed
the concept of profession-sponsored insurance plans, and he warned
the 1936 OMA annual meeting: "If we do not socialize ourselves and
develop the proper technique of service, Governments will be forced
to try their hand."[14] It was subsequently agreed that the OMA would
offer financial assistance to any model insurance plan supported by
local medical groups. However, the aim of this policy was not the
long-term maintenance of independent, profession-sponsored insurance plans, but rather the promotion of insurance along the lines
favoured by organized medicine in hopes that government intervention
would follow suit. Indeed, the 1936 OMA Committee on Inter-Relations
– later the Committee on Health Insurance – stated that "Any local
or provincial voluntary schemes should anticipate, and expect to be
absorbed by, a compulsory state health insurance plan."[15] The Essex
County scheme, known as Windsor Medical Services, won a $23,800
grant from the Rockefeller Foundation in February 1937 and soon
after received about $1,200 as a start-up loan from the OMA. In 1937
the OMA also loaned $3,800 to assist Dr Jason A. Hannah in
establishing an insurance program for members of the Ontario Civil
Service Association. This plan, eventually known as Associated
Medical Services (AMS), was originally based in Toronto and in
Norfolk County alone, but by 1942 AMS had offices in ten centres
and about 20,000 subscribers. Windsor Medical Services did not
actually begin operations until 1939 and grew more slowly. Other
plans were organized under professional auspices in Regina and
Winnipeg. And in 1940, when it was apparent that the British
Columbia Liberals had completely abandoned state health insurance,
organized medicine on the west coast introduced an insurance program
known as Medical Services Associated.[16]

We shall review these voluntary private-sector arrangements in
greater detail in chapter 6. For now, it is important simply to note
that in the early 1940s most leaders of Canadian organized medicine
still had limited expectations of the voluntary approach to health
insurance. Private-sector programs operating without formal professional sponsorship carried a threat of undue lay influence upon
conditions of medical work and remuneration, with negative reper-
cussions for both autonomy and incomes. Even where organized
medicine offered support, there was no guarantee that a private agency

would conform to the profession's preferred policies, as experience with Associated Medical Services showed. AMS rejected centralized control by the OMA, did not follow all the OMA/CMA principles of health insurance, and instituted some operating policies that were deemed unfair by Toronto specialists in particular.[17] In any case, the Blue Cross hospitalization programs and the profession's own medical services plans were too small in the early 1940s for organized medicine to accept that more than a limited proportion of the population could be insured through the voluntary approach.

Speaking to the Hamilton Academy of Medicine in February 1942, former CMA president Jonathan Meakins stressed that the profession must accept the inevitability of a state-sponsored scheme. While some of his colleagues might think that this view was "heretical, radical, socialistic, communistic," Meakins contended the opponents of state health insurance belonged in the same group as those "who opposed prison reform, asylum reform, emancipation of slaves, and other great movements."[18] Equally strong endorsements of state health insurance were offered by other medical luminaries, including the president of the Winnipeg Medical Society, who was succinct: "The socialization of medicine is coming as surely as tomorrow's dawn. It is the natural result of public demand for adequate, complete medical service."[19]

In short, for all the reasons noted above, organized medicine was prepared to view state health insurance in a favourable light. The CMA's executive now had one main task. It must ensure that any legislation was tailored to the profession's specifications.

BEHIND THE SCENES IN OTTAWA

Long before the cabinet actually agreed to appoint an official Advisory Committee on Health Insurance, senior civil servants had begun meeting with representatives of organized medicine to discuss policy. The first key meeting was on 14 July 1941, when the following men met in Ottawa to review the conceptual framework for any future health insurance legislation: the new CMA president, Dr Gordon Fahrni; the CMA executive committee chairman, Dr T.H. Leggett; Dr J.J. Heagerty; and the deputy minister of health, Dr R.E. Wodehouse. Heagerty suggested then that the CMA set up a small committee to work with him in the autumn as more concrete legislative plans were developed.[20] Thus, from the outset medical opposition was headed off; in turn, however, the CMA was clearly being given a special position of influence.

In September 1941 Dr A.E. Archer, a member of the CMA executive, wrote to Ian Mackenzie about setting up a committee of doctors to play the consultative role proposed originally by Heagerty. Mackenzie wrote back promptly to endorse the idea. Wodehouse, the deputy minister, was upset that Mackenzie had not sought his advice in this matter and sent a reproving memorandum to his minister pointing out that informal meetings on a smaller scale would have been preferable to the formal appointment of a larger and more visible CMA advisory group. Wodehouse expressed particular unease about the participation of T.C. Routley,[21] perhaps because he recognized that Routley was an excellent strategist. Nonetheless on 9 September 1941 Wodehouse wrote to T.C. Routley, confirming that several of the association's "leading members" could be selected to sit in with the ministry officials during the usually confidential process of formulating draft legislation.[22] The resulting group of senior medical politicians became known as the CMA Committee of Seven.

These advisers left their stamp on the early draft legislation prepared by J.J. Heagerty. Writing to Mackenzie in October 1941, Heagerty remarked that the federal and provincial portions of the legislation had been "revised to meet the views of the Canadian Medical Association, as expressed by the Committee on Economics of that Association." He went on to enumerate several such revisions, including provision for a majority of physicians on both the federal and the provincial administrative councils. These revisions, noted Heagerty, put "the administration largely in the control of the medical profession."[23]

On 22 October 1941 the entire executive committee of the CMA met in the library of the Department of Pensions and National Health with Mackenzie, Heagerty, and Wodehouse to review the revised departmental proposals for health insurance. At this stage the legislation met almost all the principles laid down by the 1937 CMA Committee on Economics, although there was some concern that provinces were not specifically compelled to provide full coverage for so-called indigents. The CMA representatives were sufficiently relaxed that they engaged in a free-wheeling debate among themselves about the merits of abandoning fee-for-service payment for GPs, and some of the most influential doctors openly expressed their preference for a European-style capitation system.[24] One CMA executive member, Dr H.K. McDonald of Halifax, sent a letter to the *Nova Scotia Medical Bulletin* on 27 October 1941 reporting that every member of the executive had left the meeting with the "feeling that the Department of Pensions and National Health had the interests of the profession of Canada at heart."[25]

Correspondence between the ministry officials and CMA headquarters continued through the early winter. Meanwhile, Ian Mackenzie, whose department was already progressing well with data collection and planning, had rather belatedly sought and gained cabinet approval for appointment of a formal Advisory Committee on Health Insurance, to be chaired by Dr J.J. Heagerty. The Heagerty Committee, as it was known, began meeting in February 1942, and soon after, its chairman wrote a rather unctuous letter to the *CMAJ* seeking to allay any fears in the medical community and confirming the CMA's position: "As the medical profession is the most important body concerned with the provision of medical benefits, the Committee of Seven appointed by the Canadian Medical Association is considered the 'senior' committee and no steps will be taken by 'The Advisory Committee on Health Insurance' without consulting that committee."[26] (Heagerty was even more ingratiating in private correspondence. For example, on 16 February 1942, the day of the first gathering of the Advisory Committee on Health Insurance, Heagerty wrote to Routley assuring him that the department's experts were "sound, capable men" who appreciated that the CMA Committee of Seven was "the parent committee.")[27]

The Committee of Seven met repeatedly with Dr Heagerty and his civil service co-workers, and its members were made privy to confidential information concerning the department's plans. On one occasion in early April 1942 the CMA strategists caused Heagerty to wonder just who was in charge of proceedings. Whereas the CMA Committee of Seven normally met in Heagerty's office, the entire CMA executive committee was in session at the Chateau Laurier and summoned Heagerty to meet with the Committee of Seven at the hotel. Heagerty later wrote to Mackenzie noting that Routley had violated their earlier agreements by having a stenographer present, and his overall impression was that there had been a deliberate change of procedure to put the CMA in charge of protocol for further meetings. Indeed, when Heagerty had suggested that some questions would be better fielded by the entire advisory committee, the doctors responded by asking how long it would take Heagerty's colleagues to come to the Chateau "if their presence was required." Sensing that the doctors wished even more control, Heagerty remarked at one point that the profession itself should have provided initially and could still provide greater "leadership" in the matter of health insurance. The doctors then asked "if the Minister of Pensions and National Health would consent were the Canadian Medical Association desirous of taking over health insurance with the object of educating the public in regard to the need and of preparing a comprehensive Plan. On request I agreed to place this question before you."[28] Ian Mackenzie's reply was understandably curt: "We have already *led* and asked them to co-operate. They should continue to do so. *All* discussions should be in your office" (emphasis in original).[29]

Although the CMA executive was exerting considerable influence on policy formation, it was necessary to ensure that the rank and file were actually in accord with the Committee of Seven's standpoint. The Committee of Seven had therefore mailed a questionnaire to 3,000 association members across Canada, and about 2,500 replies had been received by the spring of 1942. On a straight "yes/no" basis, over 90 percent of respondents authorized the association's involvement in planning and supported the principles of health insurance as laid down by the Committee on Economics in 1937. The only canon given less than 90 percent support was the specific restriction on voluntary enrolment in the medical services component of a state plan by those above a given income level: here, the plebiscite showed 1,912 for, and 486 against.[30] Some queries were raised, however, and in June 1942, armed with the preliminary results of this survey, the CMA general council approved further revisions to the association's principles of health insurance.

Most of the principles were left unchanged, but one important modification was made. The 1937 revisions had taken the overall administration of the prototypical plan away from the department of public health and called for control by an independent commission with medical representatives. Now it was specified that the *majority* membership of the commission should be "representatives of organized medicine." (This proviso, as we have seen, had already been written into early drafts of the health insurance legislation.) Another minor but interesting change dovetailed with this new requirement. The 1937 policy statement had left open the possibility that medical referees – doctors empowered to audit clinical records, questionable claims, and consumer complaints – might be responsible to central or local insurance boards where laymen could be in the majority. To augment professional control of any plan, the corresponding 1942 principle specified that referees must report only to the doctor-dominated provincial commission.

Three new principles were added. A pension plan for doctors was requested. As well, the CMA warned that care should be taken to ensure that any plan of health insurance had a propitious effect on medical education. This addendum largely reflected fears that public-ward patients would no longer be automatically available for teaching purposes if a state health insurance plan was introduced. Finally, any plan must be actuarially monitored. As T.C. Routley later explained: "Forty countries have instituted health insurance and as yet none has given it up. Surely the doctor has some concern that the plan be financially sound, because, if it is not, it is the medical profession who will be asked to carry the burden by accepting a lower remuneration for their services."[31] Routley also stressed that "complete control" of fee schedules was vital, since "any other course would open the scheme to dangerous interference from persons unqualified to determine a matter which comes strictly within the purview of the profession."[32] This last assertion illustrates a recurring theme in the standpoint of organized medicine: because economic issues in an insurance plan could affect clinical practice, doctors claimed that they alone had the expertise to determine the proper administrative framework of a state scheme.

On 3 July 1942 Routley wrote to the deputy minister, R.E. Wodehouse, enclosing the newly approved principles.[33] The department responded by convening a special day-long meeting of the Heagerty Committee and the CMA Committee of Seven two weeks later to review the second draft of the proposed legislation in the light of these guidelines. There was minimal controversy. Heagerty did question the concept of restricting voluntary enrolment by higher-income patients; however, Routley indicated the profession's suspicion of universal health insurance as "a very definite step towards adoption of state medicine." Interestingly, debate again arose concerning modes of payment. Routley noted that Saskatchewan then had over 100 salaried municipal doctors, but this system was to be implemented elsewhere only if the population density was too sparse for normal insurance practice. On the other hand, he stated that there was an "abundance of evidence" to support the use of capitation fees for GPs, thereby triggering another lengthy discussion about the relative merits of fee-for-service and capitation payment.[34]

Although the CMA relaxed its pressure on the Heagerty Committee during the summer, a different medical group struck up a correspondence with the health minister and his officials. The College of Physicians and Surgeons of Ontario (CPSO) had expressed interest in the federal proposals as early as 6 March 1942, and during June, July, and August its registrar, Dr R.T. Noble, wrote several times to Mackenzie asking to meet with the minister for the purpose of discussing health insurance policy.[35] The CPSO registrar justified this course by pointing out that the college had twice as many members as the OMA and was therefore in a better position to speak for Ontario doctors. Since the CPSO membership accounted for around 45 percent of Canada's medical population, he felt it unfair that the CPSO had not been given representation on the CMA Committee of Seven. As for the argument that the CPSO was a licensing and discipline body

that should not be lobbying on the profession's behalf, Noble
countered that an issue as important as health insurance naturally
fell within the college's mandate of protecting the public interest.[36]
By September 1942 Dr R.E. Wodehouse rather reluctantly advised
the health minister that the CPSO must also be given a hearing.[37]

There was, in any case, no significant breach in professional
solidarity; for on 10 December the CMA Committee of Seven met with
various members of the Ontario medical establishment in an obvious
effort to clear the air. The CPSO sent its special five-man Committee
on Health Insurance, members of the standing College Committee
on Education and Registration, and the deans of the three Ontario
medical faculties. The only area of possible disagreement was, yet
again, capitation payment for GPS, since this had been formally
endorsed by the CPSO Committee on Health Insurance. However, the
Committee of Seven skirted this controversy by contending that each
province's practitioners could choose their own preferred mode of
remuneration.[38]

By this time the Advisory Committee on Health Insurance was
nearing completion of its final report. The CMA Committee of Seven
therefore met on the very next day with Heagerty, departmental
solicitor W.G. Gunn, and a statistician, A.D. Watson, to discuss the
final form of the draft legislation for the report. In effect, the CMA
representatives were given the first and the last word on the details
of the Heagerty health insurance proposals.

CONFLICTING PERSPECTIVES

Although no group other than the CMA Committee of Seven enjoyed
a working relationship with the Advisory Committee on Health
Insurance, a variety of organizations submitted briefs to Heagerty
and his colleagues. The Canadian Dental Association, Canadian
Hospital Association, and Canadian Nurses' Association focused on
matters pertinent to their own bailiwicks. Women's organizations
contributed but were divided on issues such as payment modes for
doctors or inclusion of an income ceiling on participation. The
Canadian Life Insurance Officers gave some encouraging comments
(as already noted, investor-owned companies had barely entered the
health field). Organized labour and agriculture, however, were clearly
determined to challenge the CMA's standpoint.

The Canadian Federation of Agriculture (CFA), with an affiliated
membership of over 300,000, agreed that administration should be
by an independent commission at both federal and provincial levels.
But administration by commission was seen as a way to dilute

professional and bureaucratic power: the majority on any commission should be lay representatives. The CFA rejected the policy of an income ceiling on coverage on the grounds that it would only hamstring the plan financially. Health insurance should be supported out of the Federal Consolidated Revenue Fund with *all* Canadians included. The people would make their contribution in a manner that must inevitably "spread the cost equitably" – through the progressive income tax and other sources of general revenue such as duties, tariffs, corporate taxes, and so forth: "Any other policy is to deny democracy." The CFA also called for preventive services to be integrated fully into the plan and centred around the general practitioner. They envisioned an all-out campaign for health that would "mean an entire change in the attitude of our medical schools, the education of all health personnel, and the proper integration of research into the plan."[39]

The Heagerty committee went through four draft plans for its health insurance proposals, and claimed in its final report that "as each draft plan was formulated consultations were held on the various clauses affecting this or that group." As already noted, departmental records make it plain that the second draft was revised to meet the principles of health insurance as adopted by the CMA General Council. The third draft bill set an income ceiling of $2,400 for compulsory coverage in accord with association policy and excluded those in higher income brackets. The national director of health insurance was to be a physician. Administration was to be by a council on which "the majority of members shall be licensed medical practitioners in good standing." The draft bill also envisaged payment on whatever basis organized medicine preferred. The Trades and Labour Council of Canada (TLCC) was consulted on this draft and used its brief to launch an all-out attack on the proposed legislation. Labour objected to the specification that the national director be a physician: "These duties would be better carried out by a small commission on which those who pay for the insurance would be adequately represented." The TLCC also rejected medical control of the national and provincial councils of health insurance. Of the proposed doctor-majority on the national council, the labour leaders wrote: "We presume 'in good standing' means only those who comply with the dictates of the medical association, and thus passes over to this body powers which should remain with government authority. In our view those who pay the contributions should control the Council both in numbers and in every other way." Fee-for-service payment of doctors was mocked as "liable to incite increase in the volume of illness." "Payment," opined the TLCC, "should be wherever

possible on a salary basis and in all other cases on a per capita basis.''
Manual labourers, subject to back injuries in the workplace, believed
that spinal manipulation techniques could be helpful; but the draft
bill entirely precluded the use of chiropractic or osteopathic service.
This oversight, said labour, should be redressed.

The concluding statement of the TLCC summed up their viewpoint
in a provocative fashion:

In view of the above objections, we would respectfully urge that the Act
should be entirely reconstituted to take control away from the medical
profession and place its administration in the hands of the contributors.
Desirable as it is that health insurance should be proceeded with promptly,
it is equally important that in any measure that might be enacted, the interests
of the great mass of those whose health it is aimed to protect should
predominate and that the interest of others paid to render service necessary
for this purpose should be of secondary importance.[40]

Thus, with consumers and providers of medical services pulling
in divergent directions, a political tug of war was apparently under
way between the hundreds of thousands represented by organized
labour and agriculture on the one hand, and the 7,000-strong CMA.
T.C. Routley intensified his wartime recruiting campaign, at one
point suggesting doctors must remember not only Hong Kong and
Pearl Harbour, but also health insurance in Great Britain and New
Zealand.[41] By the end of 1942 more than 50 percent of Canadian
doctors belonged to the national association, and growth continued
the following year. Indeed, between 1939 and 1945 the CMA membership
climbed from 4,001 to 9,043. These figures, however, are somewhat
misleading. As a patriotic gesture and as a means of improving the
association's membership position in the light of legislative developments, from 1942 the CMA offered free membership to all doctors
in military service. The actual number of new dues-paying members
rose by 1,463, while 3,579 were added as military members.[42]

The end of 1942 also brought a final report from J.J. Heagerty's
Advisory Committee on Health Insurance. It was an impressive
document, 558 pages in all, offering exhaustive analyses of the vast
international experience with health insurance and a detailed sta-
tistical profile of the health and economic status of Canadians. One
draft bill set out the federal machinery necessary for health insurance,
with the understanding that, as per the recommendations of the
Rowell-Sirois Commission, administrative control would be provincial. The federal government, however, was to retain fiscal influence

through conditional-grants-in-aid to the provincial insurance schemes. A second draft bill for provincial legislation was also included.

As to the outcome of the struggle between consumers and providers, historians J.R. English and R.S. Bothwell perhaps overstated the case when they wrote that Heagerty's legislation "gave the doctors everything they wanted."[43] But on most scores the CMA came out well ahead. Although numerical representation on the national council of health insurance was not specified, the clear majority would be doctors. Each province's deputy health minister, for example, was given a seat; this post was traditionally held by a doctor – all nine were MDS at the time. The chief administrative officer of each provincial insurance plan was also to be part of the national council, and the provincial draft bill specified that these posts were open only to doctors who were licensed practitioners "in good standing." The suggested composition of the provincial commissions spread representation among professional and lay groups without a majority indicated for either side. Hence the national council would be controlled by doctors, a doctor would head each provincial plan, and the profession at large would also have a strong voice on the provincial commissions through direct representation.

Remuneration methods had been another point of contention. The TLCC had opposed fee-for-service and called for salary as the preferred payment mode. Later the farm groups took the same stance. Although some doctors supported capitation payment of general practitioners, organized medicine had totally rejected a salaried system. The provincial draft bill merely indicated that the rate and method of payment would be negotiated with the medical profession. This, in essence, was what the Committee of Seven had been recommending since July 1941.

Furthermore, the Heagerty legislation made no mention of "irregular" practitioners, and its financing was to be based largely on a set of premiums rather than general tax revenue. Indeed, the only point in the Heagerty legislation that possibly contravened the CMA's 1942 principles was the lack of a clear-cut income ceiling on participation; to maintain a separate private-practice sector where doctors could price-discriminate against a wealthier clientele, the CMA had long opposed the concept of allowing higher-income groups to purchase coverage in the public plan for any services other than hospital accommodation. Yet even here there was no real loss. In the first place, the CMA questionnaire had shown that this was the only principle of health insurance to receive less than 90 percent support. About 20 percent of doctors apparently felt that middle-class families should not be denied the choice of insuring medical services in the public plan if they so desired. Secondly, many middle-class and wealthy families would doubtless continue to make private arrangements for medical care so long as the plan was not, in fact, based on universal compulsory participation. Finally, some inter-provincial variation in income limits might be necessary, since medical fee schedules and hospital per diems were not uniform nationally. The CMA Committee of Seven accordingly decided that income limits, too, should be a provincial matter, and this decision had been communicated to the departmental draftsmen at their final meeting on 11–12 December 1942.[44]

Organized medicine therefore had good reason to be pleased. As the official release date of the report approached, the Committee of Seven urged the CMA executive to call a special meeting of the association's general council to acknowledge the forthcoming event. The profession's parliament convocated on 18–19 January 1943 – the first such event between annual meetings in the association's history. Departmental solicitor W.G. Gunn, Dr J.J. Heagerty, and Ian Mac-kenzie made appearances, with much mutual goodwill expressed on all sides. Some suggestions for improving the legislation were offered: there was concern that the state's responsibility for covering low-income and indigent groups was not clearly enough spelled out in the draft bill; and predictably, some medical spokesmen expressed reservations about the lack of a clearly specified income ceiling on participation. But many constructive comments were made, including a discussion of the potential public health benefits that would accrue if GPs were paid by capitation and had definite "lists" of patients. As capstone to this historic event, the CMA General Council passed two cautiously worded resolutions. First, the CMA approved "the adoption of the principle of health insurance"; no mention of the specific plan under consideration was made. Second, the CMA pronounced itself in favour of "a plan of health insurance which will secure the development and provision of the highest standard of health services, preventive and curative, if such plan be fair both to the insured and to all those rendering the services." In drafting these motions, the association's executive seems to have recognized that the health insurance battle was far from over.[45] There was nonetheless an overall readiness to work within a public sector framework – a readiness that was attenuated gradually over the next eighteen months.

THE SPECIAL COMMITTEE, 1943

The Department of Finance had expressed reservations about the economics of the Heagerty draft legislation, and the cabinet soon followed suit.[46] Ian Mackenzie kept the issue alive, however, by persuading his cabinet cohorts that an all-party Special House Committee on Social Security should be appointed to consider the Heagerty report and its draft legislation during the spring session. Less than a week after the throne speech announced the government's intention of setting up this body, members of the CMA's Committee of Seven began lobbying for support in Ottawa. Sixteen of twenty doctors in the House of Commons and Senate, including most of the fourteen medical MPs, dined with the CMA representatives and were given an after-dinner presentation about health insurance. T.C. Routley wrote a confidential memo to the CMA executive describing the dinner and outlining strategy:

It was a very pleasant affair ... another dinner has been planned for four weeks hence ... In looking over the list of Parliamentarians, it might be well if members of the Executive and others would keep in mind the advisability of these gentlemen being contacted by medical colleagues who know them well. When it is remembered that there are twenty doctors in the two Houses, it will be recognized that they can be a powerful force when it comes to dealing with legislation of a health insurance character. It was the opinion of your officers that the group we met were in sympathy with the aims and objects of the CMA and we hope to continue the development of relationships of an informative and friendly character.[47]

Of fourteen doctors in the Commons, nine received appointments to the Special Committee. Other professionals comprised a third of the committee's forty-one members. Seven members were successful businessmen. A sprinkling of farmers and Angus MacInnis – a Vancouver transit worker, CCFer, and son-in-law of J.S. Woodsworth – rounded off the roster. It was not a body with whom organized labour or agriculture was likely to develop close ties.

The first meeting of the Special Committee was convened on 16 March 1943 under the chairmanship of Professor Cyrus MacMillan (Liberal – Queen's), dean of arts and science at McGill University. Ian Mackenzie appeared in order to advocate adoption of the Heagerty draft legislation. He rejected the idea of an income ceiling: "If an epidemic invades a community, the bacteria do not knock only at the doors of those earning less than $1,800 a year"; and justified a contributory plan on the grounds that abolition of premiums would lead to "the pauper mentality" and foster the "delusion that the public purse is bottomless." Mackenzie did not envision direct- or extra-billing: "The big difference will be that the doctor, the nurse and the hospital will send their bills to the health insurance fund instead of to the patient." As to payment modes, the minister of national health noted that there had been less insistence by the profession on fee-for-service. He suggested that, "from a public health stand-point, the capitation system is preferable because it will encourage the physician to counsel and urge preventive measures."[48]

Later that month, as the social security committee was immersed in its early deliberations, Routley sent another confidential bulletin to the CMA executive: "20 doctors in House and Senate have met with us on three occasions and plan to meet again from time to time. They should be helpful. Veniot, their Chairman, is showing splendid leadership."[49] It was fitting that Dr Clarence J. Veniot, a New Brunswick MP, was chosen to chair the doctors' all-party discussion group; for he was a member of the CMA's Committee of Seven, the CMA executive, and the parliamentary Special Committee.

At its fourth session the committee was addressed by the nine provincial deputy ministers of health. Although they recommended that the administration of the plan be by the health departments rather than by independent commissions, the deputy ministers other-wise upheld CMA policy. They suggested that the director of each health insurance scheme should be a doctor; further, that he or she be chosen from a group of nominees put forward by the provincial medical association. The advisory council to the department of health must have two representatives of the CMA, and if the Special Committee did instead opt for provincial administration by an independent commission, it should have not only two CMA representatives, but also delegates from the provincial medical schools. Angus MacInnis (CCF – Vancouver East) finally asked the deputy ministers whether laymen had any input into these proposals. When their spokesman, Dr F.W. Jackson of Manitoba, replied in the negative, MacInnis remarked, "I thought as I listened to it that it was the representation of the union and the members have to keep in good standing if they want to get anywhere." Jackson, who from 1931 to 1937 had been both executive secretary of the MMA and the deputy minister of health, replied that the delegation was in fact "not the voice of the union": "There might be some other gentlemen here who might express the voice of organized medicine in Canada better than the health officers."

George Fulford (Liberal – Leeds), an Ontario industrialist, followed up on MacInnis's comments. Fulford pointed out that the deputy ministers' plan made no provision for "osteopaths, chiropractors and masseurs. After all," he added, "in a modern community they do form, in so far as the layman is concerned, an important group and perform a useful service." Dr J.J. Heagerty replied at the chairman's request: "The doctor has the privilege of utilizing the services of the masseur, the osteopath and the chiropractor and any other service that he thinks his patient needs. That, I think, covers all these other questions." Fulford was not satisfied: "I rose to my feet on this point. I hoped if the medical profession became all powerful that they would not outlaw the so-called drugless practitioner." Ian Mackenzie then asked Dr Heagerty if each province could make its own decision about the matter. When Heagerty indicated that the answer depended on how the province defined the term "general practitioner," a lawyer, Hughes Cleaver (Liberal – Halton), sought clarification: "Do I take it from that answer, Dr Heagerty, that a person who is ill will not be able to have the services of a chiropractor under this Act until the general practitioner recommends that he requires those services?" Heagerty confirmed this analysis. Cleaver commented, "That would appear to be highly dangerous"; and the issue was dropped temporarily.[50]

On 6 April 1943 the CMA made its presentation, with the ubiquitous T.C. Routley reading the doctors' lengthy and impressive brief. Also in attendance were A.E. Archer, the association president, and representatives from the CMA executive committee. There were no real surprises, except perhaps, the association's interest in community health centres – a new departure for the CMA. The brief reiterated and elaborated on the CMA's health insurance principles and emphasized both the need for an income ceiling and the importance of coverage of indigents. In the light of earlier discussion, the question of capitation versus fee-for-service payment of general practitioners was left to provincial discretion, but fee-for-service alone was recommended for specialist work. As a reflection of organized medicine's concern about the growth of prepayment arrangements outside professional auspices, Routley also stressed the disadvantages of voluntary plans: "Any acceptable national or provincial plan should offer more than can any individual plan. These plans deserve great credit for their pioneering service, but it is in the national interest to have all single plans absorbed ... If Canada is to have health insurance, let its action not be hamstrung by lack of vision or courage."[51]

After the brief was read, Routley and Archer diplomatically fielded a number of questions from the members of the Special Committee. At one point, barrister Maurice Lalonde (Liberal – Labelle) asked whether the CMA could claim to speak for Quebec, an apparently telling point, since the CMA in fact had only 300 French-speaking members out of 2,100 francophone physicians and surgeons in Canada. Here, however, the CMA had taken the appropriate steps. Its Quebec division, together with the predominantly francophone Féderation des Sociétés Médicales and the College of Physicians and Surgeons of Quebec, had formed a conjoint committee on health insurance which authorized the CMA in writing to speak for the Quebec profession. Dr Léon Gérin-Lajoie, a CMA executive member from Quebec, presented this authorization; and Dr C.J. Veniot (Liberal – Gloucester) intervened in the proceedings to underscore this endorsement by asking for a similar statement from the president of the Quebec division of the CMA, who was also in attendance. To finalize the matter, Dr James J. McCann (Liberal – Renfrew South) asked Gérin-Lajoie to table the letters of authorization for the record.[52]

Once the questions stopped, Dr Herbert A. Bruce (Conservative – Parkdale), a distinguished surgeon and former Ontario lieutenant-governor, capped the presentation with a lengthy monologue directed to the lay members of the Special Committee. Stressing the expertise of Routley and company, Bruce said that "it is very fortunate for this committee at this particular time ... that these gentlemen have made a study of this subject for many years – and they are able to give us out of their own knowledge just what we require to know to enable us to put on the statute books, I hope, a better Act of health insurance than any country heretofore has had." The member from Parkdale added a warning about the perils of legislating without the full co-operation of the medical profession and concluded with effusive thanks to Routley and Archer and further praise of the CMA submission.[53]

Shortly after the CMA presentation, T.C. Routley contacted Heagerty and rather boldly asked if the federal print-shop would produce a pamphlet version of the association's submission – 7,500 copies in English, 2,500 in French – for distribution to doctors coast-to-coast. Heagerty complied but subsequently decided that it would be inappropriate if the Department of Health itself paid the printer on the CMA's behalf. By 14 April one of Heagerty's assistants was able to report that all "has been fixed up and the Department need not have anything to do with it."[54]

The deferential treatment accorded the CMA contrasted markedly with the reception given other groups. For example, the Canadian Federation of Agriculture, representing about 350,000 rural residents, was allocated so short a speaking period that its spokesman, H.H. Hannam, was forced to defer his verbal presentation and reschedule his appearance before the Special Committee. The CFA's views were summarized in a widely distributed pamphlet, "Health on the March," which had been the basis for national discussions through the CBC Farm Forum radio program. Hannam therefore tabled the pamphlet in evidence before departing. Nothing was changed from the original submission to the Heagerty Committee: lay control, no premiums, funding from general revenue, universal coverage without ceilings, community health centres, and a strong emphasis on preventive services. The farmers' lobby group also suggested that either chiropractic and osteopathic services be covered, or regular practitioners be taught more about spinal manipulation techniques. The CFA's strongest language was reserved for organized medicine's claims to control over fee schedules and mode of remuneration:

The average citizen is amazed that any one group should assert such a principle. Nobody proposes to turn over medical *services* to the control of politicians. Nobody contends, for instance, that a board of aldermen should decide when to operate for appendicitis. The practice of medicine, nursing or dentistry is the responsibility of the professions concerned. But the question of how these services shall be paid for is very much the concern and responsibility of the public.[55]

The train of the argument here, of course, was exactly the opposite of that used by Routley and other CMA spokesmen – clinical expertise should not be generalized into the administrative and economic sphere. A few weeks later, when Hannam returned to discuss the CFA submission, Dr J.J. Heagerty effectively demonstrated several impractical aspects of the farmers' health service blueprint.[56]

Shortly thereafter, organized labour appeared before the Special Committee and attacked the proposed legislation. Since the final draft bill had not been altered in any way to reflect labour's earlier criticisms, the TLCC brief was virtually identical to its submission to the Heagerty Committee several months earlier. Percival R. Bengough read the brief, claiming to speak on behalf of 264,375 wage-earners. Bengough was definitely a veteran in the health insurance arena; he had served on both the Hearings Committee and the insurance commission in British Columbia eight years earlier. The TLCC brief acknowledged the need for medical representation but objected strenuously to the medical majority on the National Council on Health Insurance and the provision that the chairman of the provincial health insurance commission must be a doctor. More lay representation was demanded in all facets of administration. The TLCC also requested that chiropractic services be insured and indicated reservations about the means-testing procedures that were set out for assessment of employee contributions. In a response to the CMA's recently adopted principle relating to health insurance and medical education, the Heagerty final draft bill had stated that any patient insured under the state scheme who did not pay extra for semi-private coverage must be available for clinical teaching in hospitals affiliated with medical schools. This feature, too, provoked a sharp response: "A scheme of health insurance on a contributory basis does not mean that one in receipt of benefits automatically becomes a guinea pig for observation. This is a matter for the patient to decide." The 1943 TLCC brief concluded with precisely the same phrases quoted earlier from its 1942 submission to the Heagerty Committee: the legislation should be "entirely reconstituted to take control away from the medical profession and place it in the hands of the contributors."

In reply to a question from Percy Wright (CCF – Melfort), Bengough affirmed that labour wished to see the provincial bill rewritten to eliminate any mention of an income ceiling. However, it is perhaps understandable that the bulk of the discussion of the TLCC brief consisted in pointed exchanges between the doctors on the Special Committee and the labour spokesman. Dr John Howden, a veteran Liberal member from St Boniface, Manitoba, said, "I would like to ask the witness whether he agrees with anything in this bill at all?" Bengough indicated that labour supported the principle of the legislation, but not "the management." Herbert Bruce wondered if Bengough "seriously" believed that the Heagerty legislation was largely for the benefit of doctors.

Bengough: Not yet, it is not, doctor, but if it was operated on this basis I would be rather afraid it would be.
Bruce: Do you think this Act could be operated at all without the medical profession?
Bengough: Well, naturally their services are needed.
Dr J.J. McCann: Let the chiropractors and labour run it.

Dr Moses McGarry (Liberal – Inverness) asked Bengough from what group the chairman of the insurance commission should come, "if not the medical profession." Bengough cited workmen's compensation boards as examples of administrative bodies that paid doctors and did not always have medical representatives. Dr Thomas Donnelly (Liberal – Wood Mountain), a former municipal doctor in Saskatchewan, rejected the TLCC's attempt to change the legislation with respect to public-ward patients and medical education. Bengough agreed that patients were vital to medical education, but insisted that they should be asked to co-operate:

Donnelly: Your objection is to the one in the public ward not being consulted?
Bengough: I think so, yes.

Donnelly: If your suggestion is adopted you are going to have a nice mess.

Herbert Bruce then asserted that the medical profession would disappear in forty years if the public-ward patients were not automatically available for students under the scheme. Although Mrs F.C. Casselman (Liberal – Edmonton East) interceded to suggest that 90 percent of patients, public or private, would be glad to help the profession if requested to do so, the wrangling continued for several more minutes, Angus MacInnis weighing in on Bengough's side against McCann, Bruce, and Donnelly. Finally, Cyrus MacMillan thanked Bengough and brought the proceedings to a close.[57]

As spring gave way to summer, other providers of health services came before the committee to promote their interests. Representatives of the nation's 1,500 optometrists protested that their services were not insured by the proposed legislation. They argued that the public would logically see family physicians and ophthalmologists for spectacle prescribing, since medical services alone were to be prepaid. Dr J.J. McCann tried Heagerty's earlier argument for chiropractors: a doctor could always refer his or her patients to an optometrist. The optometrists replied that 70 percent of their patients saw them directly under normal circumstances. This referral process would simply add expenses to the health insurance plan – and accrue to the medical profession's financial benefit.[58]

A delegation from the Dominion Council of Chiropractors was next to appear. In Ontario, Saskatchewan, Alberta, and British Columbia 571 chiropractors were licensed to practise, and 100 more worked outside the law in other provinces. In the 1940s the medical mainstream was highly sceptical about the therapeutic effectiveness of spinal manipulation. Both chiropractic and osteopathic institutes were visited by European specialists in physical medicine from the mid-1920s on, and a handful of physicians did contend that spinal manipulation had a definite though limited role. Chiropractors, however, had yet to accept these limitations. In one instance, an attempt by the chiropractors to win recognition in Manitoba in 1936 was vetoed when the chiropractors sent a circular to the legislators asserting that spinal manipulation could cure 95 percent of disease, infectious or otherwise, and no diagnosis was necessary.[59]

The chiropractors were nonetheless able to muster some reasonable arguments for their inclusion in any scheme. They pointed out that a 1941 British Columbia Royal Commission on Workmen's Compensation had been petitioned by labour groups and industrialists alike for extension of benefits to cover chiropractic services. The commissioner found that 1,300 injured workmen had paid out of their own pockets to see chiropractors in the previous year, even though medical services were provided free under the terms of the compensation legislation. The law was therefore amended to include chiropractors' services. The chiropractors' council also reported that at least 200,000 persons – including several thousand servicemen with access to free medical care – had taken chiropractic treatments in the preceding year. They argued that the draft bills contravened the "democratic principle of the law of freedom of choice of health practitioner." Drs Veniot, Bruce, and McCann gave the chiropractic delegation a chilly reception. The chiropractors' case was not helped when their spokesman, in argument with an incredulous Herbert Bruce, denied that antibiotics were superior to spinal manipulation in treating bacterial meningitis.[60]

On 15 June 1943 the Canadian Osteopathic Association (COA) made a brief presentation. The COA complained that whereas osteopaths were granted legal status analogous to the regular medical profession in Alberta and British Columbia, they were categorized as drugless practitioners in Ontario. In support of coverage for osteopathic services under national health insurance, they noted that 6,000 servicemen had visited osteopaths during the war, despite the free care available from the Royal Canadian Army Medical Corps (RCAMC). The doctors on the Special Committee neatly turned this point around: if osteopathic services were effective, why had the RCAMC not provided them? A COA representative responded that the RCAMC had encouraged eight osteopaths to enlist in the air force where they were to assist in managing patients with difficult musculoskeletal problems; to the osteopaths' annoyance, the air force doctors then denied them officer status and put them to work as physiotherapists. Several more exchanges between the osteopaths and the doctors followed until the session was brought to an end by the chairman.[61]

The chiropodists were the last group of "irregular" practitioners to make a presentation to the 1943 session of the Special Committee before summer adjournment. Graduates of English and American post-secondary programs in foot care, the 150 chiropodic practitioners scattered across Canada sought recognition in the health insurance program by advancing arguments similar to those used by the optometrists. Again, it was Dr J.J. McCann who insisted that their services should be covered only on referral.[62]

It is clear, then, that many of the doctors on the 1943 Special Committee considered themselves to be acting primarily as representatives of organized medicine. They sought both to defend the draft bill as supported by the CMA executive and to protect their profession's exclusive status under the terms of insurance coverage.

The CMA's lobbying campaign is also worthy of comment. Initially, the CMA executive focused its efforts on influencing Mackenzie, Heagerty, and others involved in drafting the health insurance legislation. This focus on cabinet ministers and senior civil servants was not surprising in a parliamentary system and in the general case has long been recognized by students of pressure-group politics.[63] Later, the all-party Special Committee on Social Security afforded both an opportunity for MPs to dispense with parliamentary caucus discipline as they sought a consensus on health insurance and a chance for the CMA to undertake effective direct lobbying of legislators – an approach seen more commonly in the United States. Although the CMA's early success was considerable, its leaders soon discovered that the political process was more capricious than they had hoped.

THE SHIFTING POLITICAL WINDS

The Special Committee reported to the House in late July 1943, offering its approval of the general outline of the Heagerty draft legislation as well as the philosophy of the Heagerty report. Thus encouraged, Ian Mackenzie pressed King to take action. Mackenzie argued that socialism, once confined to British Columbia and Saskatchewan alone, had become "a national political menace." As part of the campaign to head off the CCF, a dominion-provincial conference to deal with the implications of the proposed health insurance legislation should be held as soon as possible.[64]

Mackenzie's agitation was understandable. The latter part of the Second World War was a period of political ferment which has seldom been matched in Canadian history. During the war years the number of individuals employed rose by 63 percent, and organized labour doubled its membership. Support for the CCF underwent similar growth. Between April and October 1943 the number of card-carrying CCFers in Ontario more than doubled, and in the provincial election of that year, the CCF jumped from zero to thirty-four seats and became the official opposition. Several months later, T.C. Douglas led the CCF to power in Saskatchewan for the first time.

Perhaps the clearest barometer of change was the national opinion poll taken in September 1943, following hard on the heels of the CCF's astonishing gains in the Ontario election. The CCF had the support of 29 percent of the electorate; the Liberals and Conservatives each had 28 percent. Shortly thereafter, the council of the National Liberal Federation met at Mackenzie King's request and passed a series of resolutions aimed at winning farmers' and working-class votes. The Conservatives made their own attempt to woo the west, urban wage-earners, and farmers by bringing in John Bracken, Liberal-Progressive premier of Manitoba, as national leader. At Bracken's insistence there was a name change to the Progressive Conservative party.

The CMA was therefore in an awkward position. Although the Heagerty draft legislation had been largely tailored to the profession's specifications, the proceedings of the 1943 Special Committee had demonstrated that the political arena was by no means safe. In fact, even before the 1943 session ended, the CMA twice sent lengthy bulletins to Ottawa offering "Further Comments" on the health insurance measure. They stressed the importance of clear inclusion of "those unable to pay, be they called 'indigents' or not," and warned that "strong opposition from the medical profession" would result if the health insurance plan left the doctors with any charity work. In this respect, at least, the lessons of the British Columbia dispute had been well learned. The CMA "Comments" dealt, too, with the importance of public ward patients to medical education, and emphasized that the health insurance funds at both federal and provincial levels should be clearly separated and protected against other revenue needs. To this end, a contributory plan with government paying premiums on behalf of low-income groups was strongly preferred, since full financing from general taxation revenues would put health services and provider payments in competition for funds with other government projects. Attention was also given to matters of individual and collective technical autonomy; there were to be no "referees" directly auditing accounts in doctors' offices, nor were the self-governing colleges to yield up any of their powers.[65]

Health department bureaucrats, for their part, made efforts to allay the doctors' anxieties. They resumed close contact with the CMA Committee of Seven behind the scenes during June and July, and lengthy memoranda were exchanged discussing amendments to the Heagerty draft legislation.[66] Some of these discussions hinged on minor points of wording raised by the CMA seven and the association's solicitor. Others were more substantive. For example, since the provincial bill did not specify a medical majority on the administrative commission, the CMA requested better representation from the profession at large, licensing bodies, and medical schools. A request was also made that medical commissioners be named only from panels nominated by organized medicine. A.D. Watson, the departmental actuary, remarked that this was "going pretty far," but agreed to write in the amendment to secure professional co-operation. A few CMA requests for amendments were referred by Watson to Heagerty with the suggestion that Heagerty or some other member of the Special

Committee should bring them up for discussion, and a number of
CMA requests were rejected as legally or politically unacceptable.
Nonetheless the legislation was sufficiently changed that Watson
suggested the Special Committee should be given a new set of bills
to consider, complete with all the revisions "approved by the Committee of Seven."[67]

The CMA executive remained uneasy. On 6 August 1943 T.C. Routley
mailed out a circular letter to selected members of the association,
calling for vigilance, since governments occasionally tried "to strangle
the profession."[68] The normally sanguine CMA president, A.E. Archer,
wondered in his mid-1943 valedictory address whether health insurance should not be put off until the war's end. And an August 1943
editorial in the *CMAJ* welcomed the parliamentary summer break
as a respite in which doctors could mull over the situation.[69]

On the other hand, the CMA had good reason to believe that a
state scheme of some kind was inevitable. Public support for health
insurance remained strong. A 1943 Gallup poll did show a slight
decline in the number of those definitely favourable to paying a small
part of their income toward health insurance from 75 percent in 1942
to 69 percent, but by 1944 the Gallup pollsters found the fraction
favourable to health insurance had risen to 80 percent.[70]

The CMA also knew that the Heagerty draft legislation might be
the best they could hope for. Progressive Conservative leader John
Bracken had personally commissioned a study of post-war reconstruction plans from Charlotte Whitton – a recognized authority on social
welfare. Published in the autumn of 1943, Whitton's *The Dawn of
Ampler Life* proposed a form of state medical service that would
be operated as a "social utility." The service would be integrated
with the provincial departments of health. Whitton insisted that the
only fair method of financing was to use general tax revenue; premiums
were rejected. Rural doctors should definitely be on salary, and she
implied that in some circumstances urban MDs might be made salaried
employees of their health departments. Stressing the superiority of
a state medical service to state-aided health insurance, Whitton took
specific aim at the Heagerty draft bills. She claimed doctors had an
average net income of $3,142 per year (in fact the 1941 census showed
an average gross income of $5,126 and a net income of $3,076) but
if the specific allocation for doctors' fees were divided by the number
of physicians practising in Canada, the Heagerty bill would guarantee
an average annual gross income of up to $10,000 per year, with extra
fees from wealthy patients still to be collected on top of this amount.
Whitton also argued that nurses were underpaid in comparison with
doctors.[71]

Whitton's calculations were misleading; for by late 1943 it had become obvious that while Heagerty had budgeted generously for medical services, the estimates for the plan as a whole were far too low. The unreliability of these initial financing arrangements provided yet another amber light for organized medicine, since, as the *CMAJ* editor noted, miscalculations could only damage the planners' "professional reputations," while doctors' incomes would be directly affected.[72] Nonetheless Whitton's book was widely read and must surely have signalled to the CMA executive that the political winds were blowing due left.[73]

The CCF proposals were even more alarming for organized medicine. While the Conservatives made no move to adopt Whitton's recommendations as actual party doctrine, the official CCF Health Planning Committee indicated firm support for a state medical service financed through general taxation without premiums or other contributory mechanisms. All doctors would eventually be on salary, although at the outset GPs could supplement their salaries with capitation fees, and specialists would receive partial fees for services rendered. CCF policy further decreed that doctors should be paid better than any other salaried group in society, their incomes to be equalled only by professional engineers. A network of community health centres was envisioned, each of which could provide offices for all the GPs in a given area, together with diagnostic and therapeutic equipment, secretarial aid, and ancillary services.

The CCF plan was presented to the London Academy of Medicine during the summer of 1943 by E.B. Jolliffe in one of his early appearances as leader of the newly powerful Ontario CCF caucus. Jolliffe attempted to assuage medical fears by indicating that it would be a "long time" before all doctors could be placed on salary. He also stressed the local autonomy of the community health centres in the CCF plan, contending: "It is not state medicine; that is because it is not completely controlled from the top." On the administrative end, Jolliffe addressed the profession's autonomy concerns by carefully distinguishing between the "general" and "technical" aspects. He proposed placing all technical administration under the control of commissions comprised entirely of representatives chosen by organized medicine and other health care professions. Jolliffe's address was reprinted by the *Nova Scotia Medical Bulletin*[74] and the *Ontario Medical Review*[75] and summarized, albeit with a critical editorial commentary, in the *CMAJ*.[76]

Organized medicine accordingly faced a dilemma in strategy. The CMA could, of course, try to postpone its marriage to the state until the political climate became more favourable, but this option had drawbacks. There was no guarantee that the terms of legislation would be better in future; indeed, delay might actually increase the possibility of a "shot gun wedding," with the CCF officiating. Better that Dr J.J. Heagerty's marriage contract be used by a sympathetic Liberal minister – or so the thinking seemed to run in the CMA executive committee as 1943 drew to a close.[77]

Thus, in December 1943, when T.C. Routley was dispatched by the executive to discuss health insurance on the CBC's national Farm Forum radio program, he found himself "playing a lone hand" in defending the Heagerty legislation against representatives of agriculture and the Canadian Congress of Labour (CCL), a sister organization and sometime rival of the TLCC. After the programs all nine provincial farm organizations reported that the CFA-CCL stance had been strongly supported by correspondents and callers. And Routley, later describing the event in a bulletin to the more than 200 doctors designated across Canada as a "Health Insurance Committee-at-Large," plaintively remarked:

It is my opinion that Agriculture and Labour and a good many other people would throw a harpoon into the medical profession with zest because they regard our organization as monopolistic and selfish and not in the public interest. They think . . . that the individual doctor is a grand person by himself, but becomes quite another person when coming under the hypnotic sway of his medical organization.[78]

THE SPECIAL COMMITTEE, 1944

Because there had been serious criticism inside and outside the House of the proposed financing of the Heagerty draft legislation, an interdepartmental committee on health insurance finance undertook revision of these sections of the bills in the fall of 1943. It recommended streamlining the premium structure, with the result that those at the bottom end of the wage scale paid less, but a flat rate applied to all single contributors with incomes over $1,600 and all married contributors with incomes above $2,200 per year.[79] Heagerty's team made other modifications to the draft bill at this time. The clause on mandatory availability of insured patients for medical education was rewritten, and the description of the national administrative council's composition was clarified although not substantively changed. There was also provision made for a province, at its discretion, to administer the plan under the Department of Health rather than through an independent, non-political commission, a reversal duly noted by the CMA.

The House of Commons Special Committee on Social Security resumed its deliberations on 24 February 1944 and soon after began grappling with the revised bill. A lengthy and heated debate on the question of premiums dominated the first few meetings. A vocal minority called for a non-contributory plan, but the majority, including the medical-MPs, favoured retention of premiums. Dr James J. McCann was particularly vehement: "I think I can say for every doctor upon this Committee that if this is not a contributory scheme then I might as well withdraw from this committee, and that is exactly what I would do; because if it is not a contributory scheme you put this country immediately into state medicine, and there is not a doctor in the whole country who wants to serve the state under those conditions."[80] On 30 March the Special Committee voted in support of personal premiums – an event that received the "warm approval" of the CMA Committee on Economics for the same reason advanced by McCann.[81] Maintenance of premium financing, then, appears to have had both symbolic and practical importance to the profession.

J.J. Heagerty's financial analyses, however, were subject to ongoing criticism. Early in 1944 medical economics spokesmen in British Columbia and Quebec pointed out that Heagerty's testimony on these matters was inconsistent; and during the next few months, a lively exchange between Heagerty and the BCMA commentators peppered the *CMAJ* correspondence columns.[82] Heagerty was also asked by the Special Committee to explain his thinking on medical fees allocations in the light of Charlotte Whitton's criticisms.[83]

The Special Committee meanwhile continued to receive an assortment of delegations and briefs. A.R. Mosher and Norman Dowd appeared on 30 March 1944, representing the 250,000-member Canadian Congress of Labour. The CCL emphasized the need for lay control of the health insurance commissions, arguing as had other groups that the professions had no special competence in "the economic and general aspects of administration." The CCL brief reiterated Charlotte Whitton's arguments about the generosity of payments to doctors and the relatively poor remuneration of nurses, but its strongest points were made against the bill's financing. As the CCL argued, the draft bill's premium structure would have a highly regressive incidence. Since public education was successfully funded from general tax revenue, the CCL suggested health insurance could be similarly supported. By this stage, of course, the Special Committee had just voted in favour of a contributory plan, and the CCL arguments for elimination of premiums were no longer pertinent.[84]

In Regina, where the CCF was gathering force, the State Hospital and Medical League had prepared a brief in support of the CCF health services blueprint. The brief was presented to the Special Committee on 23 May 1944 by one of the committee's own members, farmer Percy E. Wright (CCF - Melfort). The Regina-based league made a number of assertions that annoyed organized medicine, including an attempt to draw unfavourable comparisons between Canadian health services and those in the Soviet Union. It also stated, "In our opinion the Federal draft bill has been especially designed to curtail the progress of health insurance and socialized medicine. Organized medicine has always everywhere been opposed to socialized medicine and that body has the ear of the government in Canada."[85] A detailed rebuttal of the League's brief was eventually printed in the *CMAJ*.[86] In any case, the Special Committee already faced time constraints, and sweeping modification of the Heagerty draft bills at this late stage was impractical.

While the Special Committee's deliberations continued, there were signs of opposition from the business community. The Canadian Pharmaceutical Manufacturers' Association produced a pamphlet which claimed that the draft bill was in large measure a profession-sponsored ploy to boost medical incomes and exclude the irregulars. (The *CMAJ* editor replied that this was "a piece of propaganda: Our profession has had no part whatever in framing or guiding health insurance legislation."[87]) The London, Ontario, Chamber of Commerce published a widely distributed critique of the Heagerty bill in April-May 1944.[88] And by early June the *Financial Post* was already characterizing health insurance as "a vast, unwieldly and very costly piece of legislation."[89]

Although professional opinion was still more positive than negative, a trickle of letters to the *CMAJ* yielded some unflattering assessments of health insurance. From Alberta came a warning about "the paternalistic state."[90] A Nova Scotia doctor criticized the CMA's handling of the situation, claiming that the philosophy of the Heagerty proposals was "as plain an example of National Socialism and state control as one could imagine."[91] A Saskatchewan GP was equally glum: "The whole Health Insurance scheme is in the end disastrous for the profession and ultimately not at all beneficial to the country."[92]

Dr William Magner, a pathologist at St Michael's Hospital in Toronto, had a special podium to express his concern about the legislation, since he was editor of the *Ontario Medical Review*. As early as February 1944 Magner claimed that the profession should resist any plan that depended on "direct hiring of individual doctors by the state either through a department or a commission." He criticized the principles of the CMA, the OMA, and the Heagerty bills on this ground, "because experience in other countries has invariably shown that while initially there is good remuneration to induce doctors to participate, the amount is soon whittled down resulting in underpay and poor service." Magner saw the state as engaged in a "divide-and-command" exercise. The profession should respond with a "unite-and-guide" approach. Just as the government had contracted with the OMA for the provincial medical relief plan, so also should it pass funds and the total responsibility for administering health insurance to organized medicine.[93] As we shall see in chapter 6, a variation on this approach was eventually adopted as the official policy of Canadian organized medicine.

Magner carried his objections to the CMA annual meeting at Toronto in late May 1944, but other OMA officials defended the draft legislation. Dr A.E. Archer, who was now chairman of the CMA general council, took a neutral stance in an address to a special symposium on health insurance at the same meeting. Archer noted that the 1944 draft bill continued to give provinces the latitude to administer health insurance through the health department rather than an independent commission. On the other hand, he reported that the Special Committee had altered the 1944 draft bill to ensure that provinces had the option of setting an income limit on participation in the state scheme.[94]

Other participants in the symposium were idealistic and positive about the role of government and prospects for legislation. A Manitoba municipal doctor presented a strong endorsement of the salaried system for remote rural practice. An Ontario GP offered many forward-looking ideas on health services organization, and remarked: "Every day I see patients who are getting inadequate medical service, both diagnostic and curative, because they are unable to pay for it, or if they do pay they are left with insufficient money to provide a decent standard of living. Every such case is a demand, even though usually unexpressed, for some form of health insurance."[95] A spokesman for the Canadian Association of Medical Students and Interns (CAMSI) followed; while endorsing most of the CMA policies, he reported that briefs from eight medical schools across Canada showed support for a universal plan under which doctors would be paid by salary and capitation.[96]

A much more influential group than CAMSI had also registered support for state health insurance by this time – the doctors on active military service overseas. More than 3,000 MDs were enrolled in the RCAMC as of 1944, and as already noted, the CMA had offered free membership to all practitioners in the military. To keep doctors overseas informed about developments in health insurance, five separate bulletins were prepared and sent out between 1942 and 1944.

However, because of wartime conditions, not all these mailings reached their destinations. The RCAMC (Overseas) formed its own health insurance planning committee and first sent a memorandum and later a representative, Lt-Col. E.H. Botterell, indicating concern about the lack of information received. Three criticisms of CMA policy were also made. After conversations with British practitioners, the insurance committee of the RCAMC (Overseas) decided that provincial administration was not desirable. They favoured amendment of the British North America Act to place health insurance under direct federal control but would accept provincial administration by a commission if the requisite constitutional amendment could not be made. Second, the military doctors wished to see a compulsory plan covering the entire population. And third, they suggested that the CMA principle of health insurance that claimed complete control of the fee schedules, must be modified to acknowledge the need for negotiations.[97]

As noted above, the CMA Committee of Seven had found enough support for both GP capitation payments and removal of income ceilings that in late summer 1943 it privately advised the health department to leave these details in any legislation for each province to decide. By the spring of 1944 the CMA Committee on Economics publicly acknowledged the same groundswell.[98] Given these changing viewpoints and given, too, the battering of certain CMA principles of health insurance at the hands of labour and agriculture, it is understandable that yet another round of policy revisions was undertaken at the 1944 annual meeting. Several contentious principles were dropped or modified. The CMA no longer claimed majority control of the "independent non-political commission" that was to administer its ideal plan. Instead, the profession should be represented thereon, and the executive officers of the plan should be "physicians appointed by the Commission from a list submitted by organized medicine." Claims to "complete control" of fee schedules were also abandoned. Remuneration was to be by methods and at rates negotiated with the commission. And while the plans should be compulsory for those "having an annual income insufficient to meet the costs of adequate medical care," a clear income ceiling was no longer suggested; rather, each province was to make an independent decision as to who would be included.

In addition to making these revisions, the CMA General Council voted to include several new items in its list of health insurance principles. A formal statement approving the concept of contributory health insurance was placed at the head of the list, and a warning about state invasion of "the professional aspects of the doctor-patient relationship" appeared for the first time. The CMA's stand against inclusion of irregular practitioners was legitimized with a clause concerning licensing requirements. Another addendum pointed out the need for any scheme to protect the interests of the sizeable fraction of the medical population on active duty. Specific mention was made of the desirability of a contributory financing mechanism. Two more principles were borrowed almost verbatim from the British Medical Association's policy statements. The BMA was facing definite prospects of a state medical service as part of post-war reconstruction. From the BMA came the pronouncement that it was "not in the national interest" for the state to "convert the whole medical profession into a salaried service." The CMA also adopted a temporizing clause used by the BMA – one that stressed the importance of other facets of post-war reconstruction as essential handmaidens to any medical services scheme if the health of the population were to be improved.[99]

Despite certain cautionary clauses, this statement of principles was to be the strongest endorsement of state health insurance ever approved by the CMA. However, Dr A.E. Archer did warn delegates that the "trend of events" in provincial health services had not been "entirely satisfactory to the interests for which we stand."[100] The Ontario government had passed a Municipal Health Services Act in the spring which did not provide for administration by an independent non-political commission. In Saskatchewan, the College of Physicians and Surgeons was embroiled in an ongoing battle of words with the CCF and the Regina State Hospital and Medical League.[101] Worse yet, that province's Liberal government – as its last act before a summer election – had passed legislation setting out the machinery for Saskatchewan to participate in any federally sponsored health insurance plan. The College of Physicians and Surgeons objected strongly to many features of the law and were but little appeased when the Liberal health minister assured the profession that this was "merely an initiating, enabling Bill, and as such is quite innocuous."[102] The CMA Committee on Economics claimed in its 1944 report that both the Ontario and Saskatchewan enactments opened the door to "bureaucratic control" of the profession.[103] Also, notwithstanding the CMA's approval of most sections of the Heagerty legislation, there was discouraging news on the federal front: actuary Hugh H. Wolfenden, who had been retained to analyse the draft bills, reported that the costs would probably far outstrip the revenues.[104] All these developments heightened the profession's unease about state mediation.[105]

In June 1944 the Special Committee began voting on the specific provisions of the federal draft bill. The committee's votes were seldom unanimous, but clause after clause of the revised Heagerty bill was carried without significant amendment. One particularly contentious issue was the wording in clause 4 of the federal draft bill that effectively excluded coverage of services provided by practitioners other than regular medical doctors. During April both chiropractors and the Christian Scientists had submitted additional briefs protesting against this clause. Ralph Maybank (Liberal – Winnipeg South Centre) had been their strongest supporter, although other lawyers on the Special Committee took the same line in debates with Heagerty, Bruce, and the medical contingent.[106] Herbert Bruce became suspicious and telegraphed the Manitoba Medical Association for information about Maybank's connection with the chiropractors and osteopaths. Armed with a reply stating that Maybank was the paid legal adviser to the provincial chiropractors' association, Bruce asked him directly about any conflict of interest. Maybank denied a connection to the irregulars, whereupon Bruce read out the damning telegram from the MMA. At the age of ninety, Bruce still recalled the telegram's impact with obvious satisfaction: "To say the least, this had a quieting effect on him."[107]

Nonetheless on 4 July 1944 Maybank moved that the federal portion of the legislation be amended to specify that "nothing in this Act contained shall be construed as limiting the exercise by a province of any right of such province ... to employ or pay for the services of any persons (or organization of persons) where the services of such persons are considered by the province to be of value in the carrying out of such measures."[108] Committee chairman Cyrus Macmillan recommended that the matter be referred to both the justice department and a subcommittee. Deputy Justice Minister F.P. Varcoe objected to the amendment on the grounds that it was so general as to permit a province to hire unlicensed practitioners. The subcommittee vote deadlocked at 2:2, with Drs J.J. McCann and Herbert Bruce voting against, Maybank and another layman voting in favour. Cyrus Macmillan broke the tie by casting against the amendment. Maybank refused to abandon the issue, however, and on Thursday 13 July asked that the entire committee add a rider to the draft bill in support of his amendment.[109]

T.C. Routley was in Ottawa at this time and did what he could to help the profession's cause. As he put it in a "strictly confidential" memo to the CMA Committee on Economics, the amendment meant that in a given province, the irregulars might "be elevated to a status analogous to the medical profession." Routley added: "I took steps to line up the doctors on the Committee and to point out the necessity of their all being there on Tuesday. They have their backs up and

I am of the opinion that the amendment will be killed, but it will be touch and go. Of course if it should be passed, the issue becomes clear as far as the CMA is concerned and we can come out into the open and declare ourselves."[110] In the event, only about half of the doctors appeared at the last two meetings of the Special Committee, but the Maybank amendment was not accepted. Some sections of the draft bills to do with the mechanics of financing were left blank, on the grounds that insufficient data and time were available to the committee. Otherwise, the draft legislation corresponded closely to earlier outlines.[111]

The Special Committee had assumed that the Liberal government would present the draft bills at a dominion-provincial conference in the autumn of 1944. However, Mackenzie King, who was known to be uneasy about the financial ramifications of health insurance, decided against convening the conference until after the next federal election. He reminded the House of Commons on 14 August that six of nine provinces had gone to the polls since 1943, and the incumbents had been deposed in two cases. Moreover in a recent radio broadcast, George Drew, the Conservative premier of Ontario, had stressed his desire to oust the Liberals in Ottawa. King accordingly announced that there was no point in holding a conference with the provinces until the Liberals renewed their federal mandate at a general election.[112] And in the autumn, as the citizenry waited for the Liberal leader's next tactical manoeuvre, one medical spokesman disconsolately observed: "The professions are confused. The public is confounded."[113]

POLITICAL IMPASSE:
PROFESSIONAL CHANGE OF
HEART

Mackenzie King's strategic delay was perhaps the turning point in medical opinion. Organized medicine had exercised considerable influence over the framing of the health insurance legislation from 1941 to 1944. But as evidence of the capriciousness of the political process continued to mount, so too did professional anxieties. Even before the end of 1944 the tone of medical commentary had changed.[114] Dr Harris McPhedran, for example, was doubly influential as chairman of the CMA Committee on Economics and association president for 1944-5. An outstanding internist, McPhedran had publicly taken an open-minded stand on health insurance for twenty years. In a speech to the BCMA in September 1944, however, McPhedran inveighed against "Utopians" and "blueprinters." He also announced that the 1945

CMA general council would be asked by the Committee on Economics to endorse the concept of stepwise state intervention rather than any single large-scale plan. The first stage would be hospital and medical insurance for indigents, old age and blind pensioners, and those in receipt of mothers' allowances. Hospital insurance should follow, but only after "a vast plan of new hospital construction" was completed.

With these things done we would be well on the way to providing a complete health service if voluntary health insurance plans were developed at the same time. Service for those of the lower income group might then be added to that provided for those in number one group noted above ... We are not ready for the institution of a complete plan covering all the people of this Dominion. We do not want the practice of medicine to be completely state-controlled, not yet at all events, nor till such time as all men "are just men made perfect."[115]

Like Mackenzie King, the CMA executive had adopted a policy of strategic delay.

One of McPhedran's major concerns was the lack of assurance that the provinces would administer their health services through independent commissions. Indeed, far from using federal grants-in-aid as a club to force commission administration upon the provinces, Ottawa was actually moving towards a more open-ended plan. Dr Heagerty and two other senior civil servants charged with final revisions all but erased the provincial portion of the draft legislation – presumably in anticipation of provincial complaints about federal meddling in non-federal jurisdictions.

In mid-1945 the federal election took place, and King's Liberal government was returned to power with a much-reduced majority. Preparations for the postponed conference on post-war reconstruction had continued during the campaign interlude, and on 6 August 1945 formal negotiations were convened in Ottawa on a variety of domestic policy issues. In the specific area of health services, the federal government tabled a three-pronged proposal. Health Grants were offered to upgrade services in designated fields, such as mental health, tuberculosis care, venereal disease, and crippling illnesses of childhood. Financial assistance for the construction of hospitals was also made available to the provinces. As for health insurance, the federal government proposed that any province wishing to participate in a joint program should make use of a Planning and Organization Grant to survey health care facilities and set up the machinery for an insurance plan. The outline for cost-sharing in health insurance was straightforward: one-fifth of the estimated annual cost would be paid by the federal government to a given province, with a more substantial subsidy paid later to cover one-half the actual operating costs for the year. The total federal contribution was capped at not greater than $12.96 per person per year. A province that embarked on the insurance program was expected to provide prepaid general practitioner services, hospital care, and visiting nursing services, within two years. Dental, laboratory, drug, and specialist coverage could follow later.[116]

Saskatchewan's CCF government, barely twelve months in office, was keenly interested from the outset. The CCF had made a strong commitment to universal prepayment of health services, and Ottawa's financial support would be welcome. Manitoba and, to a lesser extent, British Columbia and Alberta were also interested in the health insurance proposals. However, the other provinces were either neutral or clearly opposed.

Several committees of senior civil servants worked through the rest of the summer and the autumn on the various areas where federal-provincial co-operation was needed: old age pensions, urban planning, elimination of wage and price controls, and health services. At the same time organized medicine undertook its own review of Ottawa's proposals. The 1945 CMA general council had endorsed the executive committee's recommendation that health insurance be implemented in stepwise fashion, with medical insurance for other than indigents and pensioners to be the last stage.[117] This approach clearly conflicted with the order set out by Ottawa, and two provincial medical groups made representations to their respective governments about the federal proposals. The Quebec division of the CMA suggested that the province should accept the Health Grants but reject Ottawa's specified order of implementation, since hospital care was the real priority.[118] In Ontario the College of Physicians and Surgeons joined with the OMA and delegates from four medical schools to carry a similar brief to the provincial government on 19 November 1945. The Ontario profession also contended that the government might do well to use the Planning and Organization Grant. However, neither the principle of proceeding with health insurance nor Ottawa's timetable should be adopted. Instead, the CMA's priorities were presented as guidelines for implementation.[119]

Ontario, which had been King's bête noire when he first decided to delay the dominion-provincial conference, proved in fact to be a strong opponent of the cost-sharing framework of health insurance. So far as Premier George Drew was concerned, Ottawa would gain too much taxation authority unless the financing were restructured. Ontario's rejection came in January 1946, and a few weeks later Quebec followed suit for the same reasons. When the formal negotiations were reconvened in April, it was apparent that Alberta, Saskatchewan, and Manitoba remained interested, but the opposition of Quebec and Ontario stalled any progress. Ontario finally tabled a counter-proposal that would have added to Ottawa's costs by a minimum of $134 million per year – a burden far too great for the federal government to shoulder. Negotiations broke off, and the conference adjourned *sine die* on 3 May 1946.[120] Commenting in the *CMAJ*, T.C. Routley welcomed the impasse: "Health insurance is not dead by any means. One day it will be here, but it is a credit to our people that they are not rushing into a costly piece of social legislation such as this would be until they see more clearly what it all means, what it will cost and on what basis it can be adequately and fairly financed."[121]

Another decade would pass before Ottawa and the provinces agreed on a national hospital insurance program, and yet another decade would elapse before the legislative framework of a national medicare program was passed in Ottawa. Dr Harris McPhedran had remarked during the Second World War on the need for the profession "to see things in their proper perspective, swinging neither too much to the right or left."[122] But if "left" meant a stronger role for state mediation in the medical services marketplace, then organized medicine in truth swung sharply right in the post-war period. Hereafter Canada's doctors placed increasing faith in the private sector, hoping to find an optimum blend of voluntary and government prepayment for medical services – a plan that would minimize lay control, collective bargaining, and other external checks on professional incomes and autonomy.

CHAPTER SIX

Post-War Developments:
The Private Alternative

The medical profession will assume leadership in securing public co-operation and thus see to it that Government regulation shall be only such minimum as will enable us to exercise proper control over ourselves and the public.

> J.A. Hannah, "The Place of the Voluntary Plan
> in Health Services," *CMAJ*, 1945

We firmly believe that a partnership between Government and enlightened free enterprise is much to be preferred to dictatorship by the Government.

> Alberta Medical Association, Statement of
> Opinion on Hospital Insurance, September 1956.

During the late 1940s and 1950s the tenor of Canadian medical politics changed, as continuing suspicion of state mediation in the health care market combined with the spread of private prepayment mechanisms to heighten professional resistance to any universal tax-funded plan. These changes dovetailed in some measure with the mood of the nation. Canada found itself embroiled in the Korean conflict, and defence expenditures soared. Social security naturally remained a concern, but international security seemed rather more important in a period when the Cold War cast a chill over global politics. Especially in the 1950s, the ideological climate was less favourable to central planning and government intervention than had been the case in the 1930s or during the Second World War.

Nonetheless, the post-war technological revolution in medicine yielded new diagnostic and therapeutic interventions, propelled the trend to more specialized and hospital-centred care, and thereby kept the issue of prepayment arrangements for hospital and medical care very much alive. The failure of the Dominion-Provincial Conference on Post-War Reconstruction was a setback to those in Ottawa who supported a national health insurance plan. But while grandiose plans had perforce to be abandoned, an incremental approach remained feasible. The federal government therefore moved slowly ahead with some of the components of the National Health Program as outlined in August 1945. Only in Saskatchewan, however, did the wartime wave of interest in health services reorganization bear immediate fruit in a brief flurry of government activity.

SASKATCHEWAN: A SPECIAL CASE

As noted earlier, Saskatchewan led the way with municipally funded medical and hospital service programs. Its pioneering endeavours in provision of health services continued in the 1940s under a Co-operative Commonwealth Federation government led by T.C. "Tommy" Douglas.

The fusion of the Saskatchewan College of Physicians and Surgeons (SCPS) and the Saskatchewan Medical Association in 1930 created a "closed shop" professional body that was further united by the political threat of the CCF. Leaders of the Saskatchewan medical profession had viewed the rise of the CCF with suspicion almost from its inaugural convention at Regina in July 1933. The party's avowed intention of setting up a salaried state medical service worried the SCPS which, from the 1930s on, had endorsed only "state-aided Health Insurance on a reasonable fee-for-service basis." Support for the CCF position was provided by the Saskatchewan Association of Rural Municipalities and by a special lobbying group formed in 1936 – the Regina-based State Hospital and Medical League. In 1944, when the league had appeared before the Special Committee on Social Security in Ottawa, its membership included 120 rural municipalities, six cities, twenty-four towns, fifty-six villages, fraternal societies, church and farm organizations, the Saskatchewan Teachers' Federation, and co-operative groups.[1]

During the war years W.J. Patterson's Liberal government had created a parallel body to Ottawa's social security committee, and as expected, its hearings showed the public to be strongly in favour of either state medicine or a universal health insurance scheme. On 18 March 1942 the SCPS had passed a resolution in favour of state health insurance with three provisos: the plan should be contributory; payments to doctors must be on a fee-for-service basis; and administration should be by an independent commission with representation from the SCPS. Whereas the 1942 CMA survey cited in chapter 5 found

75 percent of doctors in favour of income ceilings in a public plan, the scps deliberately avoided setting any limits on enrolment. Thus, in its presentations to legislators during 1943 the scps executive emphasized the college's support for health insurance along the lines of the Heagerty draft bills, and laid out its various objections to state medicine.[2]

Anticipating the passage of the Heagerty legislation in Ottawa, the Saskatchewan Special Select Committee on Social Security and Health Services endorsed the principle of state-aided health insurance and recommended investigations begin into how Saskatchewan might administer its portion of a federal-provincial plan. Out of those investigations came an enabling act which was hastily drafted and passed during the Liberals' last session in office. The rapid passage of this bill was apparently prompted by the Liberals' desire to prove their commitment to social welfare before joining electoral battle with the ccf.

As already noted, this bill caused intense agitation in medical circles; for its provisions, kept deliberately vague because of the act's enabling or initiating nature, offered no guarantee that certain cardinal principles of organized medicine would be respected. During its passage, the Liberal health minister was confronted in the legislature by a delegation from the profession. A special Sunday meeting 'of the scps health insurance committee was convened to compile a list of objections to the bill; a protest telegram was sent to the premier; and copies of the list of objections and the protest telegram were sent to all members of the college. Professional concern about the content of the bill was clearly strengthened by the prospects of a ccf sweep in the coming election. Dr Jack F.C. Anderson, for instance, "expressed the fear that if the Bill is in effect when a dangerous element may be forming the government, it could have disastrous results."[3]

The campaign leading up to the 15 June 1944 provincial election saw Liberal party literature warning of "Socialism and Dictatorship." ccf newspaper advertisements and speeches by Tommy Douglas keyed on the health services issue and argued in essence that Saskatchewan was faring so poorly that health insurance along the lines of the Heagerty plan would prove inadequate. In fact, the ccf statements contained a number of serious errors to do with basic mortality indices. Rejoinders were given by both the scps and the Liberal party.[4] When the ballots were tallied, the ccf took forty-seven seats to the Liberals' five and formed North America's first socialist government.

T.C. Douglas underlined his party's commitment to health services reorganization by taking on the health minister's portfolio in addition to his duties as premier. A little more than two months after the election, negotiations began with the SCPS concerning a plan of medical care for indigents and other recipients of social assistance. Not surprisingly, the college proved co-operative and the bargaining sessions were amicable. By 1 January 1945 a social assistance medical care plan was in operation covering 25,000 old age pensioners, recipients of mothers' allowances, blind pensioners, and wards of the state. Payments to doctors were on a prorated fee-for-service basis. SCPS spokesmen hastened to make clear that their acceptance of the plan was not a carte blanche for government intervention: "While we feel that the Premier's move to provide care for the group of Old Age Pensioners, etc., is a commendable step, further steps or additions to the plan should not be made without the profession being satisfied that the first step is sound. It will take a period of several years to properly appraise this scheme."[5]

The CCF, however, was already moving with alacrity on a broader front. A month after the CCF victory, Douglas had sent a telegram to Dr Henry E. Sigerist, professor of the history of medicine at Johns Hopkins University, inviting him to survey the health needs of the province and make recommendations. Sigerist, as much a medical sociologist as historian, had a special interest in health care delivery and was a recognized expert on the Soviet system of socialized medicine.[6] He arrived in Regina on 6 September 1944, met with officials, then toured the province for ten days. Aided by technical advisers from the provincial health department, Sigerist compiled his report over the course of another week. His posthumously published diaries record the following comments: "I think the report is good. It is realistic and foresees a gradual socialization of services. It is by no means complete, but it is the best I could do in less than four weeks."[7] Indeed, far from suggesting any radical upheavals, Sigerist suggested a stepwise approach. The municipal doctor schemes should be strengthened, a system of universal health insurance begun in certain cities, and one or two regions of the province used as trial areas for a comprehensive plan of medical-hospital services.[8] As a medical observer later remarked: "It is much milder than might have been expected from one known to be such an enthusiastic advocate of the Russian system."[9]

To facilitate the extension of coverage beyond recipients of social assistance Sigerist had suggested that a permanent Health Services Planning Commission be established. On 10 November 1944 a statute creating this body received royal assent. This legislation also gave the government a broad mandate to initiate prepayment of health services in the province. Despite the SCPS's repeated calls for direction of government activities by an independent non-political commission, the three appointees to the planning body had all served as technical advisers to Dr Sigerist. Two of the three had very close ties to the government: Dr Mindel Sheps, a CCF activist on staff as assistant to the health minister; and T.H. McLeod, an economist who was also an assistant to Premier Tommy Douglas. The deputy minister of health served ex-officio. The college was asked to nominate a doctor to be chairman of the Health Services Planning Commission (HSPC), but for reasons that remain unclear, no nomination was forthcoming. Fifteen months elapsed before the government filled the position unilaterally. The SCPS was also offered representation on the Advisory Committee to the HSPC, and two college spokesmen – Drs J.F.C. Anderson and C.J. Houston – joined citizens from various walks of life in this capacity.

Early in 1945 the HSPC followed Sigerist's schema and recommended the division of the province into health regions. In the rural areas the municipal doctor arrangements would be expanded into a salaried general practitioner service. Where possible, group practice patterns would prevail, organized around community diagnostic centres. The planners further envisioned that doctors should have a pension fund, paid holidays, and paid leave for continuing education. Salaries would be graded according to post-graduate studies, specialty training, and responsibilities. The HSPC openly rejected the concept of adminis-tration by an independent commission. Public funds could not be passed to a body that was not accountable to the taxpayers, nor should powers that properly belonged to the government and the department of public health be delegated away to a non-elected organization.[10]

These proposals were unveiled at the first meeting of the Advisory Committee on 2 March 1945. Two weeks later the college met with the premier and registered its objections to the plan as well as to the planning commission. The college spokesmen stressed the CMA principle that called for salaried doctors only in those underserviced areas where such subsidies constitued a necessary incentive and reiterated their preference for fee-for-service payments. The HSPC proposals were rejected as a step on the road to state medicine. Perhaps because of concern that regional administration would fragment the profession and undermine college authority the SCPS delegation also repeated its demand for centralized administration under an inde-pendent commission.

Negotiations continued into the summer of 1945. In the interim, the HSPC began the organization of two health regions. Number 3, based around Weyburn, was to have a system of hospital insurance. Health Region Number 1, based around Swift Current, took in about

50,000 people and was considering a full system of hospital *and* medical care insurance. These developments caused further alarm among college leaders. The college registrar, Dr J.G.K. Lindsay, went so far as to recommend in writing at one point that doctors in and around Swift Current boycott a meeting with the regional health officer.[11] In December 1945 the region's residents voted by plebiscite to proceed with a prepayment scheme. A twelve-member district health board was then elected from among municipal councillors; hence the board was composed entirely of laymen – another facet of the regional approach that displeased scps spokesmen.[12] However, cordial relations between lay administrators and medical practitioners had been nurtured over a long period in this part of the province. By 1945 there were already five municipal doctor schemes and several municipal hospitals operating in the Swift Current region. The local medical community had also suffered somewhat because of repeated crop failures in the area, and a prepayment scheme meant income security.[13] Thus, despite the disapproval of the scps executive, productive negotiations were maintained between the regional health board and the Swift Current Medical Society.

By this time the scps had already recognized one important fact: T.C. Douglas was a politician – not a planner. As such, his concern was to implement programs of health services as amicably and rapidly as possible. Leaders of the college repeatedly bypassed the hspc and members of his staff to negotiate with Douglas directly, thereby winning a variety of concessions. Given the province's chronic shortage of doctors, a point of special concern to Douglas was the scps's warning that sweeping changes in the provincial health care system might drive practitioners out of Saskatchewan and discourage immigration. The extent to which Douglas gave way is indicated in a letter dated 19 September 1945 and addressed to the head of the College Health Services Committee. Douglas noted the lack of progress in the Dominion-Provincial Conference on Post-War Reconstruction. Since some time would elapse before a universal health insurance plan could be adopted by the province, the premier emphasized the need for ongoing negotiations of a flexible and friendly nature concerning administration of any plan. He nevertheless agreed that administration should be by a representative commission chaired by a physician "in good standing." Moreover, the doctors' professional services committee not only would have "unrestricted jurisdiction over all scientific, technical and professional matters"; it would also have the power to determine "the general character of the agreement and arrangements whereunder the profession will provide medical services."[14]

Douglas had clearly abandoned the party's commitment to a salaried medical service under department of health auspices. scps spokesmen felt this was part of a larger trend and later reported that "the public has become better informed on the issues at stake, and during the year 1945 evidence became apparent to all that public opinion now favoured a system of state-aided Health Insurance. The Minister of Health has recognized the changed public opinion and has consistently referred to his health plans as on a Health Insurance basis and contributory in character."[15] However, there was still the issue of regionalized health services, and despite the premier's letter, the administration of this program remained under the auspices of the department of health.

The scps therefore turned to T.C. Routley and the cma for advice. Routley was mindful of the success of the cma's Committee of Seven in Ottawa during the Second World War, and he suggested that a seven-man Medical Advisory Committee be chosen to work closely with the premier-cum-health minister. Dr A.E. Archer of Alberta, a past-president of the cma and the association's special consultant in economics, was seconded to the new negotiating team. Douglas agreed to this concept on 24 January 1946.[16] In consequence, an informal and direct conduit to the premier was created which assisted the college in by-passing the HSPC.

On the other hand, rather than acceding to the profession's request that "immediate steps" be taken "to withdraw all administrative authority" from the HSPC,[17] on 27 February Douglas appointed Dr Cecil G. Sheps as acting chairman. The scps had already made no secret of its disapproval of Dr Mindel Sheps, and her husband's appointment on a pro tem basis exacerbated the tensions between the planning body and the profession.[18] Also of concern to the college was the administrative framework of the government's other step forward in the health services field – universal hospitalization insurance. The scps was on record as supporting the hospitalization program, despite its understandable misgivings about the adequacy of hospital resources to deal with the increased load that would result. Indeed, before the plan became operational the council of the scps approved a resolution favouring the extension of coverage to outpatient diagnostic services on the grounds that too many admissions to take advantage of insured in-patient tests were liable to occur. However, the legislation for state hospital insurance, introduced and passed during March and April 1946, contravened scps policy by vesting administrative authority in the HSPC, and the same enactment transferred direction of the social assistance medical care scheme from the department of health to the HSPC. Meeting at Moose Jaw on 26

May 1946, the doctors on the profession's Central Health Services Committee passed a motion requesting that all administration be delegated to a commission "similar to the one outlined in the letter from Premier T.C. Douglas ... to this committee dated 19th September 1945."[19] The new hospitalization program was to be funded by a flat rate levy of about $5 per person, although a family ceiling was added to soften the otherwise regressive incidence of this premium. It would take effect from 1 January 1947.

The SCPS reported on these various developments at the CMA annual meeting in late spring 1946. It stressed the college's preference for "centralized administrative control as opposed to regional control," and criticized the HSPC for promoting health services "along lines which are unsound." Certain personnel on the HSPC were "entirely lacking the confidence of the medical profession," and first on the SCPS's list of "Immediate Objectives and Aspirations" was the following: "To actively assist the Minister of Health in obtaining a qualified chairman for the Health Services Planning Commission, such chairman to be appointed chairman of the independent Administrative Commission upon its creation." As a reflection of fears arising from the Swift Current Medical Society's decision to proceed on its own terms, the list also included a statement of "Insistence on Health Region negotiation for medical services through official College of Physicians and Surgeons channels."[20]

In the event, the Swift Current doctors successfully bargained for fee-for-service payment at 75 percent of 1938 SCPS rates, and the medical insurance program went into effect on 1 July 1946. Doctors working in the region as well as official representatives of the SCPS and CMA praised the program generously, finding no disruption of doctor-patient relationships or other features of normal practice. Perhaps the most telling evidence of its acceptability came from the rise in number of GPs in the region: in 1946 twenty-one were active; by 1948 thirty-six GPs were kept busy.[21] Relations between the profession and the government were further improved when the Shepses departed and Dr Fred Mott was appointed chairman of the HSPC in the summer of 1946. Mott, an American who took his medical degree at McGill University, was formerly a high-ranking official in the US Public Health Service, and he was well received by the profession.

Thus, in 1947 there was a slight but perceptible lessening of tension between the SCPS and the government. The college did continue to remind Douglas of his promise that administrative authority would be passed to an independent commission. But the CCF's universal hospital insurance plan proved successful,[22] and two other steps towards complete prepayment of all services – the social assistance medical care scheme and Swift Curent program – had also won the co-operation of organized medicine. Indeed, if one includes the coverage provided through full-time and part-time service contracts between municipalities or towns and general practitioners, about one-third of the province's residents had access to medical care prepaid under local or provincial government auspices. Further change, however, would come on only a piecemeal basis until the 1960s.

THE MAKING OF POST-WAR
PROFESSIONAL POLICY

The spread of private-sector health care insurance had, to all intents and purposes, begun in the nineteenth century with lodge and industrial contract practice. In the wake of the Depression came a rash of urban-centred hospitalization programs which eventually grew into Blue Cross insurance plans sponsored by provincial hospital associations. At the outset, organized medicine looked upon these plans ambivalently: hospital insurance would give doctors greater clinical freedom, but lay control, as always, caused anxieties. In Saint John, New Brunswick, for example, the local medical society gave approval to a hospitalization scheme jointly sponsored by the civic Board of Trade and labour groups on condition that prepayment contracts not be extended to medical services.[23]

As indicated in chapter 5, the late 1930s also brought the first profession-sponsored plans for medical care. By co-opting the insurance concept, organized medicine could promote good public relations, acquire administrative expertise for any later pas de deux with the state, and – if all went well – forestall or redirect government intervention. These plans also provided guaranteed payment from employees in the low- and lower-middle income brackets. Jason A. Hannah, the young pathologist who was managing director of Associated Medical Services (AMS), summed matters up this way in 1938:

If the medical men leave the building to others they may well fear state-controlled medicine. If they themselves will evolve "health insurance" they can look forward to a system which will be of equal pride and value as their endeavours along scientific lines ... From this beginning the profession in Canada can build a system of medical economics which will not only improve their financial lot but will afford us the opportunity of cleaning our dwelling which is generally recognized as being long past due.[24]

A number of profession-sponsored plans were well established before the end of the Second World War. Medical Services Associated (MSA-BC), based originally in Vancouver and New Westminster, British Columbia, took on groups of ten or more employees whose incomes were under $2,400 per year, and it had more than 20,000 subscribers by 1945. The Manitoba Medical Services (MMS), incorporated in 1942, was – in the words of one prominent Winnipeg practitioner – "brought into being with a view to demonstrating to our people that medical coverage can be obtained at a satisfactory premium without government interference and regulation."[25] Although MMS was less successful than the British Columbia scheme, the Ontario plans flourished. By 1947 AMS had over 40,000 members and Windsor Medical Services covered 22,000 persons on various contracts. Income ceilings on participation were originally imposed by all the plans except AMS, a policy clearly designed to maintain the profession's price-discriminatory market position. Defending the concept of income ceilings in any private or public plan, Dr R.E. Valin, director of the Quebec-based Association des Médecins de langue française de l'Amérique du Nord, noted in 1944: "We feel that if others than this [lower] income level group receive services, the profession will be shamefully exploited. In the Associated Medical Services men with salaries of $15,000 have been treated for minimum fees."[26]

Despite the growth of these plans, many leaders of organized medicine continued to be uncertain about the future of voluntary insurance during the early 1940s. Actuary Hugh Wolfenden, commissioned by the CMA to survey the insurance problem, had warned of the need to put the experimental medical care plans on a solid footing: "Any failure would bring a disaster set-back to the voluntary movement and might provoke immediately the very type of government intervention which the plans were designed originally to divert."[27] But trepidation about the profession's own plans was more than financial. Even if small-scale experiments proved successful, there was as yet scant evidence that most of the population could be covered by them. There was also the issue of regionalization: if local medical societies became involved in local schemes, the profession's provincial negotiating position would be undermined. This concern led the Ontario Medical Association to attempt from 1940 on to weld Windsor Medical Services and AMS into a single, province-wide, OMA-controlled scheme. By 1943, however, it had become apparent that these plans were not likely to be united under OMA auspices. The fears of the OMA Board of Directors extended beyond regionalization to the broader problem of voluntary insurance under lay control:

For a long time we have observed the growing influence of non-medical organizations on the practice of medicine. In particular, there has been increasing activity on the part of commercial assurance companies who now set medical fees and sell medical services at thirty percent commission. Governments have entered the field of therapy. Industries have asked us to provide a working plan, and in its absence, have made their own arrangements, often unsatisfactory both from their standpoint and from ours.[28]

The Board of Directors concluded that the OMA should establish its own plan "as soon as possible": "If this is not done, we will be wrong on two counts. If a state plan is not instituted, we will more and more relinquish the practice of medicine to private interest. If a state plan is instituted, we will have failed to fully demonstrate our ability as a profession to manage our own affairs. There is no other alternative."[29] (Given this incisive analysis of the situation, it is not surprising that the OMA representatives were eventually the prime movers when the CMA undertook a policy shift away from state-administered health insurance in 1949. In 1943, however, the Board of Directors' call for a new profession-sponsored insurance plan was actually rejected by the OMA council on the grounds that a national health insurance program was already imminent.)[30]

Alarm over private-sector medical insurance arrangements was not confined to Ontario. In British Columbia the College of Physicians and Surgeons had remained active in the protection of professional interests after the state health insurance feud, and its economics committee served as negotiating agent with an assortment of medical service plans other than the profession's own operation – MSA-BC. Bodies such as the West Kootenay Power and Light Company, the Teachers' Provincial Federation, and the employees' organization of Cunningham-Western Drugs operated acceptable plans; they were under direction of a doctor approved by the college, adhered to the college fee schedule minus a percentage discount for overhead, provided comprehensive coverage, and operated on a non-profit basis so that doctors and insured persons alone would reap the benefits of prepayment for medical services. At least nine medical insurance agencies, however, were regarded as indirectly exploiting the profession by operating outside the college auspices and selling policies for a profit. Because these agencies reimbursed patients rather than paying the doctors directly, the college could not bring its bargaining strength to bear on them and instead called for a scheme of government regulation.[31] (More than a decade later, some BC medical leaders would support such indemnity arrangements in tacit recognition of the fact that they might actually improve the profession's position, because doctors, individually and as a cartel, were not contractually bound to a given fee schedule, nor were practitioners subject to direct administrative controls.)

The growth of private-sector plans outside professional auspices was, as we have seen, among the reasons why the CMA in 1943 had called for abolition of voluntary health insurance agencies in favour of any comprehensive state scheme. But during the period from 1944 to 1946, as the CMA's infatuation with national health insurance waned rapidly, more and more spokesmen for organized medicine flirted with the possibility that the profession-sponsored plans might be nurtured into an alternative to universal state-sponsored health insurance.[32] In chapter 5 it was noted that Dr William Magner, the editor of the *Ontario Medical Review*, was one of the most persuasive exponents of this view. In 1945 as the OMA wrestled with the logistics of starting its own plan, Magner toured the province in his new capacity as president-elect of the association and urged support for a medical services plan entirely under OMA control. The OMA by this time had administered the provincial medical relief plan for ten years, and in 1942 the government subsidy had been extended to old age pensioners, blind pensioners, and recipients of mothers' allowances. As Magner saw it, with a well-run OMA plan it was possible that government would eventually introduce legislation to put all medical insurance under the profession's administrative control.[33]

Administrators with the non-profit health insurance plans played a part in fostering the profession's faith in the private alternative. For example, in April 1945 Ruth Wilson, the executive director of the Maritime Hospital Service Association, gave a special address to the Halifax Medical Society on the desirability of a profession-sponsored medical insurance plan. After one and a half years, the Maritime Blue Cross program had over 90,000 subscribers, and Wilson urged organized medicine on the eastern seaboard to institute a parallel program.[34] As a direct result of this speech, an inquiry into "repayment Medical Schemes" was carried out by a committee of Halifax practitioners chaired by Dr R.O. Jones. This group was sceptical in its report,[35] but a few months later the Committee on Economics of the Nova Scotia Medical Society endorsed the concept of profession-approved insurance.[36]

Perhaps the most persistent advocate of the voluntary approach was Dr Jason A. Hannah, the managing director of Associated Medical Services. Hannah was a renegade of sorts in that he repeatedly rejected OMA demands for control of AMS; but his addresses to medical audiences during the Second World War and thereafter resounded with warnings about "state-controlled" health insurance.[37] Hannah contended that rather than accepting a government scheme, the profession should bank on gradual growth of its own voluntary plans. Those who could not afford to enrol in private schemes should be covered separately under government arrangements which would "remove the burden of the indigent from the shoulders of the profession and spread it over the whole population through taxation."[38]

By 1946 professional opinion was beginning to swing in that direction. The failure of the Dominion-Provincial Conference on Post-War Reconstruction made it clear that a full-scale national health insurance plan would be delayed indefinitely. The CMA Committee on Economics had already suggested that medical services for the self-pay group should be the last item covered in the stepwise implementation of a state plan; and it now recommended that each provincial division should try "to meet public demand ... wherever it exists by providing a plan of prepaid medical care sponsored by the medical profession."[39]

Apart from these domestic developments, happenings on the international scene also influenced the evolution of organized medicine's policy during the post-war period. From 1927[40] the *CMAJ* had carried a "London Letter" which kept the Canadian profession posted on happenings in the British medical arena – including the political battles over the National Health Service (NHS). Editorial commentary in the *CMAJ* from 1944 to 1949 traced the planning and implementation of the NHS with distinct disapproval.[41] While the British Medical Association's travails steered Canadian doctors away from state intervention on any sweeping scale, American Medical Association policy nudged them towards use of profession-controlled plans as an instrument to deflect government action. The AMA had generally taken a dim view of voluntary prepayment for medical services, linking consumer-sponsored schemes to past patterns of lodge practice and dangers of lay control. But with the Wagner-Murray-Dingell health insurance bill moving through US Senate committee hearings in 1946, AMA spokesmen stressed their approval of private voluntary insurance under professional auspices as a preferable alternative to the proposed legislation.[42]

Canada's sister state in the Commonwealth – Australia – also was in the throes of a highly publicized health care skirmish at the time. The federal council of the British Medical Association in Australia had declared itself opposed to plans for an Australian state medical service, calling instead for government-subsidized enrolment in private insurance schemes; and a *CMAJ* editorial in June 1949 offered sympathy to the Australian profession.[43] Eventually, organized medicine launched legal action against the government, and the 1949 National Health Service act was declared ultra vires by the Australian

Supreme Court on the grounds that it violated a clause in the constitution barring civil conscription during peacetime.

The capstone to these international developments came from the World Medical Association (WMA). T.C. Routley, by now very much a medical elder statesman, had been a member of the commission that set up the World Health Organization, and was especially prominent in WMA affairs. From its inauguration in 1946 the WMA pondered questions of universal concern to organized medicine and the post-war push for reorganization of health services in many nations was among them. The WMA adopted a manifesto on "Medical Social Security" in 1948 which contained several important points.

The manifesto addressed the profession's technical autonomy concerns by stating: "Where medical service is to be subjected to control, this control should be exercised by physicians." There were to be no restrictions on where or how physicians chose to practice. So far as socio-economic autonomy went, the manifesto advised: "It is not in the public interest that physicians should be full-time salaried servants of the government or social security bodies." In a statement that was somewhat at odds with either budgetary discipline or actuarial principles, the WMA indicated that "Remuneration of medical services ought not to depend directly on the financial condition of the insurance organization." And, to maintain professional market strength and independence, preservation of a private sector was implied by the pronouncement that compulsory health insurance plans should apply only to those "who are unable to make their own arrangements for medical care." This document was promptly approved by the CMA executive committee.[44]

This international impetus was abetted by the ongoing spread of the physician-sponsored plans. Having failed to bring AMS and the Windsor plan under its auspices, the OMA established Physicians' Services Incorporated (PSI) in 1947.[45] PSI enrolled 20,000 members in its first year of operation and was controlled by a board of governors on which the OMA had a majority of representatives.

Again Saskatchewan was a special case. Prairie collectivism had spawned an entity most doctors mistrusted – medical services co-operatives. Of these consumer-controlled agencies, the largest was the Mutual Medical and Hospital Services Association of Saskatoon, founded in 1939. By 1946 this co-op had 16,000 members. A smaller co-op of the same vintage was based in Regina. The Regina co-op had originally arranged to hire eight doctors on salary, but under pressure from the Regina Medical Society the eight practitioners withdrew. At the same time the society itself started a small doctor-sponsored plan on a fee-for-service basis. The Regina co-op accordingly abandoned its plans for a salaried clinic and elected to run a straightforward reimbursement scheme within the extant framework of private fee-for-service practice. The operating policies of the two organizations were sufficiently similar that by 1949 the 6,000-member Regina co-op agreed to merge with the smaller doctor-sponsored plan. The resulting agency was known as Group Medical Services (GMS), and had equal representation from consumers and organized medicine on its board of directors.[46]

The political manoeuvring in Saskatoon was less subtle. The profession had given thought to establishing its own prepaid medical care plan in 1939, but after consultation with the Saskatoon co-op it agreed not to proceed on condition that a partnership of sorts exist between the doctors and the consumers' insurance agency. According to spokesmen for the Saskatoon Medical Society, the co-op reneged on this agreement and for four years refused to appoint "a mutually acceptable medical advisory committee" to liaise with the profession. The co-op secretariat had also antagonized organized medicine by attacking the profession in a variety of public forums during 1944 and 1945. In 1946 the 16,000-member co-op announced a million-dollar plan to set up a large clinic with salaried medical staff in Saskatoon, together with a variety of satellite operations in neighbouring centres. Medical Services (Saskatoon) Incorporated (MS(S)I) was therefore launched in 1946 to compete with the co-op and pre-empt this ambitious program.[47] As the directors of MS(S)I later wrote in a confidential paper, the consumer-sponsored plan had begun "to grow in strength to a sufficient degree to completely cast aside the advice and support of organized medicine and, along with what appeared to be strong offers of assistance from the Provincial Government, threatened to completely jeopardize the future of prepaid medical care in the province, and the welfare of the profession in general."[48] Doctors in northern Saskatchewan embarked on a concerted campaign to encourage their patients to enrol in their new agency.[49] By 1950 MS(S)I had 35,000 subscribers and the consumer-sponsored plan was losing ground rapidly.

In June 1947 the CMA Committee on Economics convened a meeting in Winnipeg of those involved in the profession's prepaid medical care plans. Representatives from Ontario, Saskatchewan, Manitoba, and British Columbia attended. The conference left no doubt on one score: politically, the plans were in a race with public demand and possible government responses. And as the Saskatchewan representatives remarked:

It was the threat of a compulsory plan in BC in 1935 that brought the profession in that province to its feet in one organized group to sponsor BC Medical Services Associated; it was the threat in Saskatoon which led to the setting up of MSI, and it was the general demand throughout the country which was having an influence on the political atmosphere, which made the development of these medically-sponsored plans a matter of urgency.[50]

The Winnipeg conventioneers discussed many aspects of the medical services prepayment plans. They formally recommended that any plans endorsed by the profession should be under joint lay and medical control, "but also so set up that at all times control of matters concerned with the purely professional side of the plan be determined by the medical members."[51] It was further deemed desirable to create an umbrella body with a view to standardizing insurance contracts sufficiently that the profession-sponsored plans would be more appealing to corporations with country-wide operations. A national charter obviously offered another advantage: the federal government would have less reason to enter the health insurance field.

On one score, however, government intervention was welcome. Prior to 1945 only Ontario had operated a provincial medical welfare program. As noted above, Saskatchewan introduced a social assistance medical plan before the war's end, using the Heagerty cost estimate of $9.50 per capita in the first year of operation. Doctors billed the insurance fund according to the 1942 fee schedule of the Saskatchewan College of Physicians and Surgeons, taking an initial payment of half-tariff. For the first year the final settlement was 77.5 percent of full tariff for all accounts rendered, but with increasing volume of service the settlements on the second year of operation fell to 59 percent. The SCPS therefore requested that the prorating of accounts be dropped, with implementation of a straight fee-for-service scheme at full payment of the new 1947 fee schedule. The government refused these terms and eventually accepted the profession's alternative demand of a substantial increment in the per capita payments to the insurance fund.[52]

Although the administration of the Saskatchewan plan remained in government hands, in the late 1940s two other western provinces initiated social assistance medical care programs that closely followed the Ontario precedent in delegating public funds and full responsibility to organized medicine. Alberta's plan began in 1947.[53] In British Columbia partial coverage of those in receipt of social allowances was extended in 1945 to blind and old age pensioners; and in March 1949 all these services were consolidated into a single BC provincial plan with per capita funding at $14.50.[54] The *CMAJ* saluted the BC arrangements: "It is gratifying to report that another

TABLE 4

Composition of Boards of Directors of Doctor-
Sponsored Medical Care Plans

Plan	Total Members	Medical	Non-Medical
Maritime Medical Care	9	6	3
PSI (Ontario)	10	7	3
Windsor Medical Services	10	7	3
Manitoba Medical Services	21	14	7
MS(S)I	20	10	10
GMS (Regina)	14	7	7
MSI (Alberta)	5	1	4
MSA-BC	8	2	6

Source: M.G. Taylor, *The Administration of Health Insurance in Canada* (London: Oxford University Press 1956), 207, table 33.

Province has thus recognized its obligation to finance medical care for the medically indigent, and that the administration has been entrusted to the profession."[55]

Even as coverage of those in receipt of state allowances became more widespread, the national roster of profession-sponsored plans was rounded out by two new starts in 1948. Maritime Medical Care Incorporated, based in Halifax, was controlled by organized medicine in Nova Scotia. Medical Services (Alberta) Incorporated (MSI (Alberta)), the other 1948 addition, shared with MSA-BC the distinction of a governing structure where non-medical members were in a majority. The lay directors of MSI (Alberta) were elected from among subscribers at the annual meeting, and representatives of both employers and employees sat on the MSA-BC board because of that plan's base in large groups of industrial employees. (However, another BC plan set up in 1954 to cover individuals and small groups had a clear medical majority on its board.)

Our consideration of developments shaping CMA policy would be incomplete without attention to the income status of the average private practitioner. As events in the Depression illustrated, the profession's enthusiasm for state intervention understandably tended to vary inversely with medical incomes and the precentage of accounts paid for services rendered. In 1941 Dominion Bureau of Statistics data showed that physicians and surgeons in private practice had average gross annual earnings of $5,126, which fell to $3,076 after expense deductions.[56] By 1946 the net annual earnings from professional practice had more than doubled to $6,884, with the result that mean *after-tax* income from all sources was actually higher than gross income had been in 1941. By 1949 mean net professional earnings had climbed to $8,532, an increment of another 24 percent.[57] Clearly the economic benefits to doctors from national health insurance were no longer as important as they had been during the 1930s and early 1940s.

THE 1949 POLICY STATEMENT

In the light of the foregoing, it is easy to understand the CMA's 1949 decision to add a specific and innovative policy statement to its 1944 principles of health insurance. A growing wariness of government action; establishment of state social assistance medical care schemes under professional administrative control; the spread of physician-sponsored and physician-controlled prepayment plans; steadily rising incomes; international evidence that private insurance, with or without government-subsidized enrolment for low-income groups, could be an alternative to state health insurance – all these factors contributed to the CMA policy shift. There had been one unwritten rule dating back to the late 1930s, however: namely, that the CMA should never propose a definite plan for government intervention but rather limit itself to setting down guiding principles. The catalyst for abandonment of that stategem was the appearance of a new federal initiative in health services.

In December 1946 Paul Martin had been transferred from secretary of state to minister of national health and welfare. Martin's commitment to national health insurance was well known and in late 1947 T.C. Routley presciently decided that an overture should be made to the health ministry with a view to re-establishing an advisory body like the CMA's Committee of Seven.[58] Dr G.D.W. Cameron, the deputy minister of health, put Routley off.[59] On 21 January 1948, however, Martin contacted Routley to confirm that they should meet. The minister left no doubt that he planned to proceed with stepwise implementation of the so-called Green Book proposals on post-war health and social security that had been rejected at the Dominion-Provincial Conference of 1945–6.[60] By March 1948 regular meetings were in progress between senior CMA personnel and the health ministry mandarins.[61]

A valuable addition to the CMA lobbying team was Dr Arthur D. Kelly. Kelly was a friend of T.C. Routley; he had served as secretary of the Ontario Medical Association from 1938 and in 1946 had joined the CMA staff as deputy secretary-general. Whereas Routley was imposing and courtly, Kelly brought a more relaxed tenor to relations between the ministry and the CMA. A steady flow of correspondence on a first-name basis ensured that the profession would be kept up-to-date with any federal policy proposals.

Paul Martin's behind-the-scenes work came to fruition on 18 May, when Prime Minister Mackenzie King announced a program of federal health grants to the provinces totalling $30 million per year. This program had three major objectives: to expand and improve hospital facilities; to provide free diagnosis and treatment for selected disorders, including tuberculosis, cancer, venereal disease, and mental illness; and to survey the health status and health care needs of Canadians. Having enlisted professional co-operation at the outset, Martin continued his efforts to allay medical fears. Speaking to the Royal College of Physicians and Surgeons in Ottawa on 27 November 1948, for example, the health minister stated: "I can assure you that no action taken by the present Government under this or under any other program to improve health services in Canada will stifle or destroy the liberty of the individual doctor ... Regimentation of the doctor would be ruinous to health progress."[62]

Dr William Magner, now president of the CMA after a successful term as 1946-7 OMA chief, visited each provincial division during the autumn of 1948 and spoke in support of the health grants program. However, Magner's endorsement did not extend to Paul Martin's suggestion that this latest initiative cleared the way for national health insurance. The CMA president warned of the possibility that a truly independent and non-political administrative commission could never be constituted under a government plan. Alluding to "the lack of enthusiasm for schemes of compulsory national health insurance" in British, American, "and, if I read my colleagues aright," Canadian medicine, he stated:

Motives of self-interest are powerful, and it is quite true that doctors fear, under any such plan, bureaucratic control, regimentation, and curtailment of professional liberty. But these things are feared, less because of their effect on the personal happiness and well-being of the doctor, than because they would inevitably lead to a deterioration in the quality of medical work, to a loss in spirit and initiative which has been responsible for dramatic advances in medical knowledge and medical skill during the past fifty, and particularly during the past twenty-five years.

To avoid the dangers of a state plan, Magner proposed a simple solution. Blue Cross hospital insurance and profession-sponsored medical insurance could meet most of the demand from middle-income groups in five to ten years. For the low-income group and those on pensions or welfare a precedent already existed in the form of the government subsidy paid to the OMA-administered medical welfare plan, and this subsidy could just as well be given to PSI instead. If the same principle were extended across the nation to the voluntary non-profit insurance plans operated under the auspices of the hospital and medical associations, a compulsory state program would never be needed.[63]

By 13 June, when 100 delegates convened at the Bessborough Hotel in Saskatoon for the CMA's 1949 annual meeting, the Committee on Economics had already decided that the association's health insurance policy must be revised. Each provincial division had been notified that it should prepare a statement of opinion commenting on the CMA's 1944 principles of health insurance and the 1946 protocol for gradual implementation of any state health insurance plan. Dr V.F. Stock, chairman of the economics committee, reminded delegates that certain of the 1944 principles could be construed as a tacit endorsement of state-administered health insurance – as in fact had been recognized when they were drafted. And he called on the CMA council to take a clearer stand on the issue of state health insurance.[64] Following Stock's comments, representatives of each division spoke. Their views are synopsized below.

British Columbia (Dr Frank Turnbull): The BC government had introduced a universal hospitalization insurance program earlier in the year. Although the implementation of the program had not gone smoothly, "from our point of view we feel that the initiation of compulsory hospital insurance as a part of health insurance has been a good thing." Turnbull did not take a firm stand on either government medical care insurance or the possible role of the profession-sponsored plans as an alternative.

Alberta (Drs Morley Young and Harold Orr): Hospital costs were the real problem. Dr Orr moved that the CMA "advocate the institution of a hospital insurance plan to include all the people in Canada," with details to be determined by the executive committee.

Saskatchewan (Dr J. Lloyd Brown): The 1944 principles "will hold good," and the CMA "should not go beyond the advocacy of sound principles" because interprovincial differences made a uniform national plan unworkable. "I do not believe many of us consider that the voluntary plans will be a complete answer, but they are educating the public to certain sound principles that must be included in a scheme of any kind."

Manitoba (Dr H.S. Evans): The Manitoba Medical Service was now "on a well-established working basis." The profession would "like to see it extended to indigents and those without incomes" in all parts of the province.

Ontario (Dr E. Kirk Lyon): The OMA strongly favoured the idea that the CMA should adopt a specific policy and publicize it widely. The 1944 principles were "indefinite and out of date." Given the precedent of the medical welfare plan in Ontario, the OMA recommended several new principles. In the light of later events, the most important were as follows:

The Canadian Medical Association, having approved the adoption of the principle of health insurance, and having seen demonstrated the practical application of this principle in the establishment of voluntary pre-paid medical care plans, now proposes: A. The establishment and/or extension of these plans to cover Canada. B. The right of every Canadian citizen to insure under these plans. C. The provision by the state of the Health Insurance Premium, in whole or in part, for persons who are adjudged to be unable to provide these premiums for themselves.

Quebec (Dr Vance Ward): There was considerable divergence of opinion within the Quebec medical profession, including "a considerable body of opinion" in favour of doctor-sponsored prepayment plans and "a large group" that felt "the wisest course is to accept [state] health insurance as inevitable and to try to mould the legislation as best we can." Private insurance alone "will never be the whole answer." Compulsory insurance for low-income patients might be applied to hospital care and in-patient medical services, so that office practice could continue without major upheavals. "The time has come, we feel, to move on from general principles to the sponsoring of a definite plan."

New Brunswick (Dr Arthur F. van Wart): "We feel that a voluntary prepaid plan is not the whole answer."

Nova Scotia (Dr Norman H. Gosse): The provincial government was "far removed from what might be called socialism." The government had recently decided to implement a medical welfare plan along the lines of the Ontario program, with the profession itself in charge of administration. The doctors' medical service plan was already being sold to groups, and the Nova Scotia profession hoped to extend it soon to individuals. Unemployed persons could also be covered if the government paid their premiums in whole or in part.

Representatives from Australia and Great Britain then outlined developments in their countries. Because of the diversity of viewpoints a committee was struck to draft a policy statement. Dr Jack F.C. Anderson, the incoming CMA president, chaired this group, and each province except Prince Edward Island was represented. That same evening the committee presented a set of six new principles to the general council, and matched these with a preamble that stated, among other things, that government had "a responsibility for ensuring that adequate medical facilities are available to every member of the community, whether or not he can afford the full cost." The preamble was accepted, but the principles themselves were rejected as too vague. For example, on voluntary insurance, the committee's draft policy statement simply noted: "In the field of medical care we strongly advocate the continued expansion of prepaid medical care plans." Several hours of debate followed.

At 1:15 in the morning of 14 June 1949, when the profession's parliament finally adjourned, the OMA position had carried the day. The statement from the Ontario division, quoted above, was adopted verbatim and formed the meat of the new doctrine to whose general tenets organized medicine would cling for the next decade and a half. Another statement was added, as follows:

Additional services should come into existence by stages, the first and most urgent stage being the meeting of the costs of hospitalization for every citizen of Canada. The basic part of that cost should be met by individual contribution, the responsible government body bearing, in whole or in part, the cost for those persons who are unable to provide the contribution themselves.[65]

This policy was a master-stroke. Prior to 1949 the CMA had called for administration of health insurance by an independent, non-political commission; the 1942 principles had specified a majority of doctors, and the last revision in 1944 simply called for medical representation, while noting that "matters of professional detail should be administered by committees representative of the professional groups concerned." The extension of the profession-sponsored plans would mean that both administration and "matters of professional detail" could remain largely in the hands of private medical practitioners. Indeed, since the new policy called for the state to pay premiums for those who could not afford them, public funds were to be handed over to prepayment organizations that were closely intertwined with the provincial medical associations to ensure that doctors received remuneration for all work done among indigent and low-income groups. And, with only those in lower-income brackets enrolled on a compulsory basis, the voluntary nature of the plans could still be held out as a political selling point to the public and legislators.

The CMA's emphasis on hospital insurance as the first step in any plan was nothing new: this point had been accepted by the CMA council since 1946. Government hospitalization plans had recently been introduced in British Columbia and Saskatchewan, and Alberta was known to be contemplating similar action. By suggesting that universal hospital coverage was "urgent," the CMA implicitly encouraged further government initiatives in this field. However, given its vague wording, the CMA statement could certainly be construed as favourable to the concept that the hospital associations should emulate organized medicine and request subsidized enrolment in Blue Cross plans as an alternative to any government-administered scheme. In any event, it is obvious that if government followed the CMA's advice and attended to hospital insurance first, then organized medicine would have additional time to expand its own insurance agencies into a truly credible alternative to a state-administered medical care program.

Lastly, it should be noted that the CMA continued to call for hospital and medical insurance on a contributory basis. The health insurance fund, consisting of premiums paid by subscribers and by governments on behalf of those unable to pay, would be safe from the competition for tax dollars that would ensue if all funds were not expressly earmarked for health costs and pooled separately. For medical services specifically, some resistance from both consumers and government could be expected if, say, an increase in the fee schedule led to a need for higher premium rates. Nevertheless this policy still portended much less in the way of direct economic controls and collective bargaining than would inevitably be the case in a government-administered plan.

From here organized medicine would press forward with renewed vigour to expand its private-sector prepayment agencies and ward off third-party mediation that might diminish professional market strength and autonomy. Dr Magner's valedictory presidential address to the 1949 CMA convention was a sign of the future – a stirring defence of private insurance that was unambiguously bellicose:

Socialized Medicine means a crushing burden on the taxpayer. Socialized Medicine means a harassed medical profession, deprived of all that now attracts clever and highminded men and women to a medical career. Socialized medicine means an inferior medical service, staffed, in time, by inferior men.

Socialized Medicine is the first step, and a long step, towards the Gehenna of the Welfare State.[66]

THE CONSOLIDATION PHASE

A 1949 Gallup poll asked Canadians whether they would approve or disapprove of a National Health Plan whereby a flat rate monthly payment brought assurance of complete medical and hospital care by the federal government. As in 1944, 80 percent approved, and the percentage disapproving had fallen by three points since then. State health insurance was clearly still a live issue, and the medical profession would have to push ahead rapidly if the profession-controlled plans were to be nurtured into a feasible alternative to any state plan.

A crucial step in this strategy would be obtaining a national charter for an umbrella organization co-ordinating the various regional and provincial plans. This step, it will be recalled, had been contemplated since 1947. Armed in late 1949 with a $10,000 special expenses account, the CMA Committee on Economics set about investigating the possibility of incorporating such a national body. Excursions to Ottawa proved fruitless, and in any case the Quebec division of the CMA refused to endorse the plan for a national charter. The Quebec Hospital Association offered coverage of in-hospital medical and surgical services as one of the options in its Blue Cross hospitalization scheme. This insurance, declared the Quebec division's leaders, was sufficient.[67] The CMA's economics committee refused to be deterred, especially as there was some concern that at the 1950 Dominion-Provincial conference the federal government might renew its offer of financial assistance to the provinces for a state-run health insurance scheme. As the committee's chairman put it: "We require a corporation which can function all over Canada and which could not be disregarded by any government. We must at all costs retain our professional freedom and in so doing, these voluntary agencies will form an important factor."[68]

By June of 1951 the CMA was able to announce the formation of Trans-Canada Medical Services, its long-sought umbrella body. While not yet formally incorporated, TCMS included the Nova Scotia plan, MSI (Alberta), PSI (Ontario), MSA-BC, the two Saskatchewan plans, and the Manitoba Medical Service. The problem remained, however, of a plan for Quebec and for Maritime provinces other than Nova Scotia.

In June 1952 at its first annual meeting TCMS appointed Mr C. Howard Shillington, the managing director of MS(S)I, executive director of the national organization. Shillington was instructed to explore the possibilities of extending the TCMS network to Quebec, New Brunswick, Newfoundland, and Prince Edward Island. He met first with the executive of the Quebec division of the CMA and made little headway. Shillington later commented: "Made up principally of oldtime specialists, closely connected with the university and large hospitals and used to receiving private fees somewhat beyond the level of the average physician, these people were not only conservative in their outlook, but almost antagonistic to the idea of any type of plan in which the physician would be financially involved."[69] Negotiations in the Maritimes proved more productive. Since the Maritime Hospital Service Association offered insurance against in-patient medical care costs, it was admitted as an associate member of the TCMS in January 1953. There had also been some discussion with L'Association des Médecins de langue française du Canada to determine whether francophone practitioners in Quebec would prove more amenable to participation in TCMS than the anglophone-dominated Quebec division of the CMA was. According to Shillington, there was a misunderstanding, due in part to "language difficulties," and a Quebec-based prepaid medical care plan – Les Services de Santé – was not brought into the national association. Finally in June 1953 the Quebec Hospital Service Association applied to become a member of TCMS. Like its Maritime counterpart, the Quebec Blue Cross scheme provided only in-patient medical services insurance, but since the Quebec division of the CMA seemed satisfied with this limited coverage, a good case could be made for accepting the application. The obvious drawback was that neither of the Blue Cross plans was founded or controlled by organized medicine. A stormy debate ensued at the TCMS meeting between the purists who wanted only doctor-controlled plans in the organization, and the pragmatists who felt that a national umbrella for the doctor-sponsored plans must include representation from as many provinces as possible to bolster its credibility. The pragmatists prevailed; the Quebec Blue Cross agency was admitted as a full voting member, and the Maritime agency was upgraded from associate to full-member status.[70]

During the early 1950s the profession's anti-government stance was strengthened by an assortment of factors. CMA spokesmen launched their own Cold War against "socialized medicine," touring the provinces to warn the rank-and-file against "enforced subservience to either the false god of paternalism or to the equally dangerous one of bureaucratic power."[71] CMA representatives inspected the National Health Service in Britain and returned to offer gloomy assessments.[72] More vitriolic attacks on Britain's NHS came in the

TABLE 5

Growth of Selected Non-Profit Medical Care Plans, 1951–9

Plan	1951	1955	1959
MSA-BC	190,415	297,658	467,939
MSI (Alberta)	31,833	116,127	427,207
MS(S)I	48,893	122,191	211,514
MMS	118,210	219,243	346,046
PSI	218,147	584,043	1,246,221
QHSA	–	588,414	680,895
MMC	44,622	64,272	128,990
Total persons in TCMP plans*	775,165	2,403,351	4,023,216
Percent of Canadian population covered	5.5	15.2	22.7

*Includes plans as listed plus others as follows (date of first inclusion in total in parentheses): MSI-BC (1955); GMS (1951); Windsor Medical Services (1951); Maritime Blue Cross (1955).
Note: See C. Howard Shillington, The Road to Medicare in Canada (Toronto: Del Graphics 1972), 202–3 for complete statistics.

early 1950s during a large-scale advertising campaign organized by the American Medical Association,[73] and some of this sentiment naturally spilled across the border. When a favourable analysis of the NHS appeared in the 1952 Manitoba Medical Review, the director of federal health insurance studies promptly wrote to CMA headquarters suggesting that either the article should be published in the CMAJ, or, failing this, the federal department of health and welfare could provide the CMA with reprints "for wide distribution" to the medical community.[74] T.C. Routley firmly rejected both options.[75]

At that, there was evidence that the profession's strategy might be successful. In accordance with the CMA's 1949 policy statement, the Nova Scotia government had set up a public assistance health scheme in 1950 using Maritime Medical Care as the administrative agency. Trans-Canada Medical Services grew rapidly, and was eventually incorporated as Trans-Canada Medical Plans (TCMP). At the consortium's formation in 1951, 775,165 persons were covered as subscribers or dependants. By 1955, 2,403,351 persons were on the TCMP lists, amounting to 15.2 percent of the population (see table 5). MSI-BC, a new British Columbia plan for individuals and small groups, joined the TCMP family in 1954. TCMP allowed interprovincial portability of coverage and services co-ordination, which in turn made it possible for the consortium to bid for national employers' medical insurance contracts.[76]

In 1952 the CMA public relations committee launched a low-key campaign in favour of the private alternative and found firm support in the business community. By late 1953 the Canadian Chamber of Commerce had already gone on record as opposing any form of compulsory health insurance or state medicine.[77] Encouragement was also provided by the reports tendered in the wake of the federal health grants program. Each province except Newfoundland (which did not join Confederation until 1949) had surveyed its health services and offered comments on how best to expand and improve them. The actual bodies set up to discharge this function had included representatives of provincial medical and hospital associations in eight of ten provinces. Ontario and Quebec offered no comments on implementation of health insurance; British Columbia temporized; but Manitoba, Nova Scotia, New Brunswick, and Prince Edward Island endorsed the CMA proposals for subsidized enrolment in profession-sponsored medical care plans and suggested that the same principle be extended to promote coverage by Blue Cross hospitalization schemes. Only in Alberta and Saskatchewan did the reports call for a state-administered scheme in line with the 1945 federal proposals. Because of the nature of their preparation, none of those reports was de facto government policy,[78] but they served notice that the profession's counsel was being heard in high places.

So far as official party policy went, during the 1953 federal election George Drew and the Progressive Conservatives promised a plan of health insurance that would utilize existing commercial and voluntary agencies. The Liberals under Louis St Laurent coasted back to power with an ample majority, but their commitment to action on health insurance was limited. The Liberal party platform advertised support for only "a policy of contributory health insurance to be administered by the provinces when most of the provinces were ready to join in a nationwide scheme."[79] There was also an encouraging sign for organized medicine on the provincial front. Although the Alberta health services survey group had endorsed state-administered health insurance, during 1954-5 the Social Credit government explicitly rejected the concept of a full-fledged state plan and made overtures to organized medicine concerning the possibility of universal coverage through government-subsidized enrolment in MSI (Alberta). An agreement to this effect was actually drafted in 1955,[80] but never applied because of opposition from investor-owned insurance companies and financial constraints.

The strength of the CMA meanwhile continued to grow. As noted in chapter 5, in 1945 the total membership was 9,043 but only 5,464 were dues-paying members. By 1955 paid CMA membership had climbed to 10,000, and the association had a reserve fund of over

$250,000. That year, the CMA Committee on Economics completed a review of the 1944 principles of health insurance and 1949 policy statement, endeavouring to determine whether any changes should be made in these key documents. Dr T.C. Routley was about to step down as CMA general secretary after thirty-three years of service, and he provided the committee members with a detailed commentary to guide them in their revisions. Routley's exegesis noted with satisfaction that the threat of a salaried state medical service had receded: "in this connection the swing of the pendulum has to some degree been influenced by the experience of other countries." He suggested that the CMA principles were still valid in most respects, and identified no major conflict with the thrust of the 1949 policy statement. Routley also emphasized that the call in 1949 for the state to pay premiums on behalf of those unable to pay for themselves, "in no manner suggests Governmental introduction of a health insurance plan. In fact, it proposes an alternative to any Governmental plan by national coverage through Voluntary Plans."[81]

At the 1955 CMA council meeting, where Routley was honoured with the presidency of the association, the two documents were therefore melded to produce a coherent doctrine for stepwise expansion of private health insurance.[82] With its basic strategy reaffirmed and Trans-Canada Medical Plans growing steadily, organized medicine now waited and watched the horizon for signs of government action. A federal hospital insurance program was the first shadow to fall across the professional barricades in the latter half of the 1950s.

THE NATIONAL HOSPITAL
INSURANCE PLAN

As already noted, Saskatchewan and British Columbia had introduced universal state-administered hospital insurance plans in 1947 and 1949, respectively. Whereas Saskatchewan had used a municipal collection system for the hospital insurance premiums, British Columbia attempted to implement both payroll deductions and individual direct-pay arrangements for the collection of premiums. The administrative problems arising from this system became a public scandal that contributed to the defeat of the Liberal-Conservative coalition government in 1952. The new Social Credit government first attempted to streamline the collection system and then on 1 April 1954 abolished premiums altogether, funding the program instead with an increase in retail sales tax. A co-insurance charge of $1 per hospital day was maintained.[83]

In contrast to the centrally administered plans in British Columbia and Saskatchewan, Alberta's Social Credit government initiated a system of subsidies on 1 July 1950. Each municipality made its own decision as to participation, ratepayers contributing via increases in property taxes and those who did not own property paying a fixed annual premium. The local hospital would then qualify for a subsidy from the provincial treasury.[84] Yet another variation in provincial programs was offered by Newfoundland's famous "Cottage Hospitals." Serving 1,500 communities scattered along 7,000 miles of coastline, these provincially owned small hospitals were usually staffed by general practitioners, who received a basic salary. As in the municipal doctor programs of western Canada, the GPs were able to supplement their incomes by performing surgery on a fee-for-service basis. Families paid a premium of $10 each towards the costs of the program, and almost half of Newfoundland's population prepaid its hospital and medical services on this basis.[85]

Apart from these foci of government coverage, voluntary hospital insurance had proved even more popular than the various private-sector medical care prepayment plans. By 1952 almost 5.5 million Canadians were insured against the costs of hospitalization through one means or another. By far the two most popular modes of private coverage were Blue Cross plans offered by the provincial hospital associations and a host of schemes offered by the insurance industry on a for-profit basis. The problem, however, was one of who was covered and how they were covered. Individual contracts were sold at relatively high rates, and unless one were fortunate enough to enrol as part of an employees' group, the costs of hospital insurance could prove prohibitive. Nor did the Blue Cross or commercial plans necessarily offer comprehensive coverage. A long-term illness or a serious accident could still destroy a family's savings. Given the success of Saskatchewan's program and, eventually, British Columbia's plan, extension of government-sponsored hospital insurance to other provinces seemed highly probable. A major stumbling block was the need for federal-provincial financial agreements that would make such a plan feasible and appealing to all the provinces. And as the failure of the 1946 Dominion-Provincial Conference had proved, these agreements were not always easy to come by.

There was no agreement, moreover, on how government intervention should be structured. In a stance that neatly paralleled the CMA's position on medical services the Canadian Hospital Association (CHA) called for government to limit its role to paying the premiums for those who could not otherwise afford to join the Blue Cross plans. The CHA's viewpoint was hardly surprising. Many of the nation's great hospitals had been founded through religious or capitalist philanthropy, and while state support came increasingly into play to build or maintain hospital facilities, administration had remained with more or less independent governing boards of directors and executives. The situation of the hospitals was therefore somewhat analogous to that of the medical profession. Both were vitally important social institutions whose terms of existence owed much to government intervention; both were nonetheless jealous of their autonomy and sought to retain a blend of private- and public-sector funding that would obviate competition for tax dollars, minimize accountability to third parties, and reinforce rather than alter the status quo. As well, the Catholic Hospital Conference, wary of the secular tide of statism and proud of its long tradition of Christian service, looked upon the prospect of a state health insurance plan with definite unease.[86]

Investor-owned insurance interests, backed by the Canadian Chamber of Commerce, offered another variation on the subsidy theme: government should support enrolment in *all* private plans. Whereas the Blue Cross plans operated like the profession-sponsored medicare schemes on a non-profit basis, investor-owned carriers were registering premium/payment surpluses of 30 percent and more on their contracts for health services. In essence, they were asking the provincial and federal governments to underwrite the underwriters and augment the industry's profit margins by paying premiums for low-income and high-risk groups. This option had been weighed during the mid 1950s by Ontario legislators, and dismissed by Premier Leslie Frost as "a bad deal for the government."[87]

In any event, pressure mounted for the federal government to take more definitive action than the subsidy route allowed. Interprovincial inequities in hospital services had been clearly shown by the federally funded surveys earlier in the 1950s. And at least in the minds of health minister Paul Martin and his staff, the health grants had been made as a step towards implementation of a national prepayment program for medical and hospital services. Organized labour encouraged this view. The TLCC and CCL amalgamated in 1956 to form a national body with over 1 million members, and in its first brief to Ottawa the new Canadian Labour Congress reiterated the union movement's support for a comprehensive health insurance system to cover all Canadians on an equal footing. Perhaps most important, Ontario, Saskatchewan, Alberta, and British Columbia all favoured federal action to provide them with funding for their comparatively high hospitalization expenditures.

For organized medicine the issue of state-administered hospital insurance was less clear-cut than medical services insurance. Both the BC and the Saskatchewan divisions of the CMA had come to appreciate that universal hospital insurance under state auspices could actually augment rather than diminish the clinical freedom of private practitioners. And since 1949 the CMA had been on record as supporting the concept that hospitalization insurance for all Canadians was the first priority if and when the federal government entered the pre-payment arena to promote universal coverage. On the other hand, in 1952 the CMA general council voted against a resolution presented in support of universal hospital insurance.[88] The CMA's caution in part reflected an awareness that the association should not make pronouncements that could be construed as undermining the Blue Cross schemes. After all, the CHA position very closely paralleled that taken by the CMA. And as T.C. Routley remarked in 1954, "some Canadian citizens, particularly those interested in hospitalization, felt that the CMA had gone too far in speaking for the hospital authorities" with its 1949 policy statement. Routley added that the CMA was simply in favour of the principle of contributory hospital insurance for all Canadians.[89] Indeed, this caution remained evident in the 1955 combined statement of policies and principles; for no specific comments on the mechanics of hospital insurance were made, and the 1949 clause to do with the urgency of hospital insurance was deleted.[90]

In late 1955 federal proposals for a national hospital insurance scheme were tabled, and a formal offer of financial assistance was tendered to the provinces on 26 January 1956. Shortly afterward, Health Minister Paul Martin contacted the CMA and the Association des Medécins de langue française du Canada to discuss these proposals.[91] Leaders of these two bodies, together with representatives of the Canadian Association of Radiologists and Canadian Association of Pathologists, met the minister and senior civil servants on 15 March.[92] At issue was the inclusion of diagnostic services in any federal-provincial hospital insurance agreement.

Radiologists and pathologists working in the hospital setting generally made individualized arrangements to receive a salary plus a bonus scaled to the volume of services delivered. These hospital-based specialists feared the new programs would place them in a position to be bargaining directly with their respective provincial health ministries – a fear acknowledged in a resolution passed by the CMA General Council in June 1956: "The Canadian Medical Association affirms that radiological and clinical pathological services are physicians' services and not hospital care, and should not be so treated in any insurance plans."[93] In some provinces, radiologists and pathologists took the prospective implementation of hospital insurance as their cue to press for fee-for-service remuneration and an end to contract-salary arrangements; if reinstated as wholly private practitioners, they proposed to reimburse the hospital for part of the operating expenses of radiology departments and laboratories. Their fees would then be insurable through the doctor-sponsored prepayment plans. However, this viewpoint was strongly rejected by the Canadian Hospital Association.[94]

Apart from the issue of radiologists' and pathologists' services, the 1956 CMA general council also weighed the broad question of a federal-provincial hospitalization program. The executive noted that "medical opinion generally is favourable to the institution of universal hospital care insurance," but a resolution asking the general council to go on record in support of universal hospital insurance was extensively debated and ultimately defeated.[95] Although details of that debate are not available, the perspective of those who voted against the resolution can be surmised from a "Statement of Opinion" adopted in September 1956 by the Alberta division of the CMA. This statement contended that the Ottawa plan would place an "unnecessary financial burden" on the taxpayers, and lead to "Government control over the type and quality of medical care ... On a more general plane, the Association recognizes the Proposals as a first step towards complete Government control of all medical care." To back up this assertion, the Alberta doctors quoted a comment by Louis St Laurent to the 1955 Dominion-Provincial Conference wherein the prime minister alluded to the hospital and diagnostic services proposals "as the first two elements in a *universal health care program*. It would appear that the Prime Minister was speaking on behalf of a Government which has as its ultimate aim State Medicine." Calling for voluntary prepaid hospital and medical care as preferable to any state scheme, the Alberta division concluded: "We firmly believe that a partnership between Government and enlightened free enterprise is much to be preferred to dictatorship by the Government."[96]

No such "partnership" was forthcoming. In late 1956 and early 1957 the terms of the program were finalized. A key proviso was the requirement that participating provinces must make insured services available to all on uniform conditions. This precluded adoption of the policy of means-testing the needy to ascertain whether they qualified for government subsidies on their hospital insurance premiums with subsequent enrolment in private sector plans. (The actual motivation for this federal-provincial strategy probably reflected as much a desire to retain control of public funds as egalitarian ideals). In April 1957 the Hospital Insurance and Diagnostic Services Act (HIDS) was passed by unanimous roll-call votes in the House of Commons and Senate. In the election that followed several weeks later, the Liberals were narrowly defeated by the Conservatives under John Diefenbaker. The prairie lawyer and his cabinet colleagues had strongly supported the HIDS legislation, and proceeded steadily towards its implementation. The national hospital insurance program, essentially unchanged from the original blueprint, was brought into effect on 1 July 1958.

Five provinces – Saskatchewan, British Columbia, Alberta, Manitoba and Newfoundland – already had programs eligible for cost sharing, and the other provinces soon introduced operations that would qualify them for funds from the federal government. The role of the Blue Cross plans shifted to coverage of "extras" such as semi-private and private hospital accommodation, although Blue Cross insurance in Quebec and the Maritimes continued to cover medical and surgical services for hospital in patients. For investor-owned companies in the private insurance industry, a similar shift was necessary, together with redoubled attention to sale of medical care insurance contracts in an effort to win a share of the market from TCMP. For organized medicine, the success and popularity of the national hospital insurance program was a constant reminder that the future of the profession-sponsored plans remained uncertain.

THE SIGNIFICANCE OF THE MEDICAL PREPAYMENT PLANS

By 1 January 1961, when Quebec entered the program, all ten provinces were participating in the HIDS cost-sharing arrangements, and every Canadian was insured against the costs of hospitalization and in-patient diagnostic services. In the interim private prepayment for medical care had undergone impressive growth. Only 6 percent of the population had some form of medical/surgical coverage in 1945; by 1961, 53 percent were enrolled in a medical insurance plan of one kind or another. However, of that number, 9 percent or 1.6 million Canadians had coverage for in-hospital professional services at most. Of the other 44 percent, almost 1.5 million persons did not have comprehensive coverage. Another 8 million had no direct coverage for medical care whatsoever.[97] The case for proceeding with further state mediation rested in part on such statistics. Nonetheless, it is obviously important to review the political economy of medical services prepayment as it unfolded in the 1950s, paying particular attention to professional interests and strategies.

The medical insurance market was dominated by two consortia. Trans-Canada Medical Plans, the umbrella body for agencies sponsored or approved by organized medicine, rose to a total enrolment in the early 1960s of over 25 percent of the population. Almost an equivalent percentage was covered by the Canadian Health Insurance Association (CHIA), a syndicate formed from more than 100 private carriers. An assortment of much smaller organizations – including non-profit co-operatives – rounded out the roster of medical insurance agencies.

At the outset the profession-sponsored plans were intended to forestall consumer-sponsored initiatives and redirect government intervention. But investor-owned insurance agencies were not above suspicion: as noted earlier, the 1943 OMA executive had been concerned over "commercial assurance companies" that "set medical fees and sell medical services at thirty percent commission"; and non-approved carriers in British Columbia had also provoked criticism from organized medicine. By implication, organized medicine resented the idea of a third party trafficking profitably in professional services, and this was part of the underpinning for the rivalry that grew up between TCMP and the commercial consortium.

Other issues, however, were at stake. The organized profession was desirous of building its plans into a solid alternative to state-administered health insurance and to do so sought to maximize their enrolment. The expansion of private medical insurance offered by investor-owned companies undercut TCMP's chances of achieving this end. Bidding for major contracts was understandably intense; for example, TCMP won the national railway employees contract in 1956 but lost the national civil service contract to CHIA in 1959. According to Howard Shillington, the executive director of TCMP, the non-profit consortium found that interprovincial co-ordination was a source of conflict in the TCMP family of agencies; and after 1959 the national office more or less retreated from the field.[98]

Each consortium had advantages for consumers. The investor-owned carriers had to weigh the benefits to be offered against the need to make a profit and pay dividends to policy-holders with other branches of the corporation. Individual contracts were often prohibitively expensive, and there were, variously, age limits on enrolment, medical conditions that precluded coverage, and long waiting periods before an insuree could claim benefits for certain operations. The latter limitation was to prevent a family or individual from joining a plan to deal with a number of pressing problems, then departing before paying a fair share of premiums. All these limitations caused problems for consumers. On the other hand, the private insurance agencies were able to experience-rate employee groups and offer discounts on low-risk contracts. The CHIA companies also offered a wide variety of policies, so that customers could select whatever level of coverage they felt was appropriate for their needs.

The physician-sponsored plans, in contrast to the investor-owned companies, were set up as non-profit corporations. Premium/payment ratios were accordingly improved, and a potential was created for offering either more comprehensive coverage or lower premium rates. Strategists on the CMA Committee on Economics were well aware that consumer demand for complete coverage was high, and any government plan was likely to operate on such a basis. From the mid-1950s there was unease about the lack of out-patient coverage in the two Blue Cross plans affiliated with TCMP that served Quebec, Newfoundland, New Brunswick, and Prince Edward Island.[99] Elsewhere the TCMP member plans took on greater numbers of individuals in all risk categories who might be rejected as unprofitable by the commercial carriers. These persons were included for several reasons. Conscientious doctors and administrators were dismayed that the voluntary insurance movement was failing to reach those who most needed security against the costs of medical care.[100] Strategically, too, such expansion was necessary, both to meet increasing competition for subscribers and to demonstrate a service-orientation that would encourage governments to back the CMA-TCMP proposals for medical insurance. Extension of coverage by the TCMP plans did have the effect, however, of raising their operating costs and eroding the competitive edge provided by their non-profit corporate structure.

One important difference between the doctor-sponsored and investor-owned plans lay in billing arrangements. The private companies contracted not with doctors but with patients; they were therefore unable to bind doctors to accept the insurance rates as payment in full unless the doctor and patient agreed to an "assignation" whereby the practitioner billed the commercial carrier directly. In the absence of an "assignation," commercial policies operated on a straightforward indemnity basis. The policy-holder received a bill from a practitioner, paid the bill directly to the doctor, and then claimed indemnification at pre-set rates for his or her expenses. There was no guarantee that the rates of reimbursement set by the insurance company would be sufficient to cover the doctor's bill; for the private carrier did not always indemnify to the minimum fee recommended by the provincial medical association, and doctors were free to bill above the minimum tariff. The cost of care therefore remained somewhat uncertain even for insured patients.

But whereas the indemnity contracts of the investor-owned carriers left doctors free to bill directly and set their fees as they saw fit, most of the contracts initially offered by the doctor-sponsored organizations had what was known as a *service* clause: participating doctors would be bound not to extra-bill the patient. Instead, the practitioners billed the TCMP agency and accepted its payment as full settlement of the account. These service clauses were used both to give the doctor-sponsored plans greater market appeal than their commercial counterparts and to bring their modus operandi into line with that likely to be deemed desirable by government.

As time went by, however, the service element in the doctors' plans was challenged and, in some cases, eroded. Removal of income limits was one reason for this change in approach. In the 1940s most plans had put a ceiling on incomes of those who could enrol, thereby allowing doctors to improve their market position by price-discriminating against higher-income groups. Since income limits on participation also put a ceiling on the number of subscribers, they were gradually abandoned. Once income ceilings were eliminated, pressure was exerted by doctors for the right to extra-bill the wealthier individuals now able to join the profession-sponsored schemes. The TCMP agencies faced a conflict here between their ideals of service to subscribers and their responsibilities to organized medicine. There was also the question of competition from the investor-owned agencies: service contracts were a major selling point in favour of the profession-sponsored plans. Thus, in Ontario, the OMA Board of Directors pressed repeatedly between 1950 and 1956 for PSI to establish income limits above which service clauses limiting extra-billing would not apply; but the PSI Board of Directors refused. The OMA's frustration at this situation was such that between 1956 and 1958 the association looked into various means of asserting more definite control over PSI's management.[101] In contrast, both Windsor Medical Services and the Quebec-based Services de Santé did decree that all subscribers above a fixed income level could be extra-billed by GPs and specialists; for lower-income subscribers extra-billing was prohibited and the full service contract applied.

The rising influence of specialists also contributed to the spread of extra-billing. As their numbers climbed from less than 20 percent of all practitioners in the late 1940s to 40 percent by the early 1960s,[102] specialists were usually able to demand economic rewards commensurate with their additional training and higher status. Rather than adopt a dual tariff for specialists and general practitioners, some plans simply gave them freer reign in billing. MS(S)I, which had originally barred extra-billing by GPs and specialists alike, allowed specialists to bill extra on any but the first referral. MSA-BC, starting from the same global ban on extra-billing, produced a more flexible policy: specialists were strongly discouraged from extra-billing if a patient were referred by a general practitioner; but eventually both MSA and MSI-BC allowed it if a prior agreement existed and if "extra care beyond the contract or extra skill is involved." MSI (Alberta) recommended against specialist extra-billing on the first referral only, while Maritime Medical Care and the Regina plan prohibited GP extra-billing and left specialists unbound almost from the outset. In fact, during the 1950s Manitoba Medical Services was the only TCMP agency that had no provision for extra-billing by participating specialists.[103]

Firm data on the actual prevalence of extra-billing are not available. However, a 1960 nationwide survey of practitioners organized by the CMA makes it clear that most doctors accepted the "minimum provincial tariff" as full payment, whether it came from a profession-sponsored plan, directly from a patient, or from an investor-owned insurance agency to which doctor and patient had made an "assignation." Eighty-seven percent of respondents stated that they "always or usually" accepted payments directly from insurance carriers, effectively forgoing an opportunity to extra-bill. The only circumstance under which the majority of doctors did make extra charges was where a private carrier paid less than the tariff set by the provincial medical association.[104] In short, despite group pressure to obtain extra-billing privileges from the doctor-sponsored plans, most practitioners were content to keep money matters out of their dealings with patients. It is also plain that the growth of private medical insurance in all forms accustomed practitioners to the concept of settling accounts with a third party.

These survey findings underscore the growing importance of the provincial medical association's fee schedules. Whereas the old fee schedules had been somewhat sketchy, the spread of medical services insurance forced organized medicine to develop detailed tariffs. With more detailed tariffs and guaranteed third-party payment came a change in the approach to billing:

Customarily, for self-pay patients an office call was a kind of collective entity that included history, examination, one or more diagnostic procedures, a prescription or two and advice. For this a flat office call fee was charged. With insured patients, however, the fee for an office call has been likened to the cover charge at a night club: it pays for the visit, but any services given require an additional charge.[105]

In addition, pre-insurance schedules had shown a range of charges, reflecting patients' differing abilities to pay. The new schedules listed only one charge – a minimum fee around which doctors, investor-owned carriers, and the non-profit agencies could be expected to operate.[106]

The standardization of fees, however, was simply an epiphenomenon in a more politically significant process – the entrenchment of fee-for-service payment and private practice. As indicated in the previous chapter, during the Second World War the CCF, Trades and Labour Council of Canada, Canadian Federation of Agriculture, and Canadian Congress of Labour were all on record as favouring medical remuneration by salary. Although a salaried medical service had been firmly rejected by the CMA, many prominent physicians publicly endorsed capitation as a payment mode for general practice. In fact, both the Canadian Public Health Association and the Health Insurance Committee of the Ontario College of Physicians and Surgeons had spoken in favour of a capitation-based general practitioner service. The 1943 CMA submission to the Special House Committee on Social Security acknowledged this groundswell; as already noted, the CMA contended that specialist work should be remunerated on a fee-for-service basis but referred to GP services as remunerable by capitation, fee-per-item, or some combination thereof.[107]

In the more conservative post-war period, and with the spread of private-sector insurance, this willingness to consider alternative payment modes disappeared. Commenting in 1954 on the CMA health insurance principle pertaining to negotiations over payment, T.C. Routley remarked that "the vast majority of Canadian doctors approve . . . fee-for-service."[108] It is understandable, then, that in the combined statement of policy and principles adopted at the annual meeting in 1955, the CMA added the following clause: "In the provision of personal health services where the usual doctor-patient relationship exists, it is the view of the Canadian Medical Association that remuneration on a basis of fee for service rendered promotes high quality of medical care." Hereafter, a salaried state medical service with primary care based in community health centres and specialists employed by "polyclinics" and hospitals was even less feasible politically; nor was it likely that state medical care insurance could be organized around capitation payments for GPs.

Private non-profit and investor-owned plans also helped erode the bases for consumerist initiatives. Labour and farm groups might still press the provinces and Ottawa for universal medical insurance or even "state medicine," but as experience in Regina and Saskatoon demonstrated, local community efforts to create salaried clinics were liable to be fruitless in the face of organized medical opposition and competition from the popular doctor-sponsored insurance plans.

The exact impact of the spread of private medical insurance on physicians' incomes is difficult to evaluate. However, there is no question that the 1950s brought marked growth in average medical incomes. Two published estimates of mean net annual professional earnings by self-employed physicians vary by about 10 percent,[109] but both confirm the upward trend. For 1951 the higher estimate is $9,257, with an increase to $14,590 in 1959.[110] Taking the lower estimate relative to the national average of wages and salaries, in 1951 the ratio was 3.1:1, and by 1959 it had climbed to 3.7:1.[111] Thus, during a period of economic growth when the national average of wages and salaries outstripped the Consumer Price Index by a healthy margin,[112] the mean medical income in turn grew faster than the national average income. The result was a sustained and substantial improvement in standard of living that could only have hardened the profession's resistance to large-scale government mediation in the medical services marketplace.

The factors driving the increase in medical incomes were several, and their relative contributions are debatable. Certainly the government social assistance medicare plans contributed to the upward trend by providing fees for hitherto non-remunerative work in several provinces. Technological innovation expanded the medical armamentarium and from a purely economic standpoint gave GPs and specialists new services to "sell." Moreover, private medical insurance either eliminated charges at point of service altogether or, in the case of indemnity plans, offered consumers substantial security against doctors' bills; hence consumer-initiated demand was also likely to expand.[113] Health economist Robert G. Evans has used TCMP data to study the growth in volume of medical services per capita during this period; he argues that much of the increase was in fact supplier induced. According to Professor Evans, the prices of supplier-controlled services actually rose faster on average than other fee schedule items.[114] This interpretation, however, is by no means uncontested.

It remains only to place the physician-sponsored insurance movement in the broader context of the sociology of the profession. While the investor-owned agencies entered the prepayment market in response to profit opportunities, the doctor-sponsored plans obviously represented a classic co-optation response by organized medicine as an interest group. Professor Malcolm G. Taylor has suggested that these plans might be viewed as the revenue system for the medical profession qua private government[115] – an appropriate analogy but one that can be deepened by applying Max Weber's theory of collegiality. Weber presented collegiality as a form of social organization that was often used by groups seeking to win or maintain status and autonomy. Rather than granting authority to outside agencies, such groups would regulate themselves. Internal self-regulation might tend to level out within-group differences but would buttress the group against the threat of external control.[116] This concept, used in chapter 2 to explain aspects of professional ethics and self-government, is clearly pertinent to the doctor-sponsored insurance plans. By (1) promoting adherence to a single, detailed fee schedule, (2) placing some restrictions on extra-billing, (3) initially prorating fees until the insurance funds covered all billings at 90 or 100 percent of minimum tariff, and (4) vetting doctors' accounts to curb physician-generated abuses of third-party payment guarantees, the doctor-sponsored insurance plans sought to govern professional behaviour in a fashion that would impose a certain degree of equality on the collective, while buttressing its position against outside control. The socio-economic autonomy of individual practitioners would at times be compromised in the short run; the collective socio-economic autonomy of the profession might be protected in the longer term.

We shall be examining the profession's retreat from collegially organized prepayment in greater detail in chapter 8. For now, suffice it to note that some of the younger practitioners chafed at collegial controls. Differentiated to a greater extent into specialty groups, this new generation resented the restrictions on billing and the auditing of doctors' accounts imposed by the TCMP service contracts. Prorating of payments to doctors was another grievance; however, as the TCMP agencies gained a firmer financial base, actual prorating was seldom necessary. On the other hand, there was ongoing complaint about the 10 percent deduction from doctors' accounts made by most of the TCMP agencies. (This deduction was justified by the agencies as an administrative expense, since participating physicians no longer had to bill patients or risk unpaid accounts.) The critics of TCMP accordingly saw in the indemnity contracts of the private industry an opportunity for doctors to set their own fees and to practise without interference by a prepayment agency.[117]

Judging from CMA survey data,[118] as late as 1960 only a small minority of practitioners actually preferred the indemnity approach and the investor-owned agencies. Nonetheless, any dissatisfaction with TCMP's modus operandi was an ominous harbinger of things to come; for in an effort to meet public demand the profession-sponsored plans had taken on characteristics that would necessarily be part of any state-sponsored scheme. In any case, the reactions of organized medicine to public medical care insurance were soon to be tested. Saskatchewan's CCF government had been financially burdened by its decision to pioneer with a comprehensive hospitalization plan. To expand further in the medicare field would have required tax increases that might erode CCF support among the province's increasingly prosperous - and centrist - farm communities. Once federal funds amounting to 45 percent of the hospitalization budget were made available through HIDS cost sharing with Ottawa, T.C. Douglas and his colleagues could afford to take another innovative step - one that would launch Saskatchewan into an extraordinarily bitter medicare dispute, the intensity of which surpassed even the conflict in British Columbia during the 1930s.

CHAPTER SEVEN

Medicare in the Crucible
I: The Saskatchewan Dispute

Whatever the outcome may be, I believe that the medical profession will, as always, conduct themselves with the poise and posture of honourable men and adhere to the principles that have guided our profession since its inception, namely that our first duty as doctors is to care for sick people.

> Dr E. Kirk Lyon, deputy-president of the CMA,
> June 1960

The doctors of Saskatchewan are no different from doctors elsewhere; they just happened to be in front of the gun. They did not forget their principles; they acted like men of honour in war.

> Dr William W. Wigle, CMA president-elect,
> September 1962

Political scientists have argued that the well-known dispute over the introduction of Canada's first universal medicare plan[1] should be seen not simply as an example of medical pressure group activity but rather as a full-blown "community conflict."[2] The escalation of the dispute to the point of actual strike action by the majority of Saskatchewan doctors can of course be attributed in part to a fundamental ideological disagreement between a tightly knit professional body and a government emboldened by a decade and a half in power. However, it is also plain that the medicare issue – and the medical profession itself – served as a stalking horse for a variety of groups, not least the Saskatchewan Liberal party, which hoped to undermine the electoral credibility of the CCF government.

THE SASKATCHEWAN BACKGROUND

As noted in chapter 6, although the post-war initiatives in health care had spent themselves in Saskatchewan by the end of 1948, the CCF already had made sizeable strides towards its stated goal of complete prepayment of health services for the entire population. All residents – some 800,000 – had free access to hospital care, and free treatment for tuberculosis, mental illness, cancer, and venereal disease was available. Through the Swift Current scheme, the social assistance medicare program, and the municipal doctor contract arrangement about one-third of the population had more or less comprehensive coverage for medical services.[3]

Even before the CMA offered official endorsement of state-subsidized enrolment in profession-sponsored prepayment plans, the Saskatchewan College of Physicians and Surgeons (SCPS) had been alert to this alternative. During negotiations over the Swift Current plan, the profession's spokesmen had put forward the idea that the Regina-based Group Medical Services (GMS) and Saskatoon-based Medical Services Incorporated (MS(S)I) might be used as carrier agencies. However, the college reaffirmed its support for state-aided universal health insurance at its annual meeting in October 1948. The CMA's new policy was adopted the following year at a convention in Saskatoon. The SCPS promptly endorsed the CMA's 1949 policy statement but added an important rider: "When and if the people of Canada, or the province of Saskatchewan, want an all-inclusive prepaid health insurance plan," the SCPS would accept a state-administered program that met its 1948 principles, provided the necessary personnel and facilities were available. Indeed, the 1949–50 CMA president, Dr Jack F.C. Anderson of Saskatoon, commented in the *CMAJ* that there was a contrast in viewpoints between west and east: "The professions in both British Columbia and Saskatchewan seem much more ready to accept some form of compulsory Health Insurance, and have already accepted compulsory hospitalization in principle and practice (although objecting to its timing and some of its administrative practices)."[4] In 1951, as the two profession-sponsored prepayment plans showed steady growth, the SCPS finally gave an unqualified endorsement of the CMA policy statement of 1949. It was the last provincial medical group to do so.

Details of several early skirmishes between the CCF and the profession were reviewed in chapter 6. As we have seen, the success of the Swift Current Health Region, social assistance medicare plan, and hospital services program had helped ease government-SCPS tensions. Premier Douglas in particular was trusted by the profession as a pragmatic counterweight to the personnel of the Health Services Planning Commission. Overburdened with his double duty as premier and health minister and aware that the first period of health services reorganization was over, Douglas relinquished the portfolio in 1949 to T.J. Bentley, a farmer and former Saskatchewan wheat pool executive. Bentley indicated to college representatives in March 1950 that he did not personally agree with the concept of public insurance administration by an independent commission. Instead, he suggested that the Health Services Planning Commission (HSPC) be expanded to include representatives from the public and the profession. The SCPS was taken aback by this apparent reversal of the position set out by the premier in 1945. Despite further discussion, no clear agreement was reached. It was not until 1954 that the HSPC was restructured, and by this time it had already been divested of administrative authority and transformed back to a planning and advisory agency. In short, relations between the government and the SCPS were once again strained.[5]

In the meantime, growth of the doctor-sponsored prepayment plans had continued at a rapid rate. By 1955, the same year that the CMA reaffirmed its commitment to the voluntary insurance/subsidization strategy with a combined statement on policies and principles for health insurance, the two organizations in Saskatchewan boasted a total enrolment of 185,000. In a successful attempt to head off expansion of the salaried municipal doctor scheme and increase subscription lists, the profession-sponsored plans had negotiated prepayment contracts with sixty municipalities[6] (see table 6). There were two definite advantages for the municipalities in this new approach: residents would be insured for medical care delivered by practitioners anywhere in the province, including referrals to specialists in Regina and Saskatoon; and no administrative commitment was required. In the view of E.A. Tollefson, a legal authority on the Saskatchewan dispute, these contracts amounted to universal compulsory health insurance on a local basis, since all residents were required to pay taxes towards the insurance premiums.[7]

1955 also brought further skirmishing between the SCPS and the government when an effort was made to extend the Swift Current prepayment experiment to other regions. The college had never been pleased by what it perceived as a divide-and-rule element in the regionalization strategy of the CCF, and local administration by lay municipal councillors was also against SCPS principles. Another concern had arisen in 1949 when the Swift Current Health Region faced financial difficulties. Again contravening SCPS recommendations, the Swift Current doctors agreed to the imposition of a ceiling on the per capita funding of medical services, with the result that their fees were prorated and settlements consistently ran below the initial

TABLE 6
Enrolment in Medical Service Plans vs Number
of Municipal Doctor Contracts, Saskatchewan,
1951-61

Year	GMS	MS(S)I	Contracts*
1951	17,186	48,893	173
1953	26,768	92,530	157
1955	38,348	122,191	160
1957	62,173	164,573	154
1959	69,305	211,514	136
1961	78,787	217,795	126

*The actual number of GPs under contract was always lower,
since some practitioners held contracts to serve more than one
municipality.
Source: Data in this table are derived from C. Howard Shillington, The Road to Medicare in Canada (Toronto: Del Graphics
1972), 202-3; and Kenneth MacTaggart, The First Decade: The
Story of the Birth of Medicare in Saskatchewan (Ottawa: CMA
1973), 7.

level of 75 percent of SCPS minimum tariffs. To cut utilization and
reverse the trend to diminishing marginal returns for extra work done,
in 1953 the Swift Current Medical Society negotiated the imposition
of small deterrent fees on selected services. This move improved the
local doctors' position but did nothing to alter those basic aspects
of the program to which the SCPS objected. In the autumn of 1955,
when it became plain that the government would proceed with four
regional plebiscites on the medical insurance issue, the Central Health
Services Committee of the college met and devised strategies whereby
a united, strong front could be maintained by the profession.[8] In
the event, only two Health Regions voted – Regina Rural and
Assiniboia-Gravelbourg. The government campaigned for a "yes"
vote, while the profession lobbied the regional health boards and
other community groups and widely publicized its opposition to the
proposals. The extent to which these competing campaigns affected
voters' decisions is difficult to know. Farmers had reason to fear that
a regional plan would impose an undue burden on them, since the
bulk of revenue necessarily would be generated through property
taxes. Nonetheless, the voting was strongly against the extension of
the Swift Current experiment. For the college, which had orchestrated
the profession's campaign, this was confirmation both of the public
appeal of the private insurance strategy and of its own strength as
a political force in the province.[9]

Another clash occurred in 1957. The "ceiling" principle that led to prorating of payments to doctors in the social assistance medical care plan had been disputed by the SCPS since 1948, and, as noted above, the application of this budgetary cap to medical insurance in the Swift Current Health Region had also been condemned by the college.[10] In 1954, the CMA Committee on Economics reviewed the operations of the four provincial social assistance medicare plans then in existence, with Dr J. Lloyd Brown of the SCPS in charge of the study group. The CMA Committee on Economics reported that none of these plans truly conformed to organized medicine's policies:

The [CMA principles of health insurance] do not approve of the per capita rate as a means of finance and do not agree to provide full medical care under such a rigid fund, with therefore a ceiling on costs. It was realized that great care must be exercised to safeguard against precedents in any interim scheme which might later militate against us, when and if the Social Assistance group is incorporated into voluntary plan type of care.[11]

By 1957, federal-provincial negotiations on hospital insurance offered the prospect of a multi-million dollar subsidy to the Saskatchewan government, and the SCPS was well aware that the CCF would now be able to proceed with a provincial medicare plan. The time had therefore come to remove the cap on government expenditures lest it find more general application. The SCPS accordingly asked to be paid on a straightforward fee-for-service basis in the social assistance medicare plan; in return, the doctors would accept 50 percent of the fee schedule for each item of service billed. As in 1948 the government responded with an offer to increase the per capita payments to the medical insurance pool. The SCPS executive held firm: if the prorating of fees were not eliminated, doctors would refuse to participate in the program. Once more the Douglas cabinet was forced to acknowledge defeat.

The stage obviously was set for a confrontation. From the 1930s, the strength of the CCF· had forced the college to formulate clear counter-policies and fostered a cohesiveness that was enhanced by the amalgamation of the licensing body and voluntary association. Political clashes during the 1950s produced a "battle-hardened" SCPS leadership. And in keeping with the doctors' viewpoint on health insurance was the impressive enrolment in MS(S)I and GMS: by 1959 they had 211,514 and 69,305 subscribers, respectively. It has also been suggested that change in the composition of the profession contributed to anti-government feeling. Those who had weathered the Depression, when health insurance appeared as an economic boon, were now in a clear minority. By the early 1960s not only were about half the province's doctors residents of ten years' standing or less, but also the increasing concentration of practitioners in Saskatoon and Regina meant that "the cloistering influence of the medical societies and their leaders was felt more strongly."[12]

On the other hand, CCF party doctrine ever since the Regina Manifesto of 1933 had supported state medicine or universal state-aided health insurance. The government's promise of a comprehensive system of tax-funded health services was now fifteen years old, and its electoral popularity was waning. Despite the combined coverage offered through private plans, co-ops, municipal doctors, the Swift Current scheme, the social assistance plan, and the profession-sponsored insurance companies, fully one-third of the province's population still had no way of being certain that medical care costs would not prove too burdensome. There was also a deep personal dedication on Tommy Douglas's part to the principle that doctors' services should be equally available to all without regard for ability to pay. As a child in Scotland before the First World War, Douglas had contracted chronic osteomyelitis in his leg; later he found himself, at the age of nine, in the public or charity ward of the Winnipeg General Hospital facing the prospect of amputation. Only when a surgeon singled him out for medical student teaching did he receive sensibly conservative treatment; amputation was forestalled and the leg healed. Douglas later reminisced: "That experience had a profound effect on me. I thought that if my parents had been rich I'd have had the best doctor in Winnipeg or gone to Rochester or New York. Why was it that a poor boy almost lost his leg?"[13] Hence, for the former Baptist minister public access to medical services in the same fashion as public access to primary or secondary education should be "an inalienable right of being a citizen of a Christian country."[14] Once the federal-provincial cost-sharing arrangements went into effect for hospital insurance, Douglas was in a position to proceed with universal medical insurance. On 29 April 1959, speaking at a by-election rally, the premier announced that a province-wide tax-funded medicare plan was to be implemented.

THE THOMPSON COMMITTEE AND THE 1960 ELECTION

In October 1959 the SCPS met for its annual convention and made the profession's position clear. Aware that a draft bill was already in the works and angered that the profession had not been consulted, the delegates resolved unanimously "that we, the members of the College of Physicians and Surgeons of Saskatchewan, oppose the introduction of a compulsory Government-controlled province-wide medical care plan and declare our support of the extension of health and accident benefits through indemnity and insurance plans."[15] It is important to note two changes in terminology. First, through the 1940s when the SCPS still supported universal government health insurance, the phrase "state-aided" was used instead of the more ominous "government-controlled." Second, as suggested in chapter 6, by the late 1950s some physicians favoured indemnity rather than service contracts and exerted pressure for the CMA to endorse not only government-subsidized enrolment in the profession's own plans, but also state-subsidized purchase of policies sold by private companies. Moreover, MS(S)I had recently cut back on its benefits because of financial problems, with the result that subscribers were no longer offered comprehensive coverage. It appeared that the SCPS was now aligning itself with the investor-owned insurance agencies and defending MS(S)I by calling for support of indemnity as well as service plans. GMS and MS(S)I were, of course, still rivals for subscribers with the private insurance industry, but the threat posed by a common enemy made an alliance necessary.

Despite this indication of professional resistance, on 16 December 1959 the premier made a major policy broadcast over the provincial radio network outlining the cardinal principles upon which government action would be based. There were five. (1) Prepayment, through a combination of taxes and premiums, would spread the burden of medical services insurance over the whole population. (2) Universal coverage was vital "to cover the good risks as well as the bad." (3) High quality of services should be maintained. (4) Administration was to be by "a public body responsible to the legislature and through it to the entire population." But it was the final principle that would haunt the CCF: (5) the plan "must be in a form that is acceptable both to those providing the service and those receiving it."

Douglas elaborated on the fifth principle. The government, he proclaimed, did not intend to make all doctors civil servants on salary. The Swift Current program was proof of that. "We have no intention of pushing some pre-conceived plan down the doctors' throats. We want their co-operation and from our experience with other health programs I am convinced we will get it." An Advisory Planning Committee on Medical Care was to be appointed to suggest the best method of pursuing these goals. Douglas hoped to have a province-wide medicare program in operation before the end of 1961: "If we can do this – and I feel sure we can – then I would like to hazard the prophecy that before 1970 almost every other province in Canada will have followed the lead of Saskatchewan and we shall have a national health insurance program from the Atlantic to the Pacific."[16] This prophecy proved correct, but it is unlikely that Douglas foresaw the conflict looming ahead in Saskatchewan.

On 30 December 1959 the SCPS was offered three places on the Advisory Planning Committee; however, the college initially refused to name representatives.[17] Before it would co-operate, the profession made three basic demands. First, since the SCPS was opposed to a universal tax-funded plan, the profession understandably sought reassurance that the Advisory Planning Committee would not be totally bound by the government's preferred policy. It also asked that the terms of reference of the committee should be broadened to provide an appraisal of the overall health needs of the province; such an assessment would naturally reveal other areas where government should better direct its energies as well as delaying the committee's report. Lastly, there was disagreement over representation. The Advisory Planning Committee, as originally constituted, was to have three appointees who were civil servants from appropriate government departments. The SCPS requested removal of these officials because they would be serving as both "advocates and judges" of any plan.[18]

Quarrels over the committee's terms of reference were resolved by the end of January 1960, but bickering between J. Walter Erb – who had replaced T.J. Bentley as health minister three years before – and the SCPS leaders continued over the composition of the body. Correspondence from these negotiations reveals that the college executive was negotiating in somewhat erratic fashion,[19] a reflection no doubt of skittishness at any involvement in the committee's work. Finally, on 26 March 1960 the college council convened in Regina to review the matter in detail, and voted to appoint three representatives. This decision was communicated to T.C. Douglas on 29 March in a letter that warned: "[W]e must say that we have been disturbed to both hear and read about statements made by yourself and other members of your government which only refer to the preconceived plan of your party to institute a compulsory, province-wide and government-controlled medical care plan." The letter went on to remind Douglas both of the college's opposition to any such plan and of the agreement, made at the SCPS's insistence, that any segment of the committee should be entitled to submit a minority report.[20] Thus, as finally constituted, the committee included three members from the SCPS; three from the general public; three government employees, two of whom were medical doctors working in the department of public health; and three members representing, respectively, the University of Saskatchewan medical faculty, the provincial federation of labour, and – as suggested by the SCPS – the provincial Chamber of Commerce.

The three SCPS representatives were Drs E.W. Barootes, C.J. Houston, and J.F.C. Anderson, all veterans on the medico-political front. The committee chairman was Dr W.P. Thompson, a highly respected professor of biology and former president of the University of Saskatchewan. The Thompson Committee held its first meeting on 9 May 1960, as a provincial election approached.

The election was scheduled for 8 June 1960, and medical services insurance rapidly became the overriding issue in the campaign. The CCF stressed its commitment to implementation of a province-wide tax-funded plan. Both the Social Credit party and the Conservatives were on record as opposing the CCF plan; in essence, both parties supported the subsidization option. But while Social Credit and Conservative candidates stood in most ridings, neither party was a major electoral force in the Saskatchewan context. The Liberals, however, were hoping to end CCF rule after sixteen years in opposition. Liberal leader Ross Thatcher announced that "what the people want, they will be able to get under a Liberal government"; if elected, the Liberals would weigh the merits of various proposals and offer the electorate a choice in a plebiscite.[21]

For many years the overwhelming majority of newspapers in Saskatchewan had been owned by the Sifton family, which had strong ties to the Liberals. Connections were also forged with the SCPS. For example, it was Mr D.B. Rogers, editor of the *Regina Leader-Post*, who suggested in meetings with the SCPS leaders that, rather than refusing outright to participate in the Thompson Committee deliberations and risking bad public relations, they find ways to modify the committee's composition and terms of reference.[22] Even before the election date was fixed, the Sifton-owned *Saskatoon Star-Phoenix* had editorialized in favour of a plebiscite on medicare because a minority of voters might elect a CCF government that in turn could "foist the scheme on the majority. This would be manifestly unfair and undemocratic." The *Star-Phoenix* went on to suggest that the medical care scheme was "in reality a smoke-screen to divert the electorate's attention" from the CCF's impending transformation into a party dominated by organized labour.[23] Throughout the election, equally critical appraisals of the CCF were repeatedly presented by the entire Sifton chain of newspapers.

The SCPS also played a major role in the election. B.T. McLaughlin, the OMA's public relations co-ordinator, was sent to Saskatchewan for three weeks during February and March to help organize the profession's campaign. McLaughlin spoke at medical meetings in several cities and met with officials of both the news media and the various political parties. The OMA council was later told that he worked "with a view to unifying the thinking and actions of the profession prior to any stand they may have to take against government intervention into the practice of medicine."[24]

To assist in the SCPS campaign, a Medical Information Centre was opened in Regina. The SCPS announced that this office would be staffed by a special committee to "gather, co-ordinate, and disseminate information on health matters to both the medical profession and the public. Actions of this committee are completely non-political." The same claim of non-political intent appeared in a letter sent to every member of the SCPS levying $100 for support of public relations activities. Dr Frank Coburn, a CCF supporter and psychiatrist at the University of Saskatchewan medical school, publicly voiced his suspicion that the levy was being used to fight the CCF medicare plan. However Dr A.J.M. Davies, the SCPS president, dismissed Coburn's allegation as "completely erroneous and ridiculous." Davies then restated the college's opposition to the CCF medical care plan and again asserted that this was a "non-political" stand.[25]

The exact status of the $100 levy remained uncertain because of the college's power as a licensing and discipline body. The SCPS president was first quoted on 25 March as stating that the $100 levy on college members was neither voluntary nor compulsory – "it is just an assessment" – but three weeks later he suggested this was "not a voluntary assessment."[26] According to one would-be medical heretic, "Some doctors are afraid to speak out against the college's campaign becasue the chap who is spreading the literature can also deprive them of their license."[27] In the event, about 600 doctors paid the $100 "assessment." An additional $35,000 was donated by the CMA after the election to clear the SCPS's bank overdraft, suggesting therefore that as much as $95,000 was invested in the college's campaign. Exclusive of central funding, the Liberal candidates spent a total of some $71,000; the CCF candidates $89,000.

Sociologist Robin F. Badgley and public health specialist Dr Samuel Wolfe were members of the University of Saskatchewan medical faculty at this time. Both supported the CCF medicare plan and later described the SCPS's organizational strategy:

The profession had apparently studied the tactics of the American Medical Association in opposing legislative action in the United States. A tightly knit, anxious and militant group led the profession. Doctors campaigned in all parts of the province. Copying another AMA technique, a "key man" system was set up, and each "key man" was responsible for a small cell of doctors. Plans were passed from the profession's hierarchy to the "key man," then to rank-and-file doctors.[28]

The scps public relations team sent folders critical of the ccf plan to every household in the province. McLaughlin wrote articles for a special election broadsheet called *The Weekly Mirror*. In a report to Ontario doctors in April he advised that the Saskatchewan profession's "most difficult problem" was "finding that invisible line that divides in the public mind political and non-political action."[29] Nevertheless *The Weekly Mirror* carried photos of Liberal candidates.

Leaders of the scps spoke at public meetings, some arranged through local chambers of commerce, others at the profession's behest. A full-page advertisement appeared in the *Saskatoon Star-Phoenix* four days before the election, warning that "compulsory state medicine would be a tragic mistake" for Saskatchewan and carrying the names of 243 Saskatoon-area doctors. cma press releases backed up the college's campaign.

Most doctors in the province were also provided with a publicity kit. One item in the kit suggested that Catholic women should be made aware of the "latent but potential threat" of a government medicare plan to papal dictates on maternity and birth control. Another document aimed at female audiences warned that a state medicare plan would probably prevent doctors from discussing "emotional situations which crop up during pregnancy or other critical periods in a woman's life." Indeed, medicare meant that a menopausal woman, "subjected to many disturbances which she does not understand," could be denied necessary attention: "It could very easily be that this type of condition under state medicine must be referred to a psychiatric clinic or a mental hospital, a situation that we, as your personal physicians, would deplore."[30] Presumably the publicity kit did not find much use in the medical community.[31]

As it turned out, the ccf regained office, winning thirty-eight of fifty-four seats in the assembly and taking 41 percent of the popular vote which split four ways. Contacted by a *Toronto Telegram* reporter early in the morning of 9 June 1960, cma General Secretary Dr A.D. Kelly was asked for the association's official view of the election results. He deferred comment. But when Kelly's personal opinion was sought, he said, "This is a democracy and doctors will accept the decision in this light. Our efforts will now be bent on avoiding the defects we see in government plans elsewhere." Kelly's remark received wide coverage in the Canadian media, and he was forced to explain himself both to the cma executive committee and in the pages of the *CMAJ*.[32] One Sudbury surgeon, writing to reprimand Kelly, stressed that there should "be no compromise with or tolerance of 'state medicine' no matter how disguised such a scheme may be."[33] His sentiment was echoed by Dr A.J.M. Davies, head of the Saskatchewan college, who repudiated the CMA General Secretary and claimed that the profession remained "unalterably opposed" to the CCF proposals.

PRELUDE TO CONFRONTATION

Shortly after the election the CMA council convened at Banff for its annual meeting. Dr Glenn Sawyer, the OMA general secretary, noted that recent events in Saskatchewan created an atmosphere at the outset of "preparation for a storm."[34] In contrast to the 1940s, less effort was made to distinguish between state-administered health insurance and salaried programs that would lead to actual civil servant status for physicians. At a panel discussion on "The Future of Voluntary Pre-payment Mechanisms in the Health Care Field," Dr E.C. McCoy of Vancouver went so far as to suggest that a compulsory – or tax-funded scheme – "would result in national softness."[35] The general tone of the meeting was sufficiently alarmist that Dr J.H. MacDermot, a leading BC spokesman on medical economics during the 1920s and 1930s, wrote to the *CMAJ* calling for "calmness and patience and even generosity" in forthcoming dealings with government.[36]

The CMA general council authorized subsidies for the Saskatchewan profession – $35,000 to cover expenses incurred during the election campaign, and another $44,000 for the period from 1 July 1960 to the year's end. As well, the CMA economics department budget was increased by $20,000 for joint work with the SCPS in preparing "information briefs."[37]

Consideration of the Saskatchewan situation also entered into the report of the Special Committee on Prepaid Medical Care. This committee had undertaken a major survey of professional attitudes to prepayment earlier in the year, and received responses from 53 percent of the 20,000 doctors polled (see table 7). The survey touched on a variety of topics, but one set of responses was particularly interesting in the light of subsequent developments. Fully 25 percent of respondents did not agree that extension of voluntary prepayment plans could head off government intervention; 16 percent were unsure. Moreover a substantial number of respondents stated that a tax-supported plan was inevitable. Ninety-one percent endorsed the concept of professional organizations bargaining on their behalf with governments over the terms of a universal plan, and only 32 percent felt that doctors should actually refuse to participate in any program deemed unacceptable by organized medicine.

Dr J.F.C. Anderson, a former CMA president and SCPS representative

TABLE 7

CMA Special Committee on Prepaid Medical Care 1960 Survey: Results

Return rate on questionnaires: 53 percent (10,669 responses)

Residence of respondents

Newfoundland	106	Ontario	4,274
Prince Edward Island	51	Manitoba	597
Nova Scotia	394	Saskatchewan	615
New Brunswick	222	Alberta	847
Quebec	2,278	British Columbia	1,253
Northwest Territories–Yukon	11	Not specified	21

Form of Practice

Private general: 45 percent.

Private specialist: 38 percent.

Other: 12 percent.

Insurance Practice

Participating in doctor-sponsored plans: 77 percent.
    Non-participating: 23 percent.

If participating, never or seldom extra-bill TCMP patients: 87 percent.

Favour continued sponsorship of TCMP agencies: 85 percent.

"I like my patients to be covered by commercial indemnity insurance company plan(s)." Yes: 48 percent; No: 37 percent; Undecided: 15 percent.

Always or usually accept assignments from insurance company (i.e., forgo extra-billing): 87 percent.

If insurance assignment pays at minimum provincial tariff, always or usually accept as full settlement: 93 percent.

Always or usually extra-bill if insurance company pays below provincial minimum tariff: 74 percent.

Relations with Government

Voluntary prepayment can be extended so that the public will not request a tax-funded (universal) program. Yes: 59 percent; No: 25 percent; Undecided: 16 percent.

Introduction of a tax-supported program is – unlikely: 13 percent; probable: 58 percent; inevitable: 21 percent; imminent: 8 percent.

Administration of a universal scheme should be by TCMP agencies with addition of government representatives to boards. Agree: 74 percent.

Administration should be by Department of Health in province concerned. Disagree: 70 percent.

Remuneration by capitation rejected by 82 percent; remuneration by salary rejected by 84 percent; payment directly from plan on fee-for-service basis accepted by 87 percent.

TABLE 7 - *Concluded*

"If a tax-supported program is introduced I would accept an administrative arrangement wherein the patient paid me directly and then the patient was reimbursed by the plan." Yes: 56 percent; No: 31 percent; Undecided: 13 percent.

Source: "Transactions," *CMAJ* 83 (3 Sept. 1960): 471-2. For a concise summary of the results, see "News and Views, no. 15," *CMAJ* 83 (18 Feb. 1961).

on the Thompson Committee, was concerned about potential misinterpretation of these figures by the press. Anderson claimed that in his province a poll had shown over 90 percent of the doctors in private practice were adamantly opposed to a compulsory plan. After some discussion it was decided on a motion by Dr Harold Dalgleish that the contentious statistics would be released only after "further study."[38] (Several months later the executive committee authorized the release of these figures on the grounds that "no reason for their further suppression could be substantiated" – prompting Dr Anderson to suggest that the words "deferment of publication" be substituted for "suppression.")[39]

The CMA Committee on Economics had been equally active; for a new statement on medical services insurance was presented to the general council for consideration. It was, in many respects, a more strongly worded version of the 1955 statement, with references to hospitalization deleted. Indeed, the chairman of the economics committee stressed that the fourteen principles drafted were "essentials which should be acceptable *without negotiation*," except where specifically indicated in the policy statement.[40] The debate over the principles brought out only a minor division between moderates and militants. Principle 14 caused the longest discussion, since it stated in part that "the amount of remuneration is a matter for negotiation between the physician and his patient, or those acting on their behalf." As Dr R.M. Hines of Toronto noted, the words "those acting on their behalf" could well apply to government. Three separate motions to delete or amend the offending phrase came from the more militant delegates. All were defeated and the wording stood. As finally adopted by unanimous vote on 14 June 1960, the CMA's new "Statement on Medical Services Insurance" opened with a short preamble which included the assertion that "a tax-supported comprehensive program, compulsory for all, is neither necessary nor desirable." Most of its canons were time honoured – free choice of doctor and patient; protection of private practice, research and medical education; professional representation on any administrative commission; lack of interference with usual channels of professional self-government; and no infringement on the rights of doctors to choose either their type and location of practice, or their mode of remuneration.[41] A comparative analysis of ideological themes in this and other CMA policy statements was later carried out by sociologist Bernard R. Blishen, who found that the 1955 statement contained five clauses concerning "professional control" and "freedom," while the 1960 document registered nine such references in a shorter list of principles.[42]

In the wake of the CMA annual meeting, backstage preparations began in earnest for the next act in the Saskatchewan drama – the Thompson Committee hearings. The SCPS brief was compiled at considerable expense, and B.E. "Woody" Freamo, who had transferred from the OMA in 1957 to serve as the CMA's full-time economics adviser, was dispatched to Saskatchewan to assist in its preparation. In late October the SCPS held its own annual convention in Regina and reconfirmed its opposition to "a compulsory comprehensive government-controlled medical care plan." A resolution was also passed indicating that the college favoured premium assistance for the "small segment of the population" financially unable to participate in existing plans; means-testing would be administered at the local level. A strong editorial endorsement of this position was provided on 22 October by the *Regina Leader-Post*.[43] This pattern of editorial counterpoint was maintained by the Sifton press throughout the medicare dispute and must surely have heightened the collective resistance of the college members to the CCF proposals.

Both in Saskatchewan and elsewhere the profession's resistance to government intervention was also hardened, as it had been in the early 1950s, by international developments. Britain's National Health Service won many favourable reviews from doctors, patients, and outside observers after its initial difficulties were ironed out.[44] But by 1960 rising demand and the ongoing lack of capital investment in new hospitals or GP health centres had precipitated yet another round of criticism. Disenchanted by their slow progression up the ladder to consultant grade, junior doctors departed in droves. These problems were highlighted in a *CMAJ* editorial that warned of "Thunder in the Paradise of Britain's NHS."[45] The secretary of the Scottish division of the BMA wrote a cautionary lead article for the *CMAJ* on "Governments and Doctors."[46] And Professor John Jewkes of Oxford, a conservative economist, stringently criticized the NHS in a monograph which found wide readership among leaders of Canadian organized medicine;[47] Jewkes' work was cited by the SCPS in their brief to the Thompson Committee.

Although the CCF had at one time expressed a preference for a system similar to the NHS, there was no reason to believe that other parties were similarly disposed. Indeed, officials of Alberta's Social Credit government had confirmed in October 1960 that they favoured expansion of MSI (Alberta) rather than a state-administered scheme.[48] It was also true that the CCF had accepted the fee-for-service precedent in the social assistance medicare plan and the Swift Current Health Region. Dr A.D. Kelly had assessed the latter operation for the CMA in the autumn of 1960 and found that the forty-odd doctors in the Swift Current area were reasonably content.[49] However, the profession had no way of being certain that the CCF would follow the Swift Current precedent, and in any event the SCPS had already fought hard to prevent extension of the Swift Current plan to other regions.

Anxieties at CMA headquarters were therefore running high. The federal Liberal party policy committee was rumoured to be drafting its own medicare proposals. Certainly the remarkable growth of private insurance during the 1950s had not fully stemmed the tide of public demand for government action: a Gallup poll in late 1960 revealed that almost six out of every ten Canadians continued to support a comprehensive state medicare plan, even if this meant an increase in taxes. It was accordingly "with the object of removing the consideration of health and health insurance from the hectic arena of policital controversy"[50] that the CMA executive committee decided to act. On 12 December a letter was sent to Prime Minister John Diefenbaker requesting appointment of a royal commission "for assessing the health needs and resources of Canada with a view to recommending methods of ensuring the highest standard of health care for all Canadians."[51]

The tactic was in many ways analogous to CMA action during the 1930s, when the executive committee hoped both to defuse the British Columbia health insurance dispute and to obtain favourable federal consideration by calling for a national survey of health needs. On 21 December 1960 the prime minister responded in parliament with an announcement that a royal commission for this purpose would be constituted. Several months passed, however, before the commissioners for the federal inquiry were appointed. And in Saskatchewan the Thompson Committee hearings were at last under way.

A SASKATCHEWAN BLUEPRINT

On 12 January 1961 the SCPS opened the hearings of the Advisory Planning Committee with its lengthy brief. Representing some 850 doctors, the college indicated its willingness to accept continuation of the Swift Current scheme but otherwise hewed to the line already set out: the government should limit itself to means-testing those in the low income brackets and assisting them to enrol in private plans. The brief stressed the failings of Britain's National Health

Service and contended that Saskatchewan should emulate Australia, where a system of tax-subsidized enrolment in private indemnity programs covered about 70 percent of the population. Warnings were given about a potential exodus of doctors if the state became the "monopoly employer" of medical practitioners. E.A. Tollefson, professor of law at the University of Saskatchewan, later noted: "The prevailing mood of the brief was typified by the use of words like 'free enterprise,' which appeared with a favourable connotation in juxtaposition to words like 'state control' and government."[52] The scps had also exhaustively documented the diverse shortcomings in Saskatchewan's health services and facilities. The government was urged to attend these more pressing matters before turning to an expensive and uncertain program such as tax-supported medical care insurance for all. One of the key statements in the brief was this: "We sincerely believe that a single method of insurance, compulsory for all residents and controlled by government, would result in a service of inferior quality at higher costs."[53] Clearly, then, the college had firmly conjoined public and professional interests in the debate, ideologically mirroring the stand taken by British Columbia doctors twenty-five years before.

As had been the case in Ottawa during the 1940s, something of a political tug of war took place, with labour and agriculture pulling against the medical profession. The Saskatchewan Federation of Labour, with 28,500 members, rejected premiums and contended that the subsidization strategem would simply lead to widespread means-testing and unnecessary duplication of administrative facilities. A single tax-funded plan should be administered by the department of public health. Moreover doctors should not be paid by fee-for-service; salary, capitation, or some combination thereof was preferable.[54] The Saskatchewan Farmers' Union, representing more than 13,000 farm families, argued that public funds should not be paid over to private agencies. A single, comprehensive government plan was necessary. Understandably, the farmers were concerned that funding not rely unduly on property taxes. They accepted fee-for-service as a payment mode primarily because of its popularity with the medical profession, but they nonetheless suggested that salary was appropriate in many instances.[55]

After hearing out more than forty interested groups and individuals, the Advisory Planning Committee on Medical Care dispatched observers to Europe to study systems operating in other nations. At the time the committee had been given broadened terms of reference Tommy Douglas had publicly stated that interim reports might be requested in the event of undue delay. Perhaps anticipating this development, editorial writers for the *Regina Leader-Post* and the *Saskatoon Star-Phoenix* urged the planning body to take the widest possible view of health services and needs in the province. But as the committee's deliberations continued through the spring of 1961, the minister of health, Mr J.W. Erb, intervened in June to request an interim report on medical services insurance alone.

The minister's intervention raised a small storm of protest from the profession and its media allies, with accusations of political interference levelled at the government. The official rationale offered by Erb was that the fall session of the legislature would be reviewing provincial income taxes, and information on any medical care program should be available for tax planning purposes.[56] In fact, Professor W.P. Thompson, the committee chairman, perceived early on that no consensus on the framework of medical insurance was emerging, and he felt that Drs Barootes and Anderson, in particular, had shown no interest in compromise. A report was already eight months overdue, and Thompson himself therefore suggested to the cabinet committee that an interim report be requested.[57] For the CCF cabinet there were two political reasons for obtaining the medical insurance blueprint as soon as possible. First, the plan should be in operation before the next election to bolster the sagging electoral support for the party. Second, T.C. Douglas had agreed to stand for the national leadership of the New Democratic Party – the recently spawned offspring of the CCF. CCF loyalists argued that the premier was merely making good on his commitment to equality of access to health services before departing. But to the SCPS and other CCF adversaries it naturally appeared plain that the Thompson Committee had been rushed into producing a progress report so that Douglas could score a final provincial coup with medicare to assist him in making the transition to federal politics. The three SCPS representatives and the Chamber of Commerce delegate all voted against preparing an interim report but were overruled by the majority.

Dissidents in the Saskatchewan profession did speak out. Professor Alexander Robertson, head of the department of social and preventive medicine at the University of Saskatchewan, was known to favour the CCF proposals. Robertson had already been ousted under questionable circumstances as head of the salaried doctors' section of the college in 1960. And in June 1961 he exchanged broadsides in the *CMAJ* with Dr J.A. McMillan of Charlottetown, then head of the CMA's Special Committee on Prepaid Medical Care.[58] Dr J. Wendell MacLeod, dean of the University of Saskatchewan medical faculty since 1952, had been an active member of Norman Bethune's Montreal discussion group on socialized medicine during the 1930s. In September 1960 addressing a Liberal national policy conference, MacLeod strongly endorsed the concept of compulsory, tax-funded, medical care insurance.[59] In 1961 MacLeod published these views in the CMAJ.[60] Both Dean MacLeod and Professor Robertson had left the medical faculty for other posts by early 1962, and the departure of these two high-profile academicians weakened the already small pro-medicare camp in the provincial profession.

In June 1961 the CMA's annual convention was held in Montreal. Along with the usual extensive scientific program, special attention was paid to health insurance. Addresses on medical services coverage in Sweden and Australia were presented to demonstrate the feasibility of alternatives to a universal, comprehensive, and tax-supported plan. Dr Harold D. Dalgleish, now president of the Saskatchewan college, outlined the contents of the SCPS brief as submitted to the Thompson Committee, categorically rejecting any system other than subsidized enrolment in voluntary agencies. A special panel discussion on medical insurance brought out various arguments in support of the indemnity policies offered by commercial carriers, a sign of the profession's rightward drift away from the service contracts that had made TCMP-member plans more appealing to the public.[61] Even Dr Wilder Penfield, the distinguished head of the Montreal Neurological Institute, was persuaded by the CMA president to speak on "Government and Medicine" and offered some cautionary comments on state intervention.[62]

But one voice heard at the meeting was decisively neutral. Mr Justice Emmett Hall, chief justice of the Saskatchewan Court of Appeal, had been appointed chairman of the federal Royal Commission on Health Services, and its other personnel and terms of reference were made public just three days before the CMA annual meeting started. When Hall briefly addressed the CMA gathering on 24 June, he stated: "Our report may please you or may not . . . It may not please anyone."[63]

At about this time the Thompson Committee began work on its interim report. The committee had encouraged the SCPS to present any additional evidence it thought pertinent; and in Regina on 9 July 1961 the college tabled an impressive supplementary brief. The brief restated the doctors' case and gave detailed budget projections. The college also stressed that the subsidy route would still entail "responsibility to the appropriate public authority for spending of public moneys" and "substantial Government participation both as a regulating agent and in an auditing capacity."[64]

However, this presentation ultimately did not sway the majority of committee members, who, according to Dr Thompson, favoured a universal and compulsory plan with administration through the department of public health and payment of doctors by salary or capitation fee. The Chamber of Commerce representative joined with the three college spokesmen in supporting the subsidy approach. In an unsuccessful attempt to effect internal unanimity, and, presumably, to reduce the dimensions of outside professional protest, the majority compromised on two major points. Their interim report, submitted on 25 September 1961, recommended administration by independent commission and accepted the fee-for-service payment mode insisted upon by the scps. It was essentially what the profession's own policy had been before 1951.

The dissenting foursome submitted a minority report which restated the scps position, claimed the interim report was premature, and criticized the majority view as leading to a "monopolistic" scheme.[65] Since one concession demanded by the college before it consented to participate in the Advisory Planning Committee's deliberations was the right to submit such a memorandum of dissent, Dr W.P. Thompson bitterly commented in 1964: "it is now obvious that from the very beginning the College delegates on the Committee felt that their function was the prevention of any recommendations involving participation by the government, other than handing over subsidy money."[66] A third report was filed by the representative of the Saskatchewan Federation of Labour, who called for administration under the department of public health and payment by salary for doctors.

Seven days after the three documents were submitted the Central Health Services Committee of the scps met to declare its unanimous rejection of the majority views and its support for the minority report's recommendations. Although the administrative structure of the plan put forward by the majority was "superficially" attractive, "closer examination" revealed "a very extensive and effective government control inherent in such a proposal."[67]

Less than two weeks later, on Friday 13 October 1961, the government introduced "An Act to provide for Payment for Services rendered to Certain Persons by Physicians and Certain Other Persons." The scps was neither notified nor consulted concerning the introduction of this legislation. Reasons for such hasty action by the government remain unclear. T.C. Douglas was to depart for federal politics on 7 November, and his leave-taking may have borne on the decision. Previous professional intransigence may also have led the government to believe that consultation with the profession would be fruitless. In any event, the action was ill advised and, from all appearances, unfair. To the scps, it was simply further evidence that the government could not be trusted.

The bill empowered the government to appoint an administrative commission of six to eight persons, including the deputy minister of health and two other physicians. If a doctor were appointed chairman, two additional medical representatives would still be required. Provision was also made for both an advisory council and a medical advisory committee of college-approved physicians. Coverage would be universal and compulsory. Although the mode of remuneration was not specified, it was generally known that the government had accepted fee-for-service. The legislation implicitly acknowledged this fact by stipulating that balance-billing by specialists would be permitted if patients saw them without referral.[68]

Copies of this bill were mailed to every doctor in the province by the Department of Health. Shortly after, at the scps's October annual meeting, the bill was given a highly critical analysis. It was believed that the administrative commission would have almost unlimited powers to control the method and amount of payment under the plan. Dr G.E Wodehouse, chairman of the cma council, spoke at the meeting in support of the subsidy option. Wodehouse subsequently suggested that the bill was prepared before the Thompson Committee reported, and that the "real purpose of the Advisory Committee has ... been to provide a thick coat of political whitewash." As for the advisory council and medical advisory committee provided by the bill, Wodehouse noted that neither the original Saskatchewan Health Services Planning Commission nor the Thompson Committee gave the scps reason to trust such bodies.[69] Particularly vehement criticism of the bill was given by two scps representatives on the Thompson Committee. And on 18 October, claiming that "the maintenance and improvement of the present high standards of medical care will be adversely affected by the present bill," the college voted overwhelmingly to refuse "to accept a government-controlled medical scheme as outlined in the legislative draft" and declared "that it cannot co-operate in such a plan."[70]

THE STALEMATE

Carried along by the ccf majority in the legislature, the Saskatchewan Medical Care Insurance Act proceeded through its three readings without significant amendment. It received royal assent on 17 November 1961, shortly after Woodrow S. Lloyd took the premier's post left vacant by Tommy Douglas's departure. Four days later, J. Walter Erb, the minister of health, was demoted to the public works portfolio and William G. Davies installed in his stead. Woodrow Lloyd was apparently reshuffling the cabinet in preparation for the anticipated political poker game with the scps. The *CMAJ*'s Saskatchewan newsletter commented that Davies was a former head of the Saskatchewan Federation of Labour – and made the link to the then current sfl director who had submitted the third report to the government while serving on the Thompson Committee.[71] The editor of the *Regina Leader-Post* also pointed up Davies's trade union connections, warning that since the act did not include a definite guarantee that the fee-for-service payment mode would be used, "scope is provided for bending the medical care plan into conformity with some of Labour's demands" for a salaried service.[72]

Certainly the medical profession appears to have viewed the Saskatchewan Medical Care Insurance Act in a similarly sinister light. Adjectives such as "dictatorial" were used to describe the legislation; claims were made that it permitted the confidentiality of doctor-patient relations to be breached; and it was further asserted that the Medical Care Insurance Commission (MCIC) charged with administering the act was "given almost unlimited power, subject only to the dictates of the Government, to determine which doctors will be eligible to receive payment for services and what the method and amount of payment shall be."[73]

The actual content of the legislation was later given a detailed clause-by-clause legal analysis by Professor E.A. Tollefson, who concluded that the legislation corresponded with almost all the principals set out by the CMA in its 1960 statement on medical services insurance – a statement to which the SCPS also had subscribed.[74] However, this assessment is not entirely accurate, since the overall thrust of the enactment was obviously in conflict with the CMA-SCPS policy of state-subsidized enrolment in doctor-sponsored plans. That caveat aside, the wording of the act deserves attention; for analysts have differed on whether the legislation was framed in unduly broad terms.[75] The difficulty apparently arose from the fact that the MCIC necessarily had to be given definite legal powers to discharge its administrative and negotiating functions, and the empowering clauses were threatening to the already suspicious SCPS and its allies.[76] For example, section 49.1 of the act allowed the MCIC to "make regulations":

(a) prescribing the arrangements to be made for payment to physicians; (c) prescribing the rates of payments to be made under this Act to physicians and other persons and the method of assessing accounts submitted ... ; (e) respecting the manner and form in which payments to physicians and other persons shall be made under this Act; (g) prescribing the terms and conditions on which physicians and other persons may provide insured services to beneficiaries.

On the other hand, in section 42.3 the act specified that providers and consumers had rights of appeal to the courts concerning any aspect of the law, and it was further stated that the jurisdiction of the College of Physicians and Surgeons was not to be circumscribed.[77]

Professor Malcolm Taylor, a leading expert on Canadian health insurance legislation, has noted that the terminology of the act was so standard that its legal draftsmen were taken aback by the college's interpretations and reactions.[78] In any event, the scps clearly perceived section 49 as ominously broad. Thus, a second key consequence of the government's failure to consult with the profession before passing the Medical Care Insurance Act was the difficulty this oversight posed in ironing out or explaining the wording and implications of contentious clauses.

Though the legislation had provided that two members of the MCIC should be medical doctors, during November and December 1961 the college president, Dr Harold Dalgleish, twice refused invitations from the new minister of health, W.G. Davies, either to appoint representatives to the MCIC, or to discuss the implementation of the legislation. Dalgleish stated flatly that the legislation could not serve as a basis for negotiation. Attempts to recruit doctors directly to sit on the commission proved equally unproductive, since at its annual meeting in October the scps had passed a motion stating that no member of the college was to accept such an appointment without prior consulation with the college executive.[79] Reporting to the CMA executive committee in December, Dalgleish indicated that the scps had taken legal advice and believed that the legislation incorporated "powers and controls that could fundamentally change the practice of medicine." He also claimed that "the present leaders of the Saskatchewan Government ... are firmly dedicated to the principle that government should provide *all* medical services to *all* citizens with *all* doctors as salaried servants of the government." The scps was already planning means to assist doctors economically "through a period of resistance to participation" in the government program. The CMA executive committee agreed to solicit statements favourable to the college's stand from every provincial division. To maximize their media impact they were to be released at intervals between January and March 1962.[80]

On 5 January 1962, with time running short to the proposed 1 April implementation date, Davies announced the appointment of Mr Donald D. Tansley, a senior civil servant, to the post of commission chairman. Three doctors took positions on the MCIC as well. Neither Dr Sam Wolfe, an assistant professor of social and preventive medicine at the Saskatchewan medical school, nor Dr F.B. Roth, the deputy minister of health who served ex officio, was a practising physician. Dr O.K. Hjertaas of Prince Albert, the third doctor on the MCIC, was a general practitioner but already marked as a CCF sympathizer because of previous work done as secretary of the Health Services Planning Commission. Hence none of the MDS had close ties with the college, and the scps leaders publicly reminded the government that the trio served as private citizens rather than professional representatives. Three laymen – a Saskatoon labour lawyer, a farmer who was chairman of the Melfort Health Region Board, and the secretary-treasurer of the Swift Current Health Region – completed the commission. Commenting editorially on 9 January 1962, the *Saskatoon Star-Phoenix* observed pointedly that Tansley's appointment was necessitated by the government's inability to find a doctor who would serve as chairman. The *Star-Phoenix* also objected to the government's new taxes to fund the medicare program, especially since there was no sign that the doctors intended to participate.[81]

On 8 February Donald Tansley again wrote to Dr Harold Dalgleish requesting a meeting to discuss regulations to be adopted for implementation of the law. Two weeks later, Dalgleish replied, citing instances in which the government had failed to consult with the medical profession, and noting: "Your Commission receives its authority under the Saskatchewan Medical Care Insurance Act, 1961 and as such is a child of this Act. We regard this Act as a form of civil conscription of the profession of medicine and an attempt to put us under the control of government by political and economic pressure."[82] Dalgleish therefore advised that the scps would not negotiate with the mcic. In December he had suggested to W.G. Davies that the scps would be willing to meet the government only if the agenda included discussion of items such as a plan to improve mental health services in Saskatchewan and a comprehensive home care program.[83] The February letter referred to these suggestions, indicating that the scps would be happy to discuss the province's "health needs" with the mcic. In short, just as with the Thompson Committee, the scps pursued a strategy of delay and sought to control the agenda for discussion and government action.

On 26 February the mcic chairman wrote to each doctor in the province, seeking individual negotiations. The professional ranks held firm: many indignant replies were received, and several doctors pointed out that since the college was functioning as the profession's trade union in collective bargaining, they had no intention of breaking ranks.[84] By this time the legislature was again in session. Health minister William Davies wrote to the college to indicate the government's willingness to make amendments in the law, and backed this offer up with a radio appeal for co-operation. On the same day (2 March) citing administrative difficulties, Davies announced that the implementation of the act would be delayed until 1 July.

Heartened by its apparent success in forcing a postponement and supported strongly by ongoing editorial commentary in the *Regina Leader-Post* and *Saskatoon Star-Phoenix*,[85] the college council took a hard-line stand. On 15 March, Dalgleish finally replied that the college members were "not willing to provide our services through a compulsory government controlled medical care plan, as set forth in the Saskatchewan Medical Care Insurance Act." Grievances against the government were cited, including the attempt "to impair the unity of the profession" by direct mailings. The recommendations of the Thompson Committee minority report were again rehearsed, and the letter concluded "We would wish to know whether the specific changes in the Act referred to in your letter would be of such a nature as to permit the implementation of our recommendations. If so, these could form the basis of the proposed discussions."[86] Arrangements were nonetheless made to meet with an open agenda. Since neither side had moved from its original position despite an impasse of five months' duration, two crucial and interrelated questions remained unanswered. First, was there any compromise that could satisfy both sides? Second, what exactly would happen if the act came into force on 1 July 1962 as scheduled?

The first face-to-face meetings in the entire dispute were on 28 March and 1 April. A letter from Premier Lloyd to Dr Dalgleish dated 4 April indicated that the government had given some ground, and was prepared to give more. Lloyd suggested that the MCIC could serve as a "registration authority" with control over the private plans. Subject to "the persuasiveness of negotiations," it would control the premiums charged by the private plans, and "the amount, if any, of extra-billing or co-insurance charges." Further, the MCIC would operate a public plan for "those not members of other plans," and in its capacity as "registration authority" would negotiate with the college to establish "a remuneration pattern."

However, in a written statement, the college contended that these and other proposed amendments "did not fundamentally change the legislation": "Even if the legislation were so amended, the Act would remain completely unacceptable to the profession, as government would be the monopoly buyer and seller of all medical services."[87] What the SCPS understandably feared, then, was a concentration of purchasing power in government hands that could countervail the profession's own considerable market strength and potentially lead to interference with the doctors' clinical autonomy as well.

On 11 April the college negotiators offered their "final concession." Again taking their cue from Australian arrangements, the SCPS representatives suggested that the registration agency be a government board functioning through the provincial auditor's office. Government would then pay the premiums for low-income groups to insure with registered agencies. And in a clearly retrogressive step, the college

negotiators now totally abandoned the service principle, which had
been the most positive feature of their own plans. Doctors would
not receive payment directly from the insuring agency but must instead
bill all patients except indigents; the registered carrier would indemnify the patient for all or "a major portion" of the bill. Participation
was to be voluntary. As Badgley and Wolfe pointed out, this program
"would have made the cost of care unpredictable even for those who
were fully insured."[88] The government had already been apprised
of the college's proposals and was predictably unimpressed. The third
face-to-face meeting on 11 April was quickly adjourned by the premier.

The outstanding issue now was what would happen if the plan
went into effect as originally legislated. When the federal Health
Services Commission chaired by Mr Justice Emmett Hall had convened hearings in Regina on 22 January, the scps leaders had indicated
their opposition to the act but added that if it came into effect: "We
would, however, continue to treat our patients in accordance with
our capabilities. We would presume that patients presenting receipts
of payment would be able to obtain reimbursement from the insurance
program."[89] To use current parlance, the scps envisioned mass opting-
out. As originally passed, the act had not clearly delineated that option.
The premier's letter of 4 April offered the alternative administrative
framework described above and also offered "to fashion or re-fashion"
sections of the legislation by clarifying a negotiation and appeal
mechanism for doctors' remuneration, adding college appointees to
the mcic, setting up regional auditing bodies with a college representative to "overview administrative matters affecting individual
physicians," and creating an appeal process to adjudicate any complaints by practitioners about the administration of the act. The most
significant concession, however, was a statement that the government
indeed was prepared to accept indirect payment methods, presumably
including the reimbursement approach.[90] Thus, on 11 April, when
negotiations had been adjourned, Dr Dalgleish advised the cabinet
that doctors would "deal directly with their patients" who would
then "make arrangements with their insuring agency."[91]

Fearing now that extra-billing would be the norm and angered
by the profession's intransigence, the cabinet acted swiftly and with
extraordinarily bad judgment, introducing amendments to the act
on 13 April that included a section conferring wider powers on the
mcic for it to serve as an agent of the beneficiaries in respect of
fees and services. This particular amendment, virtually identical to
clauses in the ms(s)i contract and embodying provisions less stringent
than those in the provincial Automobile Accident Insurance Act, was
inevitably seen by anxious and militant doctors as a sign that the

noose was tightening. The actual intent of the contentious section is reasonably clear. It did not seek to impose a total ban on extra-billing, nor did it automatically force doctors to accept payment from the MCIC at prescribed rates. However, if a patient dealt with an opted-out doctor, and if the bill for services rendered was in excess of MCIC rates, and if a patient complained to this effect to the MCIC, then the MCIC was empowered to take legal action against the doctor in that case.[92] Whether the MCIC would actually take such action – or succeed in court – remained moot.

In the atmosphere of mistrust and bitterness that had developed, there was general confusion about the legal significance of the amendments. The Liberal caucus denounced and voted against the amending bill. The Sifton press made what Premier Lloyd termed "inflammatory distortion" of the new provisions.[93] For example, the *Regina Leader-Post* claimed that the doctors would now be "pawns of the Commission, subject to dictation as to what they can charge for their services [and] when they would receive payment." [94] In the profession's view, practitioners could no longer deal directly with patients unless the patient completed "a form which will be prescribed by a regulation of the Commission." Moreover, even if patients completed this form, the amendments supposedly meant that the government would no longer reimburse them.[95] Neither of these interpretations was accurate.[96]

By this stage, the "Keep Our Doctors Committees" (KODCS) moved into action. Organized originally by four concerned housewives who were disturbed at the prospect of losing their family physicians, the KODCS rapidly became a vehicle for various interest groups with anti-government feelings. Doctors, druggists, dentists, and businessmen lent financial aid to the KODC movement. Opposition political parties, above all the Liberals, hastened to spearhead what was seen as a means of mobilizing and uniting anti-socialist opinion in the province. By the end of April the KODC movement was mushrooming. Thirty-six communities soon established KODC branches, with business and professional men playing a key organizational role in the province-wide protest.[97] Of the KODCS Grove and Hughes have written: "The atmosphere of hysteria they whipped up, the vociferous and virulent condemnations of the government, and the dire predictions of communistic gloom, could only confirm and augment the doctors' fears of the medical care insurance legislation and inflate their concept of the support which they enjoyed in the province."[98] Local boards of trade and the Saskatchewan Chamber of Commerce joined in calling for a one-year postponement of the legislation until amendments could be made to satisfy the profession. Meanwhile, church, farm, and labour organizations endorsed the government's position.[99] Thus, just as in British Columbia twenty-five years earlier, the dispute increasingly polarized the province along ideological and socio-economic lines.

Although negotiations between the cabinet and scps had failed, mcic chairman Donald Tansley wrote to Dr Dalgleish on 21 April. The mcic proposed to make payments on a fee-for-service basis at 85 percent of the scps fee schedule – the same arrangement used by ms(s)i and gms. This letter also reaffirmed that "a choice of paying physicians directly for claims or routing payment to the doctor through the patient [would] be offered to each physician."[100] Tansley invited comments or a meeting. Dalgleish did not reply.

On 3 and 4 May the college held an emergency meeting in Regina. Some 600 doctors closed their offices to attend. Premier Lloyd requested and was given permission to address the angry assembly, but shortly before the premier arrived to speak, there came a dramatic announcement. J.W. Erb, demoted from the health ministry by the premier six months earlier, had resigned as minister of public works, claiming that the medicare act violated Tommy Douglas's fifth principle of acceptability to the profession. (Erb also feared that the ndp was under the control of the labour movement.)[101] Although Woodrow Lloyd pressed on with his planned remarks, his hour-long plea for a reasoned compromise was interrupted three times by hissing from the audience.[102] Immediately afterwards, Dr Dalgleish called for a standing vote of those who would not serve under the act. In the words of the profession's newsletter: "No one present will ever forget the historic scene presented by an immediate response of 545 of the 550 present, who stood to their feet – applauding long and loudly."[103] At this meeting the profession also voted to begin preparations for a withdrawal of all but emergency services on 1 July 1962, the date set for implementation of the legislation.

The mcic now began work with the Department of Public Health to prepare for the probable doctors' strike. Dr Sam Wolfe was sent to London and undertook to recruit British doctors willing to take full-time posts in rural areas or help temporarily during the strike. Eventually more than 100 doctors were airlifted into the province from other parts of North America and the United Kingdom. During May, the kodcs also became increasingly active, organizing rallies around the province, collecting 46,000 signatures on a petition calling for delay of the program until it was approved by the profession, and generating additional publicity with a steady stream of press releases. The government's plans to recruit doctors from outside the province were satirized. Featured at one kodc rally on the steps of the legislative building was a marcher dressed in what has been described as "a large semitic nose, Chinese pig-tail, and middle-east style of clothing," carrying a sign that read "Sask Gov't Medicare Import." A cartoon in the Regina and Saskatoon papers struck a similar chord with a black African in tribal regalia and witch-doctor mask arriving for an interview with Sam Wolfe.[104]

As the days and weeks elapsed, a central issue that continued to surface was whether doctors did in fact have the right to practise privately. Legal advisers to the SCPS were uncertain, since the regulations under which the plan would operate had still not been announced by the MCIC. Moreover, despite his letter of 21 April, MCIC Chairman Tansley added to the confusion in an interview with the press. Although he indicated that the reimbursement option was open, he also stated that if a patient insisted that a doctor accept payment from the MCIC at the standard rate, the doctor had no recourse.[105] (As already noted, this was true only if the MCIC took successful court action on the patient's behalf and, more importantly, if patients were sufficiently perturbed by the magnitude of over-billing relative to reimbursement rates that they were willing to destroy their relationship with a doctor by filing a complaint.)

On 7 June Premier Lloyd again wrote to Dr Dalgleish, repeating the government's offer to revise the legislation to meet the profession's concerns, and proposing that third-party mediation would be helpful. Dalgleish replied on 11 June, suggesting that the Saskatchewan Hospital Association fill this role. No date for face-to-face negotiations was suggested.

THE STRIKE AND THE SETTLEMENT

As the 1 July deadline approached, CMA delegates began arriving in Winnipeg for the association's annual meeting. The executive committee traditionally met before the general council convened, and it devoted considerable time to the Saskatchewan situation. H.D. Dalgleish advised the committee that the regulations of the MCIC had just been released, and after study by the officers and legal counsel of the college it had been decided that the profession must proceed with its strike plan. In a sobering analysis Dalgleish nonetheless observed:

Over the past two and a half years, the public in that province seems to have accepted and approved of the fact that they will be provided with some form of plan for comprehensive all-inclusive medical care insurance. None of the groups that have advocated delay, mediation and discussion of the disputed features of the Saskatchewan Medical Care Insurance Act have given any indication that this legislation should be completely withdrawn.[106]

Although the *CMAJ* reported that there was "some lack of unanimity of opinion" about the ethicality of the mass office closure, unanimous support for the SCPS was tendered.

Indeed, the CMA could not afford to break ranks. Governments in Alberta, Manitoba, and Ontario were believed to favour the CMA's subsidy approach to medical services insurance. If Saskatchewan successfully implemented a universal state-administered program, it could have considerable influence on other provinces, not to mention the Royal Commission on Health Services and the federal government. Thus, in an impassioned speech to the general council, the CMA president, Dr G.W. Halpenny, contended that no other event in Canadian medical history had drawn doctors so closely together as the plight of the Saskatchewan profession. He warned of the suffering that lay ahead in Saskatchewan and added: "I can only hope that the unscrupulous politicians will also suffer very severely for their reckless gambling with the welfare of the citizens whom they claim to represent."[107]

One politician, in fact, was about to suffer. T.C. "Tommy" Douglas, standing for the NDP in Regina in the 18 June federal election, was badly defeated. That the riding was a safe Conservative seat and the election one in which the Conservatives swept the Prairies seemed irrelevant; Douglas's defeat was hailed as a vote against the CCF-NDP medicare plan.

At a general council session on 19 June delegates received a background paper on the Saskatchewan situation prepared by Woody Freamo, the CMA's economics secretary. This document warned repeatedly of political, economic, and legislative control of the profession.[108] Dr Dalgleish was invited to speak and stressed to council that public support for the SCPS appeared to be growing. The basis for any final negotiations, he contended, must be repeal or rewriting of the act with the legislature summoned to pass amendments into law. The council then voted unanimously in favour of authorizing the executive committee to make any expenditures necessary to assist the SCPS, even if CMA membership dues would later have to be increased. A toughly worded telegram to Premier Lloyd was also unanimously approved.[109]

Soon after, with the Saskatchewan Hospital Association serving as intermediary, the SCPS leadership and the cabinet arranged to meet on 22 June. The broader question of administrative framework was only briefly rehearsed; the SCPS called for reconsideration of its subsidy approach; the government refused. However, the cabinet negotiators went to considerable lengths to reassure the profession, offering to promulgate cabinet orders-in-council to eliminate offensive clauses that appeared to impinge on professional self-government and, above all, giving an iron-clad guarantee that doctors could practise outside the act. A binding regulation to this effect was drawn up by the cabinet and MCIC in consultation with lawyers, and the premier also gave his word that at the next session of the legislature, an amendment to this effect would be passed. During negotiations, it was explicitly suggested that the SCPS council was free to advise its members to remain opted out until individually satisfied; since the government preferred a service-type plan, it would work doubly hard to make sure that doctors found the scheme acceptable enough to opt back in.[110]

On 25 June the college tabled a clause-by-clause list of written criticisms of the act for the first time. However, by this stage naturally there were few surprises. The government replied on 26 June, explaining or defending some clauses and offering to amend or delete many others. Its memorandum emphasized twice more that doctors "will have the unfettered right to charge their patients without reference to the Plan." In a separate exchange of letters on 26 June between Lloyd and Dalgleish, the premier provided additional details about the reimbursement plan, and rejected a suggestion that GMS, MS(s)I, and the Swift Current board be allowed to act as intermediaries between the MCIC and participating doctors.[111] In a final effort to head off the withdrawal of services, the premier also sent a letter outlining the reimbursement method to every physician in the province.[112]

The college leaders had earlier said that they would simply call for members to practise outside the act and announced strike action only when they interpreted the April amendments as a bar on opting out. It is clear that the SCPS took this view of the amendments right up to the time of the meeting on 22 June. Now came the necessary assurances, yet negotiations broke off on 27 June. Why?

First, as indicated to the government on 22 June, the SCPS council began to have misgivings about the reimbursement option. The doctors' delegation contended that the profession would be divided into two camps – the opted-in and opted-out groups. Second, and more importantly, the reimbursement avenue did nothing to alter the fact that an objectionable program was to be put firmly in place, effectively closing the profession-sponsored insurance agencies.[113] Third, and of uncertain significance,[114] the college simply refused to accept the cabinet's promises. A deep distrust of government, heightened by the sometimes scurrilous propaganda of their supporters, led the doctors to indicate that neither immediate orders-in-council nor the premier's solemn word that these orders-in-council would be subsequently passed into law could be relied upon. (Indeed, Tollefson suggests that the scps leaders' remarks may have been defamatory.)[115] Further efforts to reopen negotiations were made by the Saskatchewan Hospital Association and the urban and rural municipalities associations, but they proved fruitless.

On 1 July 1962 the overwhelming majority of doctors practising in the province closed their offices. The scps had organized a highly efficient and free emergency service which utilized 240 volunteer doctors working in thirty-four hospitals. About 250 practitioners left for summer holidays. Only 35 or so actively practised under the act's terms, although this number was gradually swollen by government imports and indigenous defectors. There is little question that the closure of offices, early discharges from hospitals, and transfers of seriously ill patients from unattended hospitals to the designated emergency centres helped generate an air of hysteria in the early days of the strike. The KODCs added to the general level of anxiety by taking out alarmist advertisements in the newspapers, flooding the media with press releases, and building publicity for a mammoth rally to be held on 11 July in front of the legislature.

Media representatives in large numbers descended on the province. In the view of the scps leaders most carried an anti-doctor bias and an ad hoc public relations committee consisting of a urologist, an internist, and a GP was set up to deal with the national and international press.[116] Not unexpectedly, the provincial newspapers were sympathetic to the strike action. A few out-of-province dailies – the *Halifax Chronicle-Herald, Quebec Chronicle-Telegraph, Montreal Gazette* and *Toronto Telegram* – also produced editorials placing responsibility for the situation on the shoulders of the CCF-NDP government. But editorials in many major out-of-province newspapers – the *Star* and *Le Devoir* in Montreal, the *Globe and Mail* and *Daily Star* in Toronto, the *Citizen* in Ottawa, and the *Financial Post* – were highly critical of the profession and the strike. Whatever the editorialists thought of universal medicare itself, what was at issue was respect for a law passed by a democratically elected government.[117] Even the *Winnipeg Free Press*, a strong supporter of the CMA's subsidy proposals,[118] commented on 4 July that the government "appeared to be ready to go a considerable way toward meeting the stated objections of the doctors ... The Doctors' refusal to move from their previously held position can only lead to a widespread loss of public confidence in the sincerity of their stated motives." Eventually both the *Lancet* and the *British Medical Journal* condemned the withdrawal

of services, although American medical groups offered encouragement, donations, and relocation to jobs south of the border for the
strikers.[119] Canadian organized medicine outside Saskatchewan was
also supportive. The *CMAJ* cited George Orwell and drew parallels
between Saskatchewan's legislation and Communist clamp-downs on
private medical practice in eastern Europe.[120] The OMA wholly backed
the work action in a 12 July newsletter. And the president of the
Ottawa Academy of Medicine, calling for immediate creation of a
$25,000 "Saskatchewan Aid Fund," asserted, "They need the lift to
their morale now! Let's show them that we appreciate the fight that
they put up for *us* now!"[121]

At Premier Lloyd's request, most of the groups supporting the
government kept a low profile to avoid confrontations with the KODC
factions. Nevertheless, a pro-medicare newsletter was circulated, and
large advertisements endorsing the CCF-NDP stand were taken out in
some newspapers. One advertisement pointedly reminded doctors of
their professional creed with its caption – "A Broken Oath."[122] So
far as the beleaguered SCPS loyalists were concerned, the campaign
against doctors was extensive and centrally directed. Dr Lewis M.
Brand joined the vice-president of the KODC in an unsuccessful attempt
to obtain a legal injunction against the Medical Care Insurance
Commission and later reminisced:

In an effort to wear down the medical profession, the government pulled
out all the stops. Union public relations men from as far as Newfoundland,
together with the highly skilled propaganda team in Regina, played the
news media in every way to discredit the medical profession and divide its
members ... News stories and television specials relentlessly pictured the
doctor as a social parasite, more interested in money than patients.[123]

Further support for the medical care plan was offered by the
Community Health Services Association (CHSA). Culling membership
among farm and labour groups, CCF sympathizers, and other
factions who were disenchanted with the medical profession's work
action, the CHSA began operating community clinics even as the strike
entered its first days. By the end of July there were clinics operating
in five centres and ten more were in the planning stage. These clinics
provided premises where physicians willing to serve under the terms
of the Medical Care Insurance Act could work in salaried group
practices.

Although the CMA advised that sixty doctors had been relocated
to practices outside the province, those who were determined to stay
on began trickling back to work. By 10 July twenty-five additional

hospitals were in service, and over 100 hospitals were serving public needs by the time the strike ended. The symbolic turning point came at the much-publicized KODC rally in front of the legislature on 11 July. Liberal leader Ross Thatcher was the principal speaker, and he demanded recall of the legislature to repeal the Medical Care Insurance Act. But whereas the KODC leaders had predicted a crowd of 40,000, the actual turnout was estimated at about one-tenth that number. At this juncture the SCPS council was becoming increasingly concerned by the exodus of established practitioners from the province. Behind-the-scenes efforts to produce a compromise were already under way and hereafter they gained momentum. The college was first to soften its position. It now proposed that, if other minor issues were settled, the only major concession needed would be the retention of GMS and MS(S)I, not in their previous autonomous capacity but rather as premium-collecting intermediaries to which consumers could assign their "payment rights." The CCF-NDP annual convention was taking place in Saskatoon's Bessborough Hotel, and at the profession's request Dr Dalgleish addressed the convention on 18 July to present the college's proposals: doctors would return to work if a special session of the legislature were convened to pass into law the premier's assurances that doctors could opt out and if an amendment were also made to preserve a role for the two profession-sponsored agencies.

A catalyst in the negotiation process was the arrival of Lord Stephen Taylor on 17 July. As a doctor and former Labour MP, Taylor had been involved in the planning and implementation of Britain's National Health Service. The Labour peer was invited as a consultant to the government, but he visited the SCPS Council immediately after Dalgleish's address to the CCF-NDP convention. CMA General Secretary A.D. Kelly later noted that Taylor met the council "in an atmosphere which I can only report to be a mixture of suspicion and curiosity," but this soon changed: "Although the guest could not be classified as a mediator he immediately began to act like one ... By sheer force of an attractive and aggressive personality he rapidly reached the stage where Council was agreeing to his transmission of the doctors' case to Government and after two hours of discussion he departed to do just that."[124] Since the college headquarters in the Saskatoon Medical Arts Building were only three blocks from the Bessborough Hotel and the CCF convention, Taylor soon found himself striding back and forth between the opposing forces, at last bringing the two sides together to sign the Saskatoon Agreement on 23 July. Over the next several days doctors' offices reopened and hospitals resumed their normal function.

Under the terms of the settlement[125] the government convened a special session of the legislature in early August to pass amendments to the act. Ambiguous wording in some clauses was improved to put the doctors at ease. Three mutually acceptable medical appointees representing the scps were eventually added to the Medical Care Insurance Commission. But the key changes came in defining three separate ways a doctor could be paid. A practitioner could bill patients directly. Patients could then seek reimbursement from the commission and receive a sum equal to 85 percent of the current scps fee schedule for the services rendered. Alternatively, a practitioner could elect to participate in the plan, billing it directly, and agreeing to take 85 percent of the scps fee schedule as full payment without any extra-billing for those services. This was how gms and ms(s)i had operated. Finally, the doctor could take his or her payments through one of the profession-sponsored plans at 85 percent of full tariff, thereby dealing with an intermediary as opposed to government itself.

The first option allowed doctors the satisfaction of practising outside the plan and charging their patients 100 percent tariff or more than the fee schedule set out by the scps. The net effect was to convert a government service plan into an indemnity plan of the sort sold by investor-owned agencies. This option had, of course, been offered by the government repeatedly before the strike; (indeed, it remains unlikely that the April amendments actually could have been applied so as to cut off the reimbursement avenue in any case). Government fears about the problem of billings above the reimbursement rate had already been made plain in the premier's letter of 26 June to all practitioners in which he had warned of the possibility of public complaints about extra-billing and the need for an agreement with the college to control the billing practices of opted-out doctors.

The second option was most in keeping with the government's preference for a genuine social insurance program. Practitioners essentially forwent 15 percent of the tariff in return for the mcic's acting as their collection agency on a prepayment basis. Patients had greater security against the costs of illness without the deterrent effect inherent in the knowledge that direct out-of-pocket expenses would result.

The third alternative was obviously the most important concession given by the government. As noted above, Dr Dalgleish had raised the question of the prepayment agencies acting as intermediaries in his letter to Premier Lloyd on 26 June. It is interesting to speculate whether a strike would have been averted had the cabinet accepted that option in late June. On the other hand, on 4 April the premier had suggested that the two doctor-sponsored agencies continue operations with the mcic as a regulatory body; he was turned down. The

Saskatoon Agreement gave GMS and MS(S)I less of a role than the April proposal, since the government did not accept the SCPS request that these agencies be allowed to continue collecting premiums. Hence GMS and MS(S)I acted primarily to redirect payments from the MCIC to doctors, apparently serving little more than a post office function. Lord Taylor had nonetheless perceived that these plans were familiar agencies which in the short term defused the conflicts and resentment that might have arisen had doctors been able to bill only the MCIC. Moreover, the preference of doctors to deal with GMS and MS(S)I ensured that these intermediaries were initially the most popular conduit for financial transactions. Consumers joined by paying a small fee instead of the original premiums and in turn were guaranteed that their doctor would not extra-bill.

(Ironically, the SCPS itself had helped ensure that the two agencies were given a limited role during the Thompson Committee deliberations two years previously. At a meeting of that body, Dr Irwin Hilliard, representing the University of Saskatchewan medical faculty, moved that "this Committee recommend that in the development of a universal program, MSI, GMS, Swift Current and other existing plans should be used in such a way as to make use of their experience, administrative staff and facilities."[126] This motion was seconded by the deputy minister of health, but put aside on a tabling motion by the SCPS representatives, who were then sufficiently adamant in their opposition to a universal plan that a compromise to allow a place for the profession's insurance vehicles in such a scheme could not be brooked.)

Although retention of the two provincial TCMP agencies was obviously in part simply a face-saving device for the SCPS, important strategic considerations were also involved. The background paper prepared by the CMA secretary on economics, Woody Freamo, for the 1962 CMA annual convention provides some useful insights. Saskatchewan doctors, wrote Freamo, "are not primarily concerned about their personal incomes – *for the first few years* at least their incomes would increase above present levels" because of universal insurance. However, since the MCIC did not "have fiscal authority or autonomy," "dollars to pay for medical services must be in constant competition with dollars needed to build roads and bridges and support other health and welfare services." And just as in the Saskatchewan Hospital Services Plan, controls might eventually need to be instituted.[127] What Freamo and the SCPS foresaw and understandably feared, then, was a situation in which the private flow of funds through investor-owned or doctor-sponsored prepayment agencies was to be replaced by a single channel with tight-fisted public treasury officials at the tap.

In the final analysis it was the profession's own "fiscal authority or autonomy" that was at issue, not that of the MCIC. The strategic importance of the TCMP plans therefore hinged on the prospect of a different government's taking power and adopting a variant on the SCPS-CMA subsidy scheme. As Dr H.D. Dalgleish told a CMA executive committee meeting in mid-September 1962, "It is the hope of the College of Physicians and Surgeons ... that these agencies may survive and be able to resume a more active role as prepayment media in the event that a different government should be elected in the future."[128]

With neither side pleased by the compromises inherent in the amended legislation, the situation in the province continued to be tense for months afterwards and was described by one medical observer as "an armed truce."[129] The ceasefire was frequently shattered. SCPS representatives complained that the government and labour organizations were giving unfair support to the community clinic movement. With the spread of community health centres could come the threat of a broad-based, salaried, general-practitioner service, supplanting extant patterns of fee-for-service insurance practice. (In fact, the number of community clinics reached a peak of eight in mid-1966 and seven years later was down to two.) The status of radiologists and pathologists, caught in limbo between the medicare act and the hospital services program, remained a source of government-SCPS conflict.[130] Many practitioners made it clear that their sufferance was temporary; if the Liberals came to power, they would demand repeal of the act. And Woody Freamo, the CMA's economist who had been assigned to Saskatchewan during much of the conflict, doubtless spoke for some opponents of the program when he firmly denied the legitimacy of the government's action: "I am quite certain that in Saskatchewan there was no substantial body of public opinion which was demanding government intervention."[131]

Dr W.W. Wigle, the president-elect of the CMA, did not entirely agree. He, too, had been at the storm centre in Saskatoon; like many others, he had been caught up in the emotional maelstrom. Writing for the *CMAJ* a few weeks after the strike, Wigle accurately characterized the implementation of the act as occurring "in an atmosphere of poor understanding, distrust on both sides, and a genuine failure to establish acceptable ideologies and work towards them as men of good faith." He stressed that the doctors had acted appropriately. Any tarnishing of the profession's image outside the province would be temporary, and only those inside the province who had witnessed events at first hand could truly understand how the dispute had escalated.

Although he believed that doctors in Saskatchewan had mustered considerable public support for their stand, the CMA president-elect warned that "a large segment of the population" clearly wanted to prepay their medical care completely: "It is also obvious that many people would have no objections to the funds being raised by taxation." The lesson of Saskatchewan was plain:

The prepayment of medical care in all its phases – the collection of funds, the administration and the payment for the services – must be more diligently studied and controlled by the profession or it will be done by someone else. No one else should be acceptable to us because those who control these factors on a completely comprehensive basis, which is what the people desire, will control medicine.[132]

CHAPTER EIGHT

Medicare in the Crucible
II: A National Plan

What we seek is a method that will provide everybody in Canada with comprehensive coverage regardless of age or state of health or ability to pay, upon uniform terms and conditions.

> Royal Commission on Health Services, *Final Report*, vol. 1, 1964

The medical profession affirms that no citizen, be he patient or physician, should be forced to conform to a pattern of medical care which is unacceptable to him.

> CMA Special Committee on Policy, 1964

THE ROYAL COMMISSION ON HEALTH SERVICES

As the conflict in Saskatchewan intensified, the federal Royal Commission on Health Services began its hearings. The commission's chairman, Mr Justice Emmett Hall, was the son of a dairy farmer who had graduated from the law course at the University of Saskatchewan in 1919 alongside John Diefenbaker. A Progressive Conservative politically, Hall's distinguished legal career took him to the position of Chief Justice of the Saskatchewan Court of Appeal and later to the Supreme Court of Canada.[1] Joining Hall on the commission were Dr Leslie Strachan, a dentist; Alice Girard, dean of the University of Montreal School of Nursing; and a former economic adviser to the St Laurent government, Dr O.J. Firestone. Wallace McCutcheon, a well-to-do industrialist, was a fifth member, but he eventually resigned to take a place in the Conservative government.

Two physicians were also appointed. One was D. David M. Baltzan, a distinguished internist and chief of staff at St Paul's Hospital in Saskatoon. Dr Baltzan had treated Diefenbaker's mother; and when the prime minister sent Hall a list of twenty potential commissioners, his name was the only one singled out for definite inclusion.[2] Baltzan had been president of the Saskatchewan College of Physicians and Surgeons in 1937, and in later years was prominent in the Canadian Council of Christians and Jews. The other medical appointee was Dr Arthur F. van Wart of Fredericton, New Brunswick. Like Dr Baltzan, Dr van Wart had a record of public service and strong ties to organized medicine. He was a past president of the CMA and had been active in medical politics for over forty years.

With a national inquiry in process, the CMA was naturally forced to divide its energies between monitoring the Saskatchewan situation and devising approaches to persuade the royal commission that the private sector arrangements should not be swept aside by a state plan. And by 1961 those arrangements were extensive: a total of 4.5 million Canadians had some degree of coverage through the eleven profession-sponsored plans in the Trans-Canada Medical Plans conglomerate, while another 4.2 million held policies with investor-owned carriers. On the other hand, few in the upper echelons of the association had any illusions about the fact that some form of partnership with government was inevitable. As Dr E.K. Lyon, a Leamington surgeon and 1960 deputy-president of the CMA, put it: "Although government in itself can never render the necessary medical care to the Canadian people independent of the cooperation of the medical profession, I am just as certain that the medical profession cannot render the necessary care without a large measure of government support."[3]

The imminent threat of a government-sponsored scheme had prompted the formation of an ideological alliance between the SCPS and the private insurance industry in 1959–60. In like fashion the CMA had come to understand that closer ties with the insurance industry were imperative. The number of Canadians holding medical insurance with investor-owned companies, after all, was now so large that it was no longer reasonable to demand state-subsidized enrolment in TCMP agencies to the exclusion of other carriers. The Canadian Health Insurance Association (CHIA), representing more than 100 companies, was equally concerned to forge a bond with organized medicine, and emphasized the threat of state control when it approached the CMA. C.H. Shillington, the executive director of TCMP at this time, has reported that the investor-owned consortium insisted that "the doctors' only protection lay in the retention of multiple insurance organizations in the health field and for this reason every support should be given to the insurance companies who were fighting the profession's battle as much as were the sponsored plans."[4] Some TCMP agencies were uncomfortable with the new three-way alliance. Their approach was non-profit; and if in the first instance the sponsored plans had served professional purposes, they had also grown to have their own institutional ideals of public service which the for-profit plans apparently lacked. But in March 1961, even before the personnel of the Hall Commission had been announced, the CMA executive committee had already arranged to collaborate with CHIA in preparation of briefs for the upcoming hearings.[5]

By autumn 1961 the health service commissioners were on the road in the Maritimes, inundated at each hearing with a flood of submissions detailing deficiencies in the health care system and recommending means of improvement. (More than 400 briefs were submitted in toto). The hearings moved west, reaching Regina in January 1962. There, understandably, the mid-winter prairie chill outside was countered in heated sessions inside, as the government and the SCPS used their briefs to spar over the imminent implementation of the CCF medicare act. By spring, as the deadlock in Saskatchewan continued, the commissioners returned to central Canada.

The CMA had made a preliminary submission to the royal commission in collaboration with L'Association des Médecins de langue française du Canada eight months previously. Hearings in each provincial capital provided an opportunity for divisions of the CMA to repeat organized medicine's message: governments should concern themselves with the low-income group and should not displace the TCMP or private carriers. Finally, in the senate chambers of the University of Toronto came the full submissions from the two most powerful medical organizations in the nation – the OMA and the CMA. Representing 6,500 doctors, on 7 May 1962 the OMA tabled a brief of just under 300 pages that touched on virtually all aspects of medical and hospital services. As expected, the OMA's position on medical insurance was given priority in the verbal presentation. Dr P. Bruce-Lockhart, the OMA president, stated,

[W]e are frankly afraid of any plan, or plans, with total or major government financing because history has taught us that then the monies for medical care have to compete at the Treasury level with the other needs of society, which means that political expediency dictates the allocation of money and not individual medical needs ... In addition to these fears, we are flatly opposed to government ever being the sole purchaser of medical services, because quite simply we would consider this conscription. Would this situation not be vicious if the only way a man can change his employer is by leaving the country?[6]

Like the scps, the oma set out various other areas where government should intervene before even considering prepayment of medical services for the low-income group.[7]

Eight days later the cma's main submission was given in the same venue. Dr G.E. Wodehouse, chairman of the subcommittee charged with preparing the document, served as principal spokesman. The cma brief was an impressive analysis of the health services sector, pin-pointing short-term and long-term problem areas and suggesting an assortment of remedial measures. But mirroring their Saskatchewan colleagues, the cma health services team placed medical care insurance well down on its list of priorities for state action. And on this point the cautionary proposals stood in contrast to other sections of the brief: governments should follow the subsidy route and leave existing private-sector schemes intact.[8] A cma correspondent later described the brief's reception: "Our appearance has been referred to as the profession's day in court, and the wide-ranging discussion did at times take on the atmosphere of the adversary system of a court of law. The debate on health insurance inevitably was promoted from the fourth priority which we have assigned it, to the centre of the stage."[9]

Six weeks after the main cma submission, the doctors' strike began in Saskatchewan. As noted in chapter 7, open editorial support for the strike was offered by the *CMAJ*,[10] and it was widely known that the national association had played a part in funding earlier scps resistance and in encouraging the college to stand its ground in the latter stage of the conflict. Since most out-of-province commentary on the strike was negative, some members of the royal commission may perhaps have become more sceptical of organized medicine's intentions. It is certain, however, that they were uneasy about the possibility of another confrontation on the scale of the Saskatchewan debacle; for in October 1962, appearing at the final "rebuttal" hearings of the royal commission in Ottawa, cma spokesmen were questioned closely concerning the profession's willingness to negotiate with a government that had already decided on a compulsory universal program. Their reply was not totally reassuring. Although the professional organizations would discuss health insurance with any government, this did not mean "that we are willing to accept any preconceived conclusion which they may have reached." Nor could a Saskatchewan-style work-action be ruled out: "It is possible that a similar situation might arise in any other province, if the government decided to proceed in the same dictatorial fashion."[11]

It seemed, then, that the profession was girding its loins for further struggles, a factor that must surely have weighed on the minds of the commissioners. Furthermore, the year of hearings had brought more than thirty submissions backing the CMA's subsidy approach to medical care insurance. Chambers of commerce, insurance industry spokesmen, TCMP representatives, and ten provincial divisions of the CMA had taken up the refrain. The profession's relations with the commissioners were not as close as those with the Heagerty Committee had been during the 1940s, nor did the CMA have informal ties of the sort developed with doctors on the Special Committee on Social Security in 1943-4. But in other respects its position was stronger. Both Baltzan and van Wart were former leaders of organized medical groups. As well, the CMA had powerful allies in the business community, a clear plan of action, and a framework of agencies in place which made its approach feasible.

It is worth considering the perspectives of labour and agriculture – the CMA's long-time opponents in debates about health care. Although some 90 to 95 percent of employees had coverage consequent upon collective bargaining arrangements, organized labour continued to offer strong support for a public health care scheme. One union's research officer claimed that only between 20 and 45 percent of the costs of health care were met by these plans, and "we believe the 45 percent to be a very liberal upper estimate."[12] (These figures presumably were derived by considering all health-related expenditures, ranging from eyeglasses to prescription and over-the-counter drugs.) Hence, in its brief to the royal commission the Canadian Labour Congress showed little patience with the argument that present arrangements were satisfactory. It also rejected the concept of insurance per se. The health care system should operate as a public service, and any program must be comprehensive, universal, progressively financed, free of direct charges at point of service, administered through the department of public health with the advice and assistance of a representative advisory council, and preferably organized to pay doctors by some means other than fee-for-service.[13] Whereas organized labour had scarcely changed its viewpoint since the 1940s, its "partner" in disagreements with the medical profession – the Canadian Federation of Agriculture – was now more conservative. The CFA accepted premium financing and the fee-for-service payment mode, although the latter concession was made in the same grudging fashion that had been evident in the Saskatchewan farmers' brief to the

Thompson Committee. But the CFA also gently pointed out that the central issue was accountability:

The voluntary approach however elaborated or supplemented, leaves very much in the hands of the medical profession the question of administration of most of the plans, of remuneration, of control of misuse, of organization of medical services, of coordination with public health services, and so on. The governmental approach, even on a fee-for-service basis, does open up an avenue of review.[14]

For the commissioners, then, there was a gruelling task ahead. The accumulated information must be sifted and digested. Special research reports prepared by Canadian scholars were also to be assimilated. And at the same time, a watchful eye needed to be kept on the provinces; for even as Saskatchewan's universal plan limped into action, there were signs that other provinces were following a different course.

PROVINCIAL DEVELOPMENTS

In the months that the Hall Commission continued its behind-the-scenes deliberations, Ontario, Alberta, and British Columbia indicated their intention of implementing schemes tailored along the lines preferred by organized medicine and the insurance industry. All three provinces were under conservative governments and firmly rejected Saskatchewan's "socialistic" scheme. In April 1963, shortly before the Liberals under Lester B. Pearson ended the Diefenbaker interlude in Ottawa, the Ontario Progressive Conservatives announced that they would proceed with a program of subsidized enrolment in private-sector plans. The Ontario Liberal party had declared its support for a universal and comprehensive plan structured along the lines of the compromise act operating in Saskatchewan, and it joined the NDP caucus in criticizing the proposal. By early 1964 British Columbia's Social Credit government was also known to be considering the subsidy route.

Although neither province took immediate steps to implement such programs, Alberta's Social Credit government announced in June 1963 that it would offer those in low-income groups a subsidy for enrolment in Medical Services (Alberta) Incorporated or one of more than thirty private carriers. The "co-ordinating directorate" of the program consisted of representatives of the health minister, the Alberta College of Physicians and Surgeons, the Canadian Health Insurance Association, and MSI (Alberta). High-risk individuals were to be insured through a separate pooling agency. Those who required assistance would not be subjected to a formal means test but nonetheless were to submit a statutory declaration proving need by 30 September 1963. Despite an extension on this deadline, only 120,000 applied out of an estimated 300,000 to 400,000 eligible. Another extension was granted, and further efforts were made to promote the application process. Eventually, most Albertans were enrolled; but of the 200,000 uninsured some 150,000 were from the low-income group, and it was generally suggested that an inadequate subsidy relative to high premiums was the overriding reason for non-participation.[15] The progress of the Alberta plan was closely monitored in Ottawa.[16]

Another interesting provincial development took place in Quebec. The cleavages between the interests of GPs and specialists were minor on the broad outlines of health insurance, and a united front had apparently been kept up in all provinces. Nevertheless, there was some resentment of the declining status of GPs, and nowhere was this more pronounced than in Quebec. The council of the Quebec College of Physicians and Surgeons was dominated by specialists at this time, and it had served as negotiating body with the provincial government during the implementation phase of hospital insurance in 1961. That same year a group of GP-activists broke away to form La Fédération des Médecins omnipracticiens du Québec (FMOQ), declaring that the college could no longer pretend to protect the public interest while negotiating as the doctors' advocate.[17] Other grievances were of course involved.

Dr Lucien Joubert's *La Médecine est Malade* (1962) presented some of the GPs' complaints. General practitioners apparently resented the domination of medical faculties by specialists and were perturbed by the steady withdrawal of their admitting privileges at major hospitals in urban centres. Moreover in 1960 the College of Physicians and Surgeons had created a double tariff, wherein specialists would be paid more than a GP performing exactly the same service. Joubert asked rhetorically, "N'est-ce pas plus agréable de voir cinq malades a vingt dollars ce consultation que vingt malades a cinq dollars?"[18] The FMOQ accordingly sought to restore both a single tariff and the GPs' admitting privileges in major urban hospitals. Breaking ranks further, it also endorsed a compulsory universal medicare scheme in 1963, favouring a plan such as Saskatchewan's but without intermediary agencies.[19]

This minor insurrection, however, involved only part of the profession in a francophone province that had never been hospitable to the CMA. On other fronts there was evidence that organized medicine might carry the day. Alberta was now "safe," Ontario and British Columbia were headed in appropriate directions. Moreover on 22 April 1964 the Liberals under Ross Thatcher had come to power in Saskatchewan. Although Thatcher and his Liberal colleagues had made the CCF medicare plan a target for constant criticism during the two years prior to its implementation, the Liberals had been oddly reticent on the medicare issue during the 1964 campaign, partly, no doubt, because the Saskatchewan program was working well and also because national party policy favoured some variant on the CCF prototype. Nonetheless, there remained the possibility that the Saskatchewan program might be modified – particularly if the Hall Commission report supported the CMA/CHIA/TCMP approach.

THE ROYAL COMMISSION
REPORTS

On 19 June 1964, after nearly three full years of deliberation, the first volume of the *Final Report* of the Royal Commission on Health Services was released. It was a body blow for the medical profession and the insurance industry. The CMA had, after all, requested appointment of the commission, hoping both to stall events in Saskatchewan and to remove health insurance from "the hectic arena of political controversy."[20] Now the royal commission – after reviewing hundreds of briefs, several scholarly reports, and the experiences of other nations – was recommending precisely what the CMA had rejected: a universal, comprehensive plan that would "make all the fruits of the health sciences available to all our residents without hindrance of any kind," and do so "on uniform terms and conditions."[21]

Several factors led the commissioners to reject the means-test subsidy route proposed by the CMA. First, the CMA and CHIA contended that some 3 million Canadians might require subsidy. The commissioners found this figure to be in error; for if the whole range of health services were considered, some one-third of Canada's population might require assistance – a potential administrative nightmare. As well, less than half the nation was covered even partially for the costs of health services through voluntary insurance, and it seemed that the swift pace of scientific progress in medicine was likely to exacerbate the financial and organizational problems inherent in the voluntary approach. Third, it could prove administratively unsound to allow private carriers to participate. Their inclusion would lead to duplication of facilities and in the case of investor-owned carriers to a situation where public sector funds would needlessly underwrite private-sector profits.[22]

Although they rejected the CMA position on multiple carriers and subsidies, the commissioners were nonetheless influenced by other standpoints of organized medicine. Administration, for example, was to be by provincial commissions "representative of the public, the health professions, and Government."[23] Podiatric and chiropractic services would be insured only "when prescribed by a physician."[24] Because optometrists lacked training in diagnosis of ocular diseases, only those who updated themselves through special programs on opthalmological pathophysiology were to be eligible to provide insured refractions; optometric undergraduate education was also to be modified in this direction.[25] Above all, the commissioners averred that they were "opposed to state medicine, a system in which all providers of health services are functionaries under the control of the state."[26] And because capitation payment for GPs was associated with a sharper division between office and hospital practice than existed in Canada, their plan was to be based around fee-for-service private practice.[27]

On the other hand, the commissioners took direct aim at certain of the profession's social institutions. They stressed that "the provincial Colleges should be clearly separated from the voluntary association or associations." Their function was public – not professional – protection, and to this end, the disciplinary powers of the colleges would have to be "extended so that they may have the authority to ensure that all medical and surgical practice is of high quality."[28] As well, the era of the sliding scale of fees was over. The commissioners were seeking "a method that will provide everybody in Canada with comprehensive coverage regardless of age or state of health or ability to pay, upon uniform terms and conditions." Accordingly, a maximum fee schedule should be negotiated between the administrative agency and the provincial professional association: "Extra billing would not be permitted." Although Dr David M. Baltzan dissented on this specific point, the commissioners made it plain in the second volume of their report that they disagreed with the opting-out clauses of the Saskatoon Agreement. Doctors would be "free to practise independently of the programme, either wholly or partially" and these arrangements would operate *without* reimbursement of patients.[29]

Nevertheless the commissioners did not see their program as a threat to the integrity of the medical profession:

The most fundamental feature of the programmes recommended is that they are based on free, independent, self-governing professions. The provision of and payment for services is to be the result of a negotiated contractual relationship based principally on the fee-for-service concept. The physician continues in private practice. He renders the service which, in his judgement, his diagnosis indicates. The state does not interfere in any way with his professional management of the patient's condition, nor with the confidential nature of the physician-patient relationship.[30]

In essence, the commissioners agreed that doctors should retain their traditional control over the content, locale, and circumstances of their daily work; but they believed that since removal of financial barriers to care was the first step towards more equitable distribution of medical services, this goal would be jeopardized if the professional monopoly – or members thereof – retained unilateral pricing prerogatives within the public program.

The royal commission report touched on an extraordinary number of issues and went well beyond a consideration of medical services alone. What the commissioners envisioned was sequential introduction of a full health services program, starting with medical care and eventually including dental and optical services, and pharmaceutical and other benefits for selected groups. Detailed plans were also tendered for improving the nation's medical and paramedical manpower situation. As for the financial ramifications of the proposed program, the commissioners estimated that the then-current system cost about $180 per person per year, but their universal and comprehensive approach would, in its first stage, increase this amount by only $20 per person per year. The commission was therefore convinced that its program was feasible. And although a second volume to complete the report was scheduled for later release, the commissioners recommended that a federal-provincial conference be convened within six months of the tabling of the first volume of their report, "to initiate the necessary planning and fiscal arrangements for the co-ordinated implementation of the programme as a whole," and "to reach agreement on the implementation of the Health Services Programme we have recommended."[31]

THE CMA RESPONSE:
AN ANALYSIS

The first volume of the report of the Royal Commission on Health Services was made public just three days before the CMA convened its 1964 annual meeting in Vancouver. There was scarcely time for a coherent response, particularly since the first copies of the report made available to the predominantly anglophone conventioneers were entirely in French.[32] However, CMA President Dr Frank Turnbull was empowered to send a telex to Prime Minister Pearson conveying the profession's "initial reaction." Turnbull wrote, "We are gratified that the report and its recommendations reflect so many of our proposals even though we cannot agree with all of the recommendations as they relate to the provision of personal medical services under single provincial plans." He reiterated the CMA's concern that personnel and facilities might not be adequate to meet increased demands and sought assurances that there would be further consultations before any legislation was introduced.[33]

Notwithstanding this diplomatic telex, many doctors were angered and dismayed. Wallace McCutcheon, the industrialist who resigned from the commission to join the Diefenbaker cabinet, was also displeased. McCutcheon was in Vancouver at the time of the CMA meeting. When he met Baltzan, van Wart, and some other doctors for a drink, McCutcheon took the opportunity to castigate the two medical commissioners for endorsing the report.[34]

Even on short notice, one thing was apparent to the CMA general council: the commissioners had effectively ignored many of the profession's arguments. On the other hand, Alberta's plan was in operation, British Columbia and Ontario were likely to begin soon, and Manitoba's Conservative government had also expressed interest in the subsidy approach.[35] The first volume of the royal commission's report accordingly provided a definite challenge for the profession to clarify its strategy and produce a more convincing ideology. Fortunately, three special committees were already at work on that very task. The Special Committee on Prepaid Medical Care, although late 1950s in vintage, had received a broadened mandate during the Saskatchewan dispute. Two other special committees – one on policy and the other on means of adapting the Australian insurance plan to Canadian conditions – had also been constituted in 1962.

Hence, at the Vancouver meeting in the immediate wake of the commission's findings, two decisions were taken. First, the reports of the three special committees must be completed and circulated. Second, an extraordinary meeting of the profession's parliament must be convoked to deal with the royal commission report. It would be the first such meeting since the general council was summoned in January 1943 to offer tentative approval of the Heagerty-Mackenzie health insurance scheme (see chapter 5).

The ruminations of each of the three special committees provide a fascinating insight into the *Realpolitik* of the CMA's evolving ideology of medical care, and we shall begin with the proposals to adapt the Australian plan of medical services to Canada. Interest in the Australian medicare scheme dated back to the 1940s, but the

renewed push for study of its modus operandi had come from the
BC division of the CMA[36]. Eventually a joint delegation of BCMA and
CMA representatives was sent out to examine the Australian situation
at first hand,[37] and the special committee set up in 1962 was chaired
by Dr Peter J. Banks, a member of the BCMA executive and a rising
star in medical politics.

Three facets of the Australian scheme appealed to some leaders
of the CMA: it relied on multiple carriers with subsidized enrolment;
direct charges were made at point of service, or, in euphemistic terms,
there was "patient participation"; and government intervention was
limited more or less to financial auditing and accounting. The Banks
Committee suggested various ways such a plan could be applied to
Canada and criticized the Canadian profession-sponsored agencies
for paying 100 percent of the doctors' bills in service contracts. It
contended that since in Australia the patient paid 10 percent of the
bill directly unless the doctor waived the extra charge, a practitioner
always "must justify his account to his patient." No explanation
was given as to exactly how this process of justification was supposed
to work, nor were there any data to support the implication that
quality of service was improved.[38]

The Banks Committee did offer another use for the concept of
"patient participation." If government became involved in subsidies,
it acquired "a vested interest in the profession's fee schedule" and
might be able to "veto" fee schedule increases through its indirect
control of premium levels. The Banks Committee had suggested a
formula tying fee schedules to changes in the cost of living or "real
productivity" indices; however, successive governments might not
honour an original agreement made by some other political party.
In this case, "the existence of the patient participation factor provides
a mechanism which could be increased to offset the effect of government's refusal to accept the implementation of the formula's result."[39]
"Patient participation" was therefore at once a negotiating lever and
a means of generating extra revenue from the private sector in the
event of disagreements between a government and the profession's
bargaining unit.

Another interesting point in the Banks Committee's proposals was
the provision for "an Assessment or Mediation Committee ...
appointed *by the profession* to mediate problems arising between
members of the profession and the approved agencies."[40] The original
health insurance principles set out by the CMA Committee on Economics in 1934 had assumed that government referees accountable
to the public through the department of health would assess accounts
and deal with overservicing problems. Since then the CMA had

progressively retreated from any form of direct auditing by extra-professional authority, and the new proposal maintained this trend.

The Special Committee on Prepaid Medical Care, chaired by Dr L.R. Rabson of Winnipeg, made it clear in its report that the TCMP agencies were no longer the CMA's favoured children:

For a long time there was a similarity of interest between the objectives of the prepaid plans and those of the profession. But, while the profession is anxious that people are covered by medical care insurance best suited to each person's needs, the particular interest of each plan appears to be that people are insured through the doctor-sponsored prepaid plans which *they assume* is the best coverage for everyone.[41] (Italics in original)

The Rabson Committee went on to complain that organized medicine did not have sufficient control over the TCMP agencies. It questioned the wisdom of service contracts that provided for direct and full payment from the plan to participating physicians. A particular source of dissatisfaction was the existence of prorating agreements between the doctor-sponsored plans and organized medicine, since these agreements had been singled out by the profession's new allies in the insurance industry as the most obvious example of organized medicine's preferential treatment of the TCMP network. It will be recalled from chapter 6 that true prorating actually occurred very rarely; once a given doctor-sponsored plan had been in operation for a few years, surpluses were accumulated to cover financial overruns, and therefore the participating doctors almost never took a reduction in fees on this basis. Reviewing the Rabson report, however, it appears that the objection was not to prorating due to financial shortfalls, but rather to the so-called administrative deduction (generally fixed at 10 percent off any payment) made by all the TCMP agencies and affiliates except Associated Medical Services. The reasons for this objection are easy to surmise. First, the deduction amounted to a 10 percent donation to the TCMP agency by all participating doctors – a concession that could not be justified, since "a similarity of interest and objectives" no longer existed. Second, the broader principle of deductions from doctors' billings to ensure the solvency of an insuring agency was arguably a poor precedent to maintain in the event of government intervention.

Like the Banks Committee, the Rabson group was concerned about "the unfortunate attraction of doctors and patients" for complete prepayment mechanisms that did not involve direct financial transactions between doctor and patient. It contended that the lack of direct payments led to "over-servicing and over-utilization." The

Rabson group therefore concluded that concessions to the TCMP agencies must be reconsidered: "In order to prevent the gradual erosion of the differences inherent in the various methods of coverage developed to date, it may be necessary to adjust financial concessions so as not to discriminate against those insurers who retain a payment method which is patient-oriented or which makes payment to doctor and patient jointly."[42]

We come finally to the Special Committee on Policy. Its report was a persuasive articulation of certain key concepts that were cornerstones to the CMA's defence of the multiple-carrier / subsidies approach to medical insurance. The physician, argued the committee, should be free "to evaluate the worth of his services."[43] Since personal medical care was, in the final analysis, a matter between individual doctors and individual patients, a collectivist paradigm was inapplicable: "The individual patient has an obligation to contribute to the costs of his own medical care and, unless indigent, to pay his doctor. He should have the right to choose his method of payment, to designate an agency to assist him in this payment should he so desire, and to select the extent of coverage he may wish to purchase."[44]

The policy committee went on to assert that no one agency – private or public – should be empowered to administer medical insurance, since this agency would be in a position to restrict or ration resources and would be insufficiently flexible to accommodate changing needs and demands.[45] The Special Committee on Policy was equally concerned to end 100 percent prepayment, claiming, as did the other bodies, that direct transactions must be introduced to curb over-servicing and over-utilization. Indeed, the TCMP plans were told that they must evolve "from their present concept of total prepayment to the sounder, more economical, and more logical one of patient participation."[46]

Governments were to limit themselves to subsidizing the participation of low-income groups in the diverse plans offered by multiple carriers. Government should not be involved in the administration of any insurance program beyond auditing procedures, even though the persons insured might be receiving a subsidy from government.[47] Auditing here implied government inspection of the agencies' accounts, not any direct involvement in monitoring professional practices. The issue, as the Canadian Federation of Agriculture remarked in its brief to the Hall Commission, was accountability – or lack of it – in disposition of public funds.

It is obvious, then, that as the CMA executive committee later remarked, there was "a clash of ideologies" between the royal commission's views and those of organized medicine.[48] But underlying the CMA's new ideology were strategic considerations of considerable advantage to the profession. By reviewing their genesis we can further understand how these doctrines protected the profession's position.

It had, of course, once been the CMA's policy to promote subsidized enrolment in the profession's own plans as an alternative to direct government intervention. And to assist the TCMP agencies in winning public acceptability, organized medicine not only provided strong sponsorship for these service plans but also made certain contractual and financial concessions to boost their appeal above that of private for-profit carriers competing in the medical insurance market. In essence, the organized profession had been seeking to ward off outside control by establishing a dominant position in prepayment of medical care. Hence, the general adoption of service contracts by the TCMP agencies was not, as the CMA Special Committee on Prepaid Medical Care suggested in 1964, an attempt to force a given mode of coverage on the public. It was, in fact, a response to three factors: public demand for complete prepayment of medical services without additional direct charges; professional preference for avoidance of monetary dealings with patients; and organized medicine's own willingness to assist the doctor-sponsored plans in cornering the insurance market.

As noted in chapter 6, the retreat from acceptance of these plans had already begun in the 1950s with pressure for removal of restrictions on extra-billing. Howard Shillington, the executive director of TCMP, was in a unique position to monitor medical attitudes; he has also noted that a younger generation of practitioners, taking high incomes and paid accounts as given, was not appreciative of the strategic economic and political role played by the doctor-sponsored plans. Instead, the TCMP agencies, which by then had grown into large corporations, were seen as "impersonal mechanisms"; and the service contracts that limited extra- and direct-billing "meant for many of these new and younger doctors not a protection of their freedom, but an invasion of their rights."[49] Even as a groundswell of dissatisfaction with TCMP began, Shillington observed that "a hard-core group of doctors, some of whom seemed to regard themselves as refugees from the British health service,"[50] gained increased influence in the OMA – and through it, in the national association as well. This militant group pushed the association towards acceptance of the investor-owned carriers' approach.

Historical evidence supports Shillington's emphasis on the militant element in the Ontario Medical Association. Far more than any other provincial medical group, the OMA had taken the implementation of universal hospital insurance as a sign that state-administered medical insurance was imminent. At a special meeting of the OMA council concerning hospital insurance on 17 February 1958, delegates from Sudbury and St Catharines walked out when the chairman dismissed as "oratory" a motion that read: "No third party must ever come between the doctor and patient, no matter how indirectly."[51] A smattering of letters appeared in the *Ontario Medical Review* claiming that the profession's only salvation lay in billing all patients directly rather than allowing other parties to determine medical fees.[52] According to Dr Morris P. Wearing, a London obstetrician, "the only thing we are doing now with PSI is getting a smoothly running organization ready for government."[53] On the other side of the fence were moderates such as the OMA general secretary, Dr Glenn Sawyer, who not only urged support for PSI, but also tried repeatedly to persuade specialists to forgo their extra-billing privileges so that the doctor-sponsored plan would provide truly comprehensive coverage.[54]

In May 1959 the OMA council spent two and a half hours debating the merits of various billing practices, and motions were passed to the effect that whenever possible doctors should bill patients rather than accept payment direct from third parties. This point naturally raised the issue of how to deal with agencies such as PSI and Windsor Medical Services. Although it was actually suggested that all doctors should opt out of PSI, the matter was eventually referred to a Special Committee on Medical Care and Practice.[55] In January 1960 this committee acknowledged that certain agencies should continue to receive special treatment but encouraged doctors to direct-bill if dealing with private insurance companies.[56] Thus, it would seem that the trend of opinion in the OMA was indeed more strongly in favour of direct-billing and indemnity contracts than was the case in the other provincial medical groups.

As noted above, by the late 1950s it had also become obvious to the leaders of organized medicine that, notwithstanding the concessions given to TCMP agencies, the commercial consortium – CHIA – had taken an equal share of the market. Thus, during the early 1960s, when CHIA pressed for an alliance and the Saskatchewan feud heightened professional fears of state intervention, the CMA understandably abandoned its original plan for universal coverage through state-subsidized enrolment in its own TCMP network and instead endorsed the multiple-carriers concept.

The multiple-carriers approach obviously drew to the CMA and its provincial divisions a powerful set of allies in the business community. But by 1962 another spin-off of the multiple-carriers strategy had become clear, for the Special Committee on Prepaid Medical Care was already sounding the alert about the dangers of any public *or* private agency's becoming "a monopolistic purchaser of medical services."[57] Belatedly the CMA planners had realized that it was not, in fact, in their interest to have TCMP agencies – or any other carrier – controlling too much of the market; for then governments could either co-opt entirely the largest existing agency as part of a universal state-administered plan or at least exercise a powerful influence on fees and patterns of practice by holding a single agency accountable. Since the insurance consortium consisted of 118 separate companies, its agencies could not be co-opted in this fashion. TCMP agencies, in contrast, were usually one or two to a province and by far the largest single carrier.

Two more pieces of the jigsaw puzzle therefore fall into place. First, we can understand why, as Shillington has reported, some doctors in the early 1960s began referring to TCMP agencies as "monoliths" and "sitting ducks." Second, we can appreciate why in 1964 the CMA's three special policy committees seemed eager to strip away certain of the concessions that had once been granted TCMP agencies precisely for the purpose of augmenting their share of the market. As one of the special committee reports remarked, the insurance companies had "pointed out that impairment of the insurance industry's ability to compete could result in 'monopolistic' control of medical services insurance in each province."[58]

There is only one piece left to fit into our puzzle. Why did the CMA committees launch such a stringent attack on the service contracts used by the profession-sponsored plans? Most doctors in the professional rank and file obviously still preferred to bill the TCMP agencies rather than their patients, finding in this arrangement "convenience, simplicity, and certainty of payment."[59] Indeed, a 1962 survey of Canadian doctors carried out for the Royal Commission on Health Services had shown that 62 percent of 11,181 respondents still preferred the TCMP agencies, while 17.4 percent favoured private insurance companies and only 7.8 percent supported government sponsorship. (Not surprisingly, the data suggest that specialists, practitioners in larger centres, those in solo practice, and those licensed after the Depression, were more likely to favour the investor-owned agencies).[60] Certainly so far as the many doctors and laymen who had worked to build up the TCMP agencies were concerned, the doctrinaire call for "patient participation" was a bitter pill to swallow. For example, in 1963 Dr W.B. Stiver, the medical director of Physicians' Services Incorporated, tartly remarked in the *CMAJ*,

We have in the medical profession today an opinion that the cure of over-utilization in prepaid comprehensive care is a combination of deterrents, deductibles, and co-insurance now given the sophisticated name of "patient participation" ... I know of no published work either in Canada or the United States which would indicate that patient participation has any worthwhile influence on utilization.[61]

Howard Shillington, who termed the new proposals "a hopeless effort to counter the mass forward movement taking place in the field of medical care insurance,"[62] has suggested that the profession's leaders may have been "confused." The rationale for the attack on 100 percent prepayment, however, is easily seen. In the first place, the insurance consortium itself was split on the issue of "patient participation"; some companies felt it improved profitability; others disagreed. But so long as TCMP used service contracts as a selling point, it maintained something of a competitive edge over its commercial rivals. Since the CMA strategists now wished to keep the prepayment market as fragmented as possible, that competitive edge should be stripped away. Moreover TCMP's example encouraged certain commercial carriers to offer "assignations" with direct and complete prepayment to doctors as well. This same modus operandi – payment in full by a third party – had been advocated by the royal commission and others who favoured a full-scale government plan. It was now expedient for the CMA to put as much ideological distance as possible between itself and the advocates of complete prepayment via a government-adminstered plan. Finally, service contracts not only made possible auditing of accounts; they also limited the profession's market strength by vesting direct control over prices with a third party and cutting off the option of revenue generation from patients. As we have seen, in discussing the effects of government-subsidized participation the Banks Committee had noted that even should the profession's preferred policy be implemented, a government might bring pressure to bear on fee schedules; and it believed that direct payments from patients were a way for the profession to maintain a more powerful position vis-à-vis any third-party prepayment agency.

The three committees were therefore attempting to swing the profession's strategy into a pattern that protected professional autonomy and conferred maximum market strength on doctors, individually and collectively. The tactic was traditional: divide and conquer – diffuse government's bargaining power by forcing it to subsidize medical practitioners through large numbers of separate carriers; keep the prepayment market fragmented among competing carriers so that no one agency could be co-opted by the state or bargain at equal strength with the profession; and maintain a means of tapping individual patients directly both as the ultimate conduit for additional revenue and as a bargaining lever.[63] *Pace* Shillington, the rank and file were perhaps "confused" when asked to assimilate this new ideology, but the CMA's strategists had planned carefully, developing in the process a rather sophisticated mechanism to maintain professional autonomy and market power in the setting of universal or near-universal prepayment for medical services.

THE POLITICAL INITIATIVE

In preparation for the January meeting of the CMA's general council, the association's executive distilled the reports of the three special committees into a single memorandum for the 180 delegates who were to convene in Toronto. Discussions were protracted, with some sparring between moderates loyal to the TCMP agencies and militants who were concerned about the strategic implications of continued concessions to TCMP. It was decided that the doctor-sponsored plans should try to extend their coverage to drug costs and other treatments such as physiotherapy – an apparent response to the Hall Commission's extensive plans. However, the general council also stressed that the TCMP agencies must adopt the concept of "patient participation." And it further warned that in future doctors expected to set their own fees without reference to outside authority – governmental or otherwise. The most important issue in the general council's view was the opting-out question that had arisen in Saskatchewan. A strong statement was accordingly adopted: "We declare that the individual physician must have the right to practise privately outside any arrangements and that the individual subscriber should have the right to avail himself of services of such a physician without the loss of benefits."[64]

In an action unusual for a supreme court judge, Mr Justice Hall had already made two public speeches sharply counter-attacking medical critics of the first volume of the royal commission report.[65] The second and final volume, released shortly after the January CMA council meeting, was originally to have been a summary of the twenty-six research studies performed for the commission. Hall decided that it should also be used to provide the definitive rebuttal of the CMA and other groups – a strategy that he later acknowledged was "maybe ... sort of a dirty trick on the medical profession."[66] As noted above, a section of the second volume of the report firmly rejected both physician extra-billing and payment of benefits to patients of opted-out practitioners. Dr David Baltzan, who had rather reluctantly gone along with the rest of the commissioners on the first volume, now vacillated over the question of extra-billing and reimbursement. Despite pressure from Hall, he finally insisted on adding a dissenting memorandum that supported the CMA position on opting-out and extra-billing. Hall responded by adding the memorandum, not on the first page as Baltzan requested, but on the last page in the body of the final volume.[67]

Although the spring of 1965 brought an apparent lull in health politics activity, important events were afoot behind the scenes. Prime Minister Lester B. Pearson and his cabinet were weighing the Hall Commission's recommendations with a view to approaching the provinces about terms of a national health insurance program. The CMA Committee on Economics also had serious matters to ponder; for in the wake of the special meeting of general council in Toronto, the committee had been charged with revising the 1960 policy statement on medical services insurance.

The first public action came from the CMA. Meeting at Halifax in mid-June 1965, the general council endorsed a new doctrine. Dr Victor Goldbloom of Montreal, chairman of the Commitee on Economics, advised the press that "moderates and progressives" had won out in wording this revised policy pronouncement. However, while the tone was more temperate, the contents amounted to a confirmation of the philosophy espoused by the three special committees in 1964.[68]

The 1965 policy document presented its proposals under headings such as "freedom," "the dangers of restrictions and conflicts," and "flexibility and progress." It formalized the CMA's alliance with the insurance industry by endorsing the multiple-carriers approach and asserted "that alternative types of insurance, those which offer prepayment and those which involve various forms of patient participation, must be maintained." A strong appeal "in the public interest" was made for opted-out practitioners to retain indirect access to public funds: "If the insurance plans devised are satisfactory to all concerned, both receivers and providers of service, then private arrangements will be relatively rare. If, on the other hand, a plan is for any reason unsatisfactory, the freedom to conclude private arrangements will be an alternative to conflict and an incentive towards improvement of the plan." Since the Hall Commission had recommended a universal single-agency scheme but some provinces were following the CMA's preferred approach, the policy statement also claimed: "The development of medical services insurance is the responsibility of the provinces, and financial contributions by the federal government should not interfere with the self-determination of the provinces."[69]

The CMA's cautionary pronouncement carried little weight with Lester Pearson's minority government. Saskatchewan's plan was obviously feasible: the doctor exodus had ended and the province's doctor / population ratio had actually improved. Medical opposition had been blunted to some extent by the success of the program and a 39.6 percent increase in doctors' net incomes between 1961 and 1963. Moreover, medical education was flourishing, and the administrative expenses, far from sky-rocketing as the plan's opponents had predicted, were already on a par with the highly efficient doctor-sponsored plans.[70] Naturally the NDP opposition in Ottawa, well aware of the Liberal's forty-six-year-old promise of a national health plan, were happy to remind the government that their party's brainchild was now teething successfully under Liberal rule in Saskatchewan. And in contrast to the St Laurent era, the inner circle of the Liberal government now consisted of a younger and more innovative group of MPs. With the Hall Commission report in the foreground, and a 1963 election promise unfulfilled, internal and external pressure for concrete action built.[71]

On 19 July 1965 at a federal-provincial conference the prime minister opened proceedings with a statement that focused initially on regional inequities and unemployment. Later, however, Pearson announced "the item of our agenda which is most important of all because it can most closely affect the daily lives of all Canadians": national medical care insurance. Four basic criteria were set out for provinces that wished federal assistance in operating medicare plans: (1) comprehensive coverage, (2) portability of benefits between provinces, (3) public administration either directly or through non-profit agencies, and (4) universal coverage "on uniform terms and conditions."[72] The latter two conditions effectively precluded the CMA / CHIA / TCMP multiple-carriers approach, could end Alberta's program, and might well nip the Ontario and British Columbia initiatives in the bud. This announcement took the representatives of the provinces by surprise. Initially reticent, several premiers later issued warnings: medicare was a provincial responsibility; tight shackling of the provinces to these conditions by a federal government wielding fiscal handcuffs would not be tolerated.

The CMA executive also was startled by the proposals and angered that it had not been asked to consult with the federal cabinet concerning administrative details.[73] Although exclusion of investor-owned carriers seemed definite, it was unclear from Prime Minister Pearson's remarks whether the allowance for a non-profit agency to administer a federal-provincial medicare program applied only to a crown corporation, or whether it might permit a TCMP agency to participate. In fact, the Hall Commission report, while rejecting commercial carriers, had suggested that the valuable administrative experience and non-profit structure of TCMP agencies made them useful vehicles for a universal government plan. At the time the militant faction in the profession must surely have viewed this suggestion as further evidence that the TCMP agencies were "sitting ducks"; however, the CMA leaders now joined forces with the TCMP to lobby actively for a guarantee that the profession-sponsored plans would retain more than the "post office" function that had become their lot in Saskatchewan.[74] The agencies could not, of course, offer the profession the insulation from economic pressures and encroachments on professional autonomy that had been envisaged in the late 1940s and 1950s. The more recent multiple carriers strategy was better protection by far. But if that option was indeed to be foreclosed, some form of buffer was better than none.

The cabinet for its part was aware of the need for the doctors' co-operation in any scheme. Hence, on 16 September 1965, at the prime minister's behest, CMA representatives met with the federal government's delegates to an upcoming dominion-provincial health ministers' conference where medicare was expected to be the key topic. The six-man CMA team brought with them a seven-page memorandum detailing their various concerns. This position paper sounded all the same warnings as past statements had, and made an especially strong plea for a role for the doctor-sponsored plans on the grounds that since many of these agencies had previously been trusted to administer the provincial public assistance medicare schemes, they could equally well be allowed to handle public funds for a universal medicare scheme.[75]

The health minister, Judy LaMarsh, had initially been dubious about delegating a major administrative role to the doctor-sponsored plans. One can only presume that at the federal-provincial ministers' conference her reticence was worn down by objections from those provinces supporting the private carriers approach; for on 1 October LaMarsh wrote CMA President Dr R.O. Jones a more encouraging note. The minister suggested that "doctor-operated plans might, in certain respects under a two-tiered arrangement, act as the agent of a provincial department [of health] in the provision of medical services." The reference to a two-tiered system was meant to suggest that a crown corporation or some other public administrative body might cover high-risk and low-income groups, while the doctor-sponsored agency became the instrument for public administration of a plan for the self-sufficient and "insurables." Identical terms and conditions of coverage must, however, continue to apply.[76]

British Columbia, in fact, went part way down this road in late 1965. The details of the plan were apparently worked out a series of dinner meetings between the Social Credit premier, W.A.C. Bennett, and the president of the BCMA.[77] Rather than using the direct subsidy method still defended by Alberta, the BC government set up a crown corporation to cover individuals and families who might prove difficult to insure in the private sector. Ontario also took steps in this direction. The Ontario government's initial plan, embodied in Bill 163, was to create a non-profit corporation of private insurance carriers to pool the costs of covering high-risk subscribers. Both a full service policy and a "major medical" policy would be offered by all approved carriers, and government subsidies would be paid to those in the low-income group who wished to purchase comprehensive coverage. This approach had been endorsed by the OMA president as essentially "in keeping with the philosophies of the profession and the policies of the Association."[78] However, the position taken by the federal government in 1965 compelled a slight change of direction. On 28 January 1966 a new plan was introduced in the Ontario legislature; it was implemented later in the year. The plan dismantled the profession-administered Medical Welfare Plan and offered a standard comprehensive insurance contract to all individual citizens on a voluntary basis with premium assistance for low-income citizens. The OMA was disturbed that the new program, known as OMSIP, was open to any individual regardless of income.[79] Nevertheless, the TCMP and private carriers were free to continue operations as before, and in British Columbia, too, the crown insurance corporation did nothing to preclude continuation of private-sector medical insurance. Both provinces could therefore be expected to join Alberta in strenuous protest against the federal government's insistence that profit-making agencies be eliminated.

For the federal Liberals the question of when and whether to proceed with a national medicare plan continued to be a thorny one. A Gallup poll in September 1965 had shown that 52 percent of respondents favoured voluntary enrolment in any medicare program, with 41 percent agreeable to a compulsory universal approach and 7 percent undecided.[80] Moreover, in November 1965 the Liberals had gone to the electorate for a fresh mandate and received a lukewarm reception. They gained two seats, but so too did the Progressive Conservatives. The NDP, up by four seats, continued to hold the balance of power, and it could be expected to reject any plan that flew in the face of the Hall Commission's recommendations. There were provinces that might be sympathetic to the Liberal concept of cost-sharing. Saskatchewan would welcome federal funds to assist in financing its medicare program, and both Newfoundland and New Brunswick expected that the combination of a federal contribution and an equalization grant would draw much of the financial sting from medicare. However, the population of the opposing provinces was much greater than that of those supporting the plan.

As the Liberals settled uneasily back into their minority government position during early 1966, backstage activity in the medicare drama continued unabated. By this time Alan MacEachen had replaced Judy LaMarsh in the health ministry, and Dr A.D. Kelly, the affable and diplomatic CMA general secretary, had retired. Kelly's successor, Dr Arthur F.W. Peart, did not have the same experience in dealing with the health ministry mandarins, but he made every effort to place the CMA's viewpoint before them on a frequent basis. In January, March, and again in April CMA delegations met with the minister or senior health and welfare bureaucrats.[81]

On 8 June, with legislation known to be in the offing, yet another meeting took place. The CMA delegation reiterated its fears about loss of the "opting-out" privilege – not just in Saskatchewan, where it had been enshrined in the agreement ending the doctors' strike – but nationwide. LaMarsh had warned Dr R.O. Jones in October 1965 that while the federal government itself could not ban extra-billing, excessive direct charges could so "seriously interfere with the principles of universality and free access" as to lead Ottawa to withhold funds from affected provinces.[82] When MacEachen issued the same warning at the 8 June meeting, the CMA delegation was, if nothing else, relieved to learn that a specific ban on opting-out would not be written into the forthcoming legislation. Jones accordingly cabled the minister from the CMA annual meeting in Edmonton two days later, seeking official permission to inform the general council of this development. MacEachen's reply telegram read: "Wish confirm my statement to you that on your assurance that medical profession accepts responsibility for avoidance of abuses and excesses which would impair universality or access to patient services, it is not intended to prohibit the doctor billing his patient directly and patient claiming plan benefits."[83] The unanswered question, of course, was: at what level would extra-billing be deemed excessive?

At that same 8 June meeting and in later correspondence the CMA representatives also returned to the issue of using private agencies within the framework of the Liberal government's four medicare principles. Two fears in particular were expressed by the CMA spokesmen. On the one hand, certain preconditions of the legislation were likely to circumscribe the role of the TCMP agencies. On the other, the federal government was known to be planning to implement its medicare plans on 1 July 1967 as a means of ushering in Canada's centennial year; and if this date were used as the deadline for universal (that is, 90 percent minimum) enrolment, then those provinces following or favouring the CMA's multiple-carriers strategy might not qualify for federal aid. These provinces would first have to restructure their administration to fit Ottawa's conditions and second be tempted to abandon the "voluntary premium" approach to push their enrolments immediately up to the 90 percent required to receive funds from Ottawa.[84]

Another meeting with the CMA on 27 June did not dissuade MacEachen and his cabinet colleagues from their commitment to the four basic principles first outlined by Lester Pearson almost one year previously. On 12 July 1966 the federal medicare bill, C-227, was introduced in the House of Commons and received its first reading. It set down the criteria for federal aid but did, in fact, embody a compromise of sorts: multiple carriers could be used so long as their participation was on a non-profit basis and public auditing of their accounts was possible.[85] Approved carriers should offer "insured services upon uniform terms and conditions to all insurable residents of the province" in a fashion that allowed "reasonable access" to insured services. Before a second reading of the bill could take place, the summer recess supervened.

For the private insurance industry elimination of the profitability provision was, of course, anathema. Participation now offered them no real benefits beyond a limited ability to achieve economies of scale in administrative expenses. CMA representatives were also displeased. Immediately after the bill had undergone first reading, the CMA issued a news release expressing regret at the government's insistence on universality and seeking clarification of those parts of the bill which pertained to external carriers. On only one score did the CMA spokesmen express relief. Opting-out had been protected. Although further battles on this issue might, as in Saskatchewan, have to be fought as each province introduced its plan, the news release noted that "nothing in the legislation prohibited a doctor from practising outside the plan and a patient could presumably consult the doctor of his choice without loss of benefits."[86]

Later in July the CMA executive met with provincial medical politicians and TCMP directors to review the legislation. Howard Shillington's account makes clear that the profession-sponsored agencies hoped to maintain as much independence as possible – and in the process they might well maintain greater independence for the profession as well. August accordingly brought renewed discussions between CMA staff and health ministry personnel. These, reported the CMA executive, "confirmed our fears that the administration of the provincial plans would be restrictive, and that the voluntary plans could continue only as 'post offices'."[87]

But by the autumn of 1966, with inflation beginning to sap the vitality of the Canadian economy, the Liberal cabinet had split on the issue of implementing medicare on 1 July 1967. Mitchell Sharp, an advocate of delay, had replaced Walter Gordon, a proponent of action, in the finance portfolio, and he spearheaded a move to postpone the program for at least a year. On 8 September 1966, with Prime Minister Pearson abroad, Sharp as acting prime minister announced the postponement.[88]

The CMA was clearly heartened; within twenty-four hours of Sharp's announcement, the executive committee had sent a communiqué to the prime minister's office acknowledging the wisdom of this decision in the light of inflation and reiterating the call for organized medicine's preferred policy of simply subsidizing the low-income groups. The letter praised the governments of British Columbia, Alberta, and Ontario for taking "a realistic approach" to the problem of medical insurance for persons of limited means. If Ottawa would change its strategy, advised the CMA, the Liberals could still have a plan to implement on centennial day: "The medical coverage of the needy should not await the resolution of political or constitutional issues. Let us do what we all agree needs to be done - now."[89] Copies of this letter were sent to the provincial premiers and a selected list of federal MPs.

Many members of the Liberal caucus were displeased with the cabinet's decision. In the ensuing uproar the cabinet won its one-year postponement with the explicit understanding that no further delay would be brooked. Doubtless chastened by the groundswell of protest, the prime minister wrote a firm reply to the CMA president on 20 September rejecting the doctors' proposals and issuing another warning about "extra-billing which if excessive might create a barrier to the receipt of necessary services. I have been encouraged to learn that your Association has accepted its rightful responsibility for ensuring that such excesses do not occur."[90]

On 13 October, as Bill C-227 entered its second reading, the CMA sent another letter to the prime minister. It repeated the association's complaints about the legislation in stronger terms, warned against government inefficiency and "rigidity," and suggested that the intro-duction of the Liberal program would "create an environment which will discourage medical recruitment." Specific recommendations for altering the bill were made with a view to permitting Ontario, Alberta, and British Columbia to continue their operations more or less unchanged and allowing other provinces to follow the subsidy route.

To enhance the insulating effect of private carriers, the CMA further recommended they be given "responsibility for the collection of premiums and assessment and payment of accounts."[91] Copies of this letter were sent to the minister of national health and welfare, as well as to all members of parliament and the senate. Interestingly, the association seems to have focused its direct lobbying on the executive, and between 1965 and 1967 it arranged only one meeting with doctor-MPs in the House.[92]

A CMA delegation was dispatched to follow up this letter. Meeting with Health Minister MacEachen on 17 October, the delegation protested the delayed implementation as a betrayal of Canada's needy people. Prompt introduction of the CMA/CHIA subsidy plan would assist some 5 million Canadians without running the risks of a universal program. As Professor Malcolm Taylor has drily pointed out, "this was a sixty-six percent increase over the number they had stated would need help in their brief to the Royal Commission on Health Services."[93] CMA officials later described the discussions as "pleasant but non-productive."[94]

The meeting also provided the CMA with a chance to request that the health ministry reply in writing to a set of criticisms of Bill C-227 submitted by the association in August. Dr J.N. Crawford, the deputy minister, waited two weeks before responding that all the CMA's criticisms had been thoroughly discussed in the preceding weeks.[95] This delaying tactic was designed to forestall any further CMA attacks on the legislation, which on 25 October received its second hearing in the House. In the second vote the bill once more received the support of the Liberals, the NDP, and the overwhelming majority of Conservatives.

The CMA secretariat, perhaps aware that the health ministry mandarins were deliberately avoiding any written comments on the bill, asked yet again on 4 November 1966 for "a written official opinion" from the ministry.[96] Dr Crawford passed on the CMA request to Dr E.H. Lossing, his second-in-command for health insurance, noting, "CMA is still pressing in spite of my recent letter." Lossing replied: "I feel our decision not to provide the CMA with ammunition was sound ... If you agree I suggest we do not answer this letter."[97]

Four weeks later Bill C-227, amended slightly, received its third and final reading. The amendment, which permitted provinces the latitude to include certain dental and optometrists' services, was protested by the CMA on the grounds that "benefits under medical care acts and programs should be limited to those services performed by or under the direction of a properly qualified physician." The vote in the House of Commons, however, was a signal indicator of general recognition that a new era of health services had dawned. The bill was supported by 177 MPs; only two voted against it.

On 9 December, the day after the final reading, the CMA executive held a gloomy news conference to warn of several drawbacks to the new law. Dr R.K.C. Thomson, the CMA president, advised that the legislation's "inflexibility will make it difficult for the provinces to tailor medical services to the special needs of different parts of the country." As well as increased taxes and strains on resources and personnel, the concept of total coverage meant "the loss of one more civil liberty." Indeed, the greatest virtue of the law in the CMA's view was that "by omission" doctors could opt out and their patients would still receive medicare benefits. This was "'the only safeguard to practitioners who wish to practise medicine without any possible Government interference." However, that provision had still to be enshrined in each provincial plan as the national program came into being.[98]

EPILOGUE

Whatever their misgivings, the profession's leaders were sufficiently realistic to appreciate the shape of things to come. As early as the spring of 1966 the CMA had set up a Special Committee on Collective Bargaining and Arbitration which met with two representatives of the Canadian Labour Congress to learn the rules of a new game. The committee's very title carried too strong a trade union taint for some doctors, however, and it was renamed the Special Committee on Collective Negotiation. In fact, the committee itself had difficulty clarifying the profession's changing status. Organized medicine would not be serving as bargaining agent for a union of employees under contract, since not only were the majority of its members in each province self-employed professionals, but also the contractual element was absent.

Yet when the committee reported, it made some prescient observations:

henceforth in Canada the economic position of doctors in the community will be largely determined by the results of meetings between representatives of the doctors and representatives of the public and/or government ... It may be expected that the warm climate of co-operation that has characterized some of the current negotiations will not always prevail. It is probable that when the financial requirements for medical care insurance increase and have to compete with other fields of governmental expense the periodic negotiations will be conducted on a harder basis.[99] (Italics in original)

The CMA's general council weighed the report on collective bargaining at the association's June 1967 meeting. Against the opposition of the Ontario division it was decided that a department of the CMA permanent secretariat should be constituted to deal with this new matter. OMA Past-President Dr Ross Matthews later told reporters that "We are not prepared to put our fee schedule on the bargaining block now, or at any time in the future."[100] Members of the OMA were advised to opt out of any plan.

Further evidence of divergent attitudes came at a "Centenary Conference" on medicare and medical manpower organized under CMA and TCMP auspices in Montreal in association with the annual meeting. Dr J.A. McMillan of Charlottetown, Prince Edward Island, represented one end of the spectrum. As former chairman of the CMA's Special Committee on Prepaid Medical Care, McMillan addressed the conference in bitter tones: "Year after year, those of us who interested ourselves in the economics of medicine have endured the taunts of our confreres; we have been subjected to the ingratitude of both subscribers and fellow doctors; but worst of all, our efforts have been ignored by both politicians and government." McMillan saw in medicare an end to professional dedication and the traditional doctor-patient relationship. Technical excellence would be the sole standard of care; for "the public and the politician and government have robbed us of our cloak of noblesse oblige." "With medicare," he caustically commented, "our most important instrument will be the ballpoint pen."[101]

Yet at the same conference a representative of the British Medical Association offered sage advice born of experience on how the profession could press government for economic and other concessions. Speaking, too, was Dr Frank Turnbull of Vancouver, a veteran leader of organized medicine and head of the CMA's Special Committee on Collective Negotiations. Dr Turnbull noted that despite Ontario's stand, both the BCMA and the Alberta College of Physicians and Surgeons had negotiated fee increases with their respective health ministers under the terms of provincial medicare plans. Quebec doctors had also "displayed a striking ability to recognize the realities of the new political situation" and were bargaining through the GPs and specialists' syndicates over fees and conditions in Quebec's social assistance medicare scheme.[102] In short, collective negotiation, once seen as "unprofessional," had "broken out all over": "We cannot see the road ahead, but the journey has commenced. If it seems like a nightmare, let us recall that one can only resolve a nightmare by waking up."[103]

CHAPTER NINE

Historical Reflections and Continued Controversies

Almost two centuries ago Hegel remarked that the only lesson of history was that people and their governments had never learned anything from history. Hegel's assessment has weathered well, if only because social and technological changes have been so sweeping that the lessons of history often become irrelevant by the time they are written. In the case of this study the implementation of medicare by all the provinces and territories has sharply transformed the structure of the relationship between the medical profession and government, with the result that generalizations about the 1980s based on the pre-medicare era must be made with caution. A historian may nonetheless take some consolation from distilling the past and, where possible, relating it to the present. Let us begin that task by asking: what were the major determinants of the Canadian medical profession's perspectives, policies, and pressure group activities in the field of state health insurance between 1911 and 1966?

To begin with, there was an obvious continuity of professional concerns from the nineteenth to the twentieth century. Just as the emergence of the medical profession saw lobbying by organized medicine for legislation that would institutionalize occupational autonomy and reinforce doctors' control of the medical services market, so in turn did the state's further intervention in the marketplace draw responses designed to protect professional market strength and prevent encroachment on occupational autonomy. Organized medicine therefore endorsed policies that would limit the impact of state-sponsored or state-subsidized prepayment of medical bills, as it sought to preserve the clinical freedom and economic position of Canadian doctors.

To this end, a definite priority for organized medicine was the maintenance of a pattern of practice in which most doctors were self-employed providers of medical services operating on a fee-for-service basis. The Second World War did bring a temporary interest in the possibility of capitation payments for general practitioners under a public insurance scheme; just as in Britain, however, the general practitioners would have been self-employed. In short, no major arm of Canadian organized medicine was ever on record as supporting a prepayment plan that in effect would make large numbers of doctors employees of a third party.

On the contrary, organized medicine persistently expressed its opposition to salaried-contract arrangements except where a practitioner could not be expected to support himself in a self-employed capacity. Protests against dispensaries and public health clinics during the 1920s were an early manifestation of this concern. Agitation by the Alberta College of Physicians and Surgeons about industrial and municipal contract practice in the 1920s and 1930s was a symptom of the same phenomenon, as was the CMA's adamant rejection of the plans for a salaried state medical service put forward by the CCF, organized labour, and farm groups during the Second World War. A final example of this pattern of behaviour was the opposition of the Saskatchewan College of Physicians and Surgeons to the community clinic movement in 1962-3.

The period after 1966 cannot be analysed in detail here, but it should be noted that the doctor's status as a self-employed provider of medical services was again defended by organized medicine in the early 1970s. At that time, although only a handful of community clinics existed, there was a flurry of enthusiasm for reorganizing primary care around local health centres with GPs and other personnel on salary.[1] The potential benefits of such centres were probably exaggerated.[2] Certainly organized medicine was dubious about the concept, both because GPs would lose their self-employment situation and because early experiments led to what one former CMA president termed "a good deal of unnecessary lay interference" that made the clinics "extremely unpopular" with doctors.[3] In Quebec, the only province that introduced community health clinics on a large scale, the Federation of General Practitioners assisted in creating more than 400 private group practices as part of a successful effort to compete with the government-sponsored health centres.[4] As matters now stand, there are about 120 community clinics across Canada, almost 100 of them in Quebec. Other forms of salaried employment for doctors in patient-contact settings are well established and run the gamut from workmen's compensation board positions to medical faculty posts and from post-graduate training situations to Newfoundland's salaried system for GPs working in remote "cottage hospitals."[5] However, about two-thirds of Canada's active practitioners are self-employed on a fee-for-service basis, and there is no sign that this administratively convenient system of private practice and public payment will be changed in the immediate future.

A second major priority for organized medicine during the period studied in this book was the protection of professional market strength, an aim linked to control of fee schedules and partially dependent on maintenance of self-employment for practitioners. Concern to avoid direct bargaining with third parties – be they lodges, industries, municipalities, consumer co-operatives, or provincial governments – was evident at various times from the 1890s on. Instead, the profession defended both its collective right to set fee schedules without outside interference as well as the right of an individual practitioner to adjust prices to the perceived means of his or her patients. This concern was not purely economic. It was believed that external controls on the economic terms of practice opened the door to meddling in the clinical work of doctors. There was also an element of pride and occupational status involved. Though doctors practised in a socio-economic setting analogous to that of many small businessmen and tradesmen, their ethical code encouraged them to reject the competitive and commercial practices that prevailed in most other markets. And as Max Weber remarked, "in most instances the notion of honour peculiar to status absolutely abhors that which is most essential to the market: hard bargaining."[6]

State health insurance, of course, raised the prospect of direct negotiations with government, but even before the First World War medical spokesmen had been alert to its financial benefits in the form of guaranteed fees from low-income groups. The great increase in the number of non-paying patients during the Depression brought unprecedented interest in state health insurance on the part of doctors and prompted the CMA and various provincial medical groups to formulate specific policies on the issue for the first time. Obviously, in any state insurance scheme the profession had to make a trade-off between the benefits of subsidized incomes on the one hand and the costs of state intervention on the other. An insistence on income ceilings in any insurance program, written into official CMA policy in 1934, was therefore designed to limit the state's influence and augment professional market strength by maintaining a separate private sector where practitioners could continue to price-discriminate. These economic considerations were especially clear in the 1935–7 British Columbia health insurance dispute.

On the other hand, a predominantly economic interpretation cannot be placed on the profession's policies during the early 1940s. Certainly medical incomes had not yet returned to pre-Depression levels, and guaranteed payment from low-income patients through a federal-provincial plan would have caused an immediate increase in medical earnings. CMA submissions to the Heagerty Committee and the Special House Committee on Social Security accordingly laid special emphasis on mandatory coverage of all those who might be poor payment risks. But while stressing the need for a ceiling below which coverage would be mandatory, the CMA lobby group in Ottawa left it to the provinces to decide on coverage for those above the income ceiling. This approach contrasted with that of the 1930s, when the CMA and its provincial divisions had emphasized that state-sponsored prepayment for higher income groups should not be permitted. Indeed, as noted in chapter 5, although most CMA leaders favoured a two-tiered plan to maintain a private sector outside state auspices, there was rank-and-file support, albeit from a minority, for a universal, all-inclusive program.

It is perhaps best to view organized medicine as pursuing a loss-minimizing strategy between 1941 and 1944. One of the profession's top priorities, after all, was to avoid a system in which the bulk of practitioners would be directly employed by their health ministries. Given that federal action seemed likely and given, too, that labour, agriculture, and the CCF were pushing for a salaried state medical service, it made good political sense for the CMA's lobbyists to take a flexible stance in support of their preferred program. Leaders of organized medicine in this period also appear to have been strongly influenced by wartime collectivism and ethical concerns about the inability of uninsured wage-earners to pay for hospital and diagnostic services.

By the late 1940s the CMA was once again determined to limit state involvement to the prepayment of the bills of those who themselves would not be able to pay the doctor. In fact, protection of the profession's economic position was more definitely assured by the 1949 CMA Policy Statement than any other previous strategy. Both the 1934 CMA principles of health insurance and subsequent revisions had rested on the concept of publicly administered insurance for indigents and wage-earners with low annual incomes. Although the CMA principles between 1937 and 1944 claimed that "complete control" of fee schedules must rest with organized medicine, some form of collective bargaining with government would have been inevitable. The policy endorsed from 1949 to the early 1960s – in which some provinces co-operated – kept government involvement to a minimum. By subsidizing the enrolment of recipients of social assistance in plans sponsored or administered by the profession itself, government effectively reinforced professional control of the socio-economic terms of medical practice. The shift to a multiple-carriers strategy, discussed in chapters 6 and 8, aimed at giving doctors protection by a different means: if no one agency, public or private, controlled most of the prepayment market, the profession's autonomy and market strength could be better maintained.

Once more, it is illuminating to take a glance at events since 1966. The introduction of universal medical insurance was associated with immediate increases in average net physician earnings in seven of ten provinces. A trend of rising medical incomes relative to the national average of wages and salaries, established in the 1950s, was therefore sustained in the 1960s as the provinces instituted first-dollar medical insurance for all their residents.[7] Having stood at 3.70 times the national average of wages and salaries in 1959, private fee-for-service practitioners' pre-tax earnings were 4.85 times the national average in 1970.[8] The historic high point for doctors' incomes was reached in 1971 when Quebec, second largest of the provinces and last to enter the national medicare program, completed its first year of universal coverage. Private practitioners' average net pre-tax earnings then climbed to 5.4 times the national average of wages and salaries.

Just as many strategists in the medical associations had foreseen, this short-term gain gave way to a gradual decline in average net incomes. Pressure from inflation-plagued provincial governments held back increases in fee schedules during the early 1970s, and most medical groups accepted either a freeze or small increases. Then, from 1976 to 1978 national wage and price controls provided a rationale for continued government limits on increases in the medicare benefit schedules. Private practitioners' incomes by 1978 had fallen to 3.4 times the national average of wages and salaries.[9] The actual decline was not due to government pressure on fee schedules alone. Many other factors contributed, including a levelling-off of the trend to increased specialization, a relative decrease in numbers of those in more remunerative surgical sub-specialties, fewer practitioners in the high-productivity age bracket of thirty-five to fifty-four, and shorter working hours in response to life-style considerations.[10] There is controversy over the exact numbers, but additional downward pressure also came from a rise in the doctor-to-population ratio that may have been as high as 20 percent.

Understandably, the response of organized medicine since 1978 has been to try to restore average incomes to earlier levels. Thus, starting in 1979, medical associations in several provinces reasserted their control of fee schedules by setting new, higher tariffs independent of government. The right to opt out and deal with reimbursed patients, preserved by CMA pressure on the federal government in 1965–6 and subsequently maintained in every province other than Quebec, was exercised by many more practitioners than during the early or mid-1970s. Variations allowed by some provinces – including direct-billing of selected patients and services or billing both government and patient for the same service – also gained popularity.[11] In Quebec the refusal of the government to pay medicare benefits to patients who dealt with extra-billing doctors generated strong economic pressures that kept virtually all practitioners opted in.

By 1979 considerable public outcry had arisen over the extra-billing issue. A 1980 federal inquiry carried out by Mr Justice Emmett Hall, former chairman of the Royal Commission on Health Services (1961 – 4), led to the recommendation that Quebec-style "closed" medicare be implemented nationally, together with arbitration mechanisms to settle fee disputes.[12] This recommendation was strongly rejected by the CMA and its provincial divisions.[13] During 1981 and 1982, CMA spokesmen continued to advocate the privatization and "demonopolization" of medicare;[14] and at the 1982 CMA annual meeting the general council specifically approved the principle of supplementary private insurance for any medical services, including charges by doctors in excess of the medicare benefit schedules.[15] As noted in the introduction, the provisions of the 1984 Canada Health Act ran entirely counter to these privatization proposals by penalizing provinces that levied or permitted direct charges to patients in the form of user fees, per diem bed charges, and physician extra-billing. (This legislative development was obviously anticipated in the warnings about extra-billing given to the CMA executive by the Liberal cabinet in 1966.) Successful collective bargaining in some provinces had already yielded fee increases that reduced the incentive for doctors to extra-bill, and the financial pressure of the Canada Health Act provided an impetus for negotiations that eliminated the practice altogether in other provinces where it was continuing. However, in Alberta and Ontario the issue remains contentious as of early 1986.

There is clearly a degree of historical symmetry in the fact that CMA policies of the late 1970s and early 1980s aimed at releasing practitioners from a negotiated tariff. During the Great Depression of the 1930s Canadian doctors sought guaranteed payment from low-income patients along with the right to price-discriminate among clients in the higher-income brackets, hoping thereby to regain their income peaks of the 1920s. Decades later, with economic conditions again unsettled but with payments from all income groups assured by medicare, organized medicine returned to the idea of creating a private sector within which practitioners could price-discriminate to restore real incomes to earlier, higher levels. Protection of professional market strength by retaining partial control of the price of services thus remained a priority.

Historical continuity is also evident in the fact that some medical spokesmen perceive a close link between control of fee schedules and preservation of clinical freedom. For example, Dr Earl Myers, the 1985–6 OMA president, dismissed the Ontario government's overtures about a negotiated end to extra-billing as "nothing more than a sham intended to cover its real intentions: the eventual control and sub-jugation of the profession both economically *and medically.*"[16] In December 1985, after a government bill (Bill 94) was tabled that made extra-billing an offence punishable by fines up to $10,000, Dr Myers wrote to all OMA members warning, "This proposed legislation ... affects all of us, both opted in and opted out, since its long term effects will be to de-professionalize medicine. Once government gains complete economic control over the profession, it can exert its influence more directly on the practice of medicine as it has in other jurisdictions."[17] Thus doctors, like other professionals, continue to emphasize the interrelatedness of their technical and socio-economic autonomy, in part because they particularly fear external meddling in their daily work, and also because their undisputed claims to special technical expertise can be generalized to protect a given socio-economic position.

Given professional fears about government interference with the doctors' clinical activities, it is interesting to note that the Canadian medicare experience bears out sociologist Eliot Freidson's general observation about the durability of technical autonomy in diverse health care systems.[18] Computerized practice profiles maintained by provincial medicare agencies occasionally lead to investigation of "outliers," but direct monitoring of the actual process and quality of medical care is not performed and quality assurance ultimately rests on various programs of professional peer review. Indirect pressures can be exerted: for example, it is common for provincial medicare agencies to refuse to pay for more than one general "check-up" per beneficiary per year. However, this is the exception rather than the rule. Even the prorating payment strategies adopted by the Quebec government and mooted recently in British Columbia do not constitute a direct challenge to the doctor's freedom to diagnose and treat as he or she sees fit. Indeed, so far as fee schedules are concerned, it is common practice for provincial governments to negotiate a block increase with their respective medical associations, and the allocation of increases between various items then occurs through the tariff committee of organized medicine itself. The medical services component of national health insurance has therefore had relatively little effect on the profession's clinical freedom, and the greatest impact has probably come – again indirectly – as a result of funding constraints in the hospital setting.[19]

In fact, there is an excellent possibility that the profession's independence has been guaranteed in many respects by the very implementation of a national medical services insurance plan based around fee-for-service private practice. The popularity of medicare with patients and the ease with which newly minted specialists and GPs can enter the system make it difficult for any government to implement sweeping changes that would undercut the doctor's position as an independent contractor. In the United States, by way of contrast, salaried practice is well established in private health maintenance organizations (HMOs) that range in size from a handful to hundreds of practitioners. The number of these prepayment plans rose from thirty in 1970 to 393 by June 1985, with a total enrolment of almost 19 million persons. Although many new HMOs simply contract for medical care with multidisciplinary groups of independent practitioners, growth also continues in the sector of "staff model" HMOs, where physicians are actually salaried employees of the consumer organization. American proprietary hospitals were in decline from the late 1950s until the early 1970s. However, as noted by sociologist Paul Starr, the number of beds controlled by for-profit corporations has since increased again, and investor-owned corporations appear to be diversifying by purchasing dialysis centres, health maintenance organizations, and other health care facilities.[20] These trends have caused considerable concern in some professional quarters, since continued rapid production of doctors by American medical schools means that practitioners may be forced to compete for salaried positions in bureaucratized, private-practice settings. Potential conflicts between corporate demands for profitable practices and medical ethics have also been predicted.[21] At least for the present, no such threat looms over the Canadian medical profession.

Let us turn now to consideration of professional pressure group tactics. The need for strong organizations and collective action to deal with the state was recognized during the First World War and became a keynote during the 1930s and 1940s. Certainly by the late 1950s and early 1960s the CMA and its provincial divisions had evolved into strong political organizations. Proceedings of committees and annual meetings bear testimony to the diversity of viewpoints on health insurance within the medical associations. However, during overt conflicts in British Columbia and Saskatchewan, common interests welded the overwhelming majority of doctors into a strongly united group.

A secure membership base and attendant financial strength were unquestionably important if organized medicine were to invest in the preparation of high-quality briefs for public hearings or fund a public relations campaign such as the one waged more or less continuously in Saskatchewan from June 1960 to the summer of 1962. But personal lobbying was, in a manner of speaking, more labour intensive; for it tended to depend on the quality and quantity of contacts between the executive of medical organizations, key civil servants, and provincial or federal cabinet ministers. The most effective such lobby in the period examined above was mounted by Dr T.C. Routley and the CMA Committee of Seven between 1942 and 1944 in Ottawa. As noted in chapter 5, their effort was unique in that the importance of the deliberations of the Special House Committee on Social Security led the CMA to expend considerable energy in cultivating close ties with medical MPs as well as influencing senior civil servants. However, party discipline in a parliamentary system has generally limited the utility of direct contact with federal or provincial representatives outside the cabinet.

Predictably, then, the lobbying activity of Canadian doctors has resembled that of the British Medical Association rather than the American Medical Association.[22] A further contrast with the AMA should be noted in matters of substance as well as form, since the CMA and its provincial divisions have consistently been more open minded than their American counterparts about the need for some degree of government involvement in prepayment of medical and hospital bills.[23] On the other hand, the Canadian federal system creates dissimilarities in the structure of British and Canadian medical politics. It has provided opportunities for the CMA and its provincial divisions to play Ottawa and the provinces off against each other, while the BMA has only a single channel for political pressure. Moreover, since the 1930s Canadian medicine has gradually developed its own federal structure. Provincial divisions are autonomous within their specific sphere of profession-government negotiations, but they send delegates to CMA meetings and co-operate closely when the national association fights battles on the federal front. As is true in ordinary party politics, some leaders of the CMA emerge from the increasingly high-profile executive committees of the provincial medical associations, while others climb to prominence through committee work at the federal level.

The ultimate pressure-group tactic for doctors is withdrawal of all but emergency services. In the period under review this was deemed necessary on only two occasions. The first, highly selective work-action was in Winnipeg during 1933-4, and perhaps because it was directed only against recipients of medical relief it drew almost no out-of-province attention.[24] The aims of the work-action were primarily economic, and these goals were achieved. A well-publicized withdrawal of medical services across Saskatchewan during July 1962 was organized in support of aims that were more broadly political; it can be classified as only a limited success.

As we have seen, the profession's proposals and pressure-group activities were given additional weight on several occasions by the formation of alliances with other interested parties. Businessmen and industrialists were loosely aligned with the BCMA in its opposition to the British Columbia health insurance act of 1936. Chambers of commerce and the insurance industry supported the profession's policy stance in the early 1960s as the multiple-carriers strategy evolved. And, although it may eventually have redounded to the profession's discredit, the vociferous backing of a broad coalition of anti-CCF groups in Saskatchewan during 1961–2 unquestionably strengthened the resolve of organized medicine to see that conflict through to its bitter conclusion.

One set of allies with which the profession had an ambivalent relationship were the member agencies of Trans-Canada Medical Plans. Creation of these medically sponsored non-profit corporations was the most original and constructive tactic used by the CMA and its provincial divisions. TCMP carriers provided medical services insurance to several million Canadians. In so doing they helped entrench private fee-for-service practice, may have contributed to the upward trend in doctors' incomes during the 1950s and early 1960s, promoted good public relations for the profession, and gave organized medicine itself a claim to special experience and expertise in administration of insurance programs. Indeed, had the investor-owned insurance agencies not captured an equal share of the prepayment market, it is possible that the TCMP vehicles would have grown much larger. As the 1964 report of the CMA Special Committee on Policy contended, market dominance by a single agency might simply have led in any case to government expropriation and the much-feared "monopolistic" state control of prepayment. Alternatively, the Hall Commission and the Liberal cabinet might have been persuaded that the TCMP agencies should continue as quasi-autonomous organizations in receipt of state subsidies but not under government control. As the CMA 1949 Policy Statement envisaged, this arrangement could well have given the profession the "insulation" against direct dealing with governments that it now lacks. All such discussion, however, is speculative. As events turned out, the TCMP agencies probably hastened the advent of publicly administered, universal state medical insurance by proving that providers and consumers alike preferred first-dollar coverage without direct financial transactions. They also demonstrated that a large-scale non-profit plan could be cheaper to administer than a multiplicity of small investor-owned plans and that reasonable budgeting on an open-ended, fee-for-service basis was possible.

Again after 1966 there have been some interesting if not unexpected developments in interest group strategies. First, with the erosion of the average medical income came renewed concern in the late 1970s with strengthening medical organizations and their collective-bargaining capacity. The threat of unionization has been used by medical spokesmen for public suasion purposes,[25] but proposals for a formal union structure have never been well received by the rank and file.[26] Only the Quebec GPs' and specialists' syndicates are supported through compulsory check-off arrangements that draw dues from all practising doctors in the province, although the Manitoba Medical Association has explored implementation of a similar arrangement. Even in the absence of compulsory enrolment, the strength and importance of the provincial medical associations relative to the federal organization have been increasing. Responsibility for health care policy and resource allocation remains primarily a provincial matter, and interprovincial variation is such that the CMA's role in assisting its divisions is limited, especially in the larger provinces. Indeed, the OMA annual budget of about $6 million is almost double that of the CMA.

Since the incomes of all fee-for-service practitioners depend on the success of a provincial medical group in pressing for increases in the medicare benefit schedule, there is no lack of support for collective action despite the rejection of formal union structure. For example, in early 1982 the Ontario Medical Association staged rotating office closures and then an escalating province-wide withdrawal of routine services as it successfully pressed the provincial government for double-digit "catch-up" increases. Participation across the province was 85 to 90 percent, and many of those who remained at work were among the 14 percent of Ontario practitioners who had opted out of the medicare system and were already charging higher prices. As the rotating walk-outs began, the OMA placed two full-page advertisements in every Ontario daily newspaper. When the province-wide work stoppages were applied, seventy AM and twenty FM radio stations carried sixty second "commercials" supporting the OMA position.[27] In short, Dr Frank Turnbull's 1967 call for the development of tougher and more sophisticated collective bargaining techniques has been belatedly heeded.

The CMA has also experimented with new lobbying strategies. In a deliberate departure from the association's longstanding focus on the executive branch of government, a national "key man" system was devised in 1980 to work at a local level in each of 282 federal ridings, so that individual members of parliament might be apprised of organized medicine's concerns about legislation aimed at limiting extra-billing. The OMA, too, has established a system whereby local MDs are designated to lobby their MPPs on a regular basis. However, caucus discipline is likely to limit the effectiveness of these tactics.

The extra-billing issue itself has caused some divisions within the profession. A 1985 decision by the Manitoba Medical Association to accept elimination of extra-billing in exchange for a binding arbitration mechanism to settle fee disputes, was unfavourably received by the CMA. As well, a splinter group of opted-out practitioners, the ninety-member Association of Independent Physicians (AIP), protested vigorously against this policy.[28] However, in Ontario, where the AIP has about 1,000 members, a united front against any proposed ban on extra-billing is being maintained by the OMA and the opted-out faction. Indeed, it has been more likely that the OMA campaign might founder on a division between specialty groups with a high percentage of extra-billing members, such as urology, obstetrics and gynecology, orthopaedics and anesthesia, and groups such as internal medicine and general practice with very low percentages of extra-billing doctors.[29] To date, no serious divisions have appeared in the profession's ranks.

Let us turn finally to a question that is more difficult to address. What interpretation can best be placed on the intent of the profession's various policy proposals and the rhetoric that accompanied them? On one level, Max Weber's triad of vital interests – power, status, and income – was always at issue as an autonomous and prestigious occupational group with a strong market position sought to control the terms of state intervention. But, even as they put forward policies with these implications, medical spokesmen tended to stress that their paramount goal was to help the general public and protect individual patients. Faced with such behaviour sociologists have sometimes resorted to a crude reconstruction of political man as *homo economicus*,[30] and in this instance they might argue that the profession's "public interest" rhetoric was the result of a deliberately misleading propaganda effort. Only slightly more forgiving is Karl Mannheim's theory that, where vital interests are at stake, an individual may develop an ideology that includes "more or less conscious disguises of a situation, the true recognition of which would not be in accord with his interests. These distortions range all the way from conscious lies to half-conscious and unwitting disguises; from calculated attempts to dupe others to self-deception.''[31] This harsh judgment, too, seems inappropriate; for in their response to the development of state health insurance between 1911 and 1966, medical spokesmen and strategists appear to have been sincerely convinced that the profession's preferred policies were best for all Canadians.

As indicated at various points in the narrative, these convictions were bound up with the ideological assumptions of professionalism itself. The original success of medical professionalism as an occupational form, after all, had rested to some extent on its possibilities for self-legitimation. Licensing legislation, the sliding scale of fees, anti-competitive and monopolistic provisions in ethical codes, and statutory self-regulation – these among other aspects of professionalism permitted doctors' interests to be promoted at the same time as certain public interests. Emboldened, too, by their profession's dedication to serving the sick, medical leaders tended to presume that their preferred prescription for health insurance would automatically benefit the Canadian body politic. Thus, in its path-breaking 1934 report, the CMA Committee on Economics claimed that doctors naturally should try to shape health policy to their specifications: "This is not a selfish motive because what is best for the medical profession must be best for the public.''[32] Similarly ingenuous statements recurred often in subsequent policy pronouncements and addresses. They continue at present as the profession's spokesmen attempt to legitimize medical policies. Speaking to a gathering of Alberta doctors in the autumn of 1979, for instance, a high-ranking official of the CMA remarked: "Paying the doctor directly the way you would pay any professional for services clarifies the doctor-patient role. Patients are happier this way. It is not a matter of money.''[33] The logical extension of this viewpoint was voiced by a practitioner representing thirty-five Toronto-area psychiatrists during public hearings on Ontario's controversial Bill 94: "Discussion of fees is often an extremely useful, an extremely meaningful process within the therapy itself.''[34]

More persuasive public-interest "side effects" have also been important in legitimizing organized medicine's policies and perspectives. In the 1960s fears of a state monopoly in medical care insurance rested in part on the prospect of collective bargaining with government over fee schedules and other aspects of practice. But a related, altruistic concern was the fact that not simply medical fees but the entire health services sector would then be competing for tax dollars. Dr J. Wendell MacLeod, dean of the Saskatchewan University medical school and a supporter of universal medicare, had foretold this situation in 1960 in a speech to a Liberal policy conference: "What proportion of the gross national product should be devoted to health depends on our national scale of values. Political judgements will have to settle the competition between measures which promote the welfare of the entire population, our commitments internationally, and frills."[35] However, to many other dedicated practitioners working long hours in an occupation that produced a view of society as a series of individuals in need of medical attention, any ordering of priorities that might restrict or ration health spending was anathema. Seeking to discourage government action in 1945-6, the CMA had pointed out the importance of housing, employment, proper nutrition, recreation facilities, and measures other than medical and hospital services in promoting the health status of populations. By the 1960s some medical spokesmen were using the converse argument for the same purpose: health care was supposedly too important to compete for tax dollars alongside other services and projects organized under public sector auspices.

Today, too, there is professional concern about restrictions on overall health care spending. The economic recession of the early 1980s meant that in most provinces acute care hospitals were placed under "shotgun" budget restrictions. Chronic care beds remain in short supply, and waiting lists for in-patient and out-patient services have lengthened. Doctors therefore have many reasonable grievances against government, and these in turn permit considerable self-legitimation. For example, in reacting to Bill 94 – the "Health Care Accessability Act" that has been drafted to penalize extra-billing doctors in Ontario – spokesmen for organized medicine have contended that government "underfunding" is doing much more to limit access to health care than are the deterrent effects of additional charges levied by a minority of practitioners. Just as in the 1960s, patient-centred concerns are important in legitimizing professional interests in a given policy or perspective.[36]

One must therefore agree with Eliot Freidson, who has stressed that the medical profession is *not* simply a "baldly self-interested union" struggling thoughtlessly for "resources at the expense of others and of the public interest."[37] However, both past developments and some of organized medicine's more recent standpoints do bring to mind Freidson's charge that medicine's autonomous status and special position atop the health care hierarchy have tended to create a narrow professional perspective that is not always conducive to optimum public policy formulation.[38] As the problem of limited funds for burgeoning technology and apparently infinite demand continues to strain the Canadian health care system, it remains uncertain whether a shared interest in efficient and effective allocation of resources will bring greater rapprochement in the views of doctors, administrators, politicians, and planners.[39] A movement to either co-operation or conflict between medicine and government cannot, of course, be firmly extrapolated from the developmental history of Canadian health insurance. But whatever the trend, one thing is certain: in the future, as in the past, the profession of medicine will be a political force that cannot be ignored.

Notes

CHAPTER ONE

1 The term "medicare" should properly be reserved for the medical services component of the public health insurance programs. In common usage this distinction is seldom made.

2 National Council of Welfare, *Medicare: The Public Good and Private Practice* (Ottawa: Supply and Services pamphlet 1982), 1.

3 A summary of the debate and positions taken can be found in the National Council of Welfare pamphlet cited in n. 2, above. Mr Justice Emmett Hall has also addressed the issue of privatization and extra-billing in *Canada's National-Provincial Health Program for the 1980s: A Commitment for Renewal* (Ottawa: Supply and Services Canada May 1980), passim. For further information, see E. LeBourdais, "Extra-billing: Your Right or Privilege?" *Canadian Doctor*, April 1984, 26–9.

4 For a brief summary of the situation in each province see *Toronto Star*, 14 July 1985, F1. Developments during the latter part of 1985 and early 1986 can be easily traced in the biweekly (now weekly) Maclean-Hunter newspaper, *The Medical Post*.

5 T. Alexander McPherson, "A Message from the President: The Canada Health Act 'Illegal'?" *Canadian Medical Association Journal* 133 (15 July 1985): front insert.

6 For the profession's viewpoint, see Ontario Medical Association, "Political Update" (undated mailing to membership, October 1985). The Liberal draft bill was described as "obscene" in a letter to OMA members from Dr Earl Myers dated 30 Dec. 1985. On the immediate response of the OMA leadership, see *Toronto Daily Star*, 23 Dec. 1985. The reaction of the OMA council at an emergency session on 21 January 1986 was extremely strong, and eleven district OMA meetings held across the province to organize the profession's protest campaign have also been

well-attended. However, the true extent of militancy in the profession at large has yet to be determined as of March 1986.

7 Malcolm G. Taylor, *Health Insurance and Canadian Public Policy: The Seven Decisions that Created the Canadian Health Insurance System* (Montreal: McGill-Queen's University Press and the Institute of Public Administration of Canada 1978).

8 Malcolm G. Taylor, "The Organization and Administration of the Saskatchewan Hospital Services Plan," PH D thesis, University of California at Berkeley 1948; Robin F. Badgley and Samuel Wolfe, *Doctors' Strike: Medical Care and Conflict in Saskatchewan* (Toronto: Macmillan 1967); Edwin A. Tollefson, *Bitter Medicine: The Saskatchewan Medicare Feud* (Saskatoon: Modern Press 1963); Walter P. Thompson, *Medical Care: Programs and Issues* (Toronto: Clarke-Irwin 1964). In the light of the volume of material published about Saskatchewan medical politics, the discussions of Saskatchewan developments in the present study are included for continuity and completeness, without any claims to originality.

9 See, for example, Maurice LeClair, "The Canadian Health System," in S. Andreopoulos, ed., *National Health Insurance: Can We Learn from Canada?* (New York: Wiley 1975), 18–22.

10 Bernard R. Blishen, *Doctors and Doctrines: The Ideology of Medical Care in Canada* (Toronto: University of Toronto Press 1969). For a critique of Professor Blishen's theoretical framework see Christopher David Naylor, "The Canadian Medical Profession and State Medical Care Insurance: Key Developments, 1911–1966," D PHIL thesis, Oxford University 1983, 8–15, 354–8.

11 Robert Michels, *Political Parties: A Sociological Study of the Oligarchical Tendencies of Modern Democracies* (Toronto: Collier-Macmillan 1966). Although most of Michels's strictures are directed against socialist parties and so-called workers' movements of seventy years and more ago, his analysis applies in some measure to any political association.

CHAPTER TWO

1 Malcolm G. Taylor, "The Role of the Medical Profession in the Formulation and Execution of Public Policy," *Canadian Journal of Economics and Political Science* 25 (Feb. 1960): 125.

2 This point is made clearly in Paul Starr's capable synthesis of historical and sociological scholarship, *The Social Transformation of American Medicine* (New York: Basic Books 1982).

3 Note that a distinction can be made between scholarly and consulting aspects of professionalism. For some comments on this distinction historically in medicine, see Eliot Freidson, *Profession of Medicine: A*

Study in the Sociology of Applied Knowledge (New York: Dodd Mead 1970), 21–2.

4 See Francis M. Cornford, tr., *The Republic of Plato* (London: Oxford University Press 1960), 10–24, 28. This train of argument was used by Plato, perhaps playfully, to make a case for authoritarian government.

5 Freidson, *Profession of Medicine*, 76.

6 Ibid., 80–2, 172–6. Freidson contends that "The profession's service orientation is a public imputation it has successfully won in a process by which its leaders have persuaded society to grant and support its autonomy." See also Terence J. Johnson, *Professions and Power* (London: Macmillan 1972), 24–6, 34–5.

7 Parsons was one of the first to describe these results of medical ethics in modern psychological terms. See Talcott Parsons, *The Social System* (Glencoe: The Free Press 1951), 459–62.

8 Ibid., 463–4. For an earlier statement on this issue, see the pioneering study by A.M. Carr-Saunders and P.A. Wilson, *The Professions* [1933] (London: Frank Cass 1964), 416–46.

9 D.W. Cathell, *Book on the Physician Himself*, 10th ed. (Philadelphia: F.A. Davis 1898), 18–19.

10 R.A. Kessel, "Price Discrimination in Medicine," *Journal of Law and Economics* 1 (Oct. 1958): 20–53.

11 Lawrence Haworth makes this point clearly in his idealized portrait of professionalism: see *Decadence and Objectivity: Ideals for Work in the Post-Consumer Society* (Toronto: University of Toronto Press 1977), 54.

12 On the importance of the diagnostic monopoly in ordering the medical division of labour, see Johnson, *Professions and Power*, 57. The aspirations of paramedical groups to professional status are limited to some extent by medicine's dominant position in this regard.

13 See Freidson, *Profession of Medicine*, 86–157, 180–3. In 1972 the Ontario Hospital Association made a similar comment about practitioners in the hospital setting; see E.A. Pickering, *Report on a Special Study Concerning the Medical Profession* (np, Ontario Medical Association 1973), 73.

14 On the difference between bureaucratic and collegial systems of authority, see Max Weber (ed. and tr. G. Roth and C. Wittich), *Economy and Society* (New York: Bedminster Press 1968), vol. 1: 220–1, 271–82. See also Eliot Freidson, *Professional Dominance: The Social Structure of Medical Care* (New York: Atherton 1970), 158–61. An excellent discussion of the bureaucratic constraints on social work can be found in W.R. Scott's essay in Amitai Etzioni, ed., *The Semi-Professions and Their Organization: Teachers, Nurses, Social Workers* (New York: Free Press 1969), 82–140.

15 Friedson, *Profession of Medicine*, 23–46.

16 Ibid., 25. Freidson here begins to veer towards the view of Carr-Saunders and Wilson, who stressed in 1933 that even as salaried employees, professionals were liable to retain an allegiance to technical standards set out by their colleagues, and this allegiance ensured that they would serve clients rather than their employer alone (see n. 8, above).

17 Derek Robinson, *Patients, Practitioners, and Medical Care*, 2nd ed. (London: Heinemann 1978), 67.

18 For some of these data, see Jean-Luc Migué and Gilles Bélanger, *The Price of Health* (Toronto: Macmillan 1974), 10–17; or Eugene Vayda, "A Comparison of Surgical Rates in Canada and in England and Wales," *New England Journal of Medicine* 289 (1973): 1224–9. One CMA president said in 1945, "As long as practitioners are forced to resort to surgical procedures to make ... the difference between a bare living and a decent income, just so long will the scale be weighted against any patient who presents himself for examination": Harris McPhedran, "The Outlook in Medical Education and Other Problems," *CMAJ* 52 (March 1945): 292.

19 For the argument in favour of fee-for-service payment, see Harry Schwartz, "Conflicts of Interest in Fee for Service and in HMOs," *New England Journal of Medicine* 299 (1978): 1071–3.

20 W.G. Manning, A. Leibowitz, G.A. Goldberg, W.H. Rogers, and J.P. Newhouse, "A Controlled Trial of the Effect of a Prepaid Group Practice on the Use of Services," *New England Journal of Medicine* 310 (1984): 1505–10.

21 On the broad issue of supplier-induced demand, see Robert G. Evans, *Price Formation in the Market for Physician Services in Canada* (Ottawa: Information Canada 1973), 17–38, 111–14; and idem, "Supplier-Induced Demand: Some Empirical Observations," in Mark Perlman, ed., *The Economics of Health and Medical Care* (London: Macmillan 1974) 162–73. Much of this behaviour is doubtless not economically premeditated but rather flows from the conjunction of available office time and/or hospital space with the doctor's belief that patients would automatically benefit from more medical attention.

22 Johnson, *Professions and Power*, 57.

23 Ronald Hamowy, *Canadian Medicine: A Study in Restricted Entry* (Vancouver: The Fraser Institute 1984), 2, 4. Professor Hamowy emphasizes the cartelizing effects of licensure, but the promulgation of fee schedules has similar effects.

24 Johnson, *Professions and Power*, 65–74.

25 For a detailed study of the profession's activities in lobbying for favourable regulatory intervention by the state, see Hamowy's *Canadian Medicine*, passim.

26 One of the best accounts of this process remains Robert L. Heilbroner's *The Making of Economic Society* (Englewood Cliffs, NJ: Prentice-Hall 1962). See especially 41–60.

27 Magali S. Larson, *The Rise of Professionalism* (Berkeley, CA: University of California Press 1979), 53–63.

28 In *Professions and Power* Johnson suggests that the dependence of leading practitioners on aristocratic sufferance and generosity was such that "patronage" rather than a self-regulating collegial control system applied.

29 See Maude E. Abbott, *History of Medicine in the Province of Quebec* (Toronto: Macmillan 1931), 31; and John J. Heagerty, *Four Centuries of Medical History in Canada* (Toronto: Macmillan 1928), 1: 315–16.

30 On English developments, see Carr-Saunders and Wilson, *The Professions*, 65–83.

31 Hamowy, *Canadian Medicine*, 34. This volume must now be regarded as the definitive source on the statutes regulating the profession and the attendant political manoeuvring. Another useful and concise overview that has been helpful in preparing this material is Joseph F. Kett, "American and Canadian Medical Institutions, 1800–1870," in Samuel E.D. Shortt, *Medicine in Canadian Society: Historical Perspectives* (Montreal: McGill-Queen's University Press 1981), 189–205.

32 On Ontario developments see Elizabeth MacNab, *A Legal History of the Health Professions in Ontario: A Study for The Committee on the Healing Arts* (Toronto: Queen's Printer 1970), 4–7, and Hamowy, *Canadian Medicine*, 13–21.

33 Some lawyers in the united parliament of the two Canadas (Quebec and Ontario) did press for repeal of licensing, but the free trade movement was weak. See Hugh E. MacDermot, *History of the Canadian Medical Association, 1867–1921* (Toronto: Murray Printing 1935), 11.

34 Barbara R. Tunis, "Medical Licensing in Lower Canada: The Dispute over Canada's First Medical Degree," in Shortt, *Medicine in Canadian Society*, 137–63; and idem, "Medical Education and Medical Licensing in Lower Canada," *Histoire sociale-Social History* 14 (May 1981): 67–91.

35 On the incorporation of the college, see Abbott, *History of Medicine*, 72. See also MacDermot, *History of the CMA, 1867–1921*, 2–5. Petitions for extension of licensure to unorthodox practitioners arrived regularly in the legislative assembly: in the years 1843, 1847, 1849, 1852, and 1853 there were attempts either to license irregulars or to repeal all licensing legislation. On Thomsonians in Ontario see Charles M. Godfrey, *Medicine for Ontario: A History* (Belleville: Mika Publishing 1979), 21–3.

36 Weber, *Economy and Society*, 1: 277.

37 Among the treatments in common use were bleeding, purging with mercurial compounds such as calomel, and dosing with arsenic and strychnine. Homeopathy and eclecticism arose in part as a reaction to the therapeutic inadequacy and iatrogenic toll of mainstream or allopathic remedies.

38 Freidson, *Profession of Medicine*, 137.

39 Hamowy, *Canadian Medicine*, 35–60.

40 For an interesting analysis of the interplay between laissez-faire and liberal viewpoints on medical licensure, see Jeffrey L. Berlant, *Profession and Monopoly: A Study of Medicine in the United States and Great Britain* (Berkeley, CA: University of California Press 1975), 145–67.

41 Hamowy, *Canadian Medicine*, 60–9, 100–16.

42 Heagerty, *Four Centuries of Medical History*, 1: 282–6.

43 See generally MacDermot's *History of the CMA, 1867–1921*. MacDermot's choice of an end point for his survey was dictated by the start of the upturn in the CMA's fortunes.

44 For a detailed analysis of the CMA/AMA code, see C. David Naylor, "The CMA's First Code of Ethics: Medical Morality or Borrowed Ideology?" *Journal of Canadian Studies* 17, no. 4 (1982–3): 20–32.

45 For the text of the code see *Origin and Organization of the Canadian Medical Association with the Proceedings of the Meetings Held in Quebec, October 1867, and Montreal, September 1868* (Montreal: John Lovell 1868), 62–73.

46 A superb overview of the sociological, political, and economic functions of medical codes generally can be found in Berlant, *Profession and Monopoly*, 64–127.

47 Johnson, *Professions and Power*, 55.

48 On discipline proceedings in Ontario, for example, see MacNab, *Legal History*, 33–9, and Godfrey, *Medicine for Ontario*, 223–30.

49 On the Patrons, see Samuel E.D. Shortt, "Social Change and Political Crisis in Rural Ontario," in Donald Swainson, ed., *Oliver Mowat's Ontario* (Toronto: Macmillan 1972), 211–35.

50 The speaker was Dr William Britton, as quoted in the *Canadian Medical Review* 8 (July 1898): 9.

51 The Patrons' challenge to the profession is discussed at much greater length in C. David Naylor, "Rural Protest and Medical Professionalism in Turn-of-the-Century Ontario," *Journal of Canadian Studies* 21 (June 1986): 5–20.

52 MacDermot, *History of the CMA 1867–1921*, 19–20, 46.

53 Ross Mitchell, *Medicine in Manitoba: The Story of Its Beginnings* (Winnipeg: Stovel-Advocate Press 1954), 57–8.

54 Hilda Neatby, "The Medical Profession in the North-West Territories," in Shortt, *Medicine in Canadian Society*, 177, 187, n. 49.

55 Godfrey, *Medicine for Ontario*, 194-5; MacNab, *Legal History*, 14-24.
56 For a variety of comments on sectarianism and the rise of scientific medicine see Frank Hodgins, *Report and Supporting Statements on Medical Education in Ontario* (Sessional Papers, Ontario Legislature, vol. 1, part ix, 1918), 132-40. It is interesting that Hodgins quoted the following key statement from Abraham Flexner's influential report on medical education in North America (1910): "Prior to the placing of medicine on a scientific basis, sectarianism was of course inevitable ... Allopathy was just as sectarian as homeopathy ... But now that allopathy has surrendered to modern medicine, is not homeopathy borne on the same current into the same harbour?" On paradigms, scientific communities, and the institutionalization of progress, see Thomas S. Kuhn, *The Structure of Scientific Revolutions* (Chicago: University of Chicago Press, 1970).
57 Godfrey, *Medicine for Ontario*, 197.
58 Quoted by C.D. Howell, "Reform and the Monopolistic Impulse: the Professionalization of Medicine in the Maritimes," *Acadiensis* 11 (Fall 1981): 19.
59 *Canadian Journal of Medicine and Surgery* 1, no. 5 (1897): 222-4, 271.
60 For discussion of the legislation in several jurisdictions that limited the scope of practice of midwifery, see Hamowy, *Canadian Medicine*, 136-7, 156-9, 343 nn. 123-4, 344 n. 131, 368 n. 224. See also C. Lesley Biggs, "The Case of the Missing Midwives: A History of Midwifery in Ontario from 1795-1900," *Ontario History* 75 (March 1983): 21-35.
61 See E.R. Booth, *History of Osteopathy and Twentieth Century Medical Practice* (Cincinatti: Jennings and Graham 1905) for general background; and M.A. Lane, *Dr. A.T. Still, Founder of Osteopathy* (Waukegan, IL: Bunting 1925), especially 39-40.
62 "Medicine in Alberta," *CMAJ* 2 (Feb. 1912): 140; "The Ontario Medical Council and Osteopathy," *CMAJ* 2 (June 1912): 514-15; "The Activities of a Provincial Association," *CMAJ* 7 (July 1917): 542-3. For two overviews, see Mr Justice Hodgins's 1918 *Report on Medical Education in Ontario* and Gilles Lacroix, *Royal Commission on Chiropraxy and Osteopathy: Osteopathy* (Province of Quebec 1968).
63 See MacNab, *Legal History*, 37-9, and Hodgins, *Report on Medical Education*, 27-9, for a sense of the arguments against full licensure. Despite its anomalous position in this respect, Ontario has maintained its restrictions on oesteopathic practice into the 1980s; see "Ontario's Injustice Toward Osteopaths Rooted in the Past," *Toronto Daily Star*, 9 October 1982.
64 Hodgins, *Report on Medical Education*, 125-6.
65 Ibid. See also the *Report of the Committee on the Healing Arts* (Toronto: Queen's Printer 1970), 2: 458.

66 Howell, "Reform and the Monopolistic Impulse," 19.
67 Hodgins provides a useful overview of the situation with respect to opticians and optometrists in his *Report on Medical Education*, 40-2, 73. See also MacNab, *Legal History*, 127-38.
68 MacNab, *Legal History*, 32 nn. 170, 174. See also *Canadian Medical Review* 8 (Aug. 1898): 52. Hamowy's monograph, which appeared during the process of review and revision of this background sketch, offers extensive corroboration of the point about mixed motives in the push to upgrade educational and licensing requirements: *Canadian Medicine*, 108-9, 147, 151, 155, 177-84, 235.
69 Howell, "Reform and the Monopolistic Impulse," 13-15.
70 Abraham Flexner, *Medical Education in the United States and Canada* (New York: Arno 1972), 29-30, 35, 108, 320, 323-4.
71 "Editorials," *CMAJ* 1 (Jan. 1911): 62-70; "The Vindication of Laval," *CMAJ* 1 (April 1911): 354-6.
72 Flexner, *Medical Education*, 19, 35 n. 2, 86, 88, 139, 150.
73 For an overview of medical education in Canada post-Flexner, see "Editorials," *CMAJ* 1 (Oct. 1911): 982-94.
74 "The Proprietary School," *CMAJ* 1 (Nov. 1911): 1091-2.

CHAPTER THREE

1 Ronald L. Numbers, *Almost Persuaded: American Physicians and Compulsory Health Insurance, 1912-1920* (Baltimore: Johns Hopkins University Press 1978), 10.
2 At a professionalization level, Jeffrey L. Berlant discusses some of the tensions between physicians, surgeons, and apothecaries: *Profession and Monopoly* (Berkeley, CA: University of California Press 1975), 128-67.
3 Detailed accounts can be found in Jean L. Brand, *Doctors and the State* (Baltimore: Johns Hopkins University Press 1965), 192-7; and P.H.J. Gosden, *The Friendly Societies in England, 1815-1875* (Manchester: University Press 1961), 138-49.
4 Frank Honigsbaum, *The Division in British Medicine: A History of the Separation of General Practice from Hospital Care, 1911-1968* (London: Kogan 1979), 14-15.
5 Ibid., 13.
6 See the summary in Jan Blanpain, *National Health Insurance and Health Resources: The European Experience* (Cambridge, MA: Harvard University Press 1978), 52-9.
7 Numbers, *Almost Persuaded*, 29-30 on the American scene. This generalization is derived from a review of the table of contents of a sampling of Canadian medical periodicals from the 1880s, 1890s, and 1900s.
8 "The British Insurance Bill," *Canada Lancet* 45 (Sept. 1911): 5-6.

9 On Macphail, see Samuel E.D. Shortt, *The Search for an Ideal: Six Canadian Intellectuals and Their Convictions in an Age of Transition* (Toronto: University of Toronto Press 1976), 13-38.

10 "The Patient's Dilemma," *CMAJ* 1 (Sept. 1911): 885-8.

11 "The Insurance Act," *CMAJ* 2 (March 1912): 228-30.

12 G.S. Ryerson, "The National Insurance Act," *Canada Lancet* 45 (April 1912): 632; "Two Effects of the British National Insurance Act," *Public Health Journal* 3 (Feb. 1912): 76.

13 "Eating the Leek," *CMAJ* 2 (Sept. 1912): 822-5.

14 Numbers, *Almost Persuaded*, 32.

15 Ronald Hamowy, *Canadian Medicine: A Study in Restricted Entry* (Vancouver: The Fraser Institute 1984), 271.

16 See Royal Commission on Health Services, *Final Report* (Ottawa: Queen's Printer 1964), vol. 1: 381-6 for some comments on early developments.

17 Hamowy, *Canadian Medicine*, 195-6, 356-7.

18 W. Britton, "Presidential Address," *Canadian Medical Review* 8 (July 1898): 8.

19 *Canadian Medical Review* 8 (Aug. 1898) 59-61.

20 Margaret W. Andrews has noted that one successful Vancouver doctor was receiving regular quarterly payments from three separate Foresters' Orders in the 1890s: "Medical Attendance in Vancouver, 1886-1920," 436-7, 445 (notes 48-50), in S.E.D. Shortt, ed., *Medicine in Canadian Society* (Montreal: McGill-Queen's University Press 1981). Generally, however, we know very little about nineteenth-century Canadian medical economics.

21 Based on a sampling of Ontario-based journals between 1897 and 1905, the issue seems to have faded rapidly. A motion was again put to the council of the Ontario College of Physicians and Surgeons for a ban on lodge practice in 1898, but it was appropriately declared out of order. As late as the 1920s, however, young Jewish general practitioners apparently found it difficult to establish themselves in Toronto because of the lodges; D. Eisen, *Diary of a Medical Student* (Toronto: Canadian Jewish Congress 1974), 107 (n. 27).

22 H.A. McCallum, "President's Address," *CMAJ* 3 (July 1913): 547-55.

23 For a synopsis of Hamilton's comments, see "On Medical Education, *CMAJ* 3 (Nov. 1913): 980-2.

24 "Report of the Committee on Applied Sociology," *CMAJ* 4 (Dec. 1914): 1123-4; and "Report on behalf of the Committee on Public Health Legislation," *CMAJ* 4 (Sept. 1914): 830-1. At the time of the CMA meeting, the Fergusons commented favourably on State intervention in "State Medicine," *Canada Lancet* 47 (July 1914): 802-3.

25 A.R. Munroe, "Health Insurance and the Medical Profession," *CMAJ* 4 (Dec. 1914): 1112-4.

26 Donald Creighton, *Canada's First Century* (Toronto: Macmillan 1970), 137. For a more extended analysis, see R. Thomas Naylor, *Dominion of Debt* (Montreal: Black Rose Books 1985), 61-108.

27 Some supporting material is presented in Naylor's essay cited in n. 26, above.

28 My discussion of health insurance in America in this period relies on the articles by AALL committee members cited below and on Ronald Numbers's excellent monograph, cited in n. 1, above.

29 See I.M. Rubinow, "20,000 Miles over the Land: A Survey of the Spreading Health Insurance Movement," *Public Health Journal* 8 (April 1917): 93-100, for a summary of American developments.

30 Numbers, *Almost Persuaded*, 41, 46, 50-1.

31 Glenn Sawyer, *The First Hundred Years: A History of the Ontario Medical Association* (Toronto: Ontario Medical Association 1981), 97.

32 "In Brief," *CMAJ* 7 (May 1917): 448-9.

33 "In Brief," *CMAJ* 7 (Oct. 1917): 933.

34 "Presidential Address," *CMAJ* 7 (July 1917): 585-8.

35 C.J. Hastings, "The Modern Conception of Public Health and Its National Importance," *CMAJ* 7 (Aug. 1917): 684-703.

36 See the *Public Health Journal* 8 (Nov. 1917): 308-9 and (Dec. 1917): 313-36; also, *CMAJ* 7 (Dec. 1917): 1110-11.

37 J.G. Wishart, "Presidential Address," *Public Health Journal* 8 (Nov. 1917): 286.

38 See *Public Health Journal* 9 (May 1918): 245; 9 (Sept. 1918): 443.

39 "A Federal Department," *Public Health Journal* 9 (Feb. 1918): 92.

40 *The Canadian Medical Week* (Toronto: Macmillan/OMA 1918): 7, 13-14.

41 "Editorials," *Public Health Journal* 9 (Aug. 1918): 390-1.

42 For the CMA president's address, see *Canadian Medical Week*, 1-5. I have been unable to locate a transcript of Hastings's address, although both the *CMAJ* and *Public Health Journal* list it among the papers scheduled for the conference under the title, "Health Insurance."

43 J. Heurner Mullin, "Are We Ready for Health Insurance?" *Public Health Journal* 9 (Sept. 1918): 402-11.

44 Numbers, *Almost Persuaded*, 64-8, 73-81, 99.

45 The background material here and at other points in this section is culled from various sources, including Irving Abella, "The Canadian Labour Movement, 1902-1960" (Ottawa: Canadian Historical Association 1974); Creighton, *Canada's First Century*; E.A. Forsey, "The Canadian Labour Movement, 1812-1902" (Ottawa: Canadian Historical Association 1974); G. Horowitz, *Canadian Labour in Politics* (Toronto:

University of Toronto Press 1968); M.A. Ormsby, *British Columbia: A History* (Toronto: Macmillan 1958).

46 Numbers, *Almost Persuaded*, 85, 88–9, 95, 103.

47 P.H. Bryce, "The Scope of a Federal Department of Health," *CMAJ* 10 (Jan. 1920): 7–8.

48 G.D. Shortreed, "Abstract of Presidential Address" (to the 1919 annual meeting of the MMA), *CMAJ* 10 (March 1920): 209–16.

49 D.L. Matters, "A Report on Health Insurance: 1919," *BC Studies* 21 (Spring 1974): 28.

50 *BC Legislative Journal* (Feb.-March 1919): 80, 122, 144.

51 Malcolm G. Taylor, "The Organization and Administration of the Saskatchewan Hospital Services Plan," PH D thesis, University of California at Berkeley 1948, 15.

52 *Victoria Daily Colonist*, 20 Nov. 1919, 1.

53 Matters, "Report on Health Insurance," 29.

54 J.W. McIntosh, "The State Health Insurance Movement in British Columbia," *Canadian Public Health Journal* 21 (1930): 584.

55 *Victoria Daily Times*, 14 Jan. 1920, 6.

56 J.H. MacDermot, "Health Insurance," *CMAJ* 15 (Mar. 1925): 289.

57 Quoted by Robert S. Bothwell and John R. English, in "Pragmatic Physicians: Canadian Medicine and Health Care Insurance, 1910–1945," in Shortt, ed., *Medicine in Canadian Society*, 481.

58 Matters, "Report on Health Insurance," 30–1.

59 Martin Robin, *The Company Province: The Rush for Spoils* (Toronto: McClelland and Stewart 1972), 181–5.

60 *BC Legislative Journal* (Nov.-Dec. 1922), 108–9.

61 See "The Medical and Allied Professions in a State Service," *CMAJ* 10 (Jan. 1920): 72–3; and H.E. MacDermot, "A Short History of Health Insurance in Canada," *CMAJ* 50 (May 1944): 448. Dr A.D. Blackader had come out of retirement to serve as chairman of the editorial board and, as indicated by his presidential address to the CMA in 1917, took a positive view of health insurance. Assuming he had not changed his stand, Blackader's influence probably accounts for the thrust of this editorial.

62 "The New Relationship between the State and the Practitioner in England," *CMAJ* 10 (Nov. 1920): 949–51.

63 H.E. MacDermot, "Short History of Health Insurance," 448.

64 Numbers, *Almost Persuaded*, 105.

65 F. Billings, "Modern Medicine and the General Practitioner," *CMAJ* 11 (Sept. 1921): 637.

66 J.H. Mullin, "Medical Organizations in Ontario and the Present Necessity," *CMAJ* 11 (July 1921): 493–5.

67 Quoted by Bothwell and English, "Pragmatic Physicians," 481.

68 See *Canadian Journal of Medicine and Surgery* 15 (May 1904): 383. Again, this is unfortunately typical of the limited evidence we have on medical economics in either the nineteenth or early twentieth centuries.

69 *Report of the Committee on Economics of the CMA, as presented at the Annual Meeting in Calgary, June 18–22, 1934* (pamphlet, n.p. 1934), 23, 30. The report was also published as a supplement to *CMAJ* 31 (Sept. 1934).

70 L.A. Gagnier, *Droits et Devoirs de la Médecine et des Médecins Canadien-français* (Montreal: Devoir 1926), 12.

71 J.H. MacDermot, "Health Insurance," 289.

72 This estimate is based on census data for the city of Vancouver from 1921 (see *Sixth Census of Canada: Vol. 3*, 522–5) and the *Seventh Census of Canada: Vol. 5* where national data on percentiles of income by household head indicate that in 1931 only about 5 percent of the population would have had total household incomes of more than $3,000 per annum.

73 J.H. MacDermot, "Health Insurance," 290.

74 Ibid., 291.

75 Ibid., 292–3. One of the discussants, Dr George Young, the OMA president, later made a vague reference to health insurance in his valedictory address: *CMAJ* 15 (July 1925): 688.

76 See the remarks by Dr W. Britton, *Canadian Medical Review* 8 (July 1898): 7.

77 "Correspondence," *CMAJ* 15 (Jan. 1925): 92–3.

78 "Business Report of the Fifty-Sixth Annual Meeting of the CMA," *CMAJ* 15 (1925): supplement, xiv–xv.

79 Gagnier, *Droits et Devoirs*, 36–7, 65.

80 Robin F. Badgley and Samuel Wolfe, *Doctors' Strike: Medical Care and Conflict in Saskatchewan* (Toronto: Macmillan 1967), 9.

81 "Report of the Committee on Municipal Physicians," *CMAJ* 19 (1928): supplement, xviii.

82 "Contract Practice in Alberta," *CMAJ* 35 (Sept. 1935): 321.

83 Ibid.

84 "News Items: Alberta," *CMAJ* 36 (March-April 1937): 325, 437. About twenty doctors held contracts with mines, logging camps, or railroad employees in 1929; and several municipalities in outlying areas paid doctors a partial salary.

85 "News Items: Alberta," *CMAJ* 35 (Dec. 1936): 700. There is an interesting parallel here between the college's attempt to standardize and control prepayment arrangements and manoeuvring by German organized medicine a decade earlier. See D.A. Stone, *The Limits of Professional Power: National Health Care in the Federal Republic of Germany* (Chicago: University of Chicago Press 1980), 33–43.

86 "Organized Medicine in the Province of Alberta," *CMAJ* 35 (Sept. 1936): 320–1.

87 The Progressives achieved federal representation in 1921 and, although they lost ground in the 1925 election, held the balance of power between the Conservatives and Liberals. In Manitoba the Progressives were closely allied to the Liberals in Ottawa, even though John Bracken, the Progressive premier, was eventually persuaded to lead the Conservatives. In Alberta the UFA/Progressives held office between 1921 and 1935 and are provocatively portrayed in C.B. MacPherson's *Democracy in Alberta* (Toronto: University of Toronto Press 1953), 28–92.

88 "News Items: Alberta," *CMAJ* 18 (Feb. 1928): 244. See also the same column, 242, and *CMAJ* 19 (Sept. 1928): 388.

89 "News Items: Alberta," *CMAJ* 18 (Feb. 1928): 242.

90 Excerpted in the *CMAJ* 18 (Feb. 1928): 218–19. Not all eastern comments were negative. Addressing the Toronto Academy of Medicine in October 1927, Dr Harris MacPhedran – later to be president of the CMA – had outlined the arguments for state health insurance or direct employment of medical practitioners by the state, suggested the British system was working well, and wondered if the Alberta developments were not in part the profession's fault, since too much unnecessary surgery was being performed. See "The Relation of the Department of Public Health to the Profession," *CMAJ* 18 (May 1928): 683–5.

91 "Medical Legislation in Alberta," *CMAJ* 18 (April 1928): 435–6.

92 Taylor, "Saskatchewan Hospital Services Plan," 44–5.

93 Ibid.

94 On Wrinch, see *Who's Who in British Columbia* (Victoria: S.M. Carter Publishing 1930), 110. See also Taylor, "Saskatchewan Hospital Services Plan," 18–19. and H.H. Murphy, "Letter from British Columbia," *CMAJ* 18 (April 1928): 350.

95 *CMAJ* 19 (July 1928): supplement, xix–xx.

96 *BC Legislative Journal* (Jan.-March 1928), 7, 175–6.

97 *CMAJ* 19 (July 1928): supplement, xvii–xviii.

98 Ibid.

99 *BC Legislative Journal*, 19 Jan. 1929, 19.

100 Ibid., 1 Feb. 1929, 24.

101 *Victoria Daily Colonist*, 17 April 1929, 1.

102 Quoted in H.E. MacDermot's "Short History of Health Insurance," 448.

CHAPTER FOUR

1 Royal Commission on Dominion-Provincial Relations, *Final Report* (Ottawa: King's Printer 1940), 1: 150.

2 Dominion Bureau of Statistics, *Canada Year Book* (Ottawa: King's Printer 1945), 895.

3 Ward Woolner, "Medical Economics in the Rural Districts of Ontario," *CMAJ* 30 (March 1934): 307.

4 Robert Tyre, *Saddlebag Surgeon* (Don Mills Ont.: General Publishing 1976), 243-5.

5 *Report of the CMA Committee on Economics of the Canadian Medical Association, as presented at the annual meeting in Calgary, June 18-22, 1934* (pamphlet, n.p. 1934), 29.

6 See the summary in the *Victoria Daily Colonist*, 12 Feb. 1930, 6.

7 General accounts of the Depression in British Columbia can be found in Margaret A. Ormsby, *British Columbia: A History* (Toronto: Macmillan 1958); Martin Robin, *The Company Province: The Rush for Spoils, 1871-1933* (Toronto: McClelland and Stewart 1972); idem, *The Company Province: Pillars of Profit* (Toronto: McClelland and Stewart 1973).

8 *Victoria Daily Times*, 17 Sept. 1934, 2. In fact, the 1933 tax statistics showed that 49 percent of all private practitioners had *net* incomes under $2,000 that year.

9 Dr J.H. MacDermot of Vancouver was again the architect of this plan, and served as the BCMA spokesman to the royal commission.

10 See the *Report of the CMA Committee on Economics, 1934*, 25, where the BCMA proposals are summarized.

11 Hugh H. Wolfenden, *The Real Meaning of Social Insurance* (Toronto: Macmillan 1932), 178-9.

12 Frank Honigsbaum, *The Division in British Medicine* (London: Kogan 1979), 17-20.

13 Royal Commission on State Health Insurance and Maternity Benefits, *Final Report* (Victoria: C.F. Banfield 1932), 21-6, 59-63.

14 *Vancouver Sun*, 16 Feb. 1932, 6.

15 "News Items: BC," *CMAJ* 27 (July 1932): 110.

16 Ormsby, *British Columbia: A History*, 450-1; Robin, *Rush for Spoils*, 237-46.

17 J.H. MacDermot, "The Medical Treatment of the Indigent in British Columbia," *Manitoba Medical Association Review* 14 (Jan. 1934): 13-14.

18 Reprinted under the title "Medical Care for Citizens on Relief," *Bulletin of the Manitoba Medical Association* 13 (March 1933): 399-400.

19 "News Items: BC," *CMAJ* 29 (Oct. 1933): 456.

20 See "Recognition of Medical Services," *CMAJ* 29 (Aug. 1933): 192.

21 Extracted under the title "The Approach of Socialized Medicine," *CMAJ* 30 (Jan. 1934): 81.

22 On the platforms of the parties, see Robin, *Pillars of Profit*, 9-12, 22-7.

23 In 1934 Patullo added a constituency to the legislature, bringing the total number of seats to forty-eight. The seat was taken by a Liberal.

24 See League for Social Reconstruction, *Social Planning for Canada* (Toronto: Thomas Nelson 1935), 31, 394-8 for the league's blueprint for medical care.

25 Robin, *Pillars of Profit*, 13.

26 C.J. Veniot, "The Medical Economic Situation in New Brunswick," *CMAJ* 30 (May 1954): 551.

27 The profession's viewpoint and plight is summarized in the *Report of the CMA Committee on Economics, 1934*, 19-21. For additional details, see among others Lillian A. Chase, "The Economic Situation in Saskatchewan," *CMAJ* 29 (Dec. 1933): 661-2, and G.E. Learmonth, "The Medical Relief Problem in Alberta," *CMAJ* 30 (Feb. 1934): 201-2.

28 See "Medical Economics," *Bulletin of the Manitoba Medical Association* 123 (Nov. 1931): 12, and *Report of the CMA Committee on Economics, 1934*, 29-30, where data on incomes for Ontario and Manitoba doctors are presented to support this point.

29 "News Items: Saskatchewan," *CMAJ* 29 (July 1933): 108.

30 A detailed account of this episode is presented in C. David Naylor, "Canada's First Doctors' Strike: Medical Relief in Winnipeg, 1933-4," 1985 research paper deposited with the Public Archives of Canada and Manitoba Archives; see also an abbreviated version of this paper in *Canadian Historical Review* 67 (June 1986): 151-80.

31 Ibid. Specific figures can be found in the *Manitoba Medical Association Review* 15 (June 1935): 12.

32 *OMA Bulletin*, Jan. 1933: 4-5.

33 Ibid., June 1933: 7-8. The 1933 numbers of the *OMA Bulletin* were marked with the date only.

34 *OMA Bulletin* 1, no. 1 (March 1934): 11.

35 W.S. Caldwell, "Medical Relief in York Township," *OMA Bulletin* 1, no. 2 (April 1934): 35.

36 *Report of the CMA Committee on Economics, 1934*, 26.

37 On the growth of the CCF in Saskatchewan during the Depression, see Seymour Martin Lipset, *Agrarian Socialism* (Los Angeles: University of California 1950), 73-109.

38 *Royal Commission on Dominion-Provincial Relations*, 1: 150.

39 *Report of the CMA Committee on Economics, 1934*, 27.

40 "The Delegation to Ottawa re: Medical Care of the Unemployed," *CMAJ* 29 (Nov. 1933): 554-6.

41 *Report of the CMA Committee on Economics, 1934*, 5.

42 Ibid., 37-8.

43 Although the report is widely available as a pamphlet, it can also be found as a supplement to the *CMAJ* 31 (Sept. 1934): 25-61, with a summary of the initial debate on 61-2.

44 *Victoria Daily Times*, 17 Sept. 1934, 1-2. Weir also claimed that only nine doctors had refused outright to participate in a health insurance scheme.

45 "Provincial Association Notes: the BMCA," *CMAJ* 31 (Dec. 1934): 674.

46 "News Items: British Columbia," *CMAJ* 29 (Sept. 1933): 341.

47 Quoted by Grant Fleming in "Proceedings of the Executive Committee, October 31, 1935," *CMAJ* 34 (Feb. 1936): 204-5.

48 Ibid., 205.

49 Public Archives of Canada (hereafter PAC), Percival Bengough Papers, MG 30, A47, vol. 1: "A Plan of Health Insurance for British Columbia 1935."

50 Hugh E. MacDermot, "Health Insurance in British Columbia," *CMAJ* 33 (July 1935): 79.

51 For a biographical note on Peebles, see "News Items: BC," *CMAJ* 33 (Aug. 1935): 228.

52 *CMAJ* 34 (Feb. 1936): 206.

53 *Victoria Daily Times*, 24 Sept. 1935, 1-2. Notwithstanding the CMA's 1934 health insurance principles, it should be recalled that a CMA delegation to Ottawa in October 1933 had volunteered to accept payment for indigent care at half rates.

54 Quoted in Malcolm G. Taylor, "The Organization and Administration of the Saskatchewan Hospital Services Plan," PH D thesis, University of California at Berkeley, 1948, 26. Professor Taylor had access to a copy of the brief.

55 *Victoria Daily Times*, 24 Sept. 1935, 2.

56 Harry M. Cassidy, "The British Columbia Plan of Health Insurance," *CMAJ* 33 (Aug. 1935): 200. See also the accompanying editorial comment by Dr A. Grant Fleming.

57 *Victoria Daily Times*, 24 Sept. 1935, 2.

58 *CMAJ* 34 (Feb. 1936): 207. Several months later, Fleming resigned from the CMA economics committee.

59 Wolfenden, *Real Meaning of Social Insurance*, passim.

60 *CMAJ* 34: 207.

61 PAC, Bengough Papers, MG30, A47, vol. 1: "Private Report of the Hearings Committee on Health Insurance to the Honourable Provincial Secretary of British Columbia," 1 Nov. 1935, 4.

62 Ibid., vol. 2: "Radio Talks", number 82.

63 Robin, *Pillars of Profit*, 16-17. See also Margaret A. Ormsby, "T. Dufferin Patullo and the Little New Deal," *Canadian Historical Review* 43, no. 4 (Dec. 1962): 289-93. Professor Ormsby's informative article unfortu-

nately contains an inaccurate summary of the health insurance legislation.

64 "News Items: BC," *CMAJ* 34 (Jan. 1936): 116.

65 "News Items: BC," *CMAJ* 34 (Feb. 1936): 232. See also *Victoria Daily Times* 20 Feb. 1936, 1.

66 It seems likely that the provincial treasurer, John Hart, took a hand; for Hart was a "sound-money man," a partner in a prosperous brokerage and insurance firm, and the most conservative member of the Patullo cabinet. Taylor suggests his involvement ("Saskatchewan Hospital Services Plan," 29) and Harry M. Cassidy implies as much in his references to the BC dispute in *Public Health and Welfare Reorganization in Canada* (Toronto: Ryerson 1944), 52–3, 90–2.

67 "News Items: BC," *CMAJ* 34 (April 1936): 478.

68 *Victoria Daily Times*, 29 Feb. 1936, 1.

69 See Robin, *Pillars of Profit*, 20; *CMAJ* 34 (April 1936): 476; *CMAJ* 35 (Aug. 1936): 226.

70 This figure appears in various sources, including contemporary reports on speeches by labour leaders, but I have been unable to confirm or deny its veracity.

71 *Vancouver Daily Province*, 3 March 1936, 2.

72 Ibid., 1. See also *CMAJ* 34 (April 1936): 476.

73 PAC, Bengough Papers, MG 30, A47, vol. 1: Financial Statement of the BC College of Physicians and Surgeons.

74 Taylor, "Saskatchewan Hospital Services Plan," 31–2. The new expert was Dr G.F. Drummond, an economics professor at the University of British Columbia. Drummond was not a wholly impartial assessor, however, since he was an integral part of the Liberal "brains-trust."

75 *CMAJ* 34 (May 1936): 598.

76 *OMA Bulletin* 3, no. 5 (May 1936): 129.

77 Ibid., 135.

78 Ibid., 130–3.

79 Ibid., 136.

80 The editorial is reproduced in full in the *CMAJ*: "The Health Insurance Bill in British Columbia," *CMAJ* 35 (June 1936): 683–6.

81 Ibid., 687.

82 "News Items: BC," *CMAJ* 35 (July 1936): 108.

83 "Report of the Committee on Economics," *CMAJ* 35 (Sept. 1936): supplement, 24.

84 "Provincial Association Notes," *CMAJ* 35 (Sept. 1936): 326–7. Considerable additional detail on the Ontario medical welfare plan can be found in the various issues of the *OMA Bulletin*, and there is also an excellent summary in Glenn Sawyer, *The First Hundred Years* (Toronto: Ontario Medical Association 1981), 99–101.

85 "Provincial Association Notes," *CMAJ* 35 (Sept. 1936): 327.

86 For an interesting sidelight, see Allon Peebles, "The State and Medicine," *Canadian Journal of Economics and Political Science* 2 (Nov. 1936): 464–77; and the following commentary by Ernest S. Moorhead, who was both the main organizer of the Winnipeg doctors' strike and a member of the CMA executive.

87 Taylor, "Saskatchewan Hospital Services," 41.

88 PAC, RG 29, Records of the Department of National Health and Welfare, vol. 1111-502-1-1, part 5; H.M. Cassidy to J.J. Heagerty, 9 Nov. 1936.

89 On the changing political climate and Liberal strategy, see Robin, *Pillars of Profit*, 28–30.

90 "A Brief Analysis of the Tentative Plan suggested by the Health Insurance Commission," *CMAJ* 36 (March 1937): 299.

91 Ibid., italics in original.

92 *Vancouver Daily Province*, 4 Feb. 1937, 1.

93 The editorial was reprinted in the *CMAJ* 36 (March 1937): 300.

94 *Vancouver Daily Province*, 4 Feb. 1937, 1.

95 Ibid., 5 Feb. 1937, 1.

96 Ibid., 2 Feb. 1937, 2.

97 "News Items: BC," *CMAJ* 36 (April 1937): 438.

98 Quoted by Taylor, "Saskatchewan Hospital Services," 35–6.

99 D.E.H. Cleveland, "News Items: BC," *CMAJ* 36 (April 1937): 437.

100 "Report of the Committee on Economics," *CMAJ* 37 (Sept. 1937): supplement, 24.

101 *Victoria Daily Colonist*, 16 April 1937, 2.

102 Robin, *Pillars of Profit*, 30–2. It is interesting that both opposition parties were led by doctors: Lyle Telford, a GP, for the CCF; and Frank Patterson, an orthopaedic surgeon, for the Conservatives.

103 Ormsby described the election as a "watershed" in Patullo's career: "Little New Deal," 294.

104 "News Items: BC," *CMAJ* 38 (Jan. 1938): 95–6.

105 Quoted in the *CMAJ* 35 (June 1936): 684. On the state of general practice in Britain in the 1930s, see Honigsbaum, *Division in British Medicine*, 79–83.

106 On the control of specialization, see generally D. Sclater Lewis, *The Royal College of Physicians and Surgeons of Canada, 1920–1960* (Montreal: McGill University Press 1962).

107 H.F. Angus, "Health Insurance in BC," *Canadian Forum* 17 (April 1937): 14.

108 PAC, Norman Bethune Papers, MG 30, B55, File 1-3, N. Bethune to J.C. [sic] Woodsworth, 13 Aug. 1936.

109 Ibid., File 1-6, "Fundamental Platform," early 1936.

110 Ibid., File 1-5, N. Bethune to A.G. Fleming, 13 July 1936. The tone of this letter suggests that Bethune was increasingly impatient with his mainstream colleagues.

111 Ibid., File 1-4, "Symposium on Medical Economics," 9–10.

112 Ibid., File 1-3, Aug. 1936.

113 "Proposed Plans for the Security of Health in the Province of Quebec," *CMAJ* 35 (Aug. 1936): 205-7.

114 "Report of the Committee on Economics," *CMAJ* 37 (Sept. 1937): supplement, 22; "Medical Relief in the Province of Ontario," *CMAJ* 36 (April 1937): 422. See also Sawyer, *The First Hundred Years*, 101–2.

115 "News Items: Alberta," *CMAJ* 35 (Dec. 1936): 700, and 36 (March 1937): 325.

116 See variously the *Report of the CMA Committee on Economics, 1934*, 19; *CMAJ* 35 (Sept. 1936): 345; *CMAJ* 36 (Jan. 1937): 100; "Report of the Committee on Economics," *CMAJ* 37 (Sept. 1937): supplement, 22.

117 Taylor, "Saskatchewan Hospital Services," 98.

118 "News Items: Saskatchewan," *CMAJ* 38 (May 1938): 521.

119 "Report of the Committee on Ethics and Credentials," *CMAJ* 37 (Sept. 1937): supplement, 9.

120 The revised principles are contained in the "Report of the Committee on Economics," *CMAJ* 37 (Sept. 1937): supplement, 21.

121 "Association Notes," *CMAJ* 38 (Jan. 1938): 80-1.

122 See *A Submission by the Canadian Medical Association to the Royal Commission on Dominion-Provincial Relations* (pamphlet, n.p. 1938): 12, 17; and *CMAJ* 38 (March 1938): 286-92.

123 Quoted by H.E. MacDermot in "A Short History of Health Insurance in Canada," *CMAJ* 50 (May 1944): 451-2.

CHAPTER FIVE

1 See, for example, "Organized Medicine in the Province of Alberta," *CMAJ* 35 (Sept. 1936): 320-1; or "The Saskatchewan Medical Association," *CMAJ* 35 (Nov. 1936): 566.

2 Both the Manitoba and the Ontario movements for amalgamation originated in the voluntary associations (*Manitoba Medical Bulletin* 121 (Sept. 1931): 4, 7–15; *OMA Bulletin* 2, no. 4 (July 1935): 89–90). In Ontario, ten out of twelve district divisions of the OMA voted in favour of amalgamation, but the college rejected the concept on legal grounds. The Manitoba debate is summarized in the *Bulletin of the Manitoba Medical Association* 13 (Jan. 1933): 357-62. Dr F.D. McKenty argued against amalgamation in 1933 with the following incisive comments: "In a broad view, the CP&S is not strictly a medical body at all, but

an arm of government, whose function is to regulate medical practice of all kinds in the interest of the public. The MMA, on the other hand, has the frankly avowed aim of advancing, in every legitimate way, the interests of medicine as a sectional group. These two functions cannot be legitimately exercised at the same time by one body." *Bulletin of the Manitoba Medical Association* 13 (Aug. 1933): 541–2. The idea of amalgamation was abandoned in 1934.

3 See "The Annual Meeting," *CMAJ* 35 (Aug. 1936): 208; or "Federation," CMAJ 38 (Jan. 1938): 82–3.

4 See "Why Should I Belong to the Canadian Medical Association?" *CMAJ* 39 (Dec. 1938): 589–91; or compare the addresses by the 1936 and 1938 CMA presidents: *CMAJ* 35 (Aug. 1936): 208–10 and *CMAJ* 39 (Aug. 1938): 184–6.

5 "Provincial Association Notes," *CMAJ* 35 (Sept. 1936): 327.

6 "Why Should I Belong," *CMAJ* 39: 591.

7 Royal Commission on Dominion-Provincial Relations, *Final Report* (Ottawa: King's Printer 1940), 2: 33–43.

8 Malcolm G. Taylor, *Health Insurance and Canadian Public Policy* (Montreal: McGill-Queen's University Press and the Institute of Public Administration of Canada 1978), 16.

9 *Report of the Advisory Committee on Health Insurance* (Ottawa: King's Printer 1943), xi–xvii (hereafter, *Heagerty Report*).

10 H.E. MacDermot, "A Short History of Health Insurance," *CMAJ* 50 (May 1944): 452.

11 Taylor, *Health Insurance and Canadian Public Policy*, 93.

12 G.S. Fahrni, "Medicine and the Nation," *CMAJ* 47 (July 1942): 72.

13 *OMA Bulletin* (June 1933): 18–19.

14 *OMA Bulletin* 3 no. 6 (June 1936): 144.

15 Quoted in Glenn Sawyer, *The First Hundred Years: A History of the Ontario Medical Association* (Toronto: OMA 1981), 117.

16 On the early history of the various profession-sponsored plans, see C. Howard Shillington, *The Road to Medicare in Canada* (Toronto: Del Graphics 1972), 44–64.

17 Concern arose initially because the AMS plan had no income limits; *OMA Bulletin* 4, no. 5 (June-July 1937): 102–3. For details on later developments, see Sawyer, *First Hundred Years*, 123–4, as well as the complaints of Toronto doctors in "Associated Medical Services, Incorporated," *Nova Scotia Medical Bulletin* 20 (1941): 146–51.

18 J.C. Meakins, "Modern Trends in Medical Practice," *CMAJ* 46 (May 1942): 452.

19 J.C. Hossack, "Presidential Address," *CMAJ* 47 (Aug. 1942): 172.

20 PAC, RG 29, Records of the Department of National Health and Welfare, vol. 1111-504-2-4, part 1, J.J. Heagerty to R. Millar, 15 July 1941.

21 PAC, RG 29, vol. 858-20-C-33, part 1, Wodehouse to Mackenzie, 4 Sept. 1941.

22 Ibid., Wodehouse to Routley, 9 Sept. 1941.

23 PAC, RG 29, vol. 1111-504-2-4, part 1, Heagerty to Mackenzie, 17 Oct. 1941.

24 Ibid., "Memorandum of Comments re: Three-Draft Departmental Proposals Concerning Health Insurance and Public Health," 22 Oct. 1941.

25 H.K. MacDonald, "Correspondence," *Nova Scotia Medical Bulletin* 20 (1941): 388.

26 "Correspondence," *CMAJ* 46 (April 1941): 390.

27 PAC, RG 29, vol. 1111-504-2-4, part 1, Heagerty to Routley, 16 Feb. 1942.

28 PAC, RG 29, vol. 858-20-C-33, part 1, Heagerty to Mackenzie (Air Mail to Vancouver), 9 April 1942.

29 Ibid. See also the follow-up correspondence in the same file between Heagerty and Routley, 10, 14, and 16 April 1942.

30 *CMAJ* 47 (Sept. 1942): supplement, 3–5.

31 T.C Routley, "The Principles of Health Insurance," *CMAJ* 47 (Oct. 1942): 371. Routley's interpretation of these priniciples clearly indicates the CMA's overarching concern with professional incomes and autonomy.

32 Ibid., 370.

33 PAC, RG 29, vol. 858-20-C-33, part 1, Routley to Wodehouse, 3 July 1942.

34 PAC, RG 29, vol. 1111-504-2-4, part 1, "Minutes of a meeting of the Health Insurance Committee of the CMA with the Advisory Committee on Health Insurance, July 17, 1942," 11–12, 17–19.

35 See, generally, PAC, RG 29, vol. 1107-504-1-2, part 1. This conflict has been misinterpreted by J.P. Dicken McGinnis in her otherwise excellent essay, "Whose Responsibility? Public Health in Canada, 1919–1945," in M.S. Staum, ed., *Doctors, Patients, and Society* (Waterloo: Wilfrid Laurier Press 1981), 205–9. McGinnis confuses the CPSO with the Royal College of Physicians and Surgeons (see 220 in her article).

36 PAC, RG 29, vol. 1107-504-1-2, part 1, R.T. Noble to I. Mackenzie, 21 Aug. 1942.

37 Ibid., Wodehouse to Mackenzie, 1 Sept. 1942.

38 Ibid., "Minutes of meeting," 10 Dec. 1942.

39 *Heagerty Report*, 503–4.

40 Ibid., 525.

41 "Correspondence," *CMAJ* 46 (April 1942): 391.

42 *CMAJ* 47: supplement, 9. See also "General Secretary's Page," *CMAJ* 52 (Jan. 1945): 96.

43 Bothwell and English, "Pragmatic Physicians," in S.E.D. Shortt, ed., *Medicine in Canadian Society* (Montreal: McGill-Queen's University Press 1981), 488.

44 PAC, RG 29, vol. 1111-504-2-4, part 1, see the "Report of the Committee on Economics and the Committee of Seven to General Council, January 18, 1943".

45 CMA Archives, "Transactions of a Special Meeting of CMA General Council, January 18–19, 1943." The library at CMA House in Ottawa did not have a formal archives system in 1980 when this and other material was reviewed. Fortunately, an archivist has since been hired. See also Taylor, *Health Insurance and Canadian Public Policy*, 25–7.

46 See J.L. Granatstein, *The Ottawa Men: The Civil Service Mandarins 1935–1957* (Toronto: Oxford University Press 1982), 161–4.

47 CMA Archives, T.C. Routley to the Executive Committee; 6 February 1943.

48 *Minutes of Proceedings and Evidence of the House of Commons Special Committee on Social Security*, vol. 1, issues 1–28 (Ottawa: King's Printer 1943), 16–30 (hereafter, *Minutes*).

49 CMA Archives, T.C. Routley to the executive committee, "Happenings at Ottawa," undated but received on 29 March 1943.

50 *Minutes*, 108–18. Cleaver was obviously aware that few GPs would refer patients to irregulars. Indeed, in some provinces, they were forbidden to do so by college statute.

51 See CMA Archives, "Submission to the Special Committee on Social Security on the Subject of Health Insurance," 25–6. The CMA brief is also in the *Minutes*, 134–47.

52 *Minutes*, 154–6. See also CMA Archives, "First Report of the Provincial Conjoint Committee on Health Insurance," Quebec, n.d. but probably 1942–43.

53 *Minutes*, 159–60.

54 PAC, RG 2, vol. 1111-504-2-4, part 1, Memo to Heagerty from "Illegible," 14 April 1943. A copy of the CMA pamphlet is also in this file.

55 *Minutes*, 285–314. (Quotation from 311).

56 Ibid., 549–50. Note that an excellent synopsis of the 1943 hearings can be found in *CMAJ* 50 (Jan. 1944): 71–5.

57 *Minutes*, 330–6.

58 Ibid., 457–75.

59 "News Items: Manitoba," *CMAJ* 34 (May 1936): 598. A review of the status of chiropraxy up to the early 1960s can be found in G. Lacroix, *Royal Commission on Chiropraxy and Osteopathy: Chiropraxy* (Province of Quebec, 1968). For an update, see M. Kelner, I. Coulter, and O. Hall, *Chiropractors: Do They Help?* (Toronto: Fitzhenry and Whiteside 1980).

60 *Minutes*, 479 ff.

61 Ibid., 606–7.

62 Ibid., 657.

63 Harry Eckstein, *Pressure Group Politics: The Case of the British Medical Association* (London: Allen and Unwin 1960) remains the classic study.

64 Taylor, *Health Insurance and Canadian Public Policy*, 35.

65 "Further Comments of the CMA on the Draft Health Insurance Measure, May 21, 1943";"Further Comments respecting Health Insurance Measure by the CMA," June 22, 1943. Both documents are in the CMA Archives.

66 The bulk of this correspondence is in PAC, RG 29, vol. 1111-504-2-4, part 2.

67 PAC, RG 29, vol. 1111-504-2-4, part 1, Watson to Heagerty, 12 June 1943. See also the accompanying eleven-page bulletin, "Notes re: Changes in Bill proposed by Committee of Seven."

68 PAC, RG 29, vol. 1111-504-2-4, part 2, Routley to "Dear Doctor," 6 Aug. 1943.

69 Bothwell and English, "Pragmatic Physicians," 490.

70 The *CMAJ* regularly noted such poll results. The three years' results are conveniently brought together in the "Report of the Committee on Economics," *CMAJ* 51 (Sept. 1944): supplement, 33.

71 Charlotte E. Whitton, *The Dawn of Ampler Life: Some Aids to Social Security* (Toronto: Macmillan 1943), 129-35.

72 "Legislation on Health Insurance," *CMAJ* 50 (Jan. 1944): 72-3.

73 Some commentators saw Whitton's overall approach as too cautious; see, for example, the *Toronto Daily Star* editorial, "Looking Backward," 30 Sept. 1943. The CMA definitely knew of Whitton's work, if only because J.J. Heagerty sent Routley a copy of the *Star* editorial; PAC, RG 29, vol. 1111-504-2-4, part 2, Routley to Heagerty, 1 Nov. 1943.

74 *Nova Scotia Medical Bulletin* 23 (1944): 64-75.

75 "The CCF Health Plan," *Ontario Medical Review* 10, no. 5 (Oct. 1943): 165-99.

76 "The CCF and Health Service," *CMAJ* 50 (Feb. 1944): 162-4. See also the accompanying editorial on 161.

77 CMA suspicions had been deepened by a belief that the amended legislation would no longer specify that medical doctors were to head the federal and provincial administrative councils. This misunderstanding was cleared up in the early autumn of 1943; PAC, RG 29, vol. 1111-504-2-4, part 2, Heagerty to Routley, 30 Aug. 1943, 3 September 1943; Routley to "Dear Doctor," 4 Sept. 1943.

78 CMA Archives, untitled bulletin from T.C. Routley to the Health Insurance Committee-at-Large, 30 Dec. 1943.

79 *Minutes of Proceedings*, vol. 2 (1944), 2, 45.

80 On the debate, see *Minutes*, 75 ff. (McCann's comment is from 112).

81 *CMAJ* 51 (Sept. 1944): supplement, 32-3.

82 *CMAJ* 50 (Jan.-April 1944): 72, 173-5, 276, 380.

83 *Minutes*, 117-19, 177-83.

84 Ibid., 209–18.

85 Ibid., 256.

86 "The State Hospital and Medical League of Regina", *CMAJ* 51 (Sept. 1944): 268–71.

87 *CMAJ* 50 (March 1944): 255.

88 CMA Archives, "Health Services, Health Insurance, and the Heagerty Bill" (A Report of the Reconstruction Committee to the Board of Directors of the London Chamber of Commerce, April 27, 1944).

89 Quoted by Donald Swartz, "The Politics of Reform: Conflict and Accommodation in Canadian Health Policy," in Leo Panitch, ed., *The Canadian State* (Toronto: University of Toronto 1977), 322.

90 *CMAJ* 50 (Feb. 1944): 175–6.

91 *CMAJ* 50 (April 1944): 378.

92 *CMAJ* 50 (March 1944): 278.

93 "Should We Look Ahead?" *Ontario Medical Review* 11, no. 1 (Feb. 1944): 35–7.

94 "Symposium on Health Insurance," *CMAJ* 51 (July 1944): 62.

95 Ibid., 68. The speaker was Dr W.V. Johnston, who became the first executive director of the College of General Practice, later the College of Family Physicians. See his autobiography, *Before the Age of Miracles* (Don Mills: Paperjacks 1975).

96 Ibid., 71.

97 "The Health Insurance Planning Committee, RCAMC (Overseas) sends a Representative to Canada," *CMAJ* 50 (Feb. 1944): 160–1, 172–3. See also CMA Archives, "Report" of the RCAMC (Overseas) health insurance planning committee, n.d. but probably July-Aug. 1943, 1–3, 5.

98 "Report of the Committee on Economics," *CMAJ* 51 (Sept. 1944): supplement, 38, 40.

99 Ibid., 33–4.

100 *CMAJ* 51 (July 1944): 62.

101 *CMAJ* 50 (March 1944): 274–5; *CMAJ* 51 (Aug. 1944): 174–5.

102 "The Saskatchewan Health Insurance Act," *CMAJ* 50 (June 1944): 569.

103 *CMAJ* 51 (Sept. 1944): supplement, 36.

104 Ibid., 45–50.

105 See, for example, Magner's address as president-elect of the OMA, delivered to each district medical society: *Ontario Medical Review* 12, no. 6 (Dec. 1945): 154.

106 *Minutes*, 203–5.

107 Herbert A. Bruce, *Varied Operations* (Toronto: Longmans, Green 1958), 317–18.

108 *Minutes*, 301–2.

109 Ibid., 313–15.

110 CMA Archives, T.C. Routley, "Memorandum re: Health Insurance," 17 July 1944.

111 The draft bills are appended to the 1944 volume of the *Minutes*.

112 Taylor, *Health Insurance and Canadian Public Policy*, 44.

113 H. McPhedran, "The Outlook in Medical Education and Other Problems," *CMAJ* 52 (March 1945): 291.

114 See, for example, D. Sclater Lewis, "Problems of the Future for Organized Medicine," *CMAJ* 51 (July 1944): 3-4.

115 McPhedran, *CMAJ* 52 (March 1945): 292. See also idem, "Problems in Medical Economics," *CMAJ* 52 (Jan. 1945): 86-9.

116 Taylor, *Health Insurance and Canadian Public Policy*, 50-1. See also idem, *CMAJ* 53 (Sept. 1945): 282-9.

117 "Report of the Committee on Economics," *CMAJ* 53 (Sept. 1945): supplement, 30-31.

118 "Report of the Committee on Economics," *CMAJ* 55 (Sept. 1946): 226.

119 *Ontario Medical Review* 12, no. 6 (Dec. 1945): 164-6.

120 Taylor, *Health Insurance and Canadian Public Policy*, 58-68.

121 "General Secretary's Page," *CMAJ* 54 (May 1946): 501.

122 H. McPhedran, "How to Meet Changing Conditions in Medicine," *CMAJ* 54 (Jan. 1946): 60. This speech was delivered to the Nova Scotia division of the CMA in July 1944.

CHAPTER SIX

1 House of Commons Special House Committee on Social Security, *Minutes of Proceedings* (1944), 237.

2 "The Views of the Saskatchewan Division on the Medical Problems of the Day," *CMAJ* 50 (April 1944): 367-71.

3 "The Saskatchewan Health Insurance Act," *CMAJ* 50 (June 1944): 568-9.

4 "Politics and Medicine," *CMAJ* 51 (Aug. 1944): 173-4.

5 "Letter to Doctors from Council of College of Physicians and Surgeons of Saskatchewan," *CMAJ* 52 (March 1945): 295.

6 Henry E. Sigerist, *Socialised Medicine in the Soviet Union* (London: Victor Gollancz 1937).

7 Sigerist's diaries suggest that he was actually contacted by the CCF either before or immediately after the election. See Henry E. Sigerist, *Autobiographical Writings* (Montreal: McGill University Press 1966), 187-90, 230-1.

8 Report of the Commissioner, H.E. Sigerist, *Saskatchewan Health Services Survey Commission* (Regina: King's Printer 1944), passim.

9 CMA Archives, note accompanying copy of Sigerist report, to "Harry."

10 For a general discussion of these events in Saskatchewan, see Seymour M. Lipset, *Agrarian Socialism* (Los Angeles: University of California Press 1950), 240-2. This analysis is useful but obviously reflects Lipset's pro-CCF bias.

11 Taylor, *Health Insurance and Canadian Public Policy* (Montreal: McGill-Queen's University Press and the Institute of Public Administration of Canada 1978), 248.

12 C.J. Houston, "A Discussion of the Value of Health Regions," *Saskatchewan Medical Quarterly* 10 (March 1946): 31-2.

13 J. Lloyd Brown, "Swift Current Health Insurance Scheme," *Saskatchewan Medical Quarterly* 13 (July 1949): 251-8. Also, "Swift Current Health Service," *Saskatchewan Medical Quarterly* 14 (March 1950): 368-70.

14 This letter is reproduced in E.A. Tollefson's *Bitter Medicine: The Saskatchewan Medical Care Feud* (Saskatoon: Modern Press 1963): 36-8.

15 "Report of the Committee on Economics," *CMAJ* 55 (Sept. 1946): supplement, 229.

16 "Central Health Services Committee," *Saskatchewan Medical Quarterly* 10 (March 1946): 37-8. See also *Saskatchewan Medical Quarterly* (Dec. 1946): 11.

17 *Saskatchewan Medical Quarterly* 10 (Dec. 1946): 11.

18 Ibid.

19 "Central Health Services Committee," *Saskatchewan Medical Quarterly* 10 (July 1946): 13-14.

20 "Report of the Committee on Economics," *CMAJ* 55 (Sept. 1946): supplement, 229-31.

21 See references at n. 13. Also, G.D.G. Howden, "General Practice in Health Region No. 1," *Saskatchewan Medical Quarterly* 13 (Dec. 1949): 335-9 and Arthur D. Kelly, "The Swift Current Experiment," *CMAJ* 58 (May 1948): 506-11.

22 For a detailed analysis of the hospitalization program, see M.G. Taylor, "The Organization and Administration of the Saskatchewan Hospital Services Plan," PH D thesis, University of California at Berkeley, 1948.

23 "News Items: New Brunswick," *CMAJ* 37 (Feb. 1939): 214.

24 J.A. Hannah, "Medical Economics," *CMAJ* 39 (July 1938): 79-80.

25 A. Hollenberg, "The Manitoba Medical Service," *CMAJ* 53 (Sept. 1945): 289.

26 *Health Insurance: Proceedings of the Conference of Canadian Health Organizations, January 28-29, 1944* (Toronto: Murray Printing 1944), 19.

27 Quoted in C. Howard Shillington, *The Road to Medicare in Canada* (Toronto: Del Graphics 1972), 25.

28 Ibid., 51.

29 Glenn Sawyer, *The First Hundred Years* (Toronto: OMA 1981), 124.

30 "Voluntary Health Insurance, *Ontario Medical Review* 10, no. 3 (June 1943): 95.

31 "Medical Service Plans in British Columbia," *CMAJ* 52 (April 1945): 411-15.

32 H. McPhedran, "The Outlook in Medical Education and other Problems," *CMAJ* 52 (March 1945): 292. See also, idem, "Problems in Medical Economics," *CMAJ* 52 (Jan. 1945): 88-9; and the discussion by Dr A.F. van Wart of Hannah's paper in the *CMAJ* 53 (Oct. 1945): 390-1.

33 *Ontario Medical Review*, no. 6 (Dec. 1945): 158. In what was probably the most objective analysis of the overall role and prospects of the profession-sponsored plans, Dr Harris McPhedran presciently pointed out that there was no precedent for a voluntary insurance scheme's taking over administration of a state-sponsored tax-funded program; see H. McPhedran: "Prepaid Medical Services," *CMAJ* 52 (May 1945): 512-15.

34 *Nova Scotia Medical Bulletin* 24 (1945): 165-75.

35 *Nova Scotia Medical Bulletin* 25 (1946): 15-21.

36 Ibid., 362-5.

37 J.A. Hannah, "The Place of the Voluntary Plan in Health Services," *CMAJ* 53 (Oct. 1945): 386-90. See idem, "Some Observations on Health Insurance," *CMAJ* 52 (March 1945): 268-70.

38 J.A. Hannah, "The Development of Associated Medical Services, Inc.," *CMAJ* 54 (June 1946): 608.

39 "Report of the Committee on Economics," *CMAJ* 55 (Sept. 1946): 227-8; see also *Nova Scotia Medical Bulletin* 25 (1946): 363.

40 See Alan Moncreiff's farewell column, *CMAJ* 54 (Jan. 1946): 75.

41 See, among others, the following editorials and articles: *CMAJ* 50 (Jan. 1944): 66; 51 (Oct. 1944): 369-74; 54 (Feb. 1946): 171; (May 1946): 503-5; 60 (Jan. 1949): 80-1.

42 "Medical Economics," *CMAJ* 55 (July 1946): 72-8. See also C. Frothingham, "The Delivery of Medical Care," *CMAJ* 54 (March 1946): 288-93 and F.H. Lahey, "Government-Dominated Medicine," *CMAJ* 54 (May 1946): 494-6.

43 "National Health Services Act in Australia," *CMAJ* 60 (June 1949): 619.

44 "Association Notes," *CMAJ* 60 (April 1949): 423.

45 The establishment of PSI was a complicated legal and political affair. See Sawyer, *First Hundred Years*, 125-34.

46 For some background, see Taylor, "Saskatchewan Hospital Services," 95-8.

47 "Report on Medical Services, Saskatoon, Incorporated," *Saskatchewan Medical Quarterly* 10 (Sept. 1946): 23-6.

48 Quoted in Taylor, *Health Insurance and Canadian Public Policy*, 260.

49 Shillington, *Road to Medicare*, 53. Shillington was the first executive director of MS(S)I.

50 Quoted in Taylor, *Health Insurance and Canadian Public Policy*, 260.

51 PAC, RG 29, vol. 858-20-C-33, part 1, "Transactions of the Seventy-Eighth Annual Meeting of the CMA, Winnipeg, June 23–27, 1947," 21.

52 *Saskatchewan Medical Quarterly* 11 (Dec. 1947): 22–33, and 12 (March 1948): 31. Most of the beneficiaries under this program in Saskatchewan were old age pensioners, hence the references to it as the "O.A.P." plan in the *Quarterly*.

53 "Alberta O.A.P. Scheme," *Saskatchewan Medical Quarterly* 12 (July 1948): 28–31.

54 PAC, RG 29, vol. 1599-7, "Financing of Personal Health Care for Recipients of Public Assistance in British Columbia 1956–7 to 1963–4," (DNHW memo, June 1965). The relevant historical material is in the first pages of this research bulletin.

55 "Association News," *CMAJ* 60 (April 1949): 407. Professor Malcolm Taylor questioned the wisdom of these arrangements in 1954. See M.G. Taylor, "The Social Assistance Medical Care Plans in Canada," *American Journal of Public Health* 44 (June 1954): 750–9.

56 Special House Commitee on Social Security, *Minutes of Proceedings*, 1944: 178.

57 Ronald Hamowy, *Canadian Medicine: A Study in Restricted Entry* (Vancouver: Fraser Institute 1984): 283.

58 PAC, RG 29, vol. 1111-504-2-4, part 2, Routley to G.D.W. Cameron, 20 Nov. 1947.

59 Ibid., Cameron to Routley, 27 Nov. 1947.

60 Ibid., Martin to Routley, 21 Jan. 1948.

61 Ibid., A.D. Kelly to Cameron, 29 March 1948.

62 *CMAJ* 60 (Feb. 1949): 187.

63 W. Magner, "The National Health Program," *CMAJ* 60 (Feb. 1949): 183–6. Magner indicated that this specific policy had never been formally discussed by the CMA or any of its provincial divisions; however, it is plain that variations on this theme were privately considered by Ontario medical leaders if not others. After all, Magner himself had suggested this type of policy five years earlier in the *Ontario Medical Review*, and in 1944 Harris McPhedran alluded to the possibility of government's transferring administrative authority to the voluntary plans. See also the statement by Dr Carman White in 1948 quoted by Hugh E. MacDermot, *History of the Canadian Medical Association*, 2 (Toronto: Murray Printing 1958): 84.

64 CMA Archives, "Transactions of the General Council of the CMA, June 13–14, 1949" 25–6. See also *CMAJ* 61 (Sept. 1949): 222.

65 Ibid., 26-35. The statements by the CMA on health insurance are conveniently collected in appendices to Bernard R. Blishen's *Doctors and Doctrines* (Toronto: University of Toronto Press 1969).

66 W. Magner, "Health Insurance," *CMAJ* 61 (Aug. 1949): 196.

67 As indicated by Dr Vance Ward's comments to the CMA council in 1949, the Quebec division was divided on the issue of prepaid medical care in doctors' offices, even though there was general support for coverage of in-patient services.

68 "Report of the Committee on Economics," *CMAJ* 63 (Sept. 1950): 227.

69 Shillington, *Road to Medicare*, 98.

70 Ibid., 94-100.

71 N.H. Gosse, " Presidential Address," *CMAJ* 63 (Sept. 1950): 302. See also *CMAJ* 63 (Nov. 1950): 517, 525. Anti-government feeling had risen sufficiently that spokesmen for the newly organized College of General Practice suggested its activities could be useful "to prevent any form of state control of medicine"; *CMAJ* 70 (April 1954): 477.

72 See, for example, W. Magner, "The National Health Service in England," *CMAJ* 62 (Jan. 1950): 5. Harris McPhedran offered a slightly more positive view; "Medical Services in Great Britain," *CMAJ* 63 (Nov. 1950): 511-5.

73 Richard Titmuss, *Essays on the Welfare State* (Boston: Beacon Press 1969), 154, n. 1. The AMA hired the public relations firm of Whitaker and Baxter and spent $1.5 million in 1949 alone.

74 PAC, RG 29, vol. 111-504-2-4, part 3, F.W. Jackson to A.D. Kelly, 1 Feb. 1952.

75 Ibid., T.C. Routley to Jackson, 7 Feb. 1952.

76 Shillington makes it clear that each plan tended to seek its own autonomy, creating at times difficulties with national co-ordination; *Road to Medicare*, 111-19. A summary of the problems with national contracts as of 1954 is provided in the "Report of the CMA Committee on Economics," *CMAJ* 71 (Sept. 1954): 219.

77 The Chamber of Commerce supported use of public funds for upgrading hospitals and other health care facilities and also accepted the use of tax dollars for social assistance medical care plans.

78 M.G. Taylor, "Government Planning: The Federal-Provincial Health Survey Reports," *CMAJ* 70 (Feb. 1954): 204-9.

79 Quoted in Taylor's *Health Insurance and Canadian Public Policy*, 108.

80 See "Transactions," *CMAJ* 73 (1 Sept. 1955): 359-60. The Socreds apparently abandoned this idea after the provincial election of 1955.

81 CMA Archives, "The Canadian Medical Association Principles relating to Health Insurance 1944 and the Statement of Policy 1949, with a Commentary by T.C. Routley," mimeo, 1954.

82 See *CMAJ* 73 (1 Sept. 1955): 357-9.

83 Taylor, *Health Insurance and Canadian Public Policy*, 167-70.

84 Taylor points out that in 1954, only 38.6 percent of Alberta hospital income came from the province, versus 73 percent in British Columbia and 85.7 percent in Saskatchewan. However, this discrepancy is not surprising given the structure of the Alberta program and need not be construed as inefficient or unfair unless it can be shown either that the administrative costs were higher, or that Alberta's use of property taxes and small premiums to defray costs was more regressive in incidence than, say, the head tax used in Saskatchewan to fund the hospitalization program.

85 "The Cottage Hospitals of Newfoundland," *CMAJ* 70 (June 1954): 686-7.

86 The attitudes of various interested parties and the political process of decision-making are covered in detail in Taylor, *Health Insurance and Canadian Public Policy*, 161-238. For a shorter summary, see Irving J. Goffman's useful article, "The Political History of National Health Insurance in Canada," *Journal of Commonwealth Political Studies* 3 (July 1965): 140-7.

87 Taylor, *Health Insurance and Canadian Public Policy*, 144-5.

88 PAC, RG 29, vol. 1111-504-2-4, part 3, J.W. Willard to G.D.W. Cameron, 24 Oct. 1952.

89 CMA Archives, "The CMA Principles relating ... with a Commentary by T.C. Routley," 12.

90 The relevant clause in the 1955 document reads: "The various services should be introduced as benefits by stages, careful planning being given to the order in which each is introduced."

91 PAC, RG 29, vol. 1111-504-2-4, part 3, P. Martin to H. Trudel, 9 Feb. 1956.

92 "Transactions of the Eighty-Ninth Annual Meeting," *CMAJ* 75 (1 Sept. 1956): 340.

93 Ibid.

94 See, for example, G.H. Agnew, D.C. MacNeill, and H.G. Pritzker, "Provision and Payment of Diagnostic Services," *Canadian Journal of Public Health* 48 (Oct. 1957): 413-25.

95 "Transactions," *CMAJ* 75 (1 Sept. 1956): 340, 357.

96 CMA Archives, "Statement of opinion of the General Meeting of the CMA, Alberta Division, September 1956."

97 The extent and shortcomings of private-sector coverage are well documented in C.H. Berry, *Voluntary Medical Insurance and Prepayment* (Ottawa: Queen's Printer 1965).

98 Shillington, *Road to Medicare*, 114-19.

99 See, for example, "Report of the Committee on Economics," *CMAJ* 71 (Sept. 1954): 218 and *CMAJ* 73 (1 Sept. 1955): 359.

100 See J.A. Hannah's letter to C.H. Shillington in *The Road to Medicare*, 67.

101 Sawyer, *First Hundred Years*, 134-8. The interesting point, of course, is that the PSI House of Delegates and Board of Directors was already controlled by organized medicine, but the doctors in these positions put the interests of the prepayment agency ahead of the OMA's preferences. These developments were duly noted in Ottawa; PAC, RG 29, vol. 1066-502-2-5, J.W. Willard to F.W. Jackson, 16 March 1954; W.S. Major to J.W. Willard, 10 March 1954.

102 Gilles Dussault, *La Profession Médicale au Québec* (Laval: Institute Supérieur des Sciences Humaines 1974), 15-17.

103 See MNHW Research Division, *Voluntary Medical Care Insurance: A Study of the Non-Profit Plans in Canada* (Ottawa: MNHW memorandum no. 4 1954), 22, 35, 126-8. See also "The Story of MSA and MSI" (BCMA pamphlet, n.d. but internal evidence suggests c. 1956).

104 "Report of the Special Committee on Prepaid Medical Care," *CMAJ* 83 (3 Sept. 1960): 471.

105 Taylor, *Administration of Health Insurance in Canada*, 176.

106 It should perhaps be noted that the minimum-fee schedule for private practice was used by all the plans except two. Les Services de Santé drew up its own schedule, since francophone GPs tended to use local tariffs rather than a uniform provincial fee schedule; and the Manitoba Medical Service arranged a special discounted fee schedule with the MMA. In Saskatchewan, the SCPS drew up a "contract practice" schedule that applied to all prepaid medical care including the profession-sponsored plans. None of these variations, however, alters the fact that the status of the provincial fee schedules had changed.

107 CMA Archives, "Submission to the Special Committee on Social Security on the subject of Health Insurance," 23-4.

108 CMA Archives, "The CMA Principles Relating ... with a Commentary by T.C. Routley," 7.

109 The problems of assessing the average net incomes of doctors in private fee practice are obvious. Full-time practitioners should ideally be separated from part-time workers. The ability of self-employed professionals to write off expenses that are actually unrelated to income generation, is well known. On the other hand, independent professionals do not have pension plans and a wide variety of benefits that are available to salaried employees.

110 Hamowy, *Canadian Medicine*, 283.

111 S.G. Peitchinis, "The Canadian Occupational Wage Structure," in L.H. Officer and L.B. Smith, *Issues in Canadian Economics* (Toronto: McGraw-Hill-Ryerson 1974), 237-8. See also PAC, RG 29, vol. 1066-502-

2-5 for a number of memoranda relating to medical incomes from the 1930s on.

112 Between 1951 and 1958 the Consumer Price Index rose by less than 25 percent: *Canada Year Book 1959* (Ottawa: Queen's Printer 1959), 956-8.

113 The entire health care sector demanded more of the consumer's income in this period. For example, between 1953 and 1959 the average annual increase in personal health care expenditures was 5.1 percent for general and allied special hospitals, 4.3 percent for physician services, and 5.9 percent for prescription drugs. See Robert G. Evans, "Beyond the Medical Marketplace," in Spyros Andreopoulos, ed., *National Health Insurance: Can We Learn from Canada?* (New York: Wiley 1975), 140.

114 Robert G. Evans, *Price Formation in the Market for Physician Services* (Ottawa: Information Canada 1973), 103-6. Evans elaborates on this argument in the article cited in n. 113, above.

115 Taylor, *Health Insurance and Canadian Public Policy*, 329.

116 Max Weber (ed. and tr. by G. Roth and C. Wittich), *Economy and Society*, (New York: Bedminster 1968), vol. 1, 220-1, 271-82.

117 Shillington offers some comments on this development in *Road to Medicare*, 140-1, 144-6.

118 "Report of the Special Committee on Prepaid Medical Care," *CMAJ* 83 (3 Sept. 1960): 471.

CHAPTER SEVEN

1 As already indicated in chapter 1, the Saskatchewan affair has been thoroughly reviewed by several authors, and this account is included primarily for completeness and continuity.

2 J.W. Grove, *Organized Medicine in Ontario* (Toronto: Queen's Printer 1969), 303. Ms Carolyn Hughes, a research assistant, wrote the background paper on the Saskatchewan dispute; Professor Grove edited it.

3 Seymour M. Lipset, *Agrarian Socialism* (Los Angeles: University of California Press 1950), 239.

4 J.F.C. Anderson, "Divisional Meetings of the CMA," *CMAJ* 62 (Jan. 1950): 94-5.

5 Malcolm G. Taylor, *Health Insurance and Canadian Public Policy* (Montreal: McGill-Queen's University Press and the Institute for Public Administration in Canada 1978), 256-8. Professor Taylor's account of events in Saskatchewan is arguably the most concise and complete available and should be read by those interested in greater detail on the medicare dispute in all its aspects.

6 Ibid., 258. Taylor contends that these contracts were actually illegal.

7 Edwin A. Tollefson, *Bitter Medicine: The Saskatchewan Medical Care Feud* (Saskatoon: Modern Press 1964), 44–5.

8 *Saskatchewan Medical Quarterly* 19 (Dec. 1955): 140–4.

9 See Taylor, *Health Insurance*, 258–60; and Shillington, *The Road to Medicare in Canada* (Toronto: Del Graphics 1972), 121.

10 Taylor's account of this episode states that the "ceiling" principle had been accepted by the Swift Current Medical Society in 1957 (*Health Insurance and Canadian Public Policy*, 263). This is not correct but must be one of the few errors in his meticulous monograph.

11 "Business Reports," *CMAJ* 71 (Sept. 1954): 217.

12 Robin F. Badgley and Samuel Wolfe, *Doctors' Strike: Medical Care and Conflict in Saskatchewan* (Toronto: Macmillan 1967), 28.

13 "Beginnings," *Today Magazine*, 16 Aug. 1980, 3.

14 Quoted in Badgley and Wolfe, *Doctors' Strike*, 21.

15 Quoted in Taylor, *Health Insurance and Canadian Public Policy*, 277–8. Primary sources indicate that the word "service" in that quote should actually read "insurance."

16 From a verbatim transcript in "News and Views on the Economics of Medicine, no. 2," *CMAJ* 82 (16 Jan. 1960). The "News and Views" columns were not given page numbers in the *CMAJ*.

17 See Walter P. Thompson, *Medical Care: Programs and Issues* (Toronto: Clarke Irwin 1964), 62.

18 "News and Views no. 4," *CMAJ* 82 (5 March 1960). See also, "Provincial News: Saskatchewan," *CMAJ* 82 (26 March 1960): 698.

19 On these negotiations, see Tollefson, *Bitter Medicine*, 45–53.

20 For the college's letter, see "News and Views, no. 5," *CMAJ* 82 (9 April 1960).

21 "News and Views, no. 7," *CMAJ* 82 (11 June 1960).

22 Taylor, *Health Insurance and Canadian Public Policy*, 280.

23 *Saskatoon Star-Phoenix*, 13 Feb. 1960.

24 "Transactions of Council," *Ontario Medical Review* 27 (June 1960): 620–1.

25 B.T. McLaughlin, "Saskatchewan Report," *Ontario Medical Review* 27 (April 1960): 371.

26 Badgley and Wolfe, *Doctors' Strike*, 31, 178.

27 Ibid., 33.

28 Ibid., 31.

29 McLaughlin, *Ontario Medical Review* 27 (April 1960): 372.

30 Badgley and Wolfe, *Doctors' Strike*, 31–33. See also "News and Views, no. 7," *CMAJ* 82 (11 June 1960).

31 The entire campaign was definitely perceived as overdone and damaging by some; see, for example, Dr Arthur D. Kelly's first clipping selection

in "Yesterday's Papers," *CMAJ* 83 (1 Oct. 1960): 775. Kelly was widely known as a "moderate" on the medicare issue.

32 "Transactions," *CMAJ* 83 (3 Sept. 1960): 473.

33 "Reverberations from the Saskatchewan Election," *CMAJ* 83 (30 July 1960): 229–30. See also *CMAJ* 83 (3 Sept. 1960): 481.

34 "C.M.A. Council," *Ontario Medical Review* 27 (July 1960): 727.

35 "Association Notes," *CMAJ* 83 (6 Aug. 1960): 284. Some indication of the profession's mood is provided by letters to the *CMAJ* during early 1960; see vol. 82, pp. 44, 792, 1242.

36 "Medicine, Government and the Future," *CMAJ* 83 (13 Aug. 1960): 331. The passage of twenty-five years had obviously softened Dr MacDermot's recollection of the BC conflict.

37 "Report of the Executive Committee," *CMAJ* 83 (3 Sept. 1960): 481.

38 "Transactions," *CMAJ* 83 (3 Sept. 1960): 471–2.

39 "Transactions," *CMAJ* 85 (2 Sept. 1961): 524.

40 "Transactions," *CMAJ* 83 (3 Sept. 1960): 498.

41 Ibid., 498–501.

42 Bernard R. Blishen. *Doctors and Doctrines: The Ideology of Medical Care in Canada* (Toronto: University of Toronto Press 1969), 152.

43 "News and Views, no. 12," *CMAJ* 83 (19 Nov. 1960).

44 Richard M. Titmuss, *Essays on the Welfare State* (Boston: Beacon Press 1969), 133–214.

45 *CMAJ* 83 (6 Aug. 1960): 266–7.

46 E.R. Walker, "Governments and Doctors," *CMAJ* 83 (1 Oct. 1960): 737.

47 John and Sylvia Jewkes, *The Genesis of the British National Health Service* (Oxford: Blackwell 1961). The rise of the New Right in Britain has brought the Jewkeses a fresh audience: see their article in Arthur Seldon, ed., *The Litmus Papers* (London: Centre for Policy Studies 1980), chapter 17.

48 *Edmonton Journal*, 19 Oct. 1960.

49 A.D. Kelly, "Swift Current, Twelve Years Later," *CMAJ* 83 (8 Oct. 1960): 812–13. The Swift Current doctors, and the bulk of the local populace, did not fully reject the CCF plan until spring of 1962, when it became clear that no provision for local administration was to be made.

50 "Political Trends and the Future of Canadian Medicine," *CMAJ* 84 (14 Jan. 1961): 116–17.

51 "News and Views, no. 13," *CMAJ* 83 (24 Dec. 1960).

52 Tollefson, *Bitter Medicine*, 57.

53 "News and Views, no. 14," *CMAJ* 84 (28 Jan. 1961).

54 "Provincial News: Saskatchewan," *CMAJ* 84 (11 March 1961): n.p.

55 Saskatchewan Farmers' Union, "Presentation to the Advisory Planning Committee on Medical Care," mimeo, Jan. 1961.

56 Thompson, *Medical Care*, 65–6.

57 Badgley and Wolfe, *Doctors' Strike*, 38-9.

58 *CMAJ* 84 (10 June 1961): 1137-8.

59 *Saskatoon Star-Phoenix*, 9 Sept. 1960.

60 J.W. Macleod, "Basic Issues in Hospital and Medical Care Insurance," *CMAJ* 84 (24 June 1961): 1434-8. See also the critique of Dean Macleod by H.E. Emson of Saskatoon, *CMAJ* 85 (30 Sept. 1961): 799-800.

61 *CMAJ* 85 (12 Aug. 1961): 394-9.

62 Wilder Penfield, "Government and Medicine," *CMAJ* 85 (29 July 1961): 242-6.

63 *CMAJ* 85 (12 Aug. 1961): 396.

64 The scps supplementary brief is reproduced in the *CMAJ* 85 (9 Sept. 1961): 664-9.

65 For a summary of the minority report, see "Provincial News: Saskatchewan," *CMAJ* 85 (18 Nov. 1961): 2.

66 Thompson, *Medical Care*, 68.

67 "Provincial News," *CMAJ* 85 (18 Nov. 1961): 4.

68 Taylor, *Health Insurance and Canadian Public Policy*, 285.

69 G.E. Wodehouse, "Politics and the Extension of Medical Services Insurance through the Voluntary Plans," *CMAJ* 86 (10 Feb. 1962): 281.

70 For the profession's outlook, see "News and Views, no. 21," *CMAJ* 85 (9 Dec. 1961).

71 Ibid.

72 "Provincial News: Saskatchewan," *CMAJ* 86 (27 Jan. 1962): 2.

73 "News and Views, no. 21," *CMAJ* 85 (9 Dec. 1961).

74 Tollefson, *Bitter Medicine*, 66-87.

75 For example, Badgley and Wolfe in *Doctors' Strike*, 40-1, and Grove and Hughes in *Organized Medicine in Ontario*, 307-8, suggest the wording was too ambiguous.

76 For a negative view of the legislation that borders on inflammatory, see Morris C. Shumiatcher, "Assault on Freedom," mimeo, a series of articles reprinted from the Regina *Leader-Post*, July 1962, 5-7. Unfortunately, the scps must have received legal advice of this sort concerning the legislation.

77 *The Saskatchewan Medical Care Insurance Act* (Regina: Queen's Printer 1961).

78 Taylor, *Health Insurance and Canadian Public Policy*, 286.

79 "Provincial News: Saskatchewan," *CMAJ* 85 (30 Dec. 1961).

80 "Association News," *CMAJ* 86 (13 Jan. 1962): 86-7.

81 "News and Views, no. 22," *CMAJ* 86 (3 Feb. 1962).

82 Quoted in Tollefson, *Bitter Medicine*, 92. Having signified their interest in transferring an Australian-style health insurance scheme to Saskatchewan, it was perhaps natural that the college borrowed the term "civil conscription" from the 1949 dispute whereby the BMA in Australia

successfully appealed in the courts against a law creating a state medical service. No such provision existed in the Canadian constitution.

83 "Provincial News: Saskatchewan," *CMAJ* 86 (17 Feb. 1962): 2.

84 Badgley and Wolfe, *Doctors' Strike*, 44, 86–7.

85 See "Provincial News," *CMAJ* 86 (24 March 1962), and (14 April 1962).

86 The letter was reproduced in full in "News and Views, no. 25," *CMAJ* 86 (31 March 1962).

87 Quoted by Tollefson, *Bitter Medicine*, 98.

88 Badgley and Wolfe, *Doctors' Strike*, 46. On the government's reaction and reasons for rejecting the plan, see Taylor, *Health Insurance and Canadian Public Policy*, 294–5.

89 "Brief of the Saskatchewan College of Physicians and Surgeons to the Royal Commission on Health Services," mimeo, 22 Jan. 1962, 23.

90 Professor Taylor emphasizes that this concession was made on 4 April (*Health Insurance and Canadian Public Policy*, 292–4); however, it is worth noting that Premier Lloyd's letter simply stated: "Even though it would be costly and cumbersome, we offered to consider a method of payment whereby the physician need not accept payment directly from the Commission." This statement may well have been construed by the SCPS as applying to the government's offer to use the private plans under MCIC authority. That caveat aside, the SCPS reaction and subsequent correspondence leaves no doubt that a concession on reimbursement was made and understood at some point in early April.

91 "News and Views, no. 27," *CMAJ* 86 (28 April 1962).

92 For the actual wording of the section, see Tollefson, *Bitter Medicine*, 99. Even Professor Tollefson's dispassionate legal exegesis (100–1) reads more into this section than one suspects the government intended.

93 Taylor, *Health Insurance and Canadian Public Policy*, 296.

94 Quoted in "Provincial News: Saskatchewan," *CMAJ* 86 (26 May 1962): n.p.

95 "News and Views, no. 27," *CMAJ* 86 (28 April 1962).

96 The allusion to forms seems to have arisen because the amendment indicated that the beneficiary would be able to waive his or her right to legal protection by the MCIC "in the form and in a manner" to be set out by MCIC regulations.

97 For a description of the KODC movement, see Badgley and Wolfe, *Doctors' Strike*, 73–81.

98 Grove, *Organized Medicine in Ontario*, 317.

99 Taylor, *Health Insurance and Canadian Public Policy*, 303.

100 Tollefson, *Bitter Medicine*, 177–8.

101 "News and Views, no. 28," *CMAJ* 86 (12 May 1962).

102 Tollefson, *Bitter Medicine*, 104 fn. 14.

103 Quoted in Badgley and Wolfe, *Doctors' Strike*, 49.

104 Saskatchewan Federation of Labour, "The First Fight for Medicare," mimeo, 1963, 6–7.

105 On these points, see "Provincial News: Saskatchewan," *CMAJ* 86 (9 June 1962): 2, 4.

106 "The Ninety-Fifth Annual Meeting," *CMAJ* 87 (21 July 1962): 142.

107 *CMAJ* 87 (14 July 1962): 94.

108 B.E. Freamo, "The Saskatchewan Situation," in "News and Views, no. 32," *CMAJ* 87 (7 July 1962).

109 "'Transactions," *CMAJ* 87 (1 Sept. 1962): 432–4.

110 Taylor, *Health Insurance and Canadian Public Policy*, 305. See also Tollefson, *Bitter Medicine*, 107–8, 185–7.

111 Tollefson, *Bitter Medicine*, 180–1, 184–5.

112 Ibid., 188–9. The premier's concern about extra-billing is obvious in this memorandum.

113 Taylor, *Health Insurance and Canadian Public Policy*, 304.

114 Given the premier's mailing to individual doctors and the exhaustive reassurances given by the government on the reimbursement issue, it is not clear that the strike would have been averted even if this concession had been legislated at once. The crux of the impasse, one suspects, was that the scps had never accepted the basic framework of the government plan, and that framework was not really altered by a reimbursement option.

115 Tollefson, *Bitter Medicine*, 109–10.

116 L.M. Brand, "Saskatchewan Graffiti: Where Were You in '62?" *Canadian Doctor* (October 1979), 95.

117 See the synopses in Taylor, *Health Insurance and Canadian Public Policy*, 307–14; also, Saskatchewan Federation of Labour, "The First Fight for Medicare," mimeo, 1963, 16 ff.

118 See, for example, the editorial in the *Free Press* on 20 June 1960.

119 Brand, "Saskatchewan Graffiti," 97–8.

120 "Corrupting Euphemisms," *CMAJ* 86 (30 June 1962): 1212–13. See also "Unjust Laws Exist," *CMAJ* 87 (28 July 1962): 190–1.

121 Grove, *Organized Medicine in Ontario*, 316.

122 Badgley and Wolfe, *Doctors' Strike*, 81.

123 Brand, "Saskatchewan Graffiti," 95.

124 For this and a further description of Taylor's activities, see A.D. Kelly, "Saskatchewan Solomon," *CMAJ* 87 (25 Aug. 1962): 416–17.

125 An excellent summary of the negotiations and terms of agreement is found in "News and Views, no. 33," *CMAJ* 87 (4 Aug. 1962).

126 It is interesting to note that Howard Shillington, the executive director of TCMP, makes reference to this scps motion with some disappointment; *The Road to Medicare*, 122–3.

127 B.E. Freamo, "The Saskatchewan Situation," in "News and Views on the Economics of Medicine, no. 32," *CMAJ* 87 (7 July 1962) (italics added).

128 *CMAJ* 87 (13 Oct. 1962): 827.

129 "News and Views, no. 34," *CMAJ* 87 (18 Aug. 1962).

130 Ibid. See also "News and Views, no. 40," *CMAJ* 87 (8 Dec. 1962).

131 B.E. Freamo, "The Effect of Saskatchewan on Other Provinces," *CMAJ* 87 (27 Oct. 1962): 939.

132 W.W. Wigle, "Saskatchewan: Before, During and After," *CMAJ* 87 (8 Sept. 1962): 575.

CHAPTER EIGHT

1 See Dennis Gruending, *Emmett Hall: Establishment Radical* (Toronto: Macmillan 1985), 14, 17, 52-67, 70, 78-83.

2 Ibid., 83. Gruending erroneously refers to Dr Baltzan as a surgeon. Hall and Baltzan were acquaintances; Hall served for years as chairman of the St Paul's Hospital board.

3 E.K. Lyon, "The Medical Sundial," *CMAJ* 83 (17 Sept. 1960): 629.

4 C. Howard Shillington, *The Road to Medicare in Canada* (Toronto: Del Graphics 1972), 141.

5 *CMAJ* 84 (24 March 1961): 552.

6 "Brief submitted to the Royal Commission on Health Services by the Ontario Medical Association May 1962," 6(a).

7 Ibid., 1(b)-10(b).

8 For the complete brief, see *CMAJ* 86 (19 May 1962): 895-926.

9 "News and Views on the Economics of Medicine, no. 29," *CMAJ* 86 (26 May 1962).

10 See, for example, "Unjust Laws Exist," *CMAJ* 87 (28 July 1962): 190-1.

11 "News and Views, no. 38," *CMAJ* 87 (10 Nov. 1962).

12 Theodore Goldberg, "Canadian Labour's Approach to Providing Comprehensive Health Services Through Organized Health Centres," *CMAJ* 84 (11 Feb. 1961): 322.

13 Malcolm G. Taylor, *Health Insurance and Canadian Public Policy* (Montreal: McGill-Queen's University Press and the Institute of Public Administration of Canada 1978), 358.

14 Quoted in ibid., 359.

15 Two other important factors that have emerged from experience with medicare premium assistance programs in the 1970s and 1980s are simple apathy and a lack of awareness on the part of low-income household heads that assistance is in fact available.

16 PAC, RG 29, vol. 1599-7, Research memorandum, J.E. Osborne to J.W. Willard, "Alberta Medical Plan," c. March-April 1965.

17 Gilles Dussault, *La Profession Médicale au Québec* (Laval: Institute Supérieur des Sciences Humaines 1974), 19, 36-9, 43; L. Joubert, *La Médecine est Malade* (Montreal: Editions de l'Homme 1962), 58, 119-20.

18 Joubert, *Médecine est Malade*, 38-40, 55, 61-73, 88.

19 Dussault, *Profession Médicale*, 43, 58.

20 "Political Trends and the Future of Canadian Medicine," *CMAJ* 84 (14 Jan. 1961): 116.

21 Royal Commission on Health Services, *Final Report* (Ottawa: Queen's Printer 1964), vol. 1: 10.

22 Ibid., 724-45, for the commissioners' analysis.

23 Ibid., 20.

24 Ibid., 33.

25 Ibid., 45-50. Seen as discriminatory by some – for example, Teddy Chevalot, *La Monopole de la Médecine* (Montreal: Cahiers du Cité Libre 1969), 123-31 – these recommendations were probably a positive step in the long-term maintenance and upgrading of the optometric profession.

26 Ibid., 13.

27 Ibid., 28-9.

28 Ibid., 31, 34. Ironically enough, Dr David Baltzan, one of the commissioners, had been president of the Saskatchewan profession when the two bodies were first amalgamated there. The concurrence of Dr A.F. Van Wart in the commission's insurance proposals was also a break with the past, since in 1949 van Wart had seconded the motion of the CMA general council that introduced the subsidies-and-private-insurance strategy.

29 Ibid., 29-30. Also, *Final Report*, vol. 2: 11.

30 Ibid., vol. 2, 10.

31 Ibid., vol. 1, 91.

32 PAC, RG 29, vol. 887-20-R-28, "The Medical Profession Looks at the Report of the Royal Commission on Health Services."

33 PAC, RG 29, vol. 1107-504-1-2, part 1, F. Turnbull to L.B. Pearson, 26 June 1964.

34 Gruending, *Emmett Hall*, 95-6. Obviously, had McCutcheon not resigned, he might well have written a minority report with the dentist and two doctors.

35 The Manitoba government was receiving ample encouragement from the traditionally Liberal *Winnipeg Free Press*. Having assailed the Saskatchewan plan mercilessly, the *Free Press* apparently felt it could not perform a *volte face* as did Ross Thatcher's Liberals. For a summary

of its viewpoint, see P. McLintock, "A Health Plan for Canada: A Study of the Hall Commission Report," Winnipeg Free Press pamphlet no. 79, Sept. 1964.

36 "Association News," *CMAJ* 83 (6 Aug. 1960): 289.

37 "Medical Services in Australia," *CMAJ* 84 (29 April 1961): 965-71.

38 "Special Supplement," *CMAJ* 91 (19 Sept. 1964): 37.

39 Ibid.

40 Ibid., 40, emphasis added.

41 Ibid., 47.

42 "Special Supplement," *CMAJ* 91 (19 Sept. 1964): 50. Note that the Special Committee referred to "direct billing" and "direct payment" when doctors billed the plan directly. In current Canadian medicare parlance, direct-billing applies to patients. Resentment of the 10 percent deduction was fanned by Dr Jason A. Hannah in advertisements for Associated Medical Services: see *Ontario Medical Review* 25 (April 1958): 421.

43 Ibid., 6.

44 Ibid., 7.

45 Ibid., 12.

46 Ibid., 15.

47 Ibid.

48 Quoted in Taylor, *Health Insurance and Canadian Public Policy*, 350.

49 Shillington, *Road to Medicare*, 140, 145-6. Note, for example, that PSI by 1958 had a staff of 375 working in a six-storey headquarters.

50 Ibid.

51 For details, see *Ontario Medical Review* 25 (March 1958): 248, 265; and (June 1958): 556-8. Full council transactions can be found in the April issue, 420 ff. The rhetoric of the militants is illuminating. Dr Michael Sabia of St Catharines wrote to the *Review* warning that the "forces of socialization" were destroying the foundations of western civilization – (June 1960): 693-7. Dr Manning L. Mador of Sudbury was equally inspired: "Let us practice medicine in the light against the onslaught of the socialist agitators" – (Sept. 1959): 882-6.

52 *Ontario Medical Review* 25 (July 1958): 652; (Sept. 1958): 797-8; (Oct. 1958): 886.

53 Ibid., 652.

54 See, for example, Dr Sawyer's comments in the *Review* 25 (April 1958): 476-7; 26 (March 1959): 263.

55 "OMA Convention Toronto May 1959," *Ontario Medical Review* 26 (July 1959): 667.

56 "Transactions of Council," *Ontario Medical Review* 27 (Feb. 1960): 166-70.

57 "Report of the Special Committee on Prepaid Medical Care," *CMAJ* 87 (1 Sept. 1962): 448.

58 "Special Supplement," *CMAJ* 91 (19 Sept. 1964): 49.

59 Shillington, *Road to Medicare*, 142.

60 Bernard R. Blishen, *Doctors and Doctrines: The Ideology of Medical Care* (Toronto: University of Toronto Press 1969), 165–74. Professor Blishen emphasizes the profession's solidarity in not supporting government sponsorship but seems to have missed the significance of the divisions in the profession.

61 Quoted in Royal Commission on Health Services, *Final Report*, 2: 5. A very detailed study of Windsor Medical Services was published in 1959 by an American group who did not find evidence of abuse by subscribers. See R.B. Robson, "Windsor Medical Services Incorporated," *CMAJ* 82 (12 March 1960): 607.

62 Shillington, *Road to Medicare*, 147.

63 This provides a neat contrast with situations of lodge, municipal, and industrial contract practice, where the profession itself had lost marketpower by fragmenting in the face of consumer collectivism.

64 *Globe and Mail*, 1 Feb. 1965.

65 Gruending, *Emmett Hall*, 96–8.

66 Ibid., 98.

67 Ibid., 99–100.

68 *Globe and Mail*, 16 June 1965.

69 For the text of the statement, see Blishen, *Doctors and Doctrines*, appendix 6, 189–91.

70 On the short-term effects of the Saskatchewan plan, see Robin F. Badgley and Samuel Wolfe, *Doctors' Strike* (Toronto: Macmillan 1967), 110–29.

71 Taylor provides a detailed account of the decision and its implementation from July 1965; *Health Insurance and Canadian Public Policy*, 352–74.

72 PAC, RG 29, vol. 1599-7, "Opening Statement by the Prime Minister of Canada, the Rt Hon. L.B. Pearson," 21–7. See also in the same file "Medicare: Statement by the Prime Minister of Canada to the Federal-Provincial Conference 20 July 1965." This was Pearson's elaboration of the announcement made on 19 July 1965.

73 R.A. Wier, "Federalism, Interest Groups, and Parliamentary Government: the Canadian Medical Association," *Journal of Commonwealth Political Studies* 11 (July 1973): 169.

74 Shillington, *Road to Medicare*, 152.

75 PAC, RG 29, vol. 1599-7: "To the Hon. Judy LaMarsh and members of the federal delegation to the Health Ministers' Conference, September 23–24, 1965," 16 Sept. 1965.

76 Shillington, *Road to Medicare*, 152. See also PAC, RG 29, vol. 1599-7, J. LaMarsh to R.O. Jones, 1 Oct. 1965.

77 Wier, *Journal of Commonwealth Political Studies* 11 (July 1973): 162.

78 Glenn Sawyer, *The First Hundred Years: A History of the Ontario Medical Association* (Toronto: OMA 1981), 159.

79 Ibid., 162.

80 Taylor, *Health Insurance and Canadian Public Policy*, 367.

81 PAC, RG 29, vol. 1111-504-2-4, part 5, passim.

82 PAC, RG 29, vol. 1599-7, J. LaMarsh to R.O. Jones, 1 Oct. 1965.

83 PAC, RG 29, vol. 1111-504-2-4, part 6, Telegram to R.O. Jones from Hon. Allan J. MacEachen, 10 June 1966.

84 "Transactions," *CMAJ* 97 (9 Sept. 1967): 621.

85 Medical Care Act 1966 Statutes of Canada 14–15 Elizabeth II, section 4(1)a.

86 "Transactions," *CMAJ* 97 (9 Sept. 1967): 622.

87 Ibid. See also Shillington, *Road to Medicare*, 154–6.

88 On Mitchell Sharp's role and motivation, see Judy LaMarsh, *Memoirs of a Bird in a Gilded Cage* (Toronto: McClelland and Stewart, 1969), 323–6.

89 "Transactions," *CMAJ* 97 (9 Sept. 1967): 623.

90 PAC, RG 29, vol. 1111-504-2-4, part 6, L.B. Pearson to R.K. Thomson, 20 Sept. 1966.

91 "Transactions," *CMAJ* 97: (9 Sept. 1967): 624.

92 Wier, *Journal of Commonwealth Political Studies* 11 (July 1973): 165, 174 n. 16.

93 Taylor, *Health Insurance and Canadian Public Policy*, 373.

94 "Transactions," *CMAJ* 97 (9 Sept. 1967): 624.

95 PAC, RG 29, vol. 1111-504-2-4, part 6, J.N. Crawford to A.F. Peart, 31 Oct. 1966.

96 Ibid., B. Freamo to J. Crawford, 4 Nov. 1966.

97 Ibid., Crawford to Lossing, undated; Lossing to Crawford, 9 Nov. 1966.

98 "Transactions," *CMAJ* 97 (9 Sept. 1967): 625.

99 "Report of the Special Committee on Collective Negotiation," *CMAJ* 97 (9 Sept. 1967): 640.

100 Quoted in J.W. Grove, *Organized Medicine in Ontario* (Toronto: Queen's Printer 1969), 299 n. 39.

101 J.A. McMillan, "Factors Influencing Utilization of Medical Care," *CMAJ* 97 (16 Dec. 1967): 1515–6.

102 On those negotiations, see Chevalot, *Monopole de la Médecine*, 13–52 for developments up to the time Turnbull spoke.

103 F.A. Turnbull, "Negotiations of the Medical Profession with Government," *CMAJ* 97 (16 Dec. 1967): 1520–1.

CHAPTER NINE

1 See, for example, the *Report of the Community Health Centre Project to the Conference of Health Ministers* (Ottawa: Information Canada 1972).

2 Jean-Luc Migué and Gilles Bélanger, *The Price of Health* (Toronto: Macmillan 1974), 59–90.

3 Comment by Dr. Peter J. Banks in Spyros Andreopoulos, ed., *National Health Insurance: Can We Learn from Canada?* (New York: Wiley 1975), 191.

4 Lee Soderstrom, *The Canadian Health System* (London: Croom Helm 1978), 51. See also Victoria Kelman, "Community Health Centres," *Canadian Dimension* 13 (May 1979): 43–6.

5 R. Williams, "Newfoundland's Salaried System for Rural Areas of Benefit to Most Cottage Hospital Physicians," *CMAJ* 115 (9 Oct. 1976): 661.

6 Max Weber, *Economy and Society* (New York: Bedminster Press 1968), vol. 2, 937.

7 Robert G. Evans, "Beyond the Medical Marketplace," in Andreopoulos, *National Health Insurance*, 134.

8 Stephen Peitchinis, "The Canadian Occupational Wage Structure," in L.H. Officer and L.B. Smith, eds., *Issue in Canadian Economics* (Toronto: McGraw-Hill 1974), 237. As might be expected, different indices yield varying results for the magnitude of the gain. It has been argued, for instance, that relative to industrial wage-earners alone, doctors' net incomes rose from 480 percent in 1961 to 650 percent in 1971: see Donald Swartz, "The Politics of Reform," in Leo Panitch, ed., *The Canadian State* (Toronto: University of Toronto Press 1979), 332–3.

9 *Medical Post*, 2 Dec. 1980, 38.

10 Ibid.

11 Compare Maurice LeClair, "The Canadian Health Care System" in Andreopoulos, *National Health Insurance*, 54–5, with National Council of Welfare, "Medicare: The Public Good and Private Practice" (Ottawa: Supply and Services Canada 1982), 25–7.

12 Emmett Hall, *Canada's National-Provincial Health Program for the 1980s: A Commitment for Renewal* (Ottawa: Supply and Services 1980), 23–32.

13 *Medical Post*, 9 Sept. 1980, 1, 65.

14 *Globe and Mail*, 25 Aug. 1981; *Medical Post*, 5 Oct. 1982, 1.

15 *Medical Post*, 5 Oct. 1982, 1, 103.

16 Ontario Medical Association, "Political Update" (undated mailing to membership, Oct. 1985), italics added. Economic updates were mailed during the dispute over OHIP benefits three years earlier. These direct

mailings are commonly used to bolster solidarity by organizations involved in conflicts. They were first used extensively in Canadian medicine by the Saskatchewan College of Physicians and Surgeons during the 1961-2 medicare dispute.

17 Earl Myers, Letter to OMA members dated 30 Dec. 1985.

18 Eliot Freidson, *Profession of Medicine: A Study in the Sociology of Applied Knowledge* (New York: Dodd Mead 1970), 25.

19 The corollary of this observation is that any program of privatization must focus above all on the hospital sector. Otherwise, rather than bringing in extra revenue for new or better facilities, privatization will simply release doctors from a negotiated tariff and allow them to increase their incomes. By extension, the application of user-fees to out-patient medical services can save money only if the drop in consumer-initiated demand is not overridden by increases in prices and supplier-controlled services. Indeed, if an equitable program of user-fees in the out-patient setting could be successfully applied, it might well be expected to decrease incomes of fee-for-service practitioners.

20 Paul Starr, *The Social Transformation of American Medicine* (New York: Basic Books 1982), 430-1, 439, 442-3.

21 For a sense of the debate in American medical circles, see, among others, Arnold S. Relman, "The New Medical-Industrial Complex," *New England Journal of Medicine* 303 (1980): 963-70; D.O. Nutter, "Access to Care and the Evolution of Corporate, For-Profit Medicine," *New England Journal of Medicine* 311 (1984): 917-19; S.A. Freedman, "Mega-Corporate Health Care: A Choice for the Future," *New England Journal of Medicine* 312 (1985): 579-81; M. Schlesinger and R. Dorwart, "Ownership and Mental Health Services," *New England Journal of Medicine* 311 (1984): 959-65.

22 R.A. Wier, "Federalism, Interest Groups, and Parliamentary Government: The Canadian Medical Association," *Journal of Commonwealth Political Studies* 11 (July 1973): 164.

23 As a representative of the American Public Health Association put it in a letter to the federal director of health insurance studies: "I can only comment that the invisible border between Canada and the United States has a real influence on the behaviour of professionals"; PAC, RG 29, vol. 1111-504-2-4, part 3, J.N. Miller to F.W. Jackson, 30 Dec. 1954. However, Professor J.W. Grove's description of Canadian medicine's "generally quietist, hands-off stance" as contrasted with the AMA's strong political involvement does seem rather wide of the mark in the light of the historical evidence; *Organized Medicine in Ontario* (Toronto: Queen's Printer 1969), 291-2.

24 Apart from the capsule summary in chapter 4, a much more detailed account of events in Winnipeg is forthcoming in C. David Naylor, "Canada's First Doctors' Strike: Medical Relief in Winnipeg, 1932-4," *Canadian Historical Review* 67 (June 1986): 151-80.

25 See, for example, *Medical Post*, 21 Oct. 1980, 1; 6 May 1980, 1, 65.

26 *Medical Post*, 18 Dec. 1979, 1, 29.

27 *Globe and Mail*, 29 April 1982, 5.

28 David Woods and Teresa Radford, "Co-operation and Confrontation Highlight MMA Meeting," *CMAJ* 132 (1 June 1985): 1322-3.

29 The evidence, however, is that the leaders of the general practice section of the OMA tied their activism in the campaign against Bill 94 to a review of the discrepancy between specialist and GP incomes; *Globe and Mail*, 5 March 1986, A1.

30 Karl Mannheim, *Essays on the Sociology of Knowledge* (London: Routledge and Kegan Paul 1972), 184.

31 Karl Mannheim, *Ideology and Utopia* (London: Routledge and Kegan Paul 1968), 49.

32 *Report of the CMA Committee on Economics of the Canadian Medical Association, as presented at the annual meeting in Calgary, June 18-22, 1934* (pamphlet, n.p. 1934), 4.

33 *Medical Post*, 9 Oct. 1979, 1.

34 *Globe and Mail*, 7 March 1986, A1.

35 J. Wendell MacLeod, "Basic Issues in Hospital and Medical Care Insurance," *CMAJ* 84 (24 June 1961): 1437.

36 For examples of this self-legitimation process, see the undated letter from Dr Joan Charboneau "To All Doctors in the Province of Ontario" (c. Dec. 1985). Dr Charboneau is president of the Association of Independent Physicians of Ontario. The same train of argument has been used by leaders of the Ontario Medical Association.

37 Freidson, *Profession of Medicine*, 370.

38 Ibid.

39 To its credit, the CMA has already taken a leadership role in this area by sponsoring an independent task force report on allocation of health care resources. See *Health - A Need for Redirection* (Ottawa: CMA 1985) for an excellent and objective review of the entire problem.

Index